# THE CORN LAWS

# THE CORN LAWS

*The Formation of Popular Economics in Britain*

*Edited by*
ALON KADISH

VOLUME VI

# PROVINCIAL FREE TRADE II
# FREE TRADE FARMERS

Routledge
Taylor & Francis Group
LONDON AND NEW YORK

First published 1996 by Pickering & Chatto (Publishers) Limited

Published 2016 by Routledge
2 Park Square, Milton Park, Abingdon, Oxon OX14 4RN
605 Third Avenue, New York, NY 10017

*Routledge is an imprint of the Taylor & Francis Group, an informa business*



BRITISH LIBRARY CATALOGUING IN PUBLICATION DATA
Corn Laws: Formation of Popular Economics
in Britain
I. Kadish, Alon
941.081

Set ISBN 1 85196 410 X

ISBN 13: 978-1-13875-891-9 (hbk) (Vol-6)

LIBRARY OF CONGRESS CATALOGING-IN-PUBLICATION DATA
Kadish, Alon, 1950–
The corn laws : the formation of popular economics in Britain / Alon Kadish.
p. cm.
Includes bibliographical references and index.
ISBN 1–85196–410–X (set)
1. Corn laws (Great Britain) 2. Free trade––Great Britain.
3. Anti-Corn-Law League. I. Title.
HF2044.K33 1996
v. 1. Whig free trade I –– v. 2. Whig free trade II : Free trade and Irish nationalism I –– v. 3. Free trade and Irish nationalism I : James Wilson and the economist –– v. 4. Free trade and religion –– v. 5. Provincial free trade I –– v. 6. Provincial free trade II : Free trade farmers.
382.7'3'0942––dc20 98–1232
CIP

CONTENTS

FREE TRADE WITH ALL THE WORLD
PRESENTED
TO
BY THE
National
ANTI CORN LAW LEAGUE

Archibald Prentice, alias 'A Farmer's Son', described in his *History of the Anti Corn Law League* the beginnings of the League's pamphlet printing and distribution.

The Manchester [Anti Corn Law] association had put forth a number of hand bills and placards; it now [1839] began to publish more largely and systematically a series of pamphlets of uniform shape. Amongst these was 'Facts for Farmers,' with the view of removing from the minds of that class the prejudices against any change of the Corn Laws which had been fostered by the landowners. The 'Facts' were contained in a closely-printed octavo of eight pages, and were supplied to distributors in all parts of the kingdom, at a rate just sufficient to cover the expense of printing and paper. ... Of these first publications about 10,000 were printed. Subsequently the impressions were of 50,000 each, and when the appeals were to the electors of the kingdom, during the height of the agitation, as many as half a million each of the more popular tracts were printed at a time.[1]

J. G. Kohl who visited the League's Manchester headquarters in 1842 wrote:

All the publications of the League are not only written, but printed, bound, and published, at the League-rooms in Market-street, Manchester. I went through the various rooms where these operations were carried on, until I came at last to the great League Depot, where books, pamphlets, letters, newspapers, speeches, reports, tracts, and wafers, were all piled in neat packets of every possible size and appearance, like the packets of muslin and calico, in the great warehouses of Manchester.[2]

The method of distribution aimed at reaching every elector in England was described by one of the League's agents who, with four assistants covered the northern and southern divisions of Cheshire in two weeks in December 1842.

In the first place I wrote out, from the county register, a distinct and complete list for each township, containing the name and address, in full, of every voter who was both qualified and resident within it, and afterwards added thereto, from written documents, the names of those who were resident within the township, but qualified to vote in virtue of property situate in other parts of the county. From these written lists the packets were then addressed, ... When the men set out in the morning, each might have in his waterproof bag from fifty to one hundred packets, weighing from twenty to forty pounds. Now by having these electors, [and] number the names of the voters in the order in which they would be visited, .... But the most important purpose which these lists were intended to answer

[1] Archibald Prentice, *History of the Anti Corn Law League* vol. 1, (1853), London: Frank Cass, 1968, pp. 125–6.
[2] J. G. Kohl, *Ireland, Scotland, and England*, London: Chapman and Hall, 1844, p. 145.

was that of having inscribed upon them, in connection with every name, the various important facts which it was desirable to possess.[1]

The distributor reported he had dispensed with nearly three tons of tracts, consisting of 11,100 sealed packets in the county (10,233 electors in north and south Cheshire in 1832), 1,500 in Chester (2,028 electors in 1832), and 600 in Stockport (1,012 electors in 1832), a total of 13,200 packets, each containing a dozen publications, i.e. some 160,000 pamphlets, to which he added loose leaflets distributed separately bringing the total of publications distributed to more than 200,000.[2]

As for the effect of his work, it was the distributor's conviction that

It is not by speeches on the hustings, at the period of an election, when men's passions are excited, and their interests are supposed to be attacked, and when the candidate for their suffrages is generally supposed to have some selfish object to serve, that many converts can be made to the principles of legislation not much understood. No; but by placing in the hands of the electors such publications as will enable them, in hours of leisure and tranquil repose, when in the company of the members of their own families, to understand correctly the nature of their interests and duties.

In addition the thorough distribution of pamphlets in the country forced the landowner to read the League's publications 'either from curiosity to see what kind of virus his tenants and neighbours are about to be inoculated with, or to be prepared to meet them in argument'.

[1] 'Completion of the tract distribution in north and south Cheshire. The distributors report to the Council of the League', signed 1 May 1843, in *The Anti Bread Tax Circular* 9 May 1843.

[2] The numbers of electors in 1832 are from J. Vincent and M. Stenton's *McCalmont's Parliamentary Poll Book. British Election Results, 1832–1918*, Brighton: Harvester Press, 1971.

# DIALOGUE

ON

# THE CORN LAWS,

BETWEEN A

## GENTLEMAN AND A FARMER.

---

**The following conversation, nearly verbatim, took place on board a Steam Boat, between a Gentleman and a Farmer:**

*Gentleman*: Good morning, Sir, I see you have the *Mark Lane Express* in your hand; how do they quote the price of corn to-day?

*Farmer*: Wheat, Sir, I am sorry to say, is lower.

*Gentleman*: Last year I heard several of my agricultural friends complaining of the price being *too high*; how was that?

*Farmer*: Prices then were too high, and the effect was to enhance the value of rents, which is injurious to the farmer.

*Gentleman*: But I thought that your Corn Bill was to remedy these evils.

*Farmer*: It does not prevent the fluctuation of high and low prices, certainly. What we want is a steady remunerating price about 60s. per quarter.

*Gentleman*: And this the Corn Law cannot secure to you?

*Farmer*: No.

*Gentleman*: Then why not petition for its repeal?

*Farmer*: Because we should be worse off then than we are now.

*Gentleman*: How so? You admit that it does not protect you from the evils you wish to avoid; neither does it secure to you the good you desire to obtain.

*Farmer*: We must have *some* protection.

*Gentleman*: Why protection? Why should farmers expect to be secured from risks in their business more than others? Is it that they are less competent to manage them, or that farming is a losing concern? I should say that a farmer has already many advantages; certainly more than the manufacturer has.

*Farmer*: How so; I should like to know how you make that out?

*Gentleman*: I will prove it to you: you grow corn, do you not? You sell it all in our *home market*, and have no occasion to export any.

*Farmer*: Certainly.

*Gentleman*: A manufacturer, on the other hand, makes (we will say for example) *cottons*, and as the demand for them in the home market is not equal to the supply, he has to send the surplus abroad.

*Farmer*: Very well.

*Gentleman*: Thus you see, Sir, you have a double advantage over the manufacturer; first, as *seller* of your own corn to him, in which case you ADD the *import charges*; and secondly, as *buyer* of his cottons, off which you DEDUCT the *export charges*; this leaves you a gainer upon each transaction. Now if an impartial person was asked which of the two parties was most entitled to protection, yourself or the manufacturer, surely he must say the latter.

*Farmer*: Sir, I admit these to be advantages.

*Gentleman*: Then why not be content with them without exacting more? why desire a Corn Law to enable you to obtain a yet higher price for which you have not a shadow of a claim?

*Farmer:* It is the foreigner we want to be protected against.

*Gentleman:* But you have always this advantage over the foreigner, that you sell on the spot, and he has to convey his corn 500 to 1000 miles, and pay all the costs of transit, before he can compete with you in your own market. Now, whatever the amount of these charges may be, whether 10s., 15s., or 20s. per quarter, it is so much protection in your favour, and you add this sum to the price of your corn at the time you sell it, although you have been at neither cost nor trouble in the matter. In other words, you add to every quarter of wheat you sell the amount of the import charges, although you sell it in the home market. This, Sir, I take to be a great advantage which you have over the manufacturer. It is a natural one which your position gives you, you are entitled to it; and no one complains of the gain you make. Do you see it?

*Farmer:* I think I do. It never struck me so before: but we get none too much. But, Sir, I would just ask you, how can the English farmer, who is burdened with high taxes, compete with the foreigner who is scarcely taxed at all?

*Gentleman:* I have already shown you *one* great advantage you have over the foreigner, and *two* which you have over the manufacturer; and I am quite sure that many a high-minded land proprietor, if he could be brought to perceive the relative positions in which the agriculturist, the manufacturer, and the foreigner are placed, in regard to each other, would be the first to denounce the *protective system* as oppressive and unjust.

*Farmer:* But, Sir, you must be aware that the greatest burden of taxes falls upon the land.

*Gentleman:* Indeed I am not, Sir.

*Farmer:* Why, everything, in fact, comes out of the land, we are more heavily taxed than any other class, and are consequently entitled to greater protection.

*Gentleman:* Will you be kind enough to state in what respect you are taxed so much beyond the rest of the community?

*Farmer:* Sir, I consider *tithes* to be a burden that fall almost exclusively on the land; the *highway rates* do the same, and the *poor rates* press heavier on the farmer than any one else.

*Gentleman:* Well, Sir, these are very fair objections to make. Now let us examine them, and see what amount of benefit on each you are entitled to. Ecclesiastical tithe, properly speaking, is a civil tax levied for an ecclesiastical purpose; it was never the property of either landowners or farmers. A landlord cannot claim benefit for what he never bought, or a tenant for what he never hired. The latter, for instance, wishes to engage a farm, say of 200 acres; the full value of the land is £250, but it is subject to the annual payment by the tenant of £50 for tithe. He hires it accordingly, paying £200 as rent to his landlord, and the £50 as tithe to the parson; but he would not give £250, the value of the rent and tithe together, and then pay the tithe afterwards. In paying tithe, therefore, a farmer cannot be said to pay it out of his own capital, or out of his landlord's rent. Neither have the least claim for protection on account of tithe.

*Farmer:* Sir, you have stated the case very clearly, and I certainly see it in a somewhat different point of view to what I did before. A tenant who holds a *titheable farm*, pays no more than a tenant who occupies one that is *tithe free*.

*Gentleman:* Just so.

*Farmer:* Now, Sir, what have you to say on the Highway Rates?

*Gentleman:* The more numerous the roads are, and the better their condition, the greater is the advantage to those persons who own or occupy the surface of country over which they pass. Turnpike tolls form the great exchequer, out of which the main highways of the kingdom are kept up; lines diverge from these, by which the value of land in numerous and extensive districts has been greatly enhanced; and if in the remoter parishes the repair of the *by-ways* fall more especially on the farmer, it is because he is more largely benefited by their use. I live in a parish not more than two miles from a market town, and have to pay toll at a turnpike every time I go to it; my neighbour, a farmer, who holds most of the land around me, and who lives half a mile further back, reaches the same town by a parallel road near his residence, and pays no turnpike at all. We both contribute to the *highway rates*, but I keep but one horse, and he keeps fourteen or fifteen, besides 500 sheep and other cattle, and his carts and waggons are constantly passing to and fro upon our parish roads between the several parts of his farm. Beyond him resides another tenant, who holds four similar occupations with corresponding advantages. I fear that the plea for *protection* on the ground of *highway rates* will turn out to be untenable, particularly when it is recollected that all farmers are exempted by Act of Parliament from the payment of tolls when carrying manure, and engaged in the work of their several occupations; and further, that towns have their own streets to maintain, over which the carts and horses of the farmers pass without paying any toll.

*Farmer:* Well, Sir, I should now like to hear your observations on the *Poor Law.*

*Gentleman:* You shall have them; only let me here premise one general remark, that whatever I may say, though *pointedly* addressed to you, is not intended *personally*, but against the *protective system*, of which you are the advocate.

*Farmer:* I perfectly understand it so, and beg you will be quite free in expressing yourself. I shall not be offended.

*Gentleman:* Of the *Poor Law*, or rather the *Poor Rates*, (for the latter, I presume, are meant,) I would say that the manufacturing and agricultural interests are, perhaps, upon a par. The poor generally exist in proportion to the amount of population; their number is smaller in thinly peopled rural districts, than in the larger towns. But here again, by living in the country, I have noticed some strange anomalies. I have seen, for instance, twenty able-bodied men in a parish out of employ, and the land in that parish suffering from the want of their labour; the farmers preferring to maintain them in idleness, rather than furnish them with the work that would turn to their own profit. And before the enactment of the Poor Law, I have known farmers, friends of my own, intelligent men, and highly respectable, who, when they wanted hands, and labourers have applied to them for work, have refused to engage them, and have hinted at the same time the propriety of their applying to the parish; the poor fellows through necessity have done so; and the same farmers, under the plea of benefitting the parish, have then consented to give 6s. per week for their services, knowing well that they were worth 10s. to them; and the parish had to make up the difference. Thus were the poor pauperized; and thus had the country to pay the wages of the farmers' labourers! And what is the object of the present Poor Law? Is it not to compel every able-bodied man, whether he has been thus pauperized or not, to depend upon his own labour for support? And does not the Corn Law deprive him of the right to exchange the produce of that labour with those who would give him food in plenty in return for it? How, then, can a poor man succeed under such circumstances? Or how can the principle of the Poor Law Bill be carried out? The two laws are incompatible.

*Farmer:* Sir, I acknowledge the charges to be too true; I also admit the inconsistency of such a mode of legislation.

*Gentleman:* Your plea for a *Corn Law* on the ground of *Tithes, Highway Rates,* and *Poor Rates*, I think is a failure. Can you advance any other reasons why the agriculturists should be especially protected? Or can you show in what respect they are more heavily taxed than others?

*Farmer:* I do not recollect just now, but I always considered that we had the worst of it.

*Gentleman:* If you cannot, then, prove to me that you pay *more* in proportion than others, will you allow me to prove to you that in truth you pay *less*.

*Farmer:* I like to hear you talk, and yet I don't like to hear you, if you can make *that* out. I like your *manner* but I don't like your *doctrine*.

*Gentleman:* The sting of a remark sometimes lies in the truth of it.

*Farmer:* I suppose so. But you were going to show me how the Farmer pays *less taxes* than any other people.

*Gentleman:* Very well. How many horses do you keep?

*Farmer:* Twelve, Sir.

*Gentleman:* What tax do you pay a year for each?

*Farmer:* Tax! tax! I don't pay anything for them.

*Gentleman:* Then other people do for theirs; and the relief afforded to the agriculturists by the repeal of the tax on their horses is about £500,000 per annum; *this sum*, therefore, you pay *less;* and here let me remark, that if a given sum is required annually for the exigencies of the State, (say fifty millions,) and one class of the community is excused the payment of their portion, then that portion must fall upon the rest to pay, and such being the case in the present instance, the public are taxed £500,000 a year for the farmer's benefit.

*Farmer:* Well, Sir, you may be right; I certainly do not pay any tax for my horses.

*Gentleman:* The *Window Tax*, again. Are you charged for any window in your farm-house?

*Farmer:* No, sir.

*Gentleman:* All farm houses under a rental of £200 a year, the tenants deriving a fixed income from no other source, are exempt. Thus, here is £50,000 a year you are relieved from, and which the public has to pay for you. And as a further specimen of the protective favour you enjoy, let me remind you that a deficiency has just been declared in the public revenue, and fresh taxes are required; and how do you suppose they are to be raised? by taxing such of the farmers' windows as pay nothing? No, but by an additional tax of ten per cent. on those who are already paying twice as much as they ought; and should the people complain of this act of injustice, they would be stigmatized as factious and revolutionary by the very parties to whom the boon of exemption is granted.

*Farmer*: Go on, you'll make something out of us in time.

*Gentleman*: I am afraid but little. I presume you employ as many servants of all kinds as you please, and pay no tax for any of them.

*Farmer*: Certainly.

*Gentleman*: Other persons, if they employ grooms, gardeners, stable boys, or what not, are charged for each; and this has been another saving to you of about £50,000 a year.

*Farmer*: For one, I wish for nothing but what is fair, and certainly think that farmers ought not to require that others should be taxed for their benefit.

*Gentleman*: I think with you, but, unhappily for the country, the reverse is the case. Let me here ask you, do you pay any direct tax at all?

*Farmer*: No, I do not.

*Gentleman*: I thought so. Well, there is another singular boon you have lately received, which (since concessions are so common) may not have struck you.

*Farmer*: Gently, Sir, if you please.

*Gentleman*: I allude to your exemption from the payment of all duty on the *insurance of farming stock*. Now, if I insure my stock in trade, I must pay a tax to Government in proportion to the amount I insure; this effects a saving to the agricultural interest of *more* than £80,000 a year. I could mention other taxes expressly repealed for the farmer's benefit, and which the public has consequently to pay. I observe, for instance, that farming stock is very frequently sold by auction—does it pay any auction duty to Government?

*Farmer*: No, Sir.

*Gentleman*: But the manufacturer's or tradesman's goods, when sold by auction, bear a duty of five per cent. to the Government. So you see here is another special exemption.

*Farmer*: You have mentioned enough.

*Gentleman*: Well, it can do us no harm to look at these things, and to talk over them pleasantly.

*Farmer*: Certainly; as I said before, I like to hear, only, to tell you the truth, I don't want to be convinced; it goes against my interest.

*Gentleman*: You think so, but depend upon it your interest consists in knowing the truth; it will be the first sure step towards bettering your condition, which needs improvement.

*Farmer*: Ah! *there* I fully agree with you; it *does* need improvement.

*Gentleman*: It strikes me that the position in which the landed interest stands in reference to itself and the country, requires to be more clearly understood; and this is one object which I have had in view in mentioning these things.

*Farmer*: Sir, I am obliged to you; I quite think that you intend the farmers no harm, although you seem to state truths that I am sure they would not relish. Have you any other objections to make?

*Gentleman*: Yes; I think there is something very partial and very unjust in that law which allows a large landed proprietor to leave his estates to whom he pleases, without paying a single farthing for either *probate or legacy duty*, whilst others, who are not rich enough to hold land, and possess only *personal property*, have to pay both. A poor man who dies worth only twenty guineas, if he *wills* it to a neighbour or friend, who is not a relation, the latter, before he can touch it, must *prove the will*, and pay 10s. besides costs; and then he cannot appropriate the money to his own use till he has paid a further sum, for *legacy duty*, of *two pounds* to government! A landed proprietor, on the other hand, may leave an estate in land worth £20,000, or any amount, to whom he pleases, without being charged one farthing. To exhibit the working of this law in favour of land yet more clearly, let us suppose a nobleman who dies possessed of *real estate* to the value of £100,000; he leaves it to whom he pleases, and no cost is incurred. A merchant or manufacturer dies possessed of *personal estate*, of the same value; he pays as under:—

| | | | |
|---|---|---|---|
| Amount of probate duty.... | £1,500 | 0 | 0 |
| Legacy duty, 10 per cent.... | 10,000 | 0 | 0 |
| (Not being left to a relation.) | | | |
| Total...... | £11,500 | 0 | 0 |

And if the same rate of duty was levied upon real estate as is now levied upon personal, it would amount to from *two and a half to three millions* annually! Is this mode of taxation just?

*Farmer*: Most assuredly not.

*Gentleman*: Well, this is the way in which the people are oppressed; can we wonder then that there should be dissatisfaction?

*Farmer*: The law is very unfair and ought to be altered, but how comes it that we get such unequal laws?

*Gentleman*: Because the *landed* aristocracy have hitherto had the making of the laws, and they have always taken care of themselves. This is exemplified by reference to the subject of Land Tax, in proportion to the amount of other taxes in this country, and the different countries in Europe. In most of the latter the Land Tax yields more than all their other taxes, whereas in Britain the Land Tax produces only *One Million odd*, and the other taxes about *Fifty Millions*. The legislature has ever descended to the minutest matters to exempt the landed interest; even the shepherd's dog is liable to no duty, while the tradesman's yard dog must pay. A fresh example of partial legislation in favour of the farmers may be seen in our new Income Tax. They are to be exempt from the inquisitorial examination of their profits! All occupiers of farms under a rental of £300 per annum to pay nothing! Those above that amount are to be assessed at only half their rentals, whilst other persons with incomes of £150 a year or upwards are obliged to disclose the full particulars of their profits and pay upon the whole amount.

*Farmer*: But there is another very important point which occurs to me just now, and which I should like to have cleared up; I allude to the national debt. Now, how is the interest of this to be paid, if the farmer is not protected?

*Gentleman*: Precisely in the same way as it is now paid *by others who have no protection*. By *protection* you mean that a *monopoly price* should be given you for your corn, to enable you the better to bear your share of the general taxation. Now, what right has the farmer, by virtue of a Corn Law, to lay a surcharge on the consumer to enable him to do this? *That* is not paying the taxes; *that* is not bearing his share of the interest of the national debt; it is shifting the burden from his own shoulders upon the shoulders of his neighbour. You may very fairly ask how the interest on the national debt is to be paid, seeing that the people, in addition to the taxes levied by the state, have to pay the taxes levied on them by the LAND. If one of your teams of horses could scarcely draw your waggon, because it was loaded, would you lay on more to make them draw the better?

*Farmer*: It is quite evident that we do not see eye to eye. The very points which I considered our strongest ones, you regard as our weakest. I still think that the Corn Law is not the disadvantage to the country many suppose; because, allowing that it secures to the farmer better prices, these are afterwards laid out again with the manufacturer—he becomes a better customer to the latter in proportion.

*Gentleman*: My dear Sir, excuse me, this is a part and parcel of the wretched reasoning with which the Corn Law advocates have ever attempted to bewilder the country. If I give you a sum of money for your goods beyond what they are intrinsically worth, to enable you to be a better customer to me in return, what do I get by it? If you merely lay out with me what I have given you in the first instance, why might I not as well have retained the money in my pocket! Unfortunately the mischief does not end here; the effect of the Corn Law is to destroy manufactures and commerce, and thus to deprive the nation of the very means by which all taxes are paid. When will the people be wise or their rulers be just?

*Farmer*: But, Sir, you must surely admit that the agricultural labourer is better off when the price of corn is high than when it is low; his wages are always raised in proportion.

*Gentleman*: I by no means admit this; to be *better off*, his wages ought to be *more than raised in proportion*. Pray what may be considered the average price of wheat at the present moment?

*Farmer*: 38s. per coomb.

*Gentleman*: And what wages per week do you pay your workmen!

*Farmer*: 10s. per week.

*Gentleman*: What is the lowest average price you have known wheat to sell at?

*Farmer*: I have known it sold as low as 21s. per coomb.

*Gentleman*: And what was the rate of wages then?

*Farmer*: I should say 8s. to 9s. per week.

*Gentleman*: Then, Sir, you have upset your own argument.

*Farmer*: How so?

*Gentleman*: Why, if a labourer earned 8s. a week when wheat was 21s. per coomb, he could procure with his money about six pecks; whereas, the man who earns 10s. a week, wheat being at 38s. per coomb, can procure only about four pecks; in other words, you ought to give your workman, according to the present price of corn, 14s. a week instead of 10s. His condition, therefore, according to your own showing, is deteriorated instead of improved. But this is not all, the sudden fluctuation in the price of *corn*, to which the agricultural poor are subject, is a serious disadvantage to them. The Corn Law in the rural districts operates as a *disturbing force* on wages, but not as a *regulating one*. Between the price of *corn* and the price of *wages*, a principle of self interest on the part of the employer interposes and acts inversely upon them, keeping *corn* up to the *maximum price*, and *wages* down to the *minimum.* And you will please also to recollect that there is still a large class of persons whose wages, though affected by the price of corn, are regulated by the demand and supply of labour in the market; I allude to the manufacturing labourers, the mechanics, artizans, and workmen in other trades; on these a greater injury is often inflicted, for it happens, and not unfrequently, that when the price of their labour is *unusually low*, the price of corn is *unusually high*, and then we have, as a consequence, one of those popular outbreaks, for which the *people* are blamed, and the *government* is in fault.

*Farmer:* Oh, I give up the argument as respects the manufacturing operatives.

*Gentleman:* Let us next turn our eye upon the Polish husbandman, clad in his dress of sheep skins. He grows corn sufficient for his wants, and would be glad to exchange it for the cottons of the Manchester weaver; each is ready to supply the needs of the other to their mutual advantage; but again the cupidity of the Corn Law interferes with its protecting duty, and both are brought to a stand still. Wide prospects are sometimes seen through small openings. Reverse the picture, and suppose these men left at liberty to exchange the products of their respective industry, an impulse would immediately be given to foreign agriculture, distant markets would be opened to our manufactures, commerce would increase, and all would participate in the general benefit.

*Farmer:* I am afraid NOT the farmer; his prices would fall, and his trade would be ruined.

*Gentleman:* If so, it only proves the unsound and artificial position in which he stands, and which wants a remedy. The natural result of the change would be this; the demand for foreign corn would enhance its price; the price would augment the value of land abroad; an improved system of culture would be introduced, better implements be required, more labourers wanted, and higher wages paid; these and other concomitant circumstances, so far from tending to lower our home prices of corn, would carry the foreign price up. And when to this we add the new demand for our manufactures, with the consequent stimulus that would be given to British industry, instead of the thousands and tens of thousands now emigrating for want of employ, and the numerous manufacturing establishments formed and forming, in self defence, in nearly all the European states, we should be glad of our population at home at fair wages, and these would form so many additional customers to the British farmer, and again INCREASE rather than diminish both the price and consumption of his corn. But leaving the question of price to adjust itself, as it soon naturally would, what have we to do with the profit and loss of the landed interest, or the manufacturing interest, or the commercial interest, or indeed any other interest in its separate character? This officious management on the part of government of men's affairs, in their private instead of their public capacities, has been, and ever will be, a fruitful source of discontent and mischief. The people have a right to enjoy peaceably the fruits of their labour, and if the agriculturists attempt to deprive them of it, they have a just cause to complain.

*Farmer:* But, Sir, you would surely not have this country depend on foreign countries for the supply of corn. What should we do, if this was the case, in times of war or scarcity?

*Gentleman:* In time of war we should probably do as we are now doing with the article of *tea*, continue to buy it as if no war existed; albeit there would yet be this difference, that *tea* is grown only in China, whereas *corn* is grown in almost every country; and we are surely not intending to make a quarrel with all the world at the same time. Indeed it is well known that *during the war with France* we were to a great extent supplied with corn from that country, at a period of great scarcity, owing to the failure of our crops. Besides, as to a war, all good men must deplore it, and no public measure like *free trade* is so calculated to prevent its occurrence. It is no advantage to either individuals or nations to quarrel with their customers; for this reason, it behoves alike the statesman, the Christian, and the philanthropist, to endeavour to do away with the present system of monopoly for one of free trade. As to a *scarcity*, seeing that every country is liable to it, it is surely better not to confine our dependance to *one*, even though that one be our own; for, in the event of a scarcity, I think yourself must admit that it would be desirable to have other markets to go to. Depend upon it, the wider the surface from whence we draw our supply of corn the better, and the less is its fluctuation in price; and if that surface be the world instead of England, our risks of failure from the seasons is diminished, and our security increased.

*Farmer:* You seem determined, Sir, not to allow us farmers one argument to defend ourselves.

*Gentleman:* I allow you to advance all the arguments you please, but I think you ought to have recourse to sounder ones.

*Farmer*: If you could only show us that we should obtain as good a price for our corn, when the law is repealed, as we do now that we are protected, we would directly give it up.

*Gentleman*: Before I do this, you are bound to prove to me that you are entitled to a Corn Law, and that you would be losers by its repeal, neither of which you have yet done. However, whether conviction be produced in your mind or not, it is very evident to those who watch the signs of the times that a strong feeling is growing in the public mind in favour of the repeal of the Corn Laws; and if to this we add the consideration of a remarkable physical fact, that whilst the land of England remains in extent the same, our population is increasing at the rate of 1000 a day! it would seem as if the change could not be far distant. How much wiser, then, would it be to meet the case in a time of tranquillity, than to defer it till a time of commotion; to concede with a grace what *may be* extorted by clamour! With respect to your remark, that it would be well to show farmers that they would be no losers by the repeal of the Corn Laws, I may say that I think they would be gainers by it, certainly in the following respects:—

Farming, it must be admitted, is a pursuit rendered sufficiently hazardous by the changes of the seasons, failure of the crops, &c., without being subjected to the sudden fluctuations in price which are produced by the Corn Law. The latter converts the operation of farming into a lottery, with the chances against the tenant; for in taking a farm, he hires it not at its *natural value*, so as to benefit by any advantage which the times might subsequently confer upon him, but he hires it at a *Corn Bill* or *monopoly price*, which has the effect of transferring all the advantage to his landlord, in the shape of rent; whilst, should prices decline, the loss falls on *himself*. In this dilemma, we have had weekly announcements in the papers of the generosity of Lord A——, or the munificence of Lord B——, in returning 5, 10, or 20 per cent., at the rent audits of their tenantry; in plain English, surrendering their claims to arrears they could never get, and which in most cases they should never have attempted to exact. Liberality is a gem that ought to shine in the lease, and not in the landlord's judgment.

By this act of apparent generosity, the tenant is placed under a perpetual obligation to his landlord, and is thereby deprived of that independence of speech and action in political affairs which is enjoyed by the humblest mechanic; a position very unfavourable to the tenant, and which the landlord knows too well how to turn to account when fitting occasions offer. Nevertheless, the latter is not solely in fault; some blame attaches to the tenant, who too readily suffers himself to be placed in this state of dependence.

In times of *scarcity*, when the price of corn rises, it generally happens that the greater portion of small farmers have little or no stocks to sell; indeed, the scarcity of the article it is that occasions the advance: thus they are not only shut out from the benefit of increased profit arising from the advanced prices, but, in addition to high rents, many other things have a tendency to rise, and this when the farmer is least able to bear it.

On the other hand, in times of *abundance*, whether arising from unusually large harvests, or extensive importation, or probably both causes, the *price declines*, and they are again debarred from profit; and the consumers being supplied, no reduction in price can increase the demand, save only such a ruinous reduction as will induce speculators to buy a perishable article which they do not want, with the view of hoarding it up against they do. Thus the farmer suffers in both cases.

The Corn Laws are a cause of the farmer's uncertainty and perplexity, when he ought to be fairly and securely reckoning on regular gains.

They are a great occasion of the farmer's instability of position, sometimes deluding him with false hopes, and sometimes depressing him below his just level, and extorting from him the unavailing cry to the legislature of agricultural distress.

They are a cause of the farmer's alienation from the industrial portion of the community, connecting his advantages with their sufferings, and his losses with their gains, and thus infusing into society a bitterness of spirit unfavourable to the landed interest.

*Farmer*: Well, but I presume you don't go the length of advocating total repeal all at once?

*Gentleman*: Yes, and for this reason, that as no other settlement can be final, and as it is for the interest of the farmer to have the question set at rest, I would therefore abolish the Corn Law at once and for ever.

*Farmer*: Why not put on a low fixed duty instead of the sliding scale?

*Gentleman*: Because, for the reasons I have already given you, there is no just ground for imposing any duty whatever upon foreign corn, for the protection of the landed interest of this country. The manufacturers disclaim all desire for protection, and denounce it as a mischievous delusion. Recollect, too, that all the agitation that is now going on is against a fixed duty. The cry everywhere is, "No bread tax!" and, judging from the manner in which public opinion is every day becoming more and more opposed to any duty upon corn, I am convinced that total repeal is inevitable in the end.

*Farmer*: But you would not be so unreasonable, I should think, as to refuse to give us time; you would agree to a duty of 8s. or 10s. to begin with, going off a shilling every year?

*Gentleman*: In my opinion, *that* would be the very worst plan of all for the farmers, for then the landlord would put off the adjustment of rent from year to year, and in the end probably throw the whole of the loss, if there was any, upon the tenant; but I will explain the matter in this way. The steward would say, "Well, Farmer So-and-so, we'll see how this new Corn Law works for a year; in the mean time you must bestir yourself, and next year we'll talk the matter of rent over." The next year the tenant pays the full rent, and the steward says, "You must set to work and improve your cultivation; there are great improvements going on, and my lord (meaning his landlord) is anxious that you should not be behind your neighbours." The third year the full rent is paid, and the steward recommends the Scotch system of two-horse ploughs, under-draining, &c. The fourth year the same rent is paid, and the steward compliments the tenant upon his improved method of farming. The fifth, sixth, and seventh years pass over in the same way; the farmer exerting all his energies to increase his produce and diminish his expenses, in order to meet the rent day. The duty has now dropped to 3s. a quarter. "Well, Farmer So-and-so," says the steward, "we seem to have been more frightened than hurt by this Corn Law; there does not seem to be much to fear from foreign competition after all." In the mean time, however, whilst the old rent is continued, the foreigner has been putting more land under cultivation, to be ready to take advantage of the low duty, and the importing merchant has been holding back his corn in bond, to pour it upon the market at the same time; and thus the English farmer finds his market swamped, all of a sudden, just as he does now by the sliding scale. On the contrary, if the Corn Law were immediately abolished, there would be an instant adjustment of rents all over the kingdom, there would be no stock of corn ready abroad to throw upon the market, the farmer would take his farm upon a long lease, most likely at a *corn rent*, before he began his improvements, and then he, and not the landlord, would reap all the benefit of his exertions. I shall only add, that I have thought much upon this matter, and am convinced that the best thing for the farmers, under all the circumstances of the times, would be, *the total and immediate repeal of the Corn Laws.*

*Farmer*: There is a good deal of reason in what you say; and, at all events, I am sure you are giving me your sincere opinion. I must confess that I thought we were more burdened than we appear to be, and I was not before aware that we had so many special exemptions as you have acquainted me with. The fact that the land tax is so much heavier upon the land of the other European countries than upon our own land, is, I must admit, a very striking fact; but what goes farthest toward removing my fears for the consequences of the abolition of the Corn Laws, is the advantages we should have, and, as you say, always must have, over the foreigner, in the circumstance, that while we produce the corn where it is consumed, he must be at the expense of freight, insurance, and shipping charges; and I am almost inclined to think this would secure to us a steady and fair remunerating price.

Here the conversation between the Gentleman and the Farmer was interrupted by the termination of the voyage; to what extent it might otherwise have been carried, it is difficult to say. Both parties separated in the most friendly manner; and I have recorded their dialogue in the hope that it may be useful to others, and throw some additional light on the state of the Corn Laws.

**Issued by the National Anti-Corn-Law League, Newall's-Buildings, Manchester.**

PRINTED BY J. GADSBY, NEWALL'S-BUILDINGS, MANCHESTER.

# AUTHORITIES

# AGAINST THE CORN LAWS.

"IT WILL BE FOR YOU TO DETERMINE WHETHER THESE LAWS DO NOT AGGRAVATE THE NATURAL FLUCTUATIONS OF SUPPLY, WHETHER THEY DO NOT EMBARRASS TRADE, DERANGE CURRENCY, AND, BY THEIR OPERATION, DIMINISH THE COMFORT AND INCREASE THE PRIVATIONS OF THE GREAT BODY OF THE COMMUNITY."—*Queen Victoria.*

"The most proper method for encouraging the growth of corn at home is to multiply the number of inhabitants and eaters of bread!" "The proper method for encouraging the importation of corn from abroad is to admit the unconditional importation of it at all times and seasons, without any restraint or limitation whatever." "As to the importation of it, it is absurd to suppose that any raw material, and more especially the most momentous of all others, should be prohibited from being brought in, and the uses of it restrained, for the sake of enriching a few monopolisers."—*Dean Tucker.*

"The unlimited, unrestrained freedom of the corn trade, as it is the only effectual preventative of the miseries of a famine, so it is the best palliative of the inconveniences of a dearth."—*Adam Smith.*

"Wherever commerce is known to be always free, and the merchant absolute master of his commodity, as in Holland, there will always be a reasonable supply of corn."—*Benjamin Franklin.*

"Of all things, an indiscreet tampering with the trade of provisions is the most dangerous. My opinion is against an overdoing of any sort of administration, and more especially against this most momentous of all meddling on the part of authority, the meddling with the subsistence of the people."—*Edmund Burke.*

"In England, all other particular interests are overborne and crushed by one great particular interest, named, in the aggregate, the agricultural interest."—*Jeremy Bentham.*

"All classes, except the landlords, will be injured by the increase in the price of corn."—*David Ricardo.*

"Those countries which have depended the most upon foreign countries for their supply of corn have enjoyed beyond all other countries the advantages of a steady and invariable market for grain."—*James Mill, author of the History of British India.*

"For the sake of its moral benefit, we know of no achievement more urgently desirable than that of a free corn trade. There is not a more fertile topic of clamour and burning discontent all over the land; and were it but effectually set at rest, we are aware of nothing which might serve more to sweeten the breath of British society."—*Dr. Chalmers.*

"The larger the surface from which a country draws its supplies of food, the less likely is it to be injuriously affected by the varieties in the harvests."—*J. R. M'Culloch.*

"We cannot persuade ourselves that this law will ever contribute to produce plenty, cheapness, or steadiness of price. So long as it operates at all, its effects must be the opposite of these. *Monopoly is the parent of scarcity, of dearness, and of uncertainty.* To cut off any of the sources of supply can only tend to lessen its abundance; to close against ourselves the cheapest markets for any commodity must enhance the price at which we purchase it; and to confine the consumer of corn to the produce of his own country is to refuse for ourselves that provision which Providence itself has made for equalizing to man the variations of climate and of seasons."—*Protest by Lord Grenville, signed by ten Peers.*

"It is my unalterable conviction that we cannot uphold the corn laws, now in existence, together with the present taxation, and at the same time increase national prosperity and preserve public contentment."—*Mr. Huskisson's Speech, House of Commons, March 25th, 1830.*

"Food is the last thing upon which I would attempt to place any protection."—*James Deacon Hume, Board of Trade.*

"A FAR BETTER CASE COULD BE MADE OUT IN FAVOUR OF A BOUNTY TO INCREASE THE IMPORTATION OF CORN THAN OF A DUTY TO RESTRAIN IT."—*James Deacon Hume.*

"I consider that the taxation imposed upon the country by our duty on corn, and the provision duties and prohibitions, are far greater, probably much more than double the amount of taxation paid to the treasury."—*Evidence of J. M'Gregor, Esq., Joint Secretary to the Board of Trade.*

"All protection means robbing somebody else."—*Colonel Thompson.*

"The corn law is an extension of the pension list to the whole of the landed aristocracy of Great Britain."—*London Times.*

"To propose to enrich a nation by forcing a permanent scarcity of corn, and obstructing the natural course of trade, is indeed at variance with common sense."—*Sir James Graham's Pamphlet, "Free Trade in Corn the real Interest of the Landlord and the true Policy of the State."*

"All that has been advanced on this point is a mere excuse for keeping up high rents."—*Speech of Mr Baring (now Lord Ashburton) against the Corn Bill in* 1815.

"No better mode of cheating a nation could be devised than the present corn laws."—*Lord Morpeth.*

"Your device has been to create an artificial scarcity."—*Lord Fitzwilliam's Address to the Landowners.*

"The hon. member for Kilkenny attributes the derangement of the currency and the high rate of interest altogether to the bank. But the present state of the Corn Laws is at the root of the question."—*Mr. Chancellor Spring Rice's retiring Speech.*

"If there is any class of persons whose opinions on this question are entitled to deference and respect, they are undoubtedly political economists, men who have made the sources of national wealth the principal subject of their inquiry; and where shall we find one, from Adam Smith to the present time, who has not reprobated the interference of the legislature with the price of corn?"—*Rev. Robert Hall.*

"If the moral and religious bearings of this question were rightly understood, the room would have been filled with the clergy and dissenting ministers of London. It is impossible that they could resist such a call upon them, for they could not but feel that the objects of the society were founded in justice and humanity, and tended to the welfare of their fellow-men."—*Doctor Pye Smith's Speech at the late meeting of the Metropolitan Anti-Corn-Law Association.*

"Free trade! the plain duty and plain interest of the human race. To level all barriers to free exchange; to cut up the system of restriction root and branch; to open every port on earth to every product; this is the office of enlightened humanity. To this a free nation should especially pledge itself. Freedom of the seas; freedom of harbours; an intercourse of nations free as the winds; this is not a dream of philanthropists. We are tending towards it, and let us hasten it."—*Dr. Channing.*

"The dearth of corn may (if such were the case) serve as a stimulus to our manufactures. America and Poland, &c., will take back cotton and hardware in exchange for wheat; and, if the affliction is not by these means taken away, it may be much lightened."—*Bishop Heber.*

"Sir Thomas Robinson, talking of the evils of importation from Ireland,—'Sir Thomas,' said Dr. Johnson, 'you talk the language of a savage. What, sir! would you prevent any people from feeding themselves, if by any honest means they can do it?'"—*Boswell's Life of Johnson.*

"I BELIEVE THAT ON THE GENERAL PRINCIPLE OF FREE TRADE THERE IS NOW NO GREAT DIFFERENCE IN OPINION, AND THAT ALL AGREE IN THE GENERAL RULE THAT WE SHOULD PURCHASE IN THE CHEAPEST MARKET AND SELL IN THE DEAREST."—*Sir Robert Peel's Speech on the Tariff, May 10th,* 1842.

"An importation of 50,000 head of cattle would produce an import trade of half a million of money, a trade which, in its nature, would lead by a smooth and certain course of operation to an export trade in return of equal amount, which would contribute to an increased demand for labour and employment."—*Mr. Gladstone's Speech, May 23rd,* 1812.

"The Corn Law increases the price of bread."—*Lord Stanley, in answer to Mr. John Brooks, at his last election for North Lancashire.*

"Rents rise with the rise in the price of corn."—*Ibid.*

"Wages do not rise with the rise in the price of bread."—*Ibid.*

# THE ANTI-CORN-LAW LEAGUE

## AND THE

# DUKE OF WELLINGTON.

---

My Lord Duke,

The Anti-Corn-Law Deputies now in London for the purpose of procuring the total and immediate Repeal of the Corn and Provision Laws, have, in compliance with the suggestion of your Grace, prepared a brief statement of their case, which they beg to submit to your Grace's attentive perusal.

The Corn Law is framed to keep up the price of corn at a higher rate in this country than the natural price. The only way in which this can be effected, is by making corn scarcer here than abroad. The Corn Law, therefore, to effect its object, must make food scarce and dear.

The middle and upper classes of society being able to consume the same quantity of bread under any circumstances, the effects of scarcity and high price fall upon the working classes and the poor. Upwards of twenty millions of our population consist of working men and their families; they consume probably three-fourths of all the food produced in this country, so that it is out of their wages that the increased price of food is principally paid.

The House of Commons has repeatedly declared by its votes, and the reports of its Committees, that it is not in the power of Parliament to regulate the wages of labour, yet a law is maintained for securing an artificial price for food out of the earnings of the working classes.

Your Grace is aware that the Corn Law is defended on the ground that wages rise and fall with the price of food. The erroneousness of this statement is shown by the facts—That the rate of wages rose during the cheaper years 1835 and 1836, and has continued to fall rapidly during the last three years of dear food; wages in Ireland are 6d. a day, with wheat at 60s. a quarter; and wages are 4s. a day in America, with wheat at 40s. a quarter.

The Corn Law is said to benefit especially the Agricultural labourers; but their wages are in ordinary times lower than those in the trading and manufacturing districts, as a proof of which we call the attention of your Grace to the fact that there has been a constant migration of labourers from the rural to the manufacturing counties.

It is said that the repeal of the Corn Law would throw lands out of cultivation. The Deputies are of opinion that it would not have such an effect, and they appeal to the superior practical judgments of Lord Spencer, the late Lord Leicester, Earl Ducie, and other high authorities in support of their views.

It is contended that the British Agriculturist is not able to compete with the foreigner. The British Manufacturer is obliged to compete with foreigners at their own doors abroad, and why should not the agriculturist be able to meet their foreign rivals in this market?

The costs of freight and other charges for bringing wheat from *the place of growth* in Poland or America, to England, is upwards of 15s. a quarter. The expense is a natural protection for our agriculturists, which nothing can deprive them of. If your poorer soils produce about three quarters of wheat per acre, here is a protection against the foreigner of £2 5s. an acre. This natural protection, even under a perfectly free Corn Trade, would place the English manufacturer under a most serious disadvantage.

It is asserted that the manufacturers are protected. The protection is nominal, and not real. The manufacturers have repeatedly petitioned that all protection duties, so called, imposed professedly for their benefit, should be abolished along with the Corn Law.

Some persons seem to believe that the Corn Law keeps up prices generally. This is a grievous error. The Corn Law does not keep up the rate of wages; it keeps up the price of nothing but food; it depresses the value of everything besides. Manufactured goods are cheaper in England than in any other country.

The Corn Law has been defended on the ground that the land of this country bears exclusive burdens—such as tithe, land tax, church rates, poor rates, highway rates, and county rates. The tithe never did belong to the landowner, and therefore he cannot be justly said to pay that which has always been the property of the church. The land tax, which was settled in 1692, and has not been increased to the present day, notwithstanding that the value of land has increased probably seven-fold, bears a smaller proportion to the whole amount of taxes in this country than in any of the continental states. The trading and manufacturing population pay their own church rates. The cities and towns maintain their own streets and highways—boroughs corporate support their own police and maintain their prisons—towns not incorporate contribute equally with the agriculturists to the county rate. It is, therefore, demonstrable that the towns pay their full share of local rates. But it will be found that the landed interest are exempted from many of the *general* taxes paid by the rest of the community, of which we need only enumerate probate and legacy duties.

It is contended that the repeal of the Corn Law would injure the home trade. It is impossible to separate the home from the foreign trade. A great part of the home trade is carried on in the large manufacturing and trading towns. Manchester is a larger consumer of its own cotton manufactures than the whole county of Bucks. You cannot increase the home trade without increasing your foreign trade, or extend your foreign trade without extending your home trade. They are one and the same thing.

It is alleged by our opponents that the object of the Anti-Corn-Law League is to obtain cheap food, for the purpose of being able to reduce wages. We have frequently declared that we desired not a *reduction* of wages, *which reduction is rapidly going on at the present time*, but the *maintenance* of wages; not to be able to compete with foreigners—*that* we already do; our object is to EXCHANGE our productions for the Corn and Provisions of other countries, and thereby to extend trade, augment the supply of food, and increase the demand for labour.

We are told that if the Corn Laws were repealed, it would be impossible to pay the interest of the national debt. The bulk of the state taxes, for meeting the interest of the national debt, and the other expenses of the government, are paid by excise and custom duties upon tea, coffee, sugar, tobacco, soap, malt, and other articles of general consumption. The tax upon Corn yields no regular revenue to the state. If the trade in corn were free, by which food would be obtained at a more moderate and steady price, the people would have more money to spend upon tea, sugar, &c., and thus the revenue would be benefited. In 1835, when corn was 39s. 4d. per quarter, there was an overflowing Exchequer. During the last three years, whilst wheat has been upwards of 60s., and population greater by nearly three millions, there has been a deficient revenue. It will be found, as a general rule, that whenever food has been abundant, and consequently cheap, the revenue has flourished, and *vice versa*.

The Corn Law is defended on the ground that it would be dangerous to depend upon foreigners for a supply of food. In 1810, when we were engaged in war with almost every European power, we imported 1,491,000 quarters of wheat, nearly half a million of which were obtained from France alone. In the ten years of war, from 1805 to 1815, during part of which period we were engaged in hostilities with the whole world, we imported upwards of five millions of quarters. No country could prevent the transportation of corn to England, unless by prohibiting exportation altogether; for when once a ship has cleared out of port, even for a coasting voyage, it is beyond the control of the government, and may convey its cargo to any destination.

We would especially call your Grace's attention to the question, as to how the increasing numbers in this country are to be employed and subsisted, unless a free scope be given to our foreign trade? The agricultural population continues to increase, but the land does not offer an increasing field for their employment. They have hitherto found a resource in the towns. If this outlet be stopped, the land must support the people in idleness. The landowners must either allow their increasing population to become their customers in the manufacturing and trading towns, or submit to maintain them as paupers in the place of their birth.

We would also direct the attention of your Grace to the increase of local rates during the scarcity and high price of food, particularly of poor rates. The discontent of the people has also led to an augmentation of the army and of the rural police. The corn law was enacted amidst tumult and bloodshed, and similar scenes have attended the frequent recurrence of scarcity under the operation of the law.

We have argued the question thus far as one of policy and expediency; we finally, and above all, refer our case to the standard of eternal justice, and we appeal from the decision of parliamentary majorities, governments, and ministers, to the God of justice.

Signed on behalf of the Conference,

P. A. TAYLOR, Chairman.

Palace Yard, London, Aug., 1, 1842.

*Issued by the National Anti-Corn-Law League, Newall's Buildings, Manchester.*

PRINTED BY J. GADSBY, NEWALL'S-BUILDINGS, MANCHESTER.

# CORN LAWS.

## THE EVIDENCE

OF

# JAMES DEACON HUME, ESQ.,

### LATE SECRETARY TO THE BOARD OF TRADE,

UPON THE

# CORN LAW,

### BEFORE THE COMMITTEE OF THE HOUSE OF COMMONS ON THE IMPORT DUTIES, IN 1839.

"I find that Mr. Deacon Hume, a gentleman whose loss I am sure we must all sincerely deplore, states the consumption of this country to be one quarter of wheat for each person annually."—*Sir Robert Peel's Speech on the introduction of his alteration of the Corn Law, Feb. 9, 1842.*

"I beg to remind the house of the memorable dictum of Mr. Deacon Hume, who observed that we had abundance of untaxed coal and iron, and that we only wanted abundance of untaxed wood in order to be provided cheaply with the three great primary raw materials of employment and of necessary consumption."—*Sir Robert Peel's Speech, May 10th, 1842.*

"I wish to claim for her Majesty's government no undue share of credit for the proposals they now make, and I am bound to admit that the last occasion when the serious attention of parliament was called to this subject (the Tariff) was by the committee which sat on the import duties in 1830."—*Sir Robert Peel's Speech on the introduction of the New Tariff, May 10th, 1842.*

Chairman: How many years have you been in the Customs and Board of Trade departments?—I was 38 years in the Customs, and nearly 11 years afterwards at the Board of Trade.

You have retired within the last year?—Within these few months.

Mr. Villiers: What do you understand by the principle of protection? is it to support an existing interest that cannot support itself?—Yes; it is of no use unless the trade is naturally a losing trade.

And it cannot support itself when the community can get the article cheaper elsewhere?—Certainly not, if the protection was wanted.

Then it is always at the expense of the consumer that the protection is imposed?—I think that is manifest.

You have always considered it to have that effect?—I have always considered that the increase of price, in consequence of protection, amounted to a tax. If I am made to pay 1s. 6d. by law for an article which, in the absence of that law, I could buy for a shilling, I consider the sixpence a tax, and I pay it with regret, because it does not go to the revenue of the country; and therefore I do not, in return, share the benefit of that payment, as a contribution to the revenue. I must be taxed a second time for the state.

Chairman: Then it is your opinion that every protection of a commodity operates as a tax to the community at large?—Yes; most decidedly.

Mr. Villiers: And, further, as a misdirection of capital and labour?—Yes, it is tempting parties to embark in a trade by fictitious support, which in the end may prove a fallacious one. I have often wondered how any rulers could consent to incur the responsibility of such a policy.

Chairman: Do not all such protective duties and monopolies occasion very considerable fluctuations in that particular branch, from time to time?—I think that every trade thrown out of its natural course by protection, is more subject to fluctuations than those which are left to their natural operation.

Mr. Tufnell: Then you cannot conceive any circumstances under which a protective duty can confer a permanent and general benefit upon the community?—I think not. While it operates in favour of the party intended to be protected, it is a tax upon the community, and there is always the risk of its not being able to support itself by its own natural strength; and the protection may some day fail of keeping it up. The real question at issue is, do we propose to serve the nation or to serve particular individuals?

Mr. Villiers: Has it ever fallen within your experience to know that one protection has been made the ground of others?—I believe that has been pretty much the argument of the landed interest; they have, upon numerous occasions, treated what they consider the protection upon manufactures as a reason for protection upon corn. But the cases are as different as possible, agricultural produce never being exported, and the foreign market being the great ground of prosperity to our manufactures.

Is it not the plea with some interests that their protection should be continued because they are so highly taxed, or pay so highly for the necessaries of life, that they cannot compete with their foreign rivals?—I have heard that argument used; but I think it not only groundless, but that the opposite is the true proposition. A highly-taxed people cannot afford to give protection; an individual whose necessary expenses are great, cannot be generous.

Would it not afford a ground for not removing the system of protection in one interest, or for removing all protections?—Yes, I think it would furnish a reason for universal protection, until, in attempting to protect everybody from taxation, you protected nobody.

Chairman: Are you not aware that foreign countries, in the duties they have imposed, have very often been led by our example in England to impose protective duties?—I believe that to be a very strong impression in all foreign countries; they imagine that we have risen to our present state of prosperity through the system of protections, and that they have only to adopt the same system in order to succeed as we have done.

When you speak of giving an example to Europe, do you believe that if England would remove those which are protective duties to cotton or to any other manufacture, that might induce the other nations of Europe to adopt a more liberal system of trade, and consequently lead to the admission of a larger portion of British manufactures?—I think it very probable that even such partial removals would have that effect: but I feel the strongest confidence that if we were to give up our protective system altogether, it would be impossible for other countries to retain theirs much longer.

Would you remove our own protection without any foreign country removing theirs?—Most certainly, and without even asking them. I dislike treating with foreign countries upon any subject except navigation, and that for this reason, that there would be waste in the matter of carriage between different countries; it would end in the ship always going empty one way on both sides; this would be a dreadful waste, from which every country would suffer in its commerce. And again, a ship in one place is a ship in another; there is no difficulty in the comparison, but there is a difficulty in comparing one description of goods, which one country makes, with a totally different description made in another, and equal terms can hardly be made; but I feel quite confident if we were entirely to drop our system of protection, in a very little time it would be a race with other countries which should be first, or rather, which should avoid to be last, to come in for the benefit of that trade which we should then open.

Mr. Villiers: Do you not consider a retaliatory duty as most adding to the injury which the duty imposed by the foreign country occasions in this country?—I have always thought so; I have disliked all treating in the matter; I would take what I wanted, and leave them to find the value of our customs.

Chairman: Then that principle you would apply generally to the commercial transactions of this country?—Entirely so; I should make our laws according to what I deemed best, which would certainly be to give the freest possible introduction of the goods of other nations into our country, and I should leave others to take advantage of it or not as they thought fit. There can be no doubt that if we imported from any country any considerable quantity of goods, and the manufactures of that country were protected, the producers of those goods which we took would very soon find the great difficulty they had in getting their returns; and, instead of our soliciting the governments of those countries to admit our goods, our advocates for that admission would be in the country itself; they would arise from the exports of the goods which we received.

Mr. Chapman: Is it your opinion that the trade of this country would flourish more without the intervention of commercial treaties with other nations?—I think that we should settle our commerce better by ourselves then by attempting to make arrangements with other countries. We make proposals to them: they do not agree to those. We then after that feel a repugnance to doing that which we ought perhaps in the first instance to have done of our own accord; and I go upon the principle that it is impossible for us to import too much, that we may be quite sure that the export will follow in some form or other, and that the making of the articles to be so exported, will be an employment infinitely more beneficial to this country than that which may be thus superseded.

Chairman: Do you consider that those principles which you have laid down ought to apply equally to articles of food of this country, a great portion of which are now excluded?—I conceive myself, if I were compelled to choose, that food is the last thing upon which I would attempt to place any protection.

That is the first thing upon which you would remove the prohibition and protective duties?—Yes. It is very clear that this country stands in need of a vast deal of agricultural produce beyond its production, which is not to be measured merely by the quantity of corn which we occasionally import, because we habitually import very largely of those articles which are the produce of land, and suited to be raised in this country, besides corn, and which shows that the power of supply is very much strained. Although we view it chiefly in the article of corn, we import a very large quantity of other commodities, commonly and habitually, such as are the produce of our own soil, or fit to be so; and this proves clearly that we want more than we can produce. The exclusion of supply in such a case is cruel privation.

You are of opinion that all those protective duties are, in fact, a direct tax upon the community, by raising the price of every one of those articles to the consumer?—Most decidedly. I cannot analyze the charge which I pay in any other way than that part of it is the price of the commodity, and part is a duty, though it goes out of my private pocket into another private pocket, instead of into that of the public.

Does that, in your opinion, add to the wealth of the country, or does it check the general industry which is applied in our manufactures? I think it cannot add to the wealth of the country, because it is clear that we consume commodities at a greater price than is the necessary price; and, consequently, we waste labour and capital in the production, and waste can never ultimately do good, at least to a nation, although some individuals may thrive upon it.

Do you consider the wealth of England to be caused and maintained by her commercial and manufacturing industry?—Certainly: if meant as in contradistinction from the produce of the soil. It is only necessary to look round the world, and see what countries there are of much richer soil that are in a state of comparative poverty; and also to look back to our own history, of no long period, to see that with the same quantity of land we have now we were a poor country compared with what we are; therefore, having always had the land, but not the trade, I must conceive that the increase of our riches arises from the trade and not from the land.

Has not the wealth of the country arisen from the great increased prosperity of our manufacturing and commercial relations?—I conceive that it can be traced to no other source. The only difference that I can see in the present state of the country and the country a century ago, is that by commerce and manufactures we have acquired riches, and raised up a population which are not only able to consume, but also able to pay good prices for the produce of our land. If the same population had been raised by other means, they would have been a burden to the land instead of an advantage.

Does not every limitation in the importation of food, and every rise in the price of food, tend to undermine the manufactures of the country, upon which we depend?—I conceive that it must do so, because we place ourselves at the risk of being surpassed by the manufactures in other countries; and as soon as it happens, if ever the day should arrive, that we should be put to a severe trial as to our manufacturing power, I can hardly doubt that the prosperity of this country will recede much faster than it has gone forward.

Do you mean whenever England shall be unable to compete with foreign markets in her principal staples with other countries which are less burthened and have cheaper food than ourselves, that then the prosperity of this country must begin to wane?—Whenever foreign countries can so compete with us, from whatever cause, I conceive that our prosperity must decline, but I cannot help believing that there can be no other cause for that than other countries having cheaper food.

Is not the increased price of food in this country one of the principal ingredients of the increased cost of our manufactures, so as to prevent our competing with other countries?—I conceive that, in the long run, it must be so: it either must be so, or the manufacturers and labourers must suffer great privations. Wages would first be lowered as far as possible; and, as many masters would be withdrawing from their trade, it is possible that the supply of labour would be so much greater than the demand that the reduction might go to the limits of starving or of riots; but it is not merely that, it is the diverting of other countries from manufactures, and inducing them to take to agriculture instead, and also producing an interchange of goods, and creating markets for returns for our goods, as well as finding markets for them to go to. Altogether, I conceive that the reduction in the price of food, and particularly the admission of it from abroad, must tend to prevent other countries from being able to surpass us in manufactures.

You have often heard it stated that the people of England, being higher taxed than they are in any other country, would be unable, as regards the price of food, to compete with other countries if the Corn Laws were taken off?—I have heard that argument, but have always been surprised at it, because it appears to me that the very circumstance of our being so highly taxed for the good of the state is a reason why we should not be taxed between ourselves.

You consider that a fallacy?—The greatest fallacy I can conceive. It is the very opposite of the true proposition.

Mr. Villiers: Do you not consider that we have greater advantages in production than any other country in the world, as regards capital and skill?—I think that is the only thing that has kept us up, but I do not think that the advantages are such that we can rely upon them for ever.

We are losing markets for our goods in return for corn, and we are compelling those countries to establish interests to rival us in other countries? — I have always thought that when the great change in this world took place after the French war, before which time foreigners had not attempted manufactures to any material extent, and when they had been greatly encouraged in agricultural pursuits, because through the war we had been great importers, if from that time we had thrown open our ports for raw produce and removed protections, we should have had our manufactures in a most secure position, for the other countries who are now attempting to rival us would not have attempted it; but it would be difficult now to get back to the point at which we then were: starting at that point, we were then the only manufacturers.

Chairman: As we lost that favourable opportunity of placing the manufactures of this country on the highest and best foundation, ought we not now to be most anxious to retrace our steps, and would not the removal of protecting duties, and lowering the duties on imports generally, be one of the steps towards that end?—I did not mean to say that it is not right to do it now, because we have lost the best time for doing it; I only meant to say that the way in which we have acted, instead of being beneficial, has been injurious.

Mr. Villiers: If the prices of the continent were equal to those of this country, we still have great advantages from the skill we employ in our manufactures?—I think that other countries have not made such an advance but that we may still very well support ourselves. I do not think we have gone so far as to make the case hopeless, though I lament that we should not have taken the step at the right time.

Is there not a tendency in our capital to leave this country and establish itself on the continent?—From the low rate of interest in this country, and the degree in which money has gone abroad for various purposes, it is very evident that the capitalist here is not altogether content with this as the place of its employment; if this is very much the case as a mere question of the investment of money, it must be doubly so in the case of manufacturing employment of it.

What the people on the continent want most is large capital, is it not?—I believe it is; and I believe they are every year obtaining very considerable capital, as well as artizans, from this country, and even master manufacturers.

Then the tendency of the present system is to drive this large amount of capital to those countries which are engaged in rivalry with us?—That is the direct tendency; and one wonders that the trading part of the community have not taken this view of the matter earlier; and I can only account for it on this supposition, that the most influential and the most advanced have believed and felt confident that the shifting of the trade was a matter of slow operation, and that it would last their time. I think that this makes the great difference between the former supineness of our manufacturers on the subject of the Corn Laws and their recent activity on that subject. The day of trial is not now so distant, in the view of the present parties, as it was in that of their predecessors, or even of themselves some years ago.

So far as the duties are imposed with a view to protect native industry and to induce capital to be employed in this country, they have the opposite tendency?—Yes, speaking of national industry as a whole.

Do you believe the high cost of living induced by those protective duties on food also drives other people not engaged in trade to live on the continent?—I have generally understood that the number of persons residing abroad do go there with a view to enjoying life with a moderate income, which they cannot do here.

Do not you suppose that that must injure the home trade?—Certainly; it transfers the customers from this country to another.

Then are we not by this system undermining the very means by which publi: taxation and public revenue are supported?—I think that we not only check the collection of the revenue immediately, but that we are also undermining our resources. I cannot help often looking at the consequences with considerable alarm. I think the country cannot stand such a system as this for a long period.

Mr. Villiers: Would it not have been the natural course of things in this country for revenue to have greatly increased, considering how the taxes are imposed?—I have not a doubt that if there were no protecting duties, the revenue would flow in with a very great increase and great ease.

Owing to the increase of population and the increase of wealth? The increase of population, and the greater ability of men to pay the state taxes, being relieved from paying taxes to individuals.

If the protective system were altogether removed, the effect would be to produce a large population, and a well-employed population?—Yes.

The tendency, as we find, of the present Corn Laws, and other protective duties, is to throw the people out of work, and to diminish their employment?—Most clearly, that is the tendency; but even taking the population as it is, and its property as it is, if they were relieved from that additional price on the goods which we pay on account of their being protected, the people of this country would be able, and would, in effect, in the expenditure of their incomes, pay a larger proportion to the revenue.

Chairman: Do not the fluctuations in the employment of industry also tend very much to lessen the productive power of the country?—Yes, I conceive they do.

Produced mainly by the present system?—Yes; because it is artificial.

Mr. Villiers: You consider it can matter little to the consumer whether he pays so much more for his food as a tax to the revenue, or whether he pays so much more for his food as a tax for protection?—The enhanced price, from whatever cause, is just the same. I would suppose that, instead of protecting land by a duty on foreign corn, the country was left to get corn at the cheapest rate, and then that a revenue was raised for the express purpose of being applied to the support of the land. It would be too palpable, and could not be borne; but I conceive the effect of the present system upon the consumer to be the same. It would be even better, and perhaps cheaper, to pay directly than indirectly, because trade would then be free.

Supposing a tax was imposed upon flour ground at the mill, every person then would pay that; do you not suppose that that would afford a large revenue?—Yes, it would, according to the rate.

The people might feel it even less than the present protecting duty?—It would be less noxious.

It is quite possible that a large revenue might be collected by that means?—Yes, and the public pay the same price that they now do.

A large revenue might be collected, and the public pay even less for bread?—Yes, because it would be only a charge, and not also an impediment to trade.

I presume in my questions a perfectly free trade, and a tax upon all flour ground at the mill?—Yes, an internal duty, and importation free.

The community would not suffer so much as they do at present, and a large revenue might be collected by that means?—I conceive that, if the duty charged at the mill was only about the same amount as that which the public now pay for the purpose of protection, not only the revenue would derive a large supply, but that it would be less injurious to the people.

Certainly less injurious to trade?—Certainly, even if it were so high as to keep bread at its present price, notwithstanding the free importation of wheat.

Chairman: Have you ever made a calculation as to the amount of taxation which the community pay in consequence of the increased price of wheat and butchers' meat, which is occasioned by the monopoly now held by land?—I think that a tolerable calculation may be made of that increased charge. It is generally calculated that each person, upon the average, consumes a quarter of wheat a year. Assuming, then, the amount of duty that this wheat paid, or the price enhanced by protection, whatever that is, as far as bread goes, to be 10s., it would be that amount upon the whole population. Then you could hardly say less than, perhaps, double that for butchers' meat and other matters; so that if we were to say that the corn is enhanced by 10s. a quarter, there would be that 10s. and 20s. more as the increase of the price of meat and other agricultural productions, including hay and oats for horses, barley for beer, as well as butter and cheese. That would be £36,000,000 a year, and the public are in fact paying that as effectually out of their pockets as if it did go to the revenue in the form of direct taxes.

And, consequently, are less able to pay any taxes that the state may require for its support?—Certainly; I conceive that having paid the private taxes they are the less able to pay the public taxes.

Is not the effect of that also to cripple and limit the industry of the country?—I conceive the great evil lies in that branch of the question; it is not so calculable, but if they could have the trade which I believe they would have if all those protections were taken away, I think they could pay 30s. a head easily, compared with what they can now do.

So that the burden of this protective system generally exceeds the whole amount of taxation paid to the state?—I conceive so, taking the cost and the evil consequences together, if that evil was equally subject to computation. It is the case with many duties, such as some of the excise duties, which are more injurious in their regulations than they are in the sum taken from the people, though you cannot estimate the injurious effect. I conceive the actual money paid, and the evil effect computed in money, would be more than the whole revenue of the country.

Mr. Williams: Upon what principle could you recommend a general change of the system in levying import duties upon articles, by the introduction of which at a less duty the manufactures of this country would be seriously affected?—Upon the principle of general national benefit. The question is, whether we mean the nation, or whether we mean to serve particular individuals; I speak, whether from habit, from my own turn of mind, or from official circumstances, in behalf of the nation, or of the country at large.

In the general change you contemplate, you contemplate that a great reduction of the taxation should take place which now so heavily presses upon the working men of this country, and so disproportionately, as compared with the working men of other countries, who are producing articles to compete with the produce of their industry?—If, by the question, are meant taxes upon a particular commodity, I conceive certainly those taxes must be countervailed by at least equal taxes on the rival article imported from abroad. But if the question means the general taxation of the country falling on the subsistence and expenditure of the people, then I must beg to submit in the strongest terms in which I can possibly give any opinion, that the general taxation of the country is no ground whatever for protection; any attempt to relieve any interest from any portion of that general taxation by raising arbitrarily the price of the article which they make, is only a violent manner of shifting their share of the burthen to other shoulders. If on account of the general taxes upon subsistence paid by any class of people, you forcibly raise to the consumer the price of the article which that class produces, you then relieve them from taxation, supposing you measure the matter fairly and correctly; and I have never been able to see the least ground why any one class of the people should be relieved from taxation, and why the other parts should be compelled to pay their proportion for them as well as their own.

Sir H. Parnell: Will you explain what you mean in your last answer by general taxation and special taxation?—I will illustrate my opinion by speaking of particular articles. We pay in this country an internal tax upon soap and upon vinegar; it would be very wrong, I conceive, to suffer soap or vinegar to be imported without also being charged with an import duty equal to those taxes; but the taxes borne by the makers of vinegar and soap in the articles of their consumption, and the consumption of their families, their food, their liquors, their sugar, their tea, or anything else; the taxes they pay in that shape upon the articles of their consumption are of a very different nature, and those are the taxes with regard to which I mean to express my opinion that there is no ground whatever for a protecting duty, in order that they may be better able to compete with the foreigner, for it is impossible to do that without causing some other party to pay more taxes than they otherwise would do. The whole community bear their share of those taxes without any assistance; of course by the whole community I mean the consumers of vinegar and the consumers of soap.

Then general taxation does not add to prices?—That may be a very difficult question, and there are so many elements in price that one can hardly give a positive opinion; I think myself that price must always be determined by supply and demand.

But the cheapest manufactures we have are subject to the whole general taxation of the country?—The manufactures that are so cheap that we export them in large quantities have no protection; the parties who make them decidedly pay all their taxes of consumption; but this shows a power of supply and a foreign demand.

Chairman: Do you mean the manufacture of cotton and other articles, of which we export large quantities?—It may truly be said so of cottons, because, though there is a duty upon foreign cottons having the character of a protective duty, I believe it to be inoperative, particularly when we consider how much is exported; and as I consider that duty to be of no service to the people concerned in the cotton manufacture, I conceive that they pay, out of their produce and their labour, all the taxes upon all they consume in this country.

Then the only import duty which they require on the cotton manufactures would be a duty equal to that imposed on the raw material which they import?—Yes, or any other ingredient which they may use in the manufacture, such as their dyes and gums.

Mr. Williams: If it can be proved that one-half of the wages of the working men in this country are taken from them in taxes, and that a very small amount of taxation, comparatively, is taken from the wages of the working men in other countries, who compete with our working men in the production of certain articles, is it your opinion, in such a case, that if the foreigner can produce an article cheaper by his paying less taxes, the production of his labour should be admitted into this country, and that the trade should be entirely lost to our manufacturers?—The comparison which I should draw is not between the taxes which would be paid by the manufacturer of the goods alluded to here, and the taxes paid by the manufacturers abroad, which must vary greatly. I should consider what taxes fall properly upon that class of manufacturers in this country, and those which fall upon the other operatives who cannot be protected in any way. I conceive that every person in this country must pay, out of his own sources, the taxes which fall upon the quantity of taxable commodities which he consumes, and that there is no question as to relieving him of those taxes that can ever afford the slightest ground for throwing them upon other people by protection against the foreign article of the same nature as that which he makes.

Then is it your opinion that the working men of this country, so large a portion of whose wages are taken from them in taxes, ought not to have any protection at all against the cheaper productions of the working men of countries that comparatively pay no taxes?—Certainly, that is my decided opinion; I think the small amount of taxes paid by persons abroad is no ground for giving protection to the commodity here; for this reason, that it is only in such a case shifting the taxes from the party intended to be relieved to others here who are to be the consumers of those commodities. You cannot throw the tax on the foreigner, but only on other British subjects.

In the case of a working man in a foreign country receiving wages of 6s. per week, with which he can get as many of the necessaries of life as the working man of this country with 10s. a week; if the skill of those two workmen is equal, would you say that the production of the labour of the foreign workman should entirely supersede the labour of the English workman, or that the English workman must come down from 10s. a week to 6s. a week, so as to be upon an equality in point of production of the article he manufactures with the foreign workman?—I should not consider the taxes or the wages paid or received in this and the foreign country as one of the elements of my calculation. If there is any commodity made in this country that stands really in the predicament supposed in the question, then I must conclude that that is one of those things which we should cease to make here; we do not make every thing, but we do know that we make an enormous quantity of things, and that we export a great quantity of articles, and therefore I must suppose that we can very safely and properly leave the interests of parties to determine what they shall make and what they shall not make in this country; and without enabling some of them to live tax-free.

You are aware that but for the protective

duties, the silk trade of this country, and the stocking trade of this country, and some other important branches of trade, would be entirely lost on account of the ability of the foreign manufacturers to produce the article cheaper than they can in this country; would you in that case say that the great interests, both as to the master manufacturers and the working men that are now employed in those trades, should be annihilated, which would be the natural consequence of allowing silks, stockings, and the other articles I have alluded to, to be imported into this country free of duty?—I do not conceive that it is so clear a case that those trades would be annihilated if the protection was taken from them as a part of a general system of relinquishing all protection, but I am far from supposing that a change to a totally free system would not make many changes in the employment of the industry of this country, and it is possible that that change might lead to the relinquishing of some branches of the silk, and even of cotton manufactures. But with the reliance that I have upon the effect of a general system of free trade, I cannot bring my mind to believe that we should not make stockings, or manufacture silk very largely in this country, if all protection were removed, provided that the system was general, so that the expense of living of the labourers in those cases which the several questions have so particularly pointed at, should be reduced to their natural amount. That must certainly be understood to mean that the corn trade should be free, that meat, that every article of consumption should for the future be free; and were that the case, no change being made in the revenue, I can scarcely believe that the natural effect would not be to raise the product of the revenue a fourth, or perhaps a third greater than it is, without laying on a single additional duty; and in that case we clearly see how easy it would be to relieve those parties who are now much pressed by competition from those taxes, which were considered to oppress them to the greatest degree, and to place them on a fairer footing with the foreign competitors than they now are. I believe the necessity of protection is occasioned almost entirely by protection itself.

Then I understand you, in the opinion you have given, to contemplate placing the working men of this country upon the same, or nearly the same footing as the workmen of other countries?—I would place them on the same footing.

Chairman: Do you mean by placing them on the same footing, that you would abolish all those monopolies as regards food in this country, and which are the cause of the great difference between the condition of the labouring people here and abroad?—Most certainly; I should never think of exposing trades situated in the manner which is contemplated in the previous question, to an open competition with foreigners, while I left them burdened,—not with taxes, I beg to be understood, but with the operation of protections in other cases, and for the emolument of other nations.

Mr. Villiers: I understand you to say that if there is any difference in the cost of living in this country and in other countries, or that we are under disadvantage in competition with them, it chiefly arises from the protective system?—That is my opinion; with our great command of trade, our navigation, our capital, and our geographical position, if trade in this country was perfectly free, and we were enabled to obtain in the cheapest markets, upon even terms, all the commodities we want, I can see no reason why this should not be one of the cheapest countries to live in that any civilized populous country can be. There are many matters in which density of population leads to cheapness.

Then when you speak of competition from cheaper labour abroad, you mean when the people here being heavily taxed to the state, their burdens are increased by taxes to support particular interests?—Exactly; I conceive protection to be a positive increase of taxes, not less positive than if an additional tax were put upon the commodity itself; whatever the compulsory amount is that you pay more than the natural amount, it is to the consumer as effectual a tax as if it were collected by the tax-gatherer, the custom-house officer, or the excise.

You did not mean to say that general taxation did not affect prices, but that it afforded no excuse for protection?—Certainly; what I mean is, that the general taxation is not a ground for taking the burden off one portion of the community, and laying it, as it must be borne by some one, on another portion, that second portion paying double, the other paying none. If I might illustrate this, I would take the article of corn; supposing the taxes paid by the landed interest in their personal and domestic expenditure should amount to 10s. a quarter upon the corn raised upon their lands, and you put 10s. upon foreign corn, while you habitually import it and pay that 10s., thus raising the price of all that is produced at home by 10s., I conceive that 10s. to be a burden thrown upon the other parts of the community, and that the landed proprietor literally lives in this country without paying any tax at all.

You observed, in a former part of your evidence, that one protection was constantly a ground for claiming another?—It furnishes a plea always to parties who are ever seeking pleas for asking for protection: it is particularly and everlastingly, as far as my own observation goes, alluded to by the landed interest.

And it frequently occurs that when one interest has thus got itself exempt from taxation, it has re-imposed the tax upon itself by having to pay it as a protection upon other productions?—Whatever the proportion may be between the protected goods produced by the party and his expenditure in the general articles of consumption, he gives and receives in that proportion; if they are equal, then he certainly does, in my opinion, restore the money back again to the other protected parties. I will suppose that there are 100 trades and 100 commodities, and that you give a certain measure of protection to every one of them, well measured as far as the nature of the goods will admit, then I conceive that those 100 parties would find all their cases completely neutralized: each would receive from the system a benefit as one, and would pay it away in dribblets to the ninety-nine, and thus they would all be brought to the same position as if none were protected at all.

But if one interest was more powerful than the other ninety-nine, it is possible that it might get some advantage over the others?—The great evil of protection is, that it cannot be made just, equal, and equitable. In my illustration just now, I supposed that you could find a way of protecting each in an equal proportion, but that is not possible.

Sir C. Douglas: Is the abolition of the Corn Laws inseparable from the opinion you entertain that the removal of import duties ought to take place?—Just so; that is the great article, and I conceive that otherwise we should expose our manufacturers to the most unfair competition with foreigners, not because of the light taxes which foreigners pay, but because of the general cheapness of living, from having corn and other provisions upon better terms than we have. I think that the first necessaries of life should be the first articles to be set free.

Then, from that last answer, the committee may understand that you mean a total abolition of the Corn Laws?—Certainly; and I should prefer the total abolition. I cannot see any ground whatever for any countervailing tax upon corn; I cannot perceive anything in the principle of protection that is peculiar to corn. British corn does not contribute to the public revenue. there is, therefore, no charge upon it to be countervailed.

Then you would not allow even a small fixed duty?—My opinion is that there is no ground for any duty; the only ground I can conceive is to countervail charges in the production of corn. I know that there are a great many charges which the landed interest conceive to be peculiarly on them, and to fall upon their productions; but as far as I have been able to investigate those charges, I think they have services in return for them, and they do not go to the public revenue; they are of a local nature, and I think the farmers are so much better off, and so much more enabled to raise the commodity with advantage, by reason of those local charges, since they have facilities in return equal to the payment: and I do firmly believe that any country that has not the system of raising funds for the purposes for which those local funds are raised, would be at a great disadvantage in the production of agricultural produce.

Mr. Villiers: You are only alluding to what is just, and not to what it may be wise to do: you are referring to what the landed interest might or might not claim in justice, not to what it might be necessary to concede to them?—To what they claim in justice, and upon that the only thing that can be urged as a plea is the countervailing duty to set against positive taxes paid to the state, not their local rates and charges. It may be sometimes wise to concede what you have not the power to refuse.

Sir C. Douglas: If the Corn Laws were totally abolished, and consequently that part of our provisions and food were brought in from other countries, do you agree with those who think that a great deal of land would be thrown out of cultivation?—By throwing land out of cultivation I presume is meant converting arable into grass land. It is a wrong term, I think, to use, though I know it is a common term. I believe that much land would be thrown out of arable cultivation, and I believe that one of the great evils of our agriculture is the misappropriation of the soil; I believe there is a great deal too large a proportion of land under the plough, and too small a portion under grass. The difficulty of rearing lean stock in this country, for the purpose of fattening, is so great that it is the chief cause of the high price of meat; and I am quite persuaded that if a very large breadth of that arable land which can scarcely be cultivated to advantage were turned back to grass, the effect would be to reduce the quantity of corn produced in this country so much as to make it impossible for the foreigner to fill the vacuum at a low price, and that the general result would be that it would produce a lower price of meat, there being a power of increased consumption in the present state of the country in the article of meat that is almost immeasurable. When we reflect upon the extremely small portion of meat eaten every day by the most robust labourers in the country, who are, of course, by far the most numerous portion of the population, if we were only to suppose them to have every day a fair, moderate meal of meat, the increase of demand for meat, and for inferior meat,—for cattle not fattened to the highest pitch of perfection, such as would be suitable to the produce of land of inferior qualities,—would be so great that there would be no want of good employment for any of the land that we possess within our boundaries.

Do not you suppose that the Corn Laws have had a tendency to bring the poor lands into cultivation?—I think they have tended to break up land which had better have remained in grass. If the question means waste land, there can be no doubt that the demand for produce has led to the breaking up of commons, and so far that is a great benefit; but it by no means follows that it should be kept permanently under plough when there is a much greater demand for grass. With regard to the effect of the protection on our corn, that can hardly be said to have been the cause of the breaking up of so much land, because I believe it is in the knowledge of most people that the era in which the lands were chiefly broken up was during the period of the war, and that corn was being imported without any restraint whatever through the whole of that period. I believe that many parties have since repented that they have broken up their lands.

Chairman: Were not prices during all that time of increased cultivation very high?—Yes, the prices were the stimulus to the conversion of the grass land into arable land, without the aid of any corn law.

Mr. Villiers: Would not the effect of population increasing, and commerce and manufactures prospering, be to lead to the breaking up of waste lands, and to a greater demand being created for the soil?—The breaking up of waste land is a process that one would always wish to see going forward; the very idea of land lying waste is repugnant to one's feelings, as long as it can be applied to any use; but that is a very different thing from having in cultivation a disproportion of arable.

But independently of those protective duties, would it not be the tendency of increased population, and the extension of manufactures, to create a greater demand for the use of the soil?—The inducement to break up waste land would not be directly the protection, but the price, and whatever was the cause of a high price would lead to the cultivation of the waste lands, whether it was a state of war, the increase of population, or any thing else; as long as there was a good price for the produce of land, parties possessing or having a right to those waste lands would bring them into cultivation.

But looking at the limited extent of this island, should you not suppose that if the manufactures prospered, and population increased, the price of land must always be high?—In looking to the increase of the population, which has doubled in the last half century, one does not know how to limit the price of land in this country, provided through no bad policy the increase of that population and its prosperity are not checked.

It is within your experience that the price of land has risen enormously in this country?—That is a matter of general notoriety, without any party being able to know precisely how the matter stands: but as far as the little information I have got upon the matter goes, I believe an exhibition of the rent-rolls of different parts of the country for the last half century would lay before the public eye one of the most astounding accounts that ever was witnessed.

Do you not connect that increase in the price of land with the start in manufactures which we took towards the latter end of the last century?—I cannot attribute it to any other cause; the war led in the first instance to what may be said to have been a wasteful consumption of food; a large portion of people who were subsisting at home with the greatest economy, were converted into soldiers and sailors, and were supported at the public expense; but the great peculiarity of that period was the commencement of the great increase of our manufactures, the bringing to perfection of Mr. Arkwright's system, the introduction of steam power, and the vast improvements of machinery; we were the first to adopt those improvements, and from the circumstance of the rest of the world being so much more disadvantageously placed in the war at that time, they were then unable to follow us, but time and peace have altered the case much, and we cannot expect to reap the same benefits after a certain period from any new discovery, however great it may be, that we did in the earlier stages. The cause of the increase in the value of land was the start in manufactures; but we kept the start the longer by reason of war.

Can you expect any decrease of the value of land from any other cause but the decline of manufactures in this country?—No, that is the only matter to which I look with any apprehension as regards the prosperity of this country.

Mr. Williams: Am I correct in understanding you to express it as your opinion that notwithstanding our heavy taxation, we could, under a system of free trade, compete with foreign countries in our manufactures and the production of corn?—I conceive that it is clearly proved that we could in those manufactures that we are calculated for, conduct them with success, because we are now conducting them successfully, although the people are not only burdened with the taxes alluded to, but according to my opinion also with a large portion of the taxes which properly belong to the protected parties; I therefore think that our best manufactures are burdened by protections, and not assisted by them.

A small portion of the £50,000,000, or £52,000,000 of taxes which are paid by the people of this country, are produced from articles on which the tax is imposed for their protection against foreign manufactures?—I conceive a very small portion, because the very circumstance of the tax being laid for the purpose of preventing importation, implies that little revenue will be received; if much were received, it would cease to be a protection.

Then it is your opinion that with the continuance of the imposition of taxes to the amount of £50,000,000, upon the people of this country, they will be able to compete with all the various productions of foreign countries where taxation is very small indeed?—They do compete now, and export in the face of those other countries £50,000,000 of the produce of their industry.

At the present time is not a most extraordinary progress being made in different branches of manufacture in Germany, and other parts of the continent, where a few years ago the manufactories were producing comparatively very small quantities?—I believe that that is the case, and it is a subject of great uneasiness, I confess, to my mind. I think I see a change taking place, and that we may find ourselves mistaken in supposing that we can always retain the trade, which having commenced with great advantage in the first instance, we are in the early stages allowed to carry on to a great extent; but it is because I fear this, because I see the power of competition rising abroad, and because I expect those countries will some day drive us out of the foreign market, and thus deprive us of our means of exportation, that I am so anxious to remove what I think are the impediments to an equal power of competition on our part with those foreign countries.

Mr. Villiers: Is not the general taxation less now than it was a few years ago, in this country?—The taxation is considerably less upon every individual. The sum raised is the same, but the taxes which we have repealed since the year 1819, when the general settlement after the war may be said to have been made, I believe in round numbers may be considered at £16,000,000 or £17,000,000 a year; the remaining taxes, in consequence of the increase of population, and what has hitherto been the prosperous state of the country, producing alone a greater amount than they formerly produced, in conjunction with those which have been repealed.

Chairman: In reference to your former answer, will you state what are the "impediments" to British commerce competing in foreign countries with that of the continent? The impediments are of the nature which has been pointed out in several of the preceding questions, namely, the expense of living in this country. It is true that the portion of that expense which consists of taxes has been expressly mentioned, but I conceive the general expense of living, and the charges upon that living, which are taken out of the pockets of the consumers by the protective system, and do not go into the revenue, are almost as large a portion as that which the revenue itself takes. Another impediment arising out of the protective system is the checking of commercial intercourse with other countries, and preventing our manufacturers from obtaining their best returns for the goods they can import.

Mr. Williams: Does it not appear to you, from the great progress which has been made of very late years indeed, in manufactures in Germany and other countries on the continent, that at no distant time the wages of the labourers and working men of this country must come down to as low a point as the rate of wages in those countries if we are to maintain our trade?—The progress in manufactures which is observably abroad is such, that unless we do take some strong measures in this country, for the purpose of putting our population upon a natural footing, and therefore upon nearly the same footing with their competitors, I do look forward with considerable apprehension to the trade of this country suffering considerably; that is a reason, in my mind, for taking off all protections, and is a very different operation from that which would go to the imposing of protecting duties for the express purpose of reimbursing particular interests for the taxes which they pay in ordinary consumption. The foreign manufacturers have shown that they can make the goods; it requires time to enable them to make enough to supplant us.

Mr. Villiers: Do you consider that the revenue presents any obstacle at all to doing away with the protective system?—No, certainly not; I conceive that the prosperity of the revenue is greatly impeded by the protective system.

But I wish to call your attention to those articles where the duties are levied, and where the operation of the duties is both protective and fiscal?—In those cases, if the protective duty were reduced to a rate which the foreigner could readily pay, a greater quantity of the article would be imported, and the revenue be increased.

Since in your opinion you ought simultaneously to reduce all the protective duties, you consider that the revenue offers no objection, but rather an argument in favour of doing away with those duties?—Certainly; my hesitation applies to the different interests that might be affected in their trade, and not to the revenue. There can be no doubt that the revenue would instantly be increased by removing or sufficiently reducing the protections.

But do you hold that you could not do away with the protection in some cases, without diminishing the revenue?—I am not aware of any case in which the revenue would be injured by removing the protection.

# EXTRACTS FROM A SERIES OF LETTERS

BY

# MR. DEACON HUME,

*Which appeared originally in the "Morning Chronicle," under the signature of H. B. T., (*Hume, Board of Trade,*) and which were afterwards published as a pamphlet by Hooper, Pall Mall East, London.*

---

## THE EVIL EFFECTS OF RESTRICTIONS ON COMMERCE.

There is scarcely a civilized spot in the globe in which the now impoverished labourer cannot produce, in excess of his own wants, some peculiar commodity with which he could provide himself with those other commodities he so greatly needs, if his right of exchange were not denied by the interposition of some arbitrary power. Mutual supply by means of such exchange is the scheme, and it is the law of nature, loudly proclaimed by the diversities of climate, soil, and capacities; it is the manifest design of a beneficent Providence for the benefit of the human race. But what is the law of man? An impious prohibition of the law of God. I figure to myself the family of a Manchester or a Birmingham workman contemplating, on a Saturday night, the true exchangeable value of their week's work, and computing how much food, as well as other commodities, it would supply them with, under the free operation of the scheme of Providence and of the law of nature. I also figure to myself the family of the Polish husbandmen longing to doff their miserable dresses of sheep-skin, and to exchange their corn for fabrics of the spindle and the loom. A greater offence can hardly be committed than to obstruct the mutual dealings of such parties, except it can be justified as a necessary national sacrifice. I stoutly deny the nationality of the object; the restraint is nothing less than a taking of the necessaries of life from those who have nothing to spare, in order to increase the luxuries of those whose command of them would bear reduction—supposing, but by no means admitting, that any reduction would ensue.

## THE CASE OF THE MANUFACTURING AND AGRICULTURAL INTERESTS STATED.

Few people are aware of the relative positions in which our manufacturing interest and our landed interest are practically placed towards each other, by reason of the different proportions which the gross quantities of their respective productions bear to the consumption of the country; and, consequently, few persons perceive the degree in which this natural inequality of advantages is aggravated by the interposition of a law which throws its weight to the side which already preponderated. *If any interference between these two interests could be justified, a far better case could be made out in favour of a bounty to increase the importation of corn, than of a duty to restrain it.*

My first position is, that the agriculturists have, under any circumstances, the enviable advantage of always selling their goods at home in a market insufficiently supplied.

My second position is, that the manufacturer, when he sells any of his goods at home, always sells them in a glutted market. These are facts which can readily be ascertained by referring to the accounts of imports and exports.

When the landowner is seller, he is enabled, in fixing the price of his wheat, to add to the amount of the foreign price, all the expense which must be incurred in bringing wheat from abroad. He stands firm in the market, and says to the manufacturer--reject my wheat if it please you to do so, and go a thousand miles by water and by land to fetch the cheap wheat you speak of.

But when the landowner changes his position, and becomes the buyer of the manufacturer's cottons, he reverses his calculations, and he deducts from the price which they would fetch in the foreign market all the expenses of sending them thither. Nor is his language less changed, though it is equally peremptory. He now says to the manufacturer—there is my offer, leave it if you like, and carry your cottons half round the world, in quest of that better price which you say will be given for them in other countries.

I am quite sure that many a high-minded land proprietor, if he could be brought to perceive the relative positions in which the agricultural and manufacturing interests are placed, would be the first to denounce the system as the most abominable piece of subtle and refined oppression he had ever met with. Yet so it is; the manufacturer stands over those very goods which are destined for a foreign market, which he knows will go to a foreign market, and for which foreign goods will assuredly be received in return; and yet he is not permitted to send them to the foreign market on his own account, nor to receive in return for them the description of foreign goods he wants for himself. The landowner is both exporter and importer; for the operation of the Corn Act is to give him a right of pre-emption of our manufactures at a maximum price.

## HOW TO PRESERVE RESPECT FOR THE RIGHTS OF PROPERTY.

When industry shall have recovered its rights, all jealousies between the rich and the poor—all invidious distinctions between the productive and the non productive—all cant about the useful and the useless—will cease; and in their place will be revived the older and better sentiment of the sacredness of property, and of respect for superiors. Let property withdraw itself into its proper limits, and relinquish all its usurpations; and let there be nothing factitious in superiority of station, and we shall see physical power and moral power always harmonizing with each other. If the working classes shall be thought to have lost any portion of their accustomed respect for the rights of property, it is solely in consequence of the unintelligible difficulties in which they find themselves placed by the attacks which property makes upon the rights of industry. Their understandings are perplexed and mystified by their situation; and as the blows they receive are inflicted by property, they are almost led to attribute to it an inherent evil quality. But the property of one man cannot, *under equal laws*, operate any injury to another. It can be no injury to me that a particular man is owner of a particular part of my country, as his exclusive estate, provided he be contented with it for its true worth, and leave me in quiet possession of any property which I may happen to own. But if he tell me that *his* property is of so peculiar a nature that it entitles him to take from me some of *mine*, in order to make his the more valuable; and, above all, if my property consist solely in my labour, then there may be some risk that I may be seduced into an opinion, that property is a sort of noxious matter, and a nuisance which I may fairly endeavour to abate.

## THE LANDOWNERS UNMASKED.

The restriction which is imposed on the rights of the workmen by the corn law, has not even the outward show of being intended for the public good; and it is in vain to tell the landowner, that the burthen of the proof that it is so intended lies on him; because we see him, on every occasion, claiming the benefit of it as his peculiar right. It is his own case which he perpetually pleads; and it is upon the merits of the case which he thinks he makes out that he demands an extra twopence of every poor man for his loaf. Nothing can exceed the indignation or resentment with which a thorough-going landlord treats every man who hesitates to admit the justice of their demands; and we occasionally see some of them, of the first rank, travelling to country meetings in splendid equipages to enforce their claim to those twopences. In the *Morning Chronicle* of the 6th instant, there is a report of such a meeting in the county of Suffolk, at which a noble lord felt himself entitled to say, that "a cry for an alteration in the corn laws proceeded from a gross democratic spirit in the country, that wanted cheap bread for its fellows, no matter what injury the agriculturists sustained." I can assure that noble lord that I have not, in my sentiments or inclinations, a particle of that democracy which he thinks is the sole enemy of his rental. So far from it, that what remains to me of my animal strength should be exerted, if necessity arose for it, in the defence of his aristocratic privileges, and of his proprietary rights. But I would remind him, at the same time, that his indignation is warmed up by feelings of a direct, personal, pecuniary interest; while it does happen, as he must know, that among those who would advocate a greater freedom in the trade of corn, are to be numbered many men of great virtue, talents, and attainments; aye, and some too of deep interest in landed property. Look at Lord Grenville's protest—was he a base democrat? As to the affected care of this Suffolk nobleman for the "agriculturists," 'tis sad meanness. Indeed, the Agricultural Report rings, from one end to the other, with evidence of the heartless depredations of the landlords upon the capital of the farmers. The agriculturist, my good lord, is in no danger, except from his landlord. It is the deduction of the "lion's share" from the gross produce which impoverishes the farmer; and these lamentations over him are only the growl of the lion while making the division. The trade of farming, as a trade, is invulnerable by competition in an importing country; and, if it is not a trade, what is it?—is it an office? The sole cause of the farmer's difficulty lies in an ill-conceived impotent corn law, and in the obstinate confidence with which the owners of their farms have relied on its efficacy in fixing their rents. But, my good lord, you have got your corn law, and you have got your distress too—what do you say to that? If "democracy" is only to be starved down, and if bread is to be made dear for that purpose, what steps will "aristocracy" take, when bread is cheap, in spite of all the corn bills it can devise and pass? How low is the country to be brought before the landed interest will admit, that their scheme works downwards instead of upwards?

## THE LANDOWNERS OUGHT TO BE FREE FROM DEBT.

The great body of landowners ought, at this day, to be the principal stockholders. The two terms should be almost synonymous; and instead of the word "mortgage" being the echo of the word "land," the possession of an estate of "five thousand a year" should imply the accompaniment of "fifty thousand consols." All mortgages ought certainly to have been paid off during the prevalence of "war prices;" but, instead of seizing so fair and unlooked for an opportunity of clearing their estates, the landowners exhibited their enlarged rentals only as security for more advances; and they became competitors with the State, in the money market, as borrowers, when they ought to have entered it as the principal lenders.

## GOOD ADVICE TO OUR ARISTOCRACY.

If our aristocracy think that, in virtue of some hereditary claims, as lords of the soil, they are to perpetuate their families and their patrimonies by any other means than their own prudent management of their estates, according to their intrinsic values, they may some day be repudiated for sentiments equally inconsistent with the natural rights and the common sense of mankind. They have the good fortune of being placed among a people strongly attached to them by disposition and by habit, and who are sensible of the advantages, while they delight in the splendour, of a high and hereditary nobility; and, therefore, if disagreement ensue, there can be no doubt as to the side on which the fault, as well as the chief suffering, must lie. But the people delight in the splendour of their nobility, only in the contemplation that it is maintained by the intrinsic resources of their own broad possessions. If the people, rich or poor, are made to support that splendour from their own means, they must cease to respect it. The landed interest, to be secure, must not touch either the poor man's loaf or the rich man's consols, neither may they resort to the expedient of clipping and coining.

## WE HAVE LONG PASSED THAT POINT UP TO WHICH THE PROSPERITY OF A COUNTRY IS BASED UPON ITS LAND.

*We have long passed that point up to which the prosperity of a country is based upon its land.* Our trade has outgrown our agriculture, because it has led to an increase of population which the land can neither profitably employ nor plentifully feed. What it is to have a redundant population the landed interest well know; and the more trade is cramped the more redundant will a given population prove, to their cost. I know they think that there is a circle of employment to be found in the *Home Trade*, in which the same internal elements of prosperity may be perpetually revolved and improved—that, as mouths increased in number, bread would get dearer, rents would rise, expenditure enlarge, home trade flourish, and the power of the people to pay for the bread increase with its price. The particular trades which act as purveyors to the luxuries of the rich, cordially believe in this view of national prosperity; and the country shopkeepers, who, during the "war prices," felt the influence of them in an unusual expenditure of the farmers' families, pant for the return of dear bread, and imagine that a price created by Act of Parliament is the same thing as a price created by actual circumstances.

But if the increase of population should not comprise a new body of manufacturers, capable of supplying commodities for the foreign market, besides having mouths enough to consume all the home-grown corn, then not only would the import trade be lost, but the home trade and the agricultural would languish together, and the country would become little else than one great poor house.

On the other hand, if the additional population consists chiefly of manufacturers, who produce commodities suitable to foreign markets, and the export of those commodities materially exceed in quantity the corn which had formerly been exported in return for the imports, the case of the country is thenceforth entirely changed, and its future prosperity will be based upon trade, and not upon land; and no imaginable measure can be so injurious to land as that which may impede the progress of trade.

## TITHES.

Of tithes it may be enough to say, that they existed long before that most abstruse and highly theoretical maxim in political economy called "Protection" was invented by "practical men;" and they have always existed as a positive charge upon land, unqualified by any right conferred on the owners of land to reimburse themselves from the moneys of the rest of the community, except so far as such a charge may, by the operation of trade, under some circumstances, infuse itself into the prices of the productions of land. If, after one-tenth part of the produce of a field has been taken for the tithe, a law is to provide that the value of the nine other parts shall be increased by one ninth, the owner of the field pays no tithe at all; and I believe that no man will say that it never was intended that the burden of tithe should be borne by the landowner. A Corn Bill, granted for the purpose of relieving the land from tithes, is a deliberate transfer of a charge from one party, who is liable to pay it, to another, who is under no such liability; and nothing but an increase of population, which has added greatly to the value of the remaining nine parts of the produce of the field, could have enabled the owner of it to execute a device for making the people pay him also for the tenth part, which never was his property.

## POOR LAWS.

The Poor Laws are of older date than the importation of corn: they existed through a long term of exportation, when the owners of land neither had, nor could have had, any protection upon the ground of the charges they incurred in supporting their poor. The circumstance of our having passed from the condition of an exporting to that of an importing country, can give them no right to be reimbursed those charges by the trading part of the community, although it supplies them with the machinery for enforcing such a claim: and, indeed, if we reflect on the number of idle persons who were supported by the great landowners out of the produce of their estates, before commerce and refinement had altered the habits of society, by converting squires into gentlemen, and boors into artizans, the poor rates would appear to be little else than a substitute for the former practice, tardily adopted after an interval of great disorder, under which the landowners were the greatest sufferers. There is nothing in the first institution of the poor law, nor in the early practice under it, upon which the landed interest can found a prescriptive or traditional right, to throw upon the rest of the community, directly or indirectly, by any device or contrivance whatever, the charge they incur in maintaining the surplus part of the population of their respective parishes.

## COUNTY RATES.

The county rates are another grievance complained of; but the occupiers of lands, and the dwellers in rural situations, are the parties most interested in the purposes for which those rates are chiefly expended. I can see no ground upon which the landed interest should throw their portion of these expenses upon the other members of the community; but this they will do if the price of corn is artificially raised upon the ground of the county rates.

**Issued by the National Anti-Corn-Law League, Newall's-Buildings, Manchester.**

J. GADSBY, PRINTER, NEWALL'S-BUILDINGS, MANCHESTER.

# AN

# ADDRESS TO FARMERS,

## ON THE WAY IN WHICH

# THEIR FAMILIES ARE TO BE PROVIDED FOR.

COUNTRYMEN AND FRIENDS,

I am the son of a farmer, whose father, grandfather, great grandfather, and great great grandfather had occupied land on the same estate from the time of Queen Elizabeth; all my relatives in the last generation were employed in agriculture; I should have been so employed myself had I been permitted to follow the bent of my own inclination; and throughout the thirty-five years of business toil in which I have been engaged, I have never ceased to cherish the hope that I should be enabled to terminate an active life on a piece of land of my own, where I could follow out the employment which had so many charms for me in youth. You may, therefore, suppose that I should regret to see you suffer any injustice from the legislature; and that my conviction that the Corn Law is injurious to your interest, arises from no prejudice against the class of men from whom I have sprung, and with whom I hope again to be associated ere I descend to the grave.

I have said that I was not allowed to follow the bent of my own inclination. My father told us that he could make no more than one son a farmer. "One of you," he used to say, "will succeed me in the farm, and the rest shall have such an education as will enable them to shift for themselves. I cannot stock four farms for you; and if I could, I would not send three of you out *to bid against my neighbours*, and to raise their rents or displace them." And thus at seventeen, when I had begun to pride myself in ploughing a furrow as straight as a mathematical line, and when the possession of a horse and gun, and the enjoyment of field sports, and the pleasant alternation of amusement and toil were most relished, I was compelled to the solitude of a great town, and to a tiresome gin-horse drudgery, which for one whole year was almost unendurable. And it was not until I came deliberately to reflect on my father's observations that I was fully reconciled to my occupation. I was then convinced that his was the wise course; and I have ever since been convinced that farmers took a very mistaken view of their own interest if they thought it could be promoted at the expense of trade, in which a great portion of their families would have to seek for employment. It is to this view of the relations between agriculture and trade to which I wish now to direct your attention.

If farmers were not too much accustomed to receive their opinions from landlords, they would very soon discover that, even if the Corn Law was advantageous to them *individually* (which I deny) it is most injurious to them as *heads of families*. What does any man labour for? Not merely that he, singly and without any ties of affinity, may obtain a subsistence, but that he may be able to secure comfort and respectability for his family. There may be exceptions to the rule, but they are exceedingly rare. The farmer can bring up one son only to his own occupation if the son be intended to hold the same station as the father, which he could not do if the farm was to be divided. For the rest of his sons he must find other employment. The church, the law, and medicine, are open to them; but in these professions a protracted and expensive education is a necessary preliminary. Trade, therefore, becomes the resource of the surplus population of the farm. If the farmer have two sons, he has, so far as their settlement in life is concerned, an equal interest in agriculture and in trade. If he have three he has twice as much interest in trade as in agriculture. If he have five or six he may find it advantageous to him (and I know several such instances) to give up farming altogether and remove into a town, in order to push them *all* forward in trade. It is to enforce this view that I proceed to lay before you the history of twelve families personally known to me.

I have taken families in which all the sons have arrived at man's estate, and after they have chosen the occupations which are likely to be followed throughout life. In like manner I have chosen, in all the cases, to include only families where the daughters have attained, or gone beyond, the usual marriageable age.

1. *Four Sons.*—One, an engineer, emigrated to Kentucky, two, farmers, who also emigrated, and one a manufacturer in Glasgow. *Five Daughters;* two married emigrants, two married farmers, and one married a person employed in iron works.

2. *Six Sons.*—One a manufacturer in Glasgow, one a banker in Lancashire, one a farmer, and three emigrated to Canada. *Six Daughters;* two married Glasgow manufacturers, one a town clergyman, and three are unmarried.

3. *Four Sons.*—Two emigrated to the United States, one a grocer in Edinburgh, and one a farmer. *Two Daughters;* one married an emigrant, and one unmarried.

4. *Six Sons.*—Two merchants in Glasgow, one a merchant in London, one a drysalter in London, and two unmarried, assistants to their father. *One Daughter* unmarried.

5. *Five Sons.*—All merchants in Manchester. *Three Daughters;* two married to manufacturers, and one to a merchant in Manchester.

6. *Four Sons.*—Calico printers in Manchester. *One Daughter* unmarried.

7. *Two Sons.*—One a merchant in Liverpool, and one a brewer in Birmingham. *Two Daughters* unmarried.

8. *Three Sons.*—One a surgeon in India, one a merchant in Edinburgh. *Two Daughters;* one married to a mechanic, and one unmarried.

9. *Five Sons.*—All employed in Glasgow. *Three Daughters;* married to Glasgow tradesmen.

10. *Two Sons.*—One a manufacturer and one a farmer. *Two Daughters* married to farmers.

11. *One Son.*—A dyer. *Three Daughters* unmarried.

12. *Five Sons* and *Two Daughters.*—All emigrated to the United States with their parents.

In these twelve families there were *forty-seven* sons who all arrived at man's estate, and only *four* of them are farmers. There were *thirty-two* daughters, the youngest of them of a marriageable age, only *four* of whom married farmers. Thus, of the whole *seventy-nine* only *eight* have any direct interest in agriculture, for the unmarried are annuitants. Of the thirty-two daughters not fewer than twelve remain unmarried; a proof that if farmers find it difficult to settle their sons around them, it is still more difficult to find suitable matches for their daughters.

In all these instances the heads of the families, with one exception, held rather extensive farms, and the sons, by emigration, or by trade at home, have sustained their fathers' station in society, and some have risen considerably beyond it. But the children of the smaller farmers, of those who held from 30 to 100 acres of land, have sunk to the class immediately below that of their fathers. Their sons have become farm labourers, masons, joiners, smiths, weavers, &c., and the daughters have married into the same class. This has been almost invariably the case where the father has not been able to confer education upon them, for without the elevating sentiments derived from knowledge there is seldom any spirit of enterprise. In a parish which I have particularly in view while writing, if the father was a *reading* man it might safely have been predicted that his family would emigrate or betake themselves to trade or to professions. If the father was uneducated and took no means to have his children well instructed, it might, with equal safety, have been predicted that they would sink into the class of mere labourers.

The landowner—the gentleman of easy or moderate fortune, has a wider range in the way of providing for his family. He can afford to educate one son for the BAR, to whom, if he possesses ability, a splendid career, with the woolsack in ultimate prospect, is open; he can afford to educate one son for the CHURCH, and is able to procure preferment for him; he can send one into the NAVY, with patronage to secure promotion; he can purchase for another a commission in the ARMY; and there are thousands of openings in our COLONIES and numerous dependencies to all who can command aristocratic influence. From all these various sources of profitable and honourable employment *your sons*—the sons of humble farmers—are almost entirely shut out. And yet, possessing all these modes of provision and advancement, the sons of landowners often find themselves compelled to descend to trade, and their daughters would often remain single if they were too proud to receive the addresses of tradesmen. Here is the history of one family belonging to what is called the Gentry:

W. D. married S. G., (his property in land reached about £1200 per annum,) and had by her one son and nine daughters. The son married, and had three sons and six daughters; one son is an emigrant in Australia; two have commissions in the Company's army; one daughter married an officer in the Company's army; the rest are unmarried. The first daughter married the eldest son of a neighbouring gentleman of landed property, who found it necessary, although the heir, to accept of a government appointment in the West Indies. To him she had three sons. One entered the Company's civil service; one obtained a commission in the army; the third obtained an appointment in the India House. Her husband had by a second wife one son, who obtained a commission in the Company's army; and by a third one son, who is an officer in the Queen's army, and two daughters, one of whom married an officer; the second is unmarried. The second daughter married a London merchant, and had to him two sons, the first of whom succeeded his father in business; the second obtained a commission in the Company's army. Her husband had by a second wife two sons, both of whom have commissions in the Queen's army. The third daughter married the son of a gentleman of landed property, to whom she had one son, a barrister. To a second husband, a man of large estate, she had a son, now a merchant in Liverpool. The fourth daughter married a clergyman, but had no family. The fifth died unmarried. The sixth married a gentleman of landed property, to whom she had three sons and seven daughters. One son tried the law and failed; tried trade and failed; married a rich merchant's daughter, and bought back the paternal acres with her portion. The second is an emigrant in Canada; the third is now in the mercantile navy. One daughter married a manufacturer; the rest are unmarried. The seventh daughter married a "bull-frog farmer," of good connexions, a dashing fellow, with a local militia commission. To him she had two sons and three daughters. One son got an appointment on a sugar estate in Jamaica, and one became a "linen draper bold." One daughter died unmarried; one married a bookseller, and one a surgeon. The eighth married a schoolmaster, to whom she had two sons and one daughter. One son had a commission in the Company's army; one is an artist; and the daughter is unmarried. The ninth daughter married a farmer, to whom she bore one son, who died young. Six males in the Company's army, and one female married to an officer of that army, one male in the Company's civil service, and one in the

India House, is tolerable quartering on India for one family, but scarcely above the average of gentlemen's families in the neighbourhood.

If thus the families of the gentry become expatriated, and we see such persons as the Hon. W. Petre and the brother of Sir William Molesworth seeking for a settlement in New Zealand, while half-pay majors, captains, and lieutenants are glad to "locate" themselves in the woods and swamps of Canada; if thus the necessities of the inferior branches of the aristocracy, with all the openings made for them at the Bar, in the Church, in the Army, in the Navy, in Colonial offices, and in Government offices at home, how are you, the Farmers of Great Britain and Ireland, to find employment for your sons? Humble Excisemen they may be, starving, like Robert Burns, on less than the salary of a valet; humble Curates they may be, like the author of "The Sabbath," with little other reward than the consciousness of discharging their sacred duties; Post-office Clerks, Stamp-office Clerks they may be, with such remuneration as was offered to John Critchley Prince, and refused by the Poet as pay not equal to that of a Manchester porter; but while TRADE is depressed, while the capital employed in it yields little or no return, and while the labour and skill exercised in it receive no adequate reward, *farmers' families must either sink into poverty, or tear themselves from all they have held dear, and seek for independence in foreign lands.*

I trust that what I have said will induce you dispassionately to consider how unrestricted commerce would affect your interests. Leave out of view for a moment the nest from whence the birds are to fly, and look to the way in which they are to find food when they are able to take wing. I know not what the conviction may be of the man who has only one son and one daughter to put "forward in the world;" but of this I am certain, that there is not an individual amongst you, having a large family to provide for, who, thinking honestly, and but for a few minutes, can deny that the chances of his family being adequately provided for, would be largely increased by a prosperous state of trade.

I have taken the subject into consideration only as it affects the provision for farmers' families. Earl Fitzwilliam, one of the largest landowners in the kingdom, declares his decided opinion that, *even as farmers*, you are injured by the operation of the Corn Law; and you will find a valuable portion of his arguments and statements in the small tract "Facts for Farmers," which I earnestly recommend to your perusal.

A FARMER'S SON.

Issued by the National Anti-Corn-Law League, Newall's Buildings, Manchester.

*Printed by J. Gadsby, Newall's-Buildings, Market-Street, Manchester.*

# FACTS FOR FARMERS.

---

WE are continually told by Sir Robert Peel, the Duke of Buckingham, Sir James Graham, the Duke of Richmond, Mr. Cayley, and others, that the corn laws benefit the *farmers* and the *agricultural labourers*: the *landlords*, who passed these laws in 1815, with the parliament houses surrounded by soldiers to keep off the enraged mob, assure us that their only aim was to put money into the pockets of the *tenants* and *labourers*,—that they derive no benefit themselves from the corn laws. One thing is certain, these laws do put a great deal of money into somebody's pockets. The difference between the price of the corn sold every year in England, and the price at which the same quantity could be bought on the continent of Europe, amounts to many millions of pounds sterling. This immense sum of money is paid by the labourer, the artizan, the widow, the orphan, the old man, and the babe, for all eat bread, or oatmeal, or barley cakes. But who pockets all this gold? The Duke of Buckingham tells us that the *farmers* and *labourers* get every farthing of it. But let us hear what Earl Fitzwilliam says on the other side of the question.

His lordship, who is himself one of the greatest landowners in the kingdom, has published three *addresses* to the landowners of England. The first appeared in February, 1831. The next came out in April, 1835. And the third and last was published in January, 1839. These three *addresses* are now printed in a cheap form, stitched together, and all may be bought of Ridgway, the publisher, Piccadilly, London, or ordered through a bookseller in any country town, at 6d. Every *farmer* or *labourer* who wishes to know the truth of this question, about which all the country is now agitated, will buy "*Lord Fitzwilliam's first, second, and third Addresses to the Landowners of England on the Corn Laws.*" We have given the title of the work to prevent mistakes; and now we shall give a few short extracts, in order that our readers may judge of the sack by the quality of the sample.

His lordship begins with an inquiry into the operations of the corn laws, upon the most numerous body of agriculturists. We give his own words:—

"First of all, let us examine the case of the *labourer* in husbandry.

"Look at his habits and circumstances, consider how large a portion of his slender income is expended in the purchase of bread and flour, and can any of you arrive at the conclusion that he is benefited by enhancing the price of corn? So far is this from being the case that, probably, there is hardly a class of labourers more interested in having corn cheap than those who are engaged in husbandry; because there is none that spends so much, comparatively, upon the necessaries, and so little upon the comforts or the luxuries of life."

His lordship now appeals to experience, and every man above the age of fifty can tell whether the following statement of facts be true:—

"Did the period of the so-called agricultural prosperity, which is supposed to have reached its highest pitch in 1810, really bring comfort into the cottage of the labourer? Did it give him a greater command over the first necessary of life? Did it enable him to obtain something beyond the necessaries of life, and thus to raise himself in the scale of society? To those *landowners* who took advantage of the times, and to those *tenants* whose landlords did not, I know well that it brought wealth; but whether it brought comfort to the *labourer*, except in districts where enclosures or other improvements, which cannot be repeated, were in actual progress, is a very different question. It is, nevertheless, a question which must be solved before we can determine whether agricultural prosperity can be truly predicated of that period of our history. Summon, therefore, into your presence the men who are old enough to remember those times, and who are both able and willing to give you an account of their then condition. Let these inquiries be made in various situations. Make them in districts of old enclosure—make them in districts of open field—make them in the north, and in the middle, and in the south of England, excluding only those particular spots where such improvements were in actual progress, as when once finished cannot be repeated. If your inquiries are so conducted, I am much mistaken if you will not conclude that the boasted period of agricultural prosperity was, to the *labourer*, a season of distress—and one during which he began to fall from his former station, to that lower condition to which we now see him reduced in many parts of England."

Lord Fitzwilliam tells us that a labourer, his wife, and three children, consume every week about five gallons and a half of wheat, or say two thirds of a bushel. Now the way in which we must judge of the condition of the *labourers*, in different years is, by first looking at the price of wheat, next at the rate of wages for the same time, and thus learning how much there is to spare over and above the money laid out for bread and flour. His lordship gives us a table of the rate of wages, the price of two thirds of a bushel of corn, and the difference over and above the money required for bread in a *labourer's* family of five persons, for a period of thirty-three years. He says that from 1803 to 1810, the *labourer's* wages in May, were steady at ten shillings per week. During these seven years, wheat rose steadily in price, and the five gallons and a half of wheat, which cost the *labourer* four shillings and eightpence in 1803, cost him eight shillings and tenpence in 1810: so that whilst he had five shillings and fourpence to spare for clothing and other comforts in 1803, he had only one shilling and twopence in 1810. The following is the table furnished by Lord Fitzwilliam. Let every reader who happens to be an old man, with a good memory, study it, and explain to younger men how far it agrees with his experience:—

TABLE

*Showing the wages in May, in each of the following years, and the difference between Wages and the price of two-thirds of a Bushel of Wheat:—*

| Year. | Wages a Week. | | Price of two-thirds of a bushel of wheat. | | Difference between wages and price being money to spare for clothing and other comforts. | |
|---|---|---|---|---|---|---|
| | s. | d. | s. | d. | s. | d. |
| 1797 | 7 | 0 | 4 | 4 | 2 | 8 |
| 1798 | 7 | 0 | 4 | 2 | 2 | 10 |
| 1799 | 7 | 0 | 5 | 9 | 1 | 3 |
| 1800 | 7 | 0 | 9 | 5 | 2 | 5* |
| 1801 | 10 | 0 | 9 | 10 | 0 | 2 |
| 1802 | 9 | 0 | 5 | 7 | 3 | 5 |
| 1803 | 10 | 0 | 4 | 8 | 5 | 4 |
| 1804 | 10 | 0 | 5 | 0 | 5 | 0 |
| 1805 | 10 | 0 | 7 | 3 | 2 | 9 |
| 1806 | 10 | 0 | 6 | 7 | 3 | 5 |
| 1807 | 10 | 0 | 6 | 0 | 4 | 0 |
| 1808 | 10 | 0 | 6 | 6 | 3 | 6 |
| 1809 | 10 | 0 | 8 | 0 | 2 | 0 |
| 1810 | 10 | 0 | 8 | 10 | 1 | 2 |
| 1811 | 12 | 0 | 7 | 10 | 4 | 2 |
| 1812 | 14 | 0 | 10 | 6 | 3 | 6 |
| 1813 | 14 | 0 | 9 | 1 | 4 | 11 |
| 1814 | 14 | 0 | 6 | 1 | 7 | 11 |
| 1815 | 12 | 0 | 5 | 4 | 6 | 8 |
| 1816 | 11 | 0 | 6 | 3 | 4 | 9 |
| 1817 | 12 | 0 | 7 | 9 | 4 | 3 |
| 1818 | 12 | 0 | 7 | 0 | 5 | 0 |
| 1819 | 12 | 0 | 6 | 1 | 5 | 11 |
| 1820 | 12 | 0 | 5 | 6 | 6 | 6 |
| 1821 | 10 | 0 | 4 | 6 | 5 | 6 |
| 1822 | 10 | 0 | 3 | 8 | 6 | 4 |
| 1823 | 9 | 0 | 4 | 5¼ | 4 | 6¾ |
| 1824 | 10 | 0 | 5 | 4 | 4 | 8 |
| 1825 | 11 | 0 | 5 | 8 | 5 | 4 |
| 1826 | 11 | 0 | 4 | 10 | 6 | 2 |
| 1827 | 11 | 0 | 4 | 8 | 6 | 4 |
| 1828 | 11 | 0 | 5 | 0 | 6 | 0 |
| 1829 | 11 | 0 | 5 | 6 | 5 | 6 |

* This is 2s. 5d. less than the money required to purchase bread alone.

If this table be correct, then it is clear that the *labourer's* comforts have always been greatest when the price of wheat was the lowest, and that he had the least to spare when the price of wheat was highest. What then becomes of the assertions of Sir Robert Peel, the Duke of Buckingham, Sir James Graham, the Duke of Richmond, Mr. Cayley, and others, who tell us that the high price of corn is good for the *labourer?* It is plain from this table that Earl Fitzwilliam speaks the honest truth when he tells the world that the corn laws are "*a system from which the agricultural labourer is suffering more than any other part of the community.*" Let it not be forgotten that, as Lord Fitzwilliam very justly observes, "the pressure of the poor rates increases with the rise in the price of corn: and if you examine the parliamentary returns, you will find that a high price of corn is immediately followed by an increase in these rates."

It is quite clear, then, that the ***labourers*** do not pocket the many millions of pounds sterling gained by somebody from the corn laws. Let us next see what Earl Fitzwilliam says about the *farmers*:—

"Having considered the effect of high price upon the great mass of the agricultural population, consisting of *labourers*, let me now call your attention to the situation in which your *tenantry*, the owners of farming stock, have been placed by, or, at least, notwithstanding the successive corn bills which were passed since the peace. The object of the law of 1815 was to keep the average price of wheat at, or as near as possible to 80s. the quarter, below which it was stated by the witnesses, and admitted by the committee of the House of Commons, in 1814, that wheat (supposing the existing rents to be continued) could not be produced in England. To this bill I gave my assent; and of all the important questions upon which I voted, in the course of the twenty-five years during which, with one short interval, I have sat in parliament, it is the only one upon which I regret the part that I took. I am, and have been for many years, satisfied that that measure was founded on the most erroneous principles, and that it has been attended with the most disastrous consequences. In this place, allow me to draw your attention solely to the effects which it produced upon our tenants. Relying upon the wisdom and power of the legislature, they were induced by it to expect those prices for their produce which the law, and the proceedings which led to its enactment, held out as the prices of grain to be maintained. They entered upon, and continued upon, farms, the rents of which were founded upon prices held out to them by act of parliament. If the prices rose to an extravagant height, as they did in 1817, in consequence of the deficient harvest of 1816, the expectations of the *farmers* and *land valuers* were raised still higher! while, on the other hand, if they fell below the parliamentary standard, the fall was attributed to some accidental add transient cause, and was disregarded in fixing rents by both the *landlord*, the *valuer*, and the *tenant*.

"During the interval from 1815 to 1822, the *farmer* experienced the most extraordinary fluctuations in the price of his merchandise, fluctuations arising from the variations of the seasons, but aggravated by the state of the law, which either rigorously prohibited, or indiscriminately admitted, foreign corn. What, however, I am particularly anxious to direct your attention to is, the utter inefficiency of the law to effect either of its two objects, that of protecting the *farmer* from too low, or the consumer from too high a price. In the spring of 1817, wheat sold at 120s. a quarter; in the winter of 1821-2, it sold at less than 40s. a quarter; the average of the year 1817 being 94s., and that of 1822 being 43s. The highest price in Oxford at Lady-Day, 1817, was 148s.; at Michaelmas, 1820, 66s.; at Michaelmas, 1822, 52s. a quarter. The consequence of this state of things cannot have escaped your recollection. Great difficulties had been felt by the *farmers* in 1814-15 and 1816; but the difficulties of all former years were surpassed by the distress of the winter of 1821-2. The insolvency of tenants, at this period, was unparalleled in the history of agricultural classes, and the inefficiency of the act of 1815 was so universally acknowledged, that an alteration in the law was made in the session of 1822! but the alteration being contingent upon circumstances which never occurred, no permanent or practical change took place till the year 1828, when the present system was adopted. During the period, therefore, from 1815 to 1828, the prohibitory system of 1815 was in virtual operation. How far it secured you from a diminution of rental, your tenants from insolvency, every landlord in England can testify. I am here, however, principally entreating your consideration of the effects produced upon the agricultural capital of the country. Year after year the value of the *farmer's* produce had been diminishing, till it fell to little more than half the price at which parliament considered that he could be remunerated for his industry. Year after year he was deluded by fallacious hopes, excited by the law itself; his rent was paid out of his capital, and not out of his profits, till that capital became insufficient for the proper cultivation of the land, and then you yourselves began to feel the calamity by which many of your tenantry had been already overwhelmed. Compare, then, the situation of that tenantry, under the protection of the Corn Law of 1815, with what it probably would have been, had the trade been avowedly free; or if you had been contented with the protection afforded by the law of 1804, under which it would have been practically free. Prices would indeed have lowered, but no such extravagant hopes would have been excited, no such erroneous calculations would have been made: rents would have fallen to a value corresponding to the price of grain, the agricultural capital of the country would have been unimpaired, and the land would have remained in a better state of cultivation. Your nominal rentals might have been diminished, but your rents would have been collected with facility, and you would not have been driven, time after time, to the wretched expedient of returning a per centage to your tenants at each successive audit, in order to induce them to remain on their farms; an expedient that proclaims to your fellow-citizens that those who resort to it are in the habit of demanding from their tenants a larger rent than they are capable of paying. Nothing, I must confess, is more distressing to me, than to witness these half-yearly annunciations of the miscalled liberality of certain portions of the landed interest. Has it never struck you, fellow-citizens, that this is no evidence of liberality, but rather of extortion; that the return of part of the rent may be proper, when called for by temporary calamity, by the effects of flood or storm, or by some accidental misfortune, overwhelming a particular tenant, or class of tenants; but that, when resorted to habitually, it is not to be justified; that it convicts those who have recourse to it of continued attempts to extract from their tenantry a rent not warranted by the value of agricultural produce; and that so far from proving the liberality of the *landlord*, it affords testimony of a very different quality?"

Thus plainly does Earl Fitzwilliam also show that the *farmers* profit as little as the *labourers* by the corn laws. He proves that these laws have been so many snares, to mislead and ruin the tenants with the delusive bait of high act-of-parliament prices. So far from their profiting by the corn laws, he has shown that *farmer* and *labourer* have been equally injured by the legislation that was pretended to be for their exclusive advantage; and at last his lordship comes to the candid admission, that "whichever effect we consider, whichever branch of the dilemma we take, the corn law is guilty."

The noble author here falls into a form of expression that does not properly express his meaning. The corn law cannot be guilty. *The law makers are guilty.* If we search a little further, we shall, however, find that he tells us very plainly who the guilty persons are who have made these laws, and why they have been made. "*The painful confession must be made,*" says his lordship, "*that our own benefit is the true object for which this obnoxious code is established.*" His lordship tells his brother *landlords* that they (the *landlords*) pocket every farthing of the profit derived from the corn laws, a profit amounting, as we have before said, to many millions of pounds sterling every year. As a *landlord*, Earl Fitzwilliam tells his brother *landlords* that they are guilty of all the evils, crimes, miseries, and physical and moral deterioration which are inflicted upon the people by the corn laws. He could not have heaped upon the consciences of a body of men a more terrible responsibility than this. He tells them, moreover, in solemn warning, that the hour of retribution is certain to arrive. We shall close our notice of his lordship's labours, by quoting the most consoling passage in the pamphlets: "Laws, based as the corn law is, in injustice and partiality, can never be of long endurance. They are only fit for fair weather; they cannot resist the storm."

**Issued by the National Anti-Corn-Law League, Newall's-Buildings, Manchester.**

*Printed by J. Gadsby, Newall's Buildings, Market-Street, Manchester.*

# CORN LAWS.

## SELECTIONS

FROM

# A PLEA FOR THE POOR.

BY THE

## HON. AND REV. BAPTIST W. NOEL, M.A.,

MINISTER OF ST. JOHN'S CHAPEL, BEDFORD ROW.

"Blessed is he that considereth the poor; the Lord will deliver him in time of trouble." Ps. xli. 1.
"He that hath pity on the poor lendeth unto the Lord; and that which he hath given will he pay him again. Prov. xix. 17.
"The righteous considereth the cause of the poor; but the wicked regardeth not to know it." Prov. xxix. 7.
"If thou draw out thy soul to the hungry, and satisfy the afflicted soul; then shall thy light rise in obscurity, and thy darkness be as the noon day. And the Lord shall guide thee continually, and satisfy thy soul in drought, and make fat thy bones; and thou shalt be like a watered garden, and like a spring of water whose waters fail not." Isa. lviii. 10, 11.

THE destitute condition of numbers among the labouring classes has been to me for some years one of the most painful subjects of reflection. My professional duties have forced me to witness something of it in London, and from gentlemen habitually occupied in visiting the poor, I have learned much more respecting it. There are many families in the metropolis half starved, the heads of which would willingly work hard to obtain a slender maintenance. In other parts of the country there is equal want. In the summer of 1839, several poor persons, with whom I conversed in Devonshire, assured me that the whole of a poor man's wages, at that time, would scarcely procure dry bread for a family of four or five children. In various agricultural counties, if I am rightly informed, the labourers and their children can scarcely ever touch meat. But the distress among agricultural labourers is not equal to that among many of the operatives in manufacturing districts. It is shocking to look down into the cellars which are tenanted by destitute thousands in the poorer parts of Liverpool and Manchester. The town missionaries in these two towns, who, living entirely among the poor, probably know more of their circumstances than almost any other persons, not excepting even clergymen, assured me last year that the distress which they witnessed in visiting among the people, was wide spread and intense beyond description. How could it be otherwise? I saw some mills closed. Others were working half time; and in the store rooms of several, I saw immense piles of goods heaped up to the very ceilings, for which the manufacturers could find no profitable sale.

* * * * * *

"In 1790," says Mr. Slaney, "the number of manufacturers and workmen living in towns was, to the labourers in country districts, as one to two. In 1840, the proportions have become exactly reversed, and the number of the former are to the latter class as two to one."* The number of families employed in agriculture was, in 1811, 895,998, and in the year 1831, it had only increased to 961,134; while the number of families employed in trade and manufactures, &c., had grown, during that period, from 1,129,049 to 1,434,873;† and on the whole, if Mr. Ward is correct, two millions of persons of agricultural origin, whose parents were employed upon the land, have, since 1811, obtained a livelihood by manufactures.‡ Should our manufacturing industry be repressed, the country labourers, already too numerous, must become an intolerable burden to the parishes; but should our manufactures flourish, many will find employment as domestic servants, porters, warehousemen, artisans, and sailors. The effect of this demand for labourers must be the same as the effect of a similar demand in towns. While labourers are abundant and labour scarce, the farmer may obtain labourers at the lowest wages which will sustain life; but when labour is abundant and labourers scarce, the labourer can make his own terms. The extension, therefore, of our commerce would speedily be felt by the labourers, who would obtain better wages and enjoy a more comfortable existence. Their number at present pauperizes them; their scarcity would then increase their comforts.

All these advantages, which appear likely to flow from a reduction of the duty on corn, to English artisans and labourers, would be ex-

* Speech on the State of the Poorer Classes, Feb. 4th, 1840.
† Porter's Progress of the Nation, p. 51.
‡ Speech of Mr. Ward to the Electors of Sheffield.

tended also to the labourers of Ireland. Nearly one third of the poor creatures who are driven by hunger from their native fields to the streets of Liverpool, are constantly, as I have been assured, without employment; in other words, nearly one third of the Irish population of Liverpool would be found, at any time, to be starving there in damp, dark, and pestiferous cellars. Not only would these find work and food, but many of their countrymen, from the wilds of Connaught and Munster, following them across the channel, would exchange the maddening contemplation of their forced idleness and hopeless want, for the habits of a cheerful and well-paid industry. In the same manner, numbers of them would be required for the lower departments of manufacturing labour throughout the cotton district; while, the farms of Ireland being thus freed from their surplus labourers, wages would rise there as well as in England; and thus the Irish peasantry, now starved when the potato crop fails, and insufficiently fed even in the best potato years, might begin, like the labourers of England, to eat cheap bread, with the potato crop to fall back upon in the years of scarcity.

It seems then clear that cheap bread would secure to the labouring classes of Great Britain and Ireland, more abundant employment, better wages, and a larger share of the comforts of life; and it is most satisfactory to think of the consequences which might result from their improved condition. Thus many would have their lives prolonged, who are now sinking prematurely to the grave from insufficient food. Children, now dwarfed and crippled in their growth from the same cause, would grow up in the enjoyment of ruddy health to a vigorous maturity. The demoralization generally attendant upon hopeless inaction and habitual mendicancy would cease. Parents who now cannot afford to pay anything for their children's education, would then be able to provide for it; and these children, now taken from school the moment that they can earn any thing, however trifling, by their labour, might then remain much longer under instruction. The new poor laws, so wise and wholesome if well administered, would be no longer felt to be a grievance, because there would no longer be able bodied labourers of good character unemployed, and anxious to obtain relief; and the millions of Chartists who lately carted their enormous petition to the door of the House of Commons, too busy and too comfortable to think of grievances, would no longer hate the constitution and the government, because the one would seem to them beneficent, and the other would have no occasion to be severe.

With these considerations before them, ought not those who have any measure of political power, to hesitate much before they employ it to prevent by law this improvement of the condition of the poor? For the poor do not ask the charity of their countrymen; all they wish is, to be permitted to buy with their own labour what other nations are willing to sell. Left alone, they could feed and clothe themselves, educate their children, and provide for the decrepitude of age. Why should the law step in and say, "You shall neither labour nor eat?" God has provided food for them in other lands; and if no law prevented, they could easily buy it. Can it be right that the law should intercept the bounty of God, and sentence them to perpetual want?

If it be replied that grave interests require this interposition of the law, let me ask what interests? It is not very likely that agriculture would suffer by a reduction of the corn duty, since the Dukes of Bedford and Devonshire, of Sutherland and Cleveland, the Marquis of Westminster, Lord Leicester, Lord Spencer, and Lord Fitzwilliam, are all favourable to the change. Too much interested in this question on account of their large possessions to adopt an opinion hastily, and too enlightened to be easily deceived, they yet believe that the change is safe; and their opinion is surely entitled to the very highest respect. Indeed, why should not competition do in this case what it has done in every other? Imaginary alarms and forebodings, never to be realized, have attended every relaxation of the system of monopoly. The East India Company opposed the opening of the trade with India in 1814, predicting the ruin of the trade, yet the exports of Great Britain to that country only increased by the change. The shipowners, in 1815, opposed Mr. Huskisson's inroads upon our navigation laws, and yet his measures have been proved to be wise. 1824 the silk manufacturers predicted the ruin of the silk trade, if the duties on silk should be lowered, and foreign manufactured silks be admitted; yet the effect of those measures was, that the average consumption of raw and thrown silk, which had been, in the ten years preceding 1824, under the protective system, 1,940,902lbs., became, in the twelve years following 1824, under a partial freedom of trade, 4,161,441lbs. Similar reductions on various raw materials of manufacture have been attended with equal success.* To turn from innovations in trade to others of a different character, I may ask what great legislative improvement has not been met by fierce opposition and numerous predictions of mischief? It was not without repeated struggles that Mr. Wilberforce was enabled to secure the admission of Christian missionaries into British India. The slave trade was obstinately defended. For many years the apprehensions of West India planters and merchants rivetted the fetters of the slave; and even to this day the fears excited by Catholic emancipation, and by the reform bill, have not wholly subsided. If other great improvements have given rise to visionary alarms, the fears excited by the proposed change in the Corn Laws may be also visionary; if in other processes of industry,

* See Report to the Chamber of Commerce at Manchester, upon restrictions in trade.

competition, though strongly deprecated, has proved advantageous, it may also be serviceable in the production of corn, and lead generally to a more scientific and less costly cultivation of the land.

* * * * *

Is it not more generous to protect the weak than the strong, those who have no political power than those who have much? If rents are the rich man's property, labour is the poor man's; and while poor men do and must pay much of the direct taxes of the country, because the most productive taxes must be ever those which are laid on articles of general consumption; is it right that their labour should be taken from them, by an indirect taxation which limits employment and depresses wages? The spirit of our constitution is to protect the poor: why else are houses beneath a certain price not rateable, and carts and ponies beneath a certain size not taxed? And still more it is the genius of the gospel to protect them. The reign of the expected Messiah was thus prophetically described by David: "He shall judge the poor of his people; he shall save the children of the needy, and shall break in pieces the oppressor." "He shall deliver the needy when he crieth; the poor also and him that hath no helper." "He shall spare the poor and the needy, and shall save the souls of the needy. He shall redeem their souls from deceit and violence, and precious shall their blood be in his sight." Agreeably, therefore, both to the practice of the legislature, and what is infinitely more to be regarded, the will of Christ, should the weak and the poor be freed from those artificial restraints upon their industry, and that unproductive taxation of their food, which, without serving the country, inflicts suffering on them.

Some persons think, indeed, that the country has prospered under the existing Corn Laws; that the repeal of them, without being advantageous to the poorer classes, would involve other classes in ruin, and that other remedies should therefore be sought for the distress occasioned by the present depression of trade.

In proof of the prosperity occasioned by these laws, it has been alleged that our exports and imports have increased between the years 1830 and 1839; the former from the value of £39,000,000 to £53,000,000 and the latter from £46,000,000 to £62,000,000.

* * * * *

Meanwhile the annual additions to the population of the United Kingdom have been nearly as follows:

| | |
|---|---|
| In Great Britain (1⅓ per cent. on 16,530,318) | 218,000 |
| Ireland (1.5 per cent. on 7,767,401) .... | 185,000 |
| In the United Kingdom .................... | 415,000 |
| Total Increase in Nine Years ............. | 3,717,000 |

It appears then that there are 3,717,000* more persons to be maintained at present, than there were in 1830. Of these very few can be maintained by agriculture, for although the quantity of produce raised has also been greatly increased of late years, yet, owing to the improvements in agriculture, this has been effected with a very slight addition to the number of labourers.

The number of agricultural families in Great Britain, which amounted in 1811 to 895,928, had only increased in 1831 to 961,131, which is at the rate of 3,260 families; or, reckoning five to a family, at the rate of 16,300 persons, each year. But the population of Great Britain, in the same period, grew from 12,069,861 to 16,529,818, *i.e.*, at the same rate of 195,972 each year. Every year therefore 179,672 persons were added to the population, none of whom could be maintained by agriculture; and in the whole 20 years, 3,851,318 persons had been added beyond those who could be so maintained. There is moreover reason to believe, that the numbers now added to the agricultural families will be less than formerly, because a large proportion of profitable wastes have already been brought into cultivation. Accordingly, the number of agricultural families, which in 1821 amounted to 978,656, had decreased in 1831 to 961,134; and Ireland is likewise over-stocked with labourers. Meanwhile the population of the United Kingdom is now increasing at the rate of 400,000 per annum; and since nearly the whole of these must be maintained by commerce and manufactures, the alleged increase of exports, amounting to the value of £14,000,000 in nine years, which is at the rate of £1,555,000 per annum, may still leave a vast number of persons unemployed, and allow a constant increase of permanent distress. To justify the present Corn Laws, it should be shown either that the amount of employment has grown faster than the population, or that, if the population has been outgrowing the means of employing them, the want of employment has not in any degree arisen from the operation of the Corn Laws. But if each workman can, on an average, manufacture annually goods to the value of £200, these additional exports have employed annually not more than 7775 additional workmen. And as the whole additional population was in each year 460,000, it is obvious that population may still have outgrown employment.

On the other hand, the want of employment has unquestionably been aggravated by the Corn Laws. Why were the annual average exports to the whole of Europe in the 5 years ending in 1836, less in value by nearly 20 per cent. than they were in the 5 years that followed the war? Because we would not allow the continent to pay for our goods with corn. Why have we been exporting large quantities of iron, steel, coals, linen, and woollen yarns, cotton twist, and machinery, to enable them to manufacture for themselves against their own interest, dearer and worse goods than they could buy of us? Because they could only pay for ours by their corn, and we would not permit them. Why has the value of fin-

* M'Culloch's Statistics, i. 415.

ished cotton goods exported to the countries of northern Europe, sunk from £4,651,681, which was its amount in 1820, to £1,607,900, which was its amount in 1838? Because by refusing to take their corn, we forced them to manufacture their goods for themselves.

Notwithstanding the Corn Laws, the industry and skill of English artisans has extended our commerce with distant nations, from whom we obtained other produce besides corn; but owing to these laws, the corn-growing nations, who from their poximity, numbers, and civilization, ought to have been our best customers, have been our worst; and although the extension of our commerce has not been entirely prevented by them, it has been so restricted as to leave a large mass of poor unemployed.

* * * * *

Nor would the farmer and the landlord suffer either from low prices or any change of cultivation, as I shall have occasion to show. The foreign market would not therefore be a substitute for the home market, but an addition to it, and the workmen will clearly have more employment and better wages.

But will the labourers derive equal advantage from the change? It seems clear that they will. In the opinion of persons of the highest authority, there will be very little loss of employment from lands being thrown out of cultivation. Mr. M'Culloch, of whom Sir Robert Peel said, in his late speech at Tamworth, that he is "one of the most intelligent and able advocates of a fixed duty," who "takes a dispassionate and able view of the case in question," "looks at it calmly, and reasons upon it closely and deliberately," "a clever and able man," writes thus, in the pamphlet which Sir R. Peel so justly eulogized: "*The truth is, that the agriculturists have nothing to fear even from the total and unconditional repeal of the Corn Laws. It admits of demonstration that it could do them no real injury. It would not throw an acre of land out of cultivation, nor sensibly affect rent.*" Mr. Porter, whose intelligent and assiduous researches into the progress of the nation are so well known, referring to the fears of some agriculturists that land would be thrown out of cultivation, adds, "It is because I am firmly convinced that there is no reasonable ground for these fears,—that, on the contrary, there can be no permanent prosperity for the agricultural classes in this country, so long as any semblance of artificial protection is continued to them, that I am induced to bring forward on this occasion my contribution towards the efforts in progress for a total repeal of the Corn Laws."*

Mr. Woolrych Whitmore, late member for Bridgenorth, who has spent his life in agriculture, derives all his income from land, has reflected many years upon the subject, and writes with equal calmness and sense; in his "Letter to the Agriculturists," writes thus: "That a great change in the Corn Laws is now probable, I need not attempt to prove. My conviction is, that it is not only probable, but certain; and that at no remote date. Whatever may be the result of this subject in the House of Commons;.... I have that confidence in the strength of the case, and in the overpowering force of public opinion in this country, when really brought to bear upon any important matter, that I entertain no doubt of the issue. That issue will be a complete change in the present system of the Corn Laws.... and my conviction is, that, although this, like all other great changes, will produce at first some loss and inconvenience to individuals, it will, in the end, be found no less beneficial to your, or rather, I should say, linked as our interests are together, *our* interests, than to the rest of the community." "If we do change this law, and at the same time, modify, with a view to the ultimate adoption of the principles of free trade, the rest of our commercial code, there is no degree of national prosperity which we may not expect; if we do not, if we are determined blindly to persevere in every species of vexatious impost and monopoly, of which the Corn Laws, as they afford the most flagrant instance, so are they the ground-work and support, we shall assuredly, at no distant period, reap the bitter fruits of our own folly, and see the prosperity we might have enjoyed pass away to other lands." "I entertain no doubt that every interest in this country, including the agricultural, would be essentially benefitted by an immediate change and ultimate repeal of the Corn Laws."*

Lastly, Lord Fitzwilliam, with immense estates to be affected by the change, and an excellent understanding to judge of its probable effects, not only shares in these opinions but has most actively promoted them. When persons so competent to judge, and so far removed from all suspicion of self-interest, concur in these opinions with many of the most intelligent men in the kingdom, there seems little reason to apprehend that any lands will be thrown out of cultivation. Could this take place, it must be by such a fall in prices as would give an enormous extension to our trade, and diffuse unparalleled comforts among all the working classes; but those whose incomes depend upon poor land, need be under no such apprehensions. It is impossible, as various writers have shown, that prices should fall to such an extent.

But should no land be thrown out of cultivation, landowners, farmers, and labourers, would all be gainers by the change.

1. The lowered price of corn would tend to diminish rents, but as the prices of all other things would fall in the same proportion, the diminished rent would be as valuable as the higher rent had been, for the purchase of all the comforts and luxuries of life. So far, therefore, the landowners

* Porter's Restrictions on the importation of Corn page 11.

* Whitmore's Letter, pp. 16, 24.

would be no losers. But, in other respects, they would be considerable gainers. The improved condition of the people would extremely reduce the poor rates. The increase of trade, by adding to the revenue, would lighten taxation, and the relief from these burdens would enable the farmer to pay a higher rent. This effect would also follow from the increased value of all kind of grass produce. Every one has observed how large a proportion of the land near great cities is turned into pasture, because of the demand for such produce. In the event of a repeal of the Corn Laws, there would be a similar demand throughout the country. The working classes, fully employed and well paid, would require more milk, butter, and cheese, more meat and leather; and arable lands would, in many cases, be turned into pasture, not because the corn would pay worse than it does now, but because grass would pay better. But, as pasture requires fewer hands than corn lands, the gross returns being equal, the farmer would be a gainer by the change, and would be enabled to pay a higher rent. Lastly, while the artificial stimulus afforded by high prices has thrown an undue proportion of land into corn cultivation, by which manure has been rendered scarce, the abundance and cheapness of manure arising from this change would render arable lands more productive, and their cultivation less costly, thereby enabling the farmer to bear a still higher rent. Taking all these important circumstances into consideration, the reduction of the rates, the removal of taxes, the increased value of grass produce, and the saving in the cultivation of corn, can we doubt that the farmers would be well able to bear a rent which, though absolutely less, would be, as compared with prices, greater than before?

In the next place, the farmers would have their share in the advantages to be derived from the repeal. Nothing can be more ruinous to them than the fluctuations in price occasioned by the present laws. In the years 1829, 1830, 1831, the average prices of wheat in the *London Gazette* were 60, 61, and 66 shillings. Such high prices would tempt the farmers to bid high for any farms which were then to be let. But these prices also led, first, to a large importation of foreign wheat; and, secondly, to an undue cultivation of wheat at home. Hence, when, in the years 1834 and 1835, the prices fell to 46 and 40 shillings, numbers of those farmers who had engaged to pay those high rents, must have been reduced to the greatest distress. A fixed and moderate price, enabling the farmer to know what would be a fair rent, would save him from that unwholesome speculation, and from those terrible reverses. Under the repeal of the existing Corn Laws, the farmer would also be in a better condition to make terms with his landlord. We have seen that he would be enabled to pay a higher rent without inconvenience, but any rent which was unfair he would be able to refuse. When respectable situations are very scarce, the children of a farmer, rather than sink down into the condition of farm servants, will consent to almost any rent which may be proposed. The competition among them for farms raises rent, as the competition among labourers for employment depresses wages. But an extension of our manufactures and commerce, providing situations for a farmer's children, as well as employment for the labourer's, must change the competition among young men for farms into a competition among landlords for tenants; hence rents will be kept down.

But the proposed change would be still more certainly beneficial to the labourers. A certain proportion of arable land being turned into pasture would lessen the amount of agricultural employment; but, meanwhile, an *unlimited* extension of our commerce would so much enlarge manufacturing and mercantile employment as to drain the country of all its superfluous labourers; and this must increase the comforts of the poor, for as rents will be kept down, not by the liberality of the landowners, but by the increased number of situations open to the children of farmers, so wages will rise, not from the liberality of the farmer, but by the increased amount of employment for the poor. The farmer will indeed be prospering; but, should he be distressed, the poor will not suffer, for so long as cultivation at all repays him, he will continue to cultivate his land: if he cultivates it, he must employ labourers, and if labourers are scarce, he must pay them equitable wages. So likewise the landowner will indeed be deriving better rents than before from his land; but, should these anticipations not be verified, his loss of rent could not in the least affect the working class, for, his whole loss of rent arising from the increase of their wages, all that he lost would be gained by them. He would have less to spend, but they would have more; his diminished power of charitable contribution would be of less moment to them than their increased power to provide for themselves. Higher wages would far more than compensate for diminished alms; and whatever might be his own loss, every equitable and humane landlord would feel that he would have no right, merely for the increase of his income, to take, by the force of law, from the cultivators of the soil, more than he could have obtained from them without that artificial aid. The advantage, therefore, to the working classes, though happily coincident with the prosperity of the farmer and the landlord, would not be dependent upon it. The change must bring them better wages and greater comforts, whatever else may happen from it.

As we have now seen that the working classes would be great gainers by the change from an artificial to a natural state, which should leave them the right of buying corn in exchange for their labour, let us consider whether this change is, on other accounts, inconvenient or dangerous.

Because large supplies of foreign corn have, of late years, been paid for in bullion, it has been argued, that they would still be so paid, were the duty fixed or altogether removed. But this is a mistake. Under the present law, the duties are so heavy that corn cannot be imported till the price is extravagantly high: when, therefore, the price rises, it stimulates to increased production; and over-production again unduly depresses the price. Besides the ruin which this brings upon farmers, it renders an exchange of foreign corn for English goods impossible. 1,491,631 quarters of wheat and flour were required in 1831, and 30,016 in 1836. Thus the stimulant given to the cultivation of corn by the high price of 1831 led to the low prices of 1835, 1836, and 1837. By these low prices, the foreigner is shut out of the market, and, consequently, can take no English goods. When the low prices have again reduced the quantity of corn, and a bad harvest ensues, then there is a sudden demand for foreign corn; but it cannot instantly create a corresponding demand for English goods, and the corn must be paid for in bullion. But the drain of bullion, which is the effect of the present sliding scale, would cease upon the duty being fixed or removed.

There is little need to anticipate the indisposition of foreigners to take our goods. As we wish to get their corn because it is cheap, they likewise wish to get our goods because they are cheap. If their surplus population can be more profitably employed on land than in manufactures, as ours can be more profitably employed in manufactures than on land, they will be as eager for the change as we.

It is as much the interest of the Germans or French to obtain cheap clothes as it is our interest to obtain cheap corn; and it is as much the interest of the merchants to obtain a profit upon English goods in the foreign market as it is to obtain a profit upon foreign corn in the English market. The Manchester Chamber of Commerce has satisfactorily shown, in its recent report on the injurious effects of restrictions on trade, that there is no indisposition in foreign nations to trade with us, their forced manufactures and their prohibitory duties being entirely the result of our own restrictive policy.

This has been repeatedly declared by foreign officials. The Prussian Government especially, in 1823, declared by its minister, "that reciprocal commercial restrictions were reciprocal nuisances, prejudicial to all nations having reciprocal interests, and particularly to those engaged in extensive commerce; and that the policy of Prussia was to substitute in the place of reciprocal prohibitions, reciprocal facilities."* Only let us be wise enough to see our interests, and they will not be so blind as to mistake theirs.

Should this trade be established, it is further impossible to conceive that foreign governments should lay prohibitory duties upon the export of their corn. France has prohibited that export, because our sudden and fitful demands only did her mischief; but for corn-growing nations generally to lay a heavy duty upon the export of corn would be the same thing as for us to lay a heavy duty upon the export of calicoes. No foreign government would be unwise enough to act thus. Besides, if they did, what would be the consequence? Such a duty at Dantzic would drive our corn-merchants to Hamburgh or the United States, and sentence Polish corn lands to lie idle; in other words, it would injure their landowners, without benefitting their government. Under these circumstances, no government would make the ruinous experiment; and we may be sure, that these corn-growing countries will very gladly welcome our traders upon equal terms.

It has been further said, that it is dangerous to England to be dependent upon other nations for its food. But the idea of independence seems to me chimerical. Not to insist upon the fact, that under the present system there is occasionally such a demand for foreign corn, from the inadequate supply at home, that the entries of foreign corn, for home consumption, during the year 1839, amounted to 2,681,390 quarters, for which the sliding scale forced the country to pay in bullion, let us bear in mind, that we are not now, and cannot be, independent of foreign countries.

If we do not get our corn from other lands, we must obtain from them our cotton, fine wool, and silk. Stop these supplies, and the disaster to the country would be little short of any which could possibly arise from the suspension of a trade in corn. Upon the arrival of such a catastrophe, the cotton, woollen, and silk mills of Great Britain must stop. The ships which supply them with their raw materials must discharge their crews, and millions of the working classes employed by spinners, weavers, bleachers, printers, and owners of warehouses, must be thrown out of work. In such circumstances, who would feed these starving millions, without employment and without money? There might be corn in the country, but how could they get it? There has been corn in the country during some of those famines which have periodically visited Ireland, but the peasantry did not get it; and there was rice in Bengal, when thousands were dying of famine, not long since, in Agra, but the labourers did not get it. On such occasions charity is inadequate. Government wants power to meet the evil, and the necessitous starve. The barns of Kent and Essex might be filled with corn, but the Lancashire artisan would still perish in his hunger. Meanwhile, all imports ceasing, and £20,000,000 of customs being withdrawn from the revenue, the nation would be bankrupt, canals would be overgrown with weeds, and roads become impassable, because there would be no trade to keep them open. The rates would be overwhelming, because the poor would be unemployed; the farmers would be ruined, because their produce would be unsaleable; and finally,

* Report to the Chamber of Commerce, p. 19.

the same ruin would seize on those landowners to whom our manufactures and commerce have given such princely incomes, as are unknown in any country which is merely agricultural.

To this dependence upon foreign nations, it would add very little that we should import any quantity of corn. If their interests secure to us a supply of cotton, they would much more secure a supply of wheat. For cotton may be sometimes held back with advantage, but wheat, which is much more perishable, must be sold speedily. Our dependence is not, therefore, greater in the one case than the other; nor would our danger from this dependence be much increased in a time of war. Hostilities would not necessarily suspend our trade with any country. If, for instance, we were at war with Russia, and that government should attempt to shut against us the port of Dantzic, the clamours of the Poles to be relieved of their crops, then rotting in the ground, would probably open it again: or should that government be in such a case unwise enough to reject the prayer of its subjects, the rest of Europe would be ready to supply us. Europe failing, we could obtain any conceivable quantity, at moderate prices, from Virginia, and from the valley of the Mississippi: and should we be even excluded from those countries, there is the rest of the world before us still.

In the event, therefore, of war with any corn-growing nation, we have little cause to fear for our supplies; but in truth one great argument for increasing as much as possible this mutual dependence of nations on each other is, that it affords the best possible guarantee against the recurrence of war. Who can doubt that the important commercial relations between Great Britain and the United States, exercised lately a considerable influence in both nations upon the question of peace or war? And the same relations between any countries would always exercise a similar influence upon them. Nations united by important interests will not quarrel about trifles, nor suffer the ambition of military glory to hurry them into an expenditure of men and money, which would exhaust their treasury, disturb their commerce, and cripple their resources.

War may be the game of ambitious potentates, but it is the horror of commercial communities; and an extensive commerce between civilized nations is therefore one of the best securities for the peace of Europe and of the world.

* * * * * * *

Should such imaginary dangers be allowed to intercept the relief which this wise measure would afford to the working classes, what other remedies can be applied to their permanent and growing distress? It has been proposed to afford increased facilities for emigration, and every enlightened friend of his country would rejoice to see this done. Let those who have sense and courage seek happier homes, if they will, under fairer skies and on less crowded shores. Let new-born nations, on the most distant wastes of the earth, give to our language, laws, literature, and religion, an almost ubiquitous influence on the world. But this vent for a distressed population must be always unsatisfactory and inadequate: unsatisfactory, because most of those who expatriate themselves would do it with the greatest pain; and inadequate, because the poorer classes, having generally less enterprise than more educated persons of the middle class, can never be induced in sufficient numbers to make the experiment. Besides, if they were disposed to submit to voluntary exile, they have not the means. Large funds would be required; and, instead of having some millions at command, the government has to provide for a deficiency in the revenue. Direct taxes have failed to afford the necessary supplies; and whence is the money to come by which 400,000 persons are annually to be enabled to emigrate? If this difficulty were removed, there are others behind. The prosperity of a new colony depends on the proper proportion being maintained between capital and labour; and if the number of labourers greatly exceeded the right proportion, so that there were no persons with capital to employ them, they would be landed on the edge of the wilderness simply to die of want. Alone, therefore, emigration can never be an adequate remedy for the prevailing distress, until there is a much greater disposition among the wealthier classes to emigrate than has ever yet been manifested. Nor even then would the proposal be in the least applicable to a manufacturing population; a colonist to Canada, Australia, or New Zealand, should be a carpenter, a bricklayer, a smith, or an agriculturist. Those colonies are not about to raise factories; and spinners or weavers would be as much out of place among them as a hedger and ditcher would be in one of Mr. Birley's mills in Manchester. For manufacturers to emigrate in numbers to distant agricultural colonies, without the slightest knowledge of the arts by which alone the colonists can live, would be to commit suicide.

One other remedy has been proposed. A distinguished opponent of the repeal of the present Corn Laws, after describing the present sufferings of the manufacturers, their lowered wages, and their increasing numbers, adds, "I confess it is frightful to contemplate such a state of things and of society, but it can no longer be concealed; *and yet the only remedy seems to be, to diminish their sources of employment*, in order to produce future or permanent good. Inadequate employment has stripped their dwellings bare, driven them to dark cellars, loaded the pawnbrokers' shops with their pledged property, taken the clothes from their backs, crowded the hospitals, withered their limbs, and broken their spirits; and when it is utterly impossible that they should emigrate, and would be fatal to them if they could, the only means suggested for the alleviation of their misery is, that there should be a greater diminution of their sources of employment." However benevolent the intentions of the writer may be, the effect of his proposal would be very similar to that mentioned by Mr. Carlyle, as made "in grim earnest," in a pamphlet bought by him in a chartist shop, "that all the children of the working people, after the third, be disposed of by painless extinction." It would be a remedy for a redundant population, exactly like a plague at Constantinople, or a famine in Bengal. No humane person who allows himself to reflect, could long entertain it. And yet there is an opinion too nearly resembling it, sometimes expressed by well-meaning persons, that we ought to keep up the agricultural population, and prevent the multiplication of great manufacturing towns, with all their disagreeable accompaniments of dirt, and smoke, and noise. But this question is surely thoughtless. The population of Great Britain and Ireland is at present growing, by an annual addition of 400,000. The land is already so thoroughly cultivated, that while the number of families in Great Britain employed in agriculture in 1821 was 978,656, the number employed in the same manner in 1831 was reduced to 961,131. The land, therefore, cannot employ the additional population; and to endeavour to prevent the multiplication of towns, and the extension of manufactories, is to endeavour to secure that the whole additional population of Great Britain and Ireland should be without employment and without food. On other grounds, too, the wish has more in it of romance than of wisdom. Manufacturing towns, though they have not the woodbined cottage and the clear stream, the scent of flowers, and the song of birds, have much that is not less attractive to a benevolent mind. They have crowding congregations of thoughtful worshippers; they have unrivalled Sunday-schools, in some of which there are from 100 to 200 regular communicants among the teachers and the pupils; and those who have seen the cottages of Mr. Ashton's workmen at Hyde, Mr. Bright's, at Rochdale, and Mr. Ashworth's, at Bank Top, near Bolton, well know that the best ordered villages in England cannot furnish dwellings more clean or convenient, or with better furniture, or, in ordinary times, with a more thriving population.

Of these two remedies, then, the one being inadequate, and the other cruel, we are driven back to the proposed change in the Corn Laws. Four hundred and thirteen thousand persons added every year to the population of the kingdom, must be employed. Emigration cannot employ them, agriculture cannot, and manufactures can. With the Corn Laws, they must starve; emancipated from them, they will prosper. Cheap bread and a regular commerce with other countries, will feed the people, supply the exchequer, promote morality, lessen the chance of war, and injure no one. In the name, then, of the unemployed poor, whose sufferings I have witnessed; on behalf of the depressed artisan, the ill-fed labourer, and the starving Irish peasant, I entreat every religious landowner, clergyman, or member of parliament, who may honour these humble pages with a perusal, to reflect seriously, and to pause long, ere he uses his influence to prolong the existence of those laws, which, in the actual condition of our country, must lead to such calamitous results.

When our Redeemer preached the gospel to the multitudes who followed him, he also healed their diseases and supplied their wants. Like him, his disciples should seize with joy the opportunity of affording a relief to the necessitous, compared with which all the charitable contributions of England are absolutely insignificant. Myriads of the working classes, whose interests are especially at stake, have implored the legislature not to vote them any public money, not to give them any unfair advantage over others, not to invade private property, but to break off the fetters which the law has laid upon their industry; to restore them their natural liberty to purchase bread in return for the produce of their labour; to permit them to maintain their families by honest and laborious exertion.

For no fault of theirs, they are suffering the pain of hunger, with all the physical and moral evils which accompany it. God has provided for them corn, not in their own crowded country, but in others less densely peopled. They have the ability to buy it by their labour, if the law forbids not; and the restoration of their natural right will invigorate every branch of British industry. Generously, therefore, as becomes the disciples of Christ, let every Christian reader overcome all party spirit, silence each ignorant prejudice, and, trampling on the suggestions of a short-sighted self-interest, labour with every friend of his country to effect that extension of our trade which, while it improves the condition of the working classes, will open the prospect of unbounded prosperity to the whole nation.

---

**Issued by the National Anti-Corn-Law League, Newall's-Buildings, Manchester.**

---

*Printed by J. Gadsby, Newall's Buildings, Market-Street, Manchester.*

# CORN LAWS.

## SELECTIONS
FROM
# MRS. LOUDON'S PHILANTHROPIC ECONOMY.*

"We measure our horses' oats to them, in return for their labour, by the feed, not by any money price, which circumstances may put on their services. Why are we thus just to them? Because they are our property; if they die, we lose money. But if we can cheat the poor operative with nominal wages, while we put such a price on corn, and all other necessaries, that he can buy but half a feed, when he should have had a whole feed, we let him take his chance, put himself on short allowance if he chooses, or work the harder; should he die in the effort, we lose nothing, we do not even suffer inconvenience; there are other labourers in the market place, who will do our work as well."—p. 73.

"What nation will the most rapidly, and most surely become wealthy, not in the mere conventional mediums of exchange, lying in motionless masses; but in true national wealth, that is, in the ability of the greatest number of its inhabitants, to enjoy the greatest quantity of necessaries, comforts, and decencies?

"That nation which is itself a skilful and adroit manufacturing community, and which can obtain, in exchange for the products of the skill and labour of its inhabitants, the greatest quantities of food to sustain them while at work, and of raw material to which again to add a new value, by new labour, and again exchange for a new profit.

"Does the artificial price, paid to the home monopolist, take wealth out of the kingdom? No; it only, like any other fraud, or breach of the principle of good-will to all, transfers wealth unjustly from one portion of the community to another. In its immediate consequences, therefore, it neither increases nor decreases the existing national fund. But we must look at its remoter consequences; if the artificial price, paid to the monopolist, whether home or foreign, be on food, or raw material, and that the goods to be manufactured are intended for any foreign market open to the competition of goods produced by those who do not pay a monopoly price for food or raw material, the labourer and capitalist must abate a portion of that part of the price of the article, which they might else have divided between them, as the wages of labour, and profit on capital; or they must give up the market, and bring their goods home again. But, if the wrought goods thus rendered useless in the foreign market, are sold much under their value in the home market, will national wealth be thereby increased, or decreased?

"Of existing wealth, itself, the transaction would be but another unjust transfer; but of the end of wealth—happiness—it would occasion considerable loss, by depriving many of subsistence, to bestow needless luxuries upon others. Of future wealth, it would also occasion incalculable loss, by causing large portions of the seeds of wealth to be consumed, without yielding the usual increase, and thus hindering the growth of national wealth, almost indefinitely."—p. 81, 82.

"Were the importation of food freely permitted, in return for value added to raw material by manufacturing labour, not only each factory workman, but each poor factory child, who could thus by certain movements of its tiny fingers, fill, as by enchantment, our granaries with the rich harvest, wafted from the fertile vale of the Mississippi, would become a sort of modern representative of the fabled old Aladin himself, with his 'Wonderful Lamp,' who,

* Philanthropic Economy, or the Philosophy of Happiness, by Mrs. Loudon. London: Edward Churton, 26, Holles-Street.

by the simple friction of his hand on the magic talisman, could summon his attendant Genii around him, and cover the festive board with supernatural abundance. For, inasmuch as the movements of the child's fingers give to the raw cotton the surplus value it acquires when wrought, whatever corn that surplus value purchases, which did not grow on territory belonging to the nation, is, as far as the nation is concerned, as much the absolute creation of those movements, out of nothing; that is, without territory to be produced upon, as though the sheaves of wheat came in obedience to a supernatural summons, wafted on fairy wings, from a world of enchantment."—p. 92, 93.

"Oh! the time will come, some generations hence, perhaps, when an Englishman's greatest anxiety will be to prove that he is not descended from any one of those whose names will then appear marked with obloquy on the pages of history, as having, in the great assembly of legislators to whom the people of England had confided the guardianship of their rights, lifted up their voices, and in the presence of their Maker and the nation, uttered sounding sophisms, with a view to gaining over a majority of the unwary, the uninformed, or the unprincipled, to join them in trampling upon those rights which they had one and all undertaken to protect!"—p. 123, 124.

"Such being the advanced state of public opinion, nay, the results of anxious research, the deductions from close reasoning on these important points, being, as they now are, reduced to self-evident propositions, and dispersed throughout the country in almost every journal of the day, leaving to none the excuse of ignorance, it becomes matter for amazement that there should yet be found a man so hardened in selfishness, so steeled against shame, as to lift up his voice in defence of that blight on every harvest which grows for Englishmen! that Egyptian seven years of scarcity, rendered by act of parliament perpetual; that doubling of the primeval curse by the edict of men, the corn laws! A scarcity of the first necessary of life, established by act of parliament; by the votes of the guardians of the welfare of the community! Is it not monstrous? Twenty-five millions of the people consuming only bread sufficient for eighteen millions; the deficiency not equally divided, but falling wholly on one class, that class the creators of plenty, the industrious poor. The class who voted for the monopoly, who benefit by the monopoly, and who, therefore, can afford to pay the monopoly price, enjoying, in the midst of this dearth of their own creating, 'bread enough, and to spare.' And not for their personal sustenance only, but also for the use, in the most wasteful profusion, of numerous non-productive establishments, consisting of all creatures or things, that can in any way contribute to their luxury, or to their vanity. 'The horses will not be fit to be seen in the carriage, unless they get their full complement of corn,' says the rich man's coachman. But who cares how wretched the double-worked, half-fed operative looks! And yet, it is our boast that we are a Christian nation; and those very animals whose sleek appearance ostentation renders more important in our eyes, than the lives and comforts of our fellow-men, are employed to draw us to the house of God, the God of equal justice, flowing from good will to all!

"Great Britain has been compared to a ship at sea, short of provisions, and not allowed to touch at any port where provisions may be had. But her case is even worse than this, for though her crew are kept on short allowance, her wardroom officers are feasting sumptuously every day, while those very officers are they who will not allow her to touch at any port where plenty may be had, because the majority of them are pursers, and have themselves the selling of the short allowance to the crew—all the dearer for being short!

"The Saviour of mankind, in setting us an example that we should follow his steps, blessed a few small loaves, and by his divine mandate made them sufficient to feed five thousand people. The parliament of Christian England follows this example—How?

"By cursing the bread of twenty-five millions of people, and changing, by their word, each poor labourer's portion into half of that which his Creator has furnished him with the natural means of obtaining for himself.

"Surely as much food as a man can buy, with as much wages as a man can get, for as much work as a man can do, is not more than the natural, unalienable birthright of every man whom God has created with strength to labour, and with hands to work. Is it, or is it not, an infringement of this right, to compel our labourers, by Act of Parliament, by law, to give as much money for half a sack of wheat, as they could purchase a whole sack of wheat for, did no such Act of Parliament, no such abuse of brief authority, no such breach of the principle of equal justice flowing from goodwill to all, no such law exist? That law, too, made law by the votes of those who put the difference into their own pockets. As Lord Fitzwilliam justly, yet in his own too temperate language, says: 'The mere circumstance of our being the most extensive proprietors, is no argument for bestowing upon us any peculiar protection. It is probably the cause of our having obtained it; but may it not have been conceded to our influence, rather than to our arguments?'"—p. 127—130.

"The pastoral poets, indeed, of our agricultural meetings, sometimes remind us, in sylvan strains, that corn fields, agricultural labourers, and sheaves of wheat, are much prettier, and more picturesque objects than factories, steam-engines, and spinning-jennies.—Granted freely! But we have not the choice. It was not the will of heaven to cast our lot on a great continent, with tracts of unappropriated territory in our rear, to fall back upon, and cultivate, in proportion as we multiply. It is only, therefore, by keeping ahead of the rest of the world in manufacturing skill and industry, and obtaining from foreign soils, in exchange for our manufactured goods, unlimited supplies of cheap food, and cheap raw material, that we can rise above our natural deficiency of surface, and become, though but a little island, the capital of great continents. Should we choose to follow a contrary policy, we must give up the vain and painful struggle, at the crisis of which we have now arrived; emigrate as fast as we increase, and content ourselves with being, what nature intended for us, a speck among the great nations of the earth.

"But we cannot eat gold, or silver, or printed calicoes, or Birmingham hardware, say the landowners; it is agricultural labour therefore, which should be encouraged; modes of making land productive, which should be thought of.

"The following, then, is a receipt for making one acre of land, produce more quarters of wheat, than ever grew on the greatest and best managed farm in the world.

"First, Abolish the Corn Laws.

"Then, take an acre of ground, (let it be the worst acre of ground in England,) and erect upon it an extensive factory. What, on an average, will be the amount of the wages each year, of all the hands employed within the walls of this factory? What, on an average, the amount of the clear yearly profits of the master of the factory?

"How many quarters of wheat will these immense sums purchase in the Amsterdam or Havre market? or in Russia, America, or Poland?

"Let the money, then, or rather goods to that amount, be sent to any of these places, and the quarters of wheat brought back and laid down, (if you will, to make conviction stronger,) at the very door of the factory.

"Are not these quarters of wheat, then, the harvest which, in one year, this one acre of the worst land has produced? Yes, as effectually, and more beneficially produced, than had every wheat ear found its way through the floor of the factory, and flourished among the wheels of the machinery, and the feet of the workmen. What prolific powers of nature could yield, what improvements of direct agriculture, or outlay of an equally great capital, in fertilizing manures, could draw from one acre of land a return of food for labour equal to that which, on the most moderate computation, would be produced by the process of indirect agriculture here described. Or should our supposed factory be so extensive as to require five or ten acres of ground on which to stand, the profits, and consequently the indirect harvest annually produced, would only be the more amazingly immense."—p. 171—174.

"On the present system, no man in England is working for himself (with the exception of members of the legislature, when throwing out honest measures). The rest of the nation is labouring hard, not only for the accommodation, but literally for the pecuniary benefit of the aristocracy or property union; the farmer is selling on commission for the landowners; the labourer toiling to buy dear bread with low wages, that the farmer, by paying him as little as possible, and getting as much as possible for his grain, may be enabled to pay as high a rent as possible to the landowners. While the manufacturer is striving hard that he may pay double for first necessaries, still for the benefit of the landowner, and one and all are rowing against the stream to pay exorbitant taxes, for the purpose of making provisions for the younger sons and brothers of the same landowners or property-union, and discharging the interest of the debt incurred by their corrupt practices."—p. 190, 191.—Note.

"Whenever freedom, from every unjust restriction, shall permit trade, wealth, and population, to progress with a daily and rapid increase, the land alone, under these favourable circumstances, continuing to be limited, must, as it becomes relatively scarce, rise to an enormous value.

"Yet, the first necessaries of life, and the raw material for manufactures, being imported in abundance, and at low prices, the new and honest, because natural monopoly which landlords would then possess, would cause neither serious privations to the labouring classes, nor limitations to trade, and, therefore, would not produce that re-action upon the land which has been occasioned by the mistaken attempt to obtain an unjust advantage over the rest of the community, by using the authority of a parliament of landowners, to starve the population into the payment of rents, disproportioned to the existing state of the prosperity of the country. Nay, should it so happen that under a system of free trade, the whole land not occupied by buildings should, one time or other, come to be required for purposes of luxury, so that the possession of a small portion of ornamental pleasure ground should confer distinction, and fresh vegetables, fresh fruit, &c., become what hot-house grapes and pines are now, the fare only of the very rich, though such an excess of competition, even for luxuries, would be very far from desirable, still, while the labouring classes found the fruit of their labour to be abundance of bread, on terms that did not oblige them to labour beyond their strength, it would be to them matter of comparative indifference, whether that bread fell from the heavens, like the manna of the Israelites; rose from the earth, responsive to their own labours; or crossed the sea in floating granaries, to supply the deficiency from geographical position, of an island empire which, from overgrown prosperity, had become almost one town.

"Should such freedom of trade, as equal justice demands, be established in this country, before our manufactures are driven abroad, the future prospects of landlords will be splendid beyond conception! It has been already shown, that, with a free trade in corn, an unlimited market for our manufactures would open before us, the natural consequences of which must be profitable employment for all the labour of a rapidly increasing population, with a field for, and fair profit upon a daily growing capital; land alone, the while, as has been already remarked, from the single circumstance of our being an island standing still, while all things else were thus rapidly changing their relative proportions to land, not only must the highest possible degree of competition for land yet known arise, but probably, a degree of competition, and a consequent rise in value, as yet unheard of. The enormous price which building land in and near great towns already brings, may give some idea of the state of things which must arise in this country, were trade allowed to prosper unmolested.

"Families change from towns to the country, or from towns of more trade or fashion, to towns of less trade or fashion, to obtain, on more moderate terms, a house, with or without, according to their plan of life, a garden, or a few acres of pleasure or accommodation ground; but the price of land must be exorbitant indeed, before people who had realized comfortable competencies would become exiles to avoid paying a high rent for their house and garden; particularly in a country in which they enjoyed the advantage of first necessaries, and general prices being reasonable.*

"It will probably be asked, in ironical triumph, if it be meant that the whole of every estate in the kingdom would be required for building land. This is not exactly the meaning intended; but it is meant to be asserted that, at no very distant period, old towns and villages would stretch, and new towns and villages arise, upon, or in the vicinity of every, or almost every estate in the kingdom; and that thus, every, or almost every landowner, by obtaining building or accommodation price or rent for a part of his property, would find the average value of the whole much increased. This would be the case, even though the actual rents of houses and gardens should not exceed what they are at present; the very lowest price of building or accommodation land being already so much higher than the very highest price of agricultural land. Indeed, so great is the difference, that the landowner who could find such a market for a very small part of an agricultural estate, would be repaid, although he should turn the remainder into beautiful parks and pleasure grounds for his own gratification.

*"But house rent would not, probably, rise; for however high ground rent might be, the proposed repeal of all taxes and monopoly-creating restrictions on timber, bricks and all building materials, would very much lessen the prime cost of erecting houses."

---

**Issued by the National Anti-Corn-Law League, Newall's Buildings, Manchester.**

PRINTED BY J. GADSBY, MARKET STREET, MANCHESTER.

# CORN LAWS.

## EXTRACTS

FROM THE WORKS* OF

# COL. T. PERRONET THOMPSON,

AUTHOR OF THE "CATECHISM ON THE CORN LAWS."

**Selected and Classified by R. Cobden, Esq., M.P., and published with the consent of the Author.**

A PROPHECY.—"So long as the necessities of the state can be supplied without any remarkable alteration in the present mode of collection, the Corn Laws may have a chance to stand. But the first necessity for any change, will probably bring them in ruins upon the heads of the monopolists. For instance, the first proposal of a Property Tax—which is a thing already whispered as possible—would set all who have property, on the discovery, that the Property Tax was only a subscription to maintain the landlords in an unjust gain. It is in fact totally incredible that any nation would acquiesce in the imposition of a Property Tax, when the whole necessity and demand for such an infliction arose out of the determination of the dominant party to lay restraints upon the industry of the community."—Vol. I., p. 94. *Westminster Review*, 1 *July*, 1829.

ANOTHER PREDICTION.——"Yes,—the tithe is to be commuted, not into a permanent payment in money, but into a permanent payment of so many quarters of corn or the value thereof. And what is the effect of this? Manifestly to attach the interests of the clergy for ever and for ever to the conservation of the Corn Laws. A clergyman is to receive annually the value of, say 100 quarters of corn. If corn is at 80s. a quarter, he is to have £400 a-year; and if at 20s., he is to have £100. But perhaps somebody will say, this is only making the substantial value of the clergyman's income permanent, or the same under all variations of the price of corn. No, simpleton, it is not; it is giving him a great deal more when corn is dear, and a great deal less when it is cheap. It makes it all the same to him, *with respect to that portion of his income which he expends on corn*; but with respect to all the rest, it makes him partake in the great plot to pillage every industry in the country for the benefit of the owners of the rent of land. If the clergyman when he has £400 a-year spends £100 of it upon bread or agricultural produce, he gets exactly the same bread which he would for £25 when corn was a quarter the price and his income £100. But for the remaining £300, does he get no more than he would get under the other circumstances for the £75? Is it not plain that he receives just the same advantage as any other corn lord?—in other words, that he has the same interest in keeping up the pillage of the commercial and manufacturing community? Do the wages of industry and the price of manufactured goods rise fourfold when corn rises fourfold? If they did, what temptation would there be to the landlords to maintain the Corn Laws? It is because they do *not* rise in the same proportion, that the landlords persist in their iniquity, and that Hull must be half a Hull, till we can muster sense, and spirit, and union, to bring them to a composition."—Vol. IV., p. 68. *Letters of a Representative*, 10 *Feb.*, 1836.

* Exercises, Political and others, by Lieut. Colonel T. Perronet Thompson, in 6 volumes. Effingham Wilson, London.

## POLITICAL ECONOMY.

"The proper business of every man and every hour, is to know as much as he can of political economy. Not but it may also be desirable that he should learn something of arithmetic and book-keeping by double entry, be acquainted with the properties of the lever and inclined plane, and have a portion of information touching the nature of the planetary motions and the divisions of the surface of the terraqueous globe. But all these acquirements may only render him a useful slave; and the other is the education which must enable him to keep the benefit of his labours for himself. It has indeed long been defined to be the science of preventing our betters from defrauding us; which is sufficient to account for its being eagerly pursued on one hand and vilified on the other."—Vol. II., p. 167. *W. R.*, 1 *July*, 1832.

"Political economy might not unreasonably be defined, the art of preventing ourselves from being plundered by our betters. It is the grand expositor of the peccadilloes of those who volunteer to benefit mankind by governing; its professors form the great Anti felony Association of modern times. It picks up swindlers of all calibres, as the *Roc* does elephants; and is a very ferret to the vermin that nestle in our barns and manufactories."—Vol. II., p. 15. *W. R.*, 1 *Jan.*, 1832.

"Object of the science which has been known by the title of Political Economy.—First, what it is not. It does not mean a politic economizing at the expense of the poor. Next then, what it is.

"*Economy* means 'keeping a house in order.'

"*Political* is that which 'relates to the many.'

"Mrs. Marcet's then, was the best definition of Political Economy. What domestic economy is to a family, that Political Economy is to a nation.

"'*National Economy*,' after the Germans, is a better term. If it had been always used, the ideas of the public would have been much clearer on the subject than they are.

"National Economy has for its object the best means of obtaining and distributing *wealth*. But what is *wealth*?

"*Wealth* is well-being. 'In all time of our tribulation, in all time of our *wealth*.'

"National Economy then, applies to the raising up of the greatest quantity of happiness, through the instrumentality of the products of industry. And what good thing is there that is not affected from this cause?

"National Economy therefore is the proper business of every man and every hour. We all practise it, either good or bad; like Moliere's man, who, without knowing it, had all his life been speaking prose.

"It is the science, in fact, of preventing our being defrauded by our betters."—Vol. IV., p. 370. *Lectures, Dec.*, 1836.

THE POOR RATES.—"The Poor Rates are God and nature's judgment on the dishonesty of the landed interest in shutting up the industry of the country by Act of Parliament; '*the eighteen-penny children are eating them up*.' Every poor man, agricultural or other, that is brought upon the poor rates for relief, is brought there by the immediate act of the men who lord it over him at quarter sessions and parish vestries, as much as if they had made an Act of Parliament saying, 'Be it enacted, that Hob Carter, and Giles Ploughman, shall never have a shilling in their pockets without the squire of the parish taking sixpence of it to keep his coach-horses.' The rural population will be long before they see this; but all things are found out in time. The object of the squirearchy now, is to preserve the wrong, and get rid of the penalty. The whole system of Poor Rate economizing, *if not combined with taking off the restrictions that create the poor*, is only improving the machinery for making the poor die quietly, and with the least disturbance to those who live sumptuously by grinding them down."—Vol. III., p. 69. *Progr. to W. R.*, 1 *April*, 1834.

WAGES AND FOOD.—"It is not true that when corn rises, the labourers will obtain the same real wages as before. For corn can only rise in consequence of its being scarce; and to say the labourers get the same real wages when food is scarce as when it is plentiful, is to say they get as much food when it is not there as when it is. If the rise in the price of food is permanent, their numbers *will not* be kept up."—Vol. IV., p. 489. *Catechism on the Corn Laws.*

## MASTERS AND MEN.

"There will always be working men desiring to have more than they get, and masters desiring to pay less than they do; and between these there may always be a sort of contest going on, and it is very likely that no way will ever be hit upon, for reducing the matter to a settled rule which shall equally satisfy all parties. But this is no excuse for anybody's overlooking the truth, that there are great and common interests in seeing the general concern go on with as much of success as it is possible to give it. The working men may be always interested in receiving a shilling more, and the master in paying a shilling less, and yet this not at all affect the fact, that the prosperity of the concern at large is what all must stand by, and that this is the thing which will settle all disputes, by making the master as glad to pay higher wages, as he now is to pay smaller. If any man says, the master is a keen hand, and will never pay the higher wages if the smaller ones will do; answer, that it is just because the smaller will not do, that he will pay the higher. An improved trade brings better profits, and more of them to the master; and the first thing this puts him upon, is bidding for more and better hands, for the sake of what he shall get by it; and so he serves out one portion of his increased profits in increased wages, to secure the other."—Vol. V., p. 234.

"The strength of the oppressors of industry at the present hour, lies in the tendency of men to look for what the Spanish proverb calls 'better bread than is made of wheat.' They are gazing after some great change they expect from the heavens, and all the time the little earthly pickpockets are ridding them of their substance. To have good trade where it can be got, and with it good wages and good profits, is really all there is in trade, and ever will be."—Vol. V., p. 452.

## POPULATION.

"It is a cruel joke to talk about the evils of an increasing population, when that population is cut off by law from the power of selling the produce of its labour, for the interest of a robber caste; who tell us plainly, that like the French *noblesse*, they will pay no taxes, unless they may have liberty to take the amount again from other people, and who, if speedy change of mind be not vouchsafed them, will come to the same rough end."—Vol. II., p. 269. *W. R.*, 1 *Oct.*, 1832.

"The time is not far off when the public will discover, that the true criterion of the general happiness, the real measure of a home statesman's talent, is in the degree in which he provides for the honest gratification of the master passion, the tyrant instinct, which alone sustains the tragedy of life, and prevents its comedy from being contemptible. To put the proposition in mathematical terms, *the fluxion of the population* is the measure of the public happiness. What a hateful world would this have been, if in addition to all the other ills of life, it had been really true, that man was sent here only to wink and nod at lovely woman through the grate of the preventive check. For moderate prudence, decent foresight, there must under all possible states of society be an incessant call. But the blunder that plays into the hands of squiree made law, and cuts off all the poetry and all the charities of life, to gratify the public enemy with wealth which after all turns only to dust and ashes in his grasp,—can last no longer than till warm hearts and cool heads apply themselves to crush the public feud by showing to all classes the folly of the whole."—Vol. III., p. 161. *W. R.*, 1 *Jan.*, 1835.

"The plenty of food leads to population and the power of populating is the measure, the gauge, of public happiness. It so happens that populating is the very first thing men like to expend their competence upon. The public, in fact, takes out its happiness in population. It is true that this populating tends directly to reduce its own materials; and so does eating a pudding. But the eating is the happiness. There are those who counsel, there should be no pudding, because, they say, eating will reduce it. The best of puddings, they are prepared to prove a temporary blessing; whence they infer that the whole race is naught. This is not an unfair representation of some arguments afloat on corn."—Vol. II., p. 396. *W. R.*, 1 *April*, 1833.

"The strength of the country must depend upon food, population, and manufactures; or upon some or other of them. And all these must be cut down together, by having two bushels of corn instead of four.

"A country which permits a legal limit to be drawn about its quantity of food, and is surrounded with rival countries which either are not confined by similar enactments, or have not reached the point where such enactments are severely felt, must decline from day to day in relative importance; —because it cuts off by its own act, the means of preserving its position in the race. Neither France nor America needs be anxious to keep down the power of Great Britain, as long as its landlords can decide that it shall not be permitted to advance."—Vol. IV., p. 485. *Catechism on the Corn Laws.*

"If Noah had shut himself up in his ark, and let his family eat nothing but what could be grown upon his decks, he would soon have had an outcry against population, and an Emigration Committee; and Shem,

Ham, and Japhet would have been 'distressed manufacturers.' And instead of reading lectures on not multiplying, his remedy would have been to let in foreign corn.

"A commercial and manufacturing nation has, or ought to have, like Noah, no limit but the world. What *he* was to do by digging, *it* can do by spinning and inducing other men to dig. The steppes of Tartary and prairies of America, are so many pledges that it need be yet but in the youth of its existence. What is to come next, when the world is filled up, it does not seem necessary to determine in this present parliament. What is clear is, that the felicity of the existing generation depends upon progression, as it did with Noah. It can make no difference, except in the size of the experiment, whether men are confined to the corn of an ark or of an island.

"There is no doubt of the general truth, that men may multiply faster than the means of support. But they have a right to demand a fair field for finding their support. They are not bound to exercise the *Malthusian* continence, upon an artificial limitation to please the landlords.

"Mr. Malthus has described to a hair's breadth the consequences of a population increasing beyond the limits of its food; and no man has been able to gainsay a word of his discoveries. He has demonstrated everything relating to the caged birds, except one thing—*why there should be a cage*. He has omitted to point out, that when God said 'Increase and multiply,' it was not added 'And let there be landlords upon the earth, to make corn laws for them that dwell therein;'—that manufactures and commerce are God's solution of the difficulty, and were given to be a dispensing and equalizing power, whereby the inhabitants of old countries should be partakers in His design of universal replenishment, with as much comfort as the more immediate actors in the process. And truly a fearful thing it is, that any men or set of men should be allowed to stand between us and God's mercies, saying to us and to God, 'Hitherto shall ye go, and no farther; and here shall ye be stayed for our unjust gain.'

"All the evils produced among us by the pressure of population, are of Corn-Law formation. The landlords said Be, and it was so."—Vol. IV., p. 505. *Catechism on the Corn Laws.*

"Suppose the case of an island newly peopled. At first, probably, the occupation of cultivator and manufacturer will be, to a great extent, combined; but as numbers increase, there will be a division of labour, and the man that makes shoes, will buy with them a portion of his neighbour's corn. In the beginning, as is found to be generally the case in new countries, these artizans will be well paid, that is, they will get a copious supply of corn in return for their day's work. But if the numbers on the island increase till they begin to press against the food which the soil can supply, they must bid one against another, and so get less and less. What will in fact be given for corn, will be just so much as will induce the people who are to eat it, to agree about the division of it. This, and this only will be the measure of the price of corn. The price of corn, therefore, will rise; and as this increase of price has no dependence on the cost of cultivating the land, the price for which the corn will sell will soon be more than the cost of production, and the difference will be *rent.* But to make this rent, the manufacturers give more hours' work for the same quantity of corn.

"This increase of toil to the manufacturing classes in the island, will be greatly and substantially alleviated, if after the population has begun to press on the limits of the supply of food, there are other islands from which food can be procured in exchange for manufactured goods. But suppose the landowners have the power to prohibit foreign exchanges for food. The consequences will be the same in kind, as if a town should shut its gates, and resolve to allow no food but such as was grown within the walls. Estimate the consequences; try all objections and proposals by this parallel.

"Suppose it were urged to you, that it would make the landowners rich within the walls, and what was good for one class must be good for another.

"Suppose it was argued, as an objection to opening the gates, that the growers of corn within the walls would be obliged to take to manufacturing pursuits, and this would ruin you by reducing wages.

"Suppose you were offered a protection a-piece in turn, as a bribe for allowing the gates to be kept shut.

"Would not each and every of these fallacies be answered by you on the spot?

"Note too, how certain it is that the landowners within the walls, and their labourers, must be brought to the grindstone in the end. When you had multiplied till you bid against one another, to starvation point, would not the agricultural labourers have done the same? Had the gates been open, and you been allowed to buy food with your manufactures outside, the children of the agriculturists might have found employment by joining in your ranks. But this is made impossible. They can, therefore, in the end, be no better off than you. There may have been a single flush of advantage to their trade at the time the gates were shut; but when that is over, they will only find they are five, instead of four, and that the five are worse off than the four, and without chance of mending their condition.

"To the landowners the evil must in time extend, through the impossibility of finding maintenance for their children, except by subdividing their estates. And this none of them can escape, except such as are either to have no children, or to have some way of keeping them at the public expense."—Vol. IV., p. 379. *Lectures, Dec.*, 1836.

"If it should be urged, that there must always come a time when population will press against food, and therefore there is no use in attempting to escape it, this would be like urging that there is no use in a man's escaping from being murdered now because he will not be immortal afterwards. There is all the difference in the world between enduring an evil by the will of Providence and by the act of man. Human life in the whole is but the procrastination of death; but that is no reason why men should be killed just now for other men's convenience. There may come a time when there will be no coal to burn, no iron to make tools, and perhaps no salt left in the sea; but this is no reason why something should not be made of the interval which must intervene. The time when population will press irremediably against food must to a great manufacturing and naval people be almost as remote as the time when there will be no salt left in the sea. And come when it may it must always come gradually, which is by itself no small diminution of the mischief. The maximum of contingent evil in prospect is only equal to what it is proposed to bring on at once now; and all the world must be cleared and peopled before the evil can arrive."—Vol. IV., p. 477. *Catechism on the Corn Laws. Feb.*, 1827.

"When Prussia wants no more manufactures, we must try Tartary; and so on till the world is filled up. As to what may take place then, it is like saying to Noah, 'Never think of going out of your ark. You have no notion how soon the world will be filled up. Show some prudence and economy, and stay where you are.'"—Vol. IV., p. 566. *Catechism on the Corn Laws.*

## THE CAGED RATS.

"Suppose now, that a hundred rats, instead of being mercifully killed in five minutes by the celebrated dog Billy, were caged up and supplied with a limited quantity of food, and encouraged to multiply till they starved each other by the subdivision of the allowance; and say whether this picture, ugly and disgusting as it is, is not a representation of the condition in which the country has been placed by the influence of the monopolists. Imagine next a well-dressed man, with all the ensigns of respectability and good fellowship about him, declaiming on the misery of the sufferers with the remains of a tartlet in his mouth, and pointing out to the spectators the different forms and aspects of the process. 'See that individual of the softer sex, with thirteen helpless young ones dependent on it for support. There whole allowance is but fifteen grains a day, and there are people who would ruin the whole rat-trap by letting in foreign corn. Observe the 'father of the cottage,' with his ribs clinging together and no fur upon his back, brooding over the fate of his suffering family, over whom his heart is yearning and breaking. That poor creature with his ear bitten off is from Congleton. The insurrectionary cock-tail in the middle is from Macclesfield. The Coventry rats are in a corner by themselves. From Rochdale, Manchester, and Barnsley they are all alike; there is not a pin to choose. Would to God my voice could reach them and be listened to [here quote sundry texts of Scripture and swallow the remains of the tartlet.] Why do not they agitate for bread? Why do not they turn tooth and nail upon the wretches who would murder them by letting in foreign produce?' The application may not be complimentary; but till it is shown in what way a starving people are to be fed by shutting out supplies and taking from each other, it is an exact representation of the politics of the monopolists."—Vol. I., p. 206. *W. R.*, 1 *Jan.*, 1830.

"When a great oppression is to be maintained, the most effectual way of doing it, whether by design or not, is to get up an outcry of another oppression somewhere else. If the rats in a cage were stocking-makers, the best thing that could be done for keeping them from resisting the master oppression which sets them all starving upon a limited quantity of food would be to persuade the workmen rats it was all the fault of the master rats, and so put them on trying their teeth on one another, instead of the cage, which is the foundation of the mischief."—Vol. VI., p. 281. *Leicestershire Mer.*

## EMIGRATION.

"The palliative proposed at present is to colonize; in other words, to force the people of England to breed, as is done by the negroes in some of the West Indian islands, for exportation. To which the direct answer is, that nobody has a right to make laws which shall force the people of England to transport themselves. They love their own country, and will not have it made uninhabitable to please the aristocracy. The plan of the landed aristocracy is this; that England shall have no more corn than *they* shall sell, and then the competition for it will ensure high prices; but to diminish the danger of resistance that might ensue, the people shall be taxed to pay for sending one another abroad. The transportation is to be the landlord's *valve*, which shall prevent the machine from blowing up, but leave the owners as much pressure as without danger can be enjoyed."—Vol. I., p. 368, *Westminster Review*, 1 *Jan.*, 1831.

"To pay a million for preventing the people from keeping themselves, and a million more for carrying part of them away, is paying twice for poverty.

"Emigration may have a tendency to let off the evil at a certain point; but there can be no right to inflict the evil till men ask for transportation as a relief. Emigration is a valve; the pains of transportation the weight upon it; and the landlords have the benefit of the high pressure.

"Every English manufacturer, therefore, who is driven to emigrate is an innocent man condemned to transportation for the interest of the landlords."—Vol. IV., p. 506. *Catechism on the Corn Laws.*

"When a man is found dying by strangulation, people do not say, 'Help him to emigrate,' but 'Take away the rope that is choking him.' If the individuals of known humanity who declare themselves friendly to emigration saw the thing in its true light, they would say to the working classes, 'Do not emigrate. Stay at home, and ask for the removal of the Corn Laws. Do not do the very thing your enemies wish you to do. Things will mend. It is no more likely that there will be Corn Laws a few years hence than that there will be a Slave Trade. The country would be worth staying in if industry was free; and it will have freedom by and by. Do not give up every thing you love because there is a majority in Parliament this year, which may be a minority the next. Every day is opening men's eyes; and the wealthier classes, who have more power and more means of removing a mischief than you have, are coming over to you, and finding out that your interests and theirs coincide. And they are not all so insensible to better motives as you may think. They remember the time when they climbed into the same apple tree, and swam in the same brook; and they would think it a sin and a shame, knowing you were wronged, not to move to your assistance. Be patient, if you can; and we will all draw together. A time will come when a poor man may sell the labour of his hands and buy bread, and then you will be better. If you must go, you must; for a man must not be starved while he can get away. But if you can contrive to hold out, stand by the old house a little longer. Let your children be born where you were born yourselves; and see if you do not get access to that fine green world of corn-fields you are now shut out from. Be persuaded of one thing, that your opponents have just as much right to ask to have you shut out from it as you have to ask that they shall grow no corn here; that they have just as much right to request to have you prevented from selling the produce of your industry for corn as you have to request to be allowed to take their parks and corn fields because it might be convenient to you. Do not go away; the thing cannot last: it is by many degrees too bad."—Vol. IV., p. 572. *Catechism on the Corn Laws.*

## COST OF THE CORN LAW.

"It occurs to me that the magnitude of the loss arising from the Bread Tax is a thing scarcely capable of being reduced to numerical calculation. What would be the numerical amount of the loss arising to a man from cutting off his four limbs in his infancy? Who can tell? It must depend upon knowing what he could have earned, and what he could have done if he had been let alone. The smallest part of the evil of the Corn Laws is what is measured by the extra price given for the bread eaten and the tax paid; the grand loss, to which the other is as nothing, is of the bread that is never eaten and never earned. The only substantial approach to a measure of the evil seems to be this. It is the difference between the value of the whole industrial produce of the country, in a free market, and the value of the agricultural by itself. Or it is the difference between the value of the estates of those whose wealth lies beneath the soil or on the water, and of those whose estates lie on the surface which grows corn. All the difference is confiscated at the command of the owners of the soil, and a fraction of it applied to their own gain: while the remainder, being the difference between what the landlords facetiously call the 'home trade' and the trade of the world at large which is cut off, is thrown into the sea for the good of nobody. Every man who has either formed industrial establishments for himself, or received them from his predecessors, suffers confiscation; and tamely allows the plunderers to run about applying the same term to anything that threatens the loss of their iniquity."—Vol. VI., p. 57. *Leicestershire Mercury.*

"Our commercial policy is a mass of confluent frauds; by which everybody robs everybody, and throws half the booty into the sea. But they all yield in individual importance to the master pustule, which is the *Corn* fraud. By this a gross sum of twelve millions and a half per annum is thrown away, in order that a certain other sum, amounting probably to five millions, may be taken from the men who work for it, and given to the landlords whose first principle of law, physic, and divinity, is not to work at all. In other words, *seventeen millions* a-year are torn from the mouths of the suffering manufacturer and his starving children, in order that *five* millions of it may find their way into the pockets of a dishonest and tyrannical class who have got a law that nobody but a landowner shall be in parliament. When pressed upon the point, they bully and appeal to their humanity and charity. The charity is easily defined; they take with a bucket and give with a spoon. They take seventeen millions a-year out of the pockets of the industrious and the poor, and urge in return that they sometimes give a crown to an old woman at Christmas."—Vol. II., p. 398. *W. R.* 1 *April*, 1833.

THE DANGER OF THE CORN LAW.

"There certainly has been no instance in history, where two-thirds of a population, not avowedly slaves and under physical restraint accordingly, have submitted to such an infliction, to please the remaining third. The process will be brief, and ought to be. Either the fundholders and the church will join with the commercial interests and the rest of the public in putting down the enormity by legislation; or their possessions will be taken in the first instance either by the operation of legislation or otherwise, and afterwards will begin the attack on all property, hard enough upon the innocent, but the inevitable consequence of the prodigious provocation. The outrageous injustice of the landlords is the key to the public danger, the spigot that confines the fermenting contents of the national beer-barrel, which must speedily burst if not relieved. If this were taken away, not all at once but by a moderately rapid progression, the debt and taxation would be made a flea-bite, not by removing them, but by increasing the ability to bear them, which comes to the same thing. The public irritation would fall, as the fierceness of a den of hungry savages might be lulled by the application of joints of meats; and there would be a great calm. It seems impossible that before the mischief goes much further, a government should not arise, possessing about as much prudence and decision as might be competent to the regulation of a regimental hospital, and, by speaking the truth and rallying the parties concerned cut off the progress of the evil by cutting off its source."—Vol. II., p. 274. *W. R.*, 1 *Oct.*, 1832.

JACOBINISM OF THE RICH.

"The origin and foundation of property, is labour. The proposal to keep up rent by restrictions virtually includes the essence of personal slavery; which consists in obliging one man to labour for the benefit of another without an equivalent. The landlords may have a property in their honest rent; but they have not a property in the power of adding to it by violence."—Vol. IV., p. 511. *Catechism on the Corn Laws.*

"The poor ought to have corn at the cheapest for which it can be got; and if they have not, they are to blame if they *are* satisfied.

"If the poor were to tell the rich, that they ought to have a 'reasonable' income, as, for instance, one or two hundred a year, and if they had this they ought to be satisfied,—and they, the poor, would take the difference; it would be pronounced to be clean *jacobinism* and spoliation. The poor have as much right to do this, as the rich man has to tell the poor that sixty shillings is a 'reasonable' price for his quarter of corn, and therefore the rich will take the difference. Much has been said of the jacobinism of the poor against the rich, but very little of the jacobinism of the rich against the poor; though one is only matter of speculation and alarm, and the other meets every man three times a-day when he sits down to eat."—Vol. IV., p. 527. *Catechism on the Corn Laws.*

PROTECTION.—"'Protection' is forcing people to buy the work of a man with one arm. It is saying to other people, 'You shall not have the thing in the way yout may have it best and cheapest, but i shall be artificially produced in some way that is worse. I am a man with one arm, in comparison of others you might have it from; and you shall pay me for working with one arm; and if we had one arm all round it would be so much the better for us all.'"—Vol. II. p. 362. *W. R.*, 1 *Jan.*, 1833.

---

BANKRUPTCY.—"Bankruptcy is the check to the indefinite multiplication of traders, as the evils arising from diminished food are the check to that of the inferior classes of labourers. Both take place where they do, in consequence of the limitation of commerce; and the engine of the limitation is the Corn Laws. He that was in the *Gazette* yesterday, came there by the Corn Laws."—*Ibid.*

---

STARVATION.—"It is certain the weakest will fail; but whether they were weak or not, somebody must fail. The case is like that of a hundred prisoners, among whom there should be thrown half enough for their daily food. The weakest will be those who starve; but whether they were weak or not, somebody must starve."—*Ibid.*

---

## HYPOCRISY OF THE FACTORY CRY.

"The appeal to 'humane and Christian feeling,' and all the tropes therewith connected, may be disposed of by the statement that the appealers created, and at this hour sustain, the evils they complain of. They have interdicted the industry of the poor; and then attach the consequences to those who oppose the attempt to relieve one sufferer by the privation of another. If a shipmaster had conveyed his crew and passengers to a month's sail from any land, with a week's provision left on board, and then instead of steering towards any port, should 'do the pathetic' on the sorrows of one part of his inmates and the cruelty of not assisting them by taking from the portions of some other, he would present the express image of such humanity and such Christianity. It would not be that there was not suffering, and that humanity did not desire to relieve it; but that the mode proposed was, like the Factory Bill, a fraud got up by the authors of the general misery, having in view the preservation and increase of that misery, through the instrumentality of the dupes who should be induced to cry out for the removal of the minor evil to the perpetuation of the greater."—Vol. II., p. 472. *W. R.*, 1 *Oct.*, 1833.

"One word of advice may be not unseasonable. Take care not to be deceived by the stratagems of the enemy. Let no man, for instance, unless he has a tail or some other asinine appendage, be taken in by such a raw jest as the Factory Bill. A Tory club have cut us off from our trade, made laws that we shall not sell the labour of our hands, reduced us and ours to the bare possibility of keeping soul and body together by labour the most excessive and toil the most extravagant; and these very men shall come forward and tell us, *that if we will send them to parliament* to support all this abuse, to maintain the Corn Laws, and keep down all chance of being allowed to sell our goods abroad, they will do, *what?* pass a bill to prevent us from working our own children more than ten hours a-day. This is kind; this is benevolent; this is worth a man's going on his knees in the mud to thank them for. Get liberty to buy and sell, ye Issachars, ye asses couching between two burdens; and then your children may live by your labour, without leave from those who starve you. If negro slaves did anything so absurd, the world would say, how debasing the effects of slavery! Feel every man for a tail, who talks of such a thing. Time was, a Yorkshireman might walk abroad, with some consciousness of being supposed as knowing as his neighbours. If fooleries of this kind go on, Gotham will be put in Schedule A, and the representation of unreason transferred into the West Riding."—Vol. II., p. 236. *W. R.*, 1 *July*, 1832.

"The truth is that we must wait till hunger brings our people to their colours, and some time or other we shall have a fair stand-up fight to know whether we are to continue to be the born thralls of the owners of the soil or not. Our Saxon ancestors wore it written on a ring about their necks; we wear it in an Act of Parliament. But we are a long way from the time yet; there must be thousands more of bankruptcies, and myriads of the wives and children of the working classes must die of hunger or overwork in factories, that a greater quantity of the produce of their industry may be given to the landlords for a bushel of corn. We are in the state of raising statues to any Tory man who will offer to limit our working hours if we on our parts will assist him to keep up the oppression that creates the inducement to over-work; and half our people might be persuaded to turn against the individual who should tell them it was an invention of the enemy. But this will mend; misery and the progress of information will alter it. I look to the last, however, most. The working classes, at least in these southern parts, have proved themselves unequal to the question. It will be when the capitalists and employers find out where they are hurt, that the real resistance will begin."—Vol. IV, p. 288. *Letters of a Representative*, 1 *July*, 1837.

THE WATER-LORDS—A SIMILE.

"Suppose, for argument's sake, that corn could be obtained for positively nothing, like water. There would be no more reason why the price of corn should be kept up for the advantage of the landlords, than why the price of water should be kept up for the advantage of men calling themselves water-lords,—by prohibiting streams and rivers, and forcing the public to buy the water of wells, from which, by dint of digging, water was obtained for half as many people as there otherwise might have been. If such an abuse was in existence, there might be reasons why it should be reduced gradually, but none why a fragment of it should finally be left.

"All the fallacies advanced in the case of corn might be repeated in such a case of water. The diligence of the water-lords to grub for the last pint, they would call improvement and zeal for the multiplication of water. They would descant on the capital they employed, and the industry they set in motion; and be pathetic on the fate of the well-digging population, if the government should restore the liberty of drink. They would assert that it was clear the country had been supplied; and if any complained that they were dying from want of water, they would tell them they were a superabundant population, and ought not to exist. They would declare that it would all be easy, if it was not for taxation; but as long as taxes were to be paid, it was impossible that water should be free."—Vol. IV., p. 515. *Catechism on the Corn Laws.*

"So far as the improvements in agriculture were the consequence of restrictions upon importation, they were only like the capital, skill, and perseverance which might be applied to digging wells, in consequence of prohibiting the water of rivers."—Vol. IV., p. 550. *Catechism on the Corn Laws.*

RECIPROCITY FALLACY.

"Reciprocity is having two good things, instead of one. But if we cannot have both the good things, it is no reason why we should reject the one we may have. The fraud of '*reciprocity*,' therefore, is like saying, 'Don't take the half-crown you may, unless somebody will give you another for taking it.'

"The first government that will fearlessly announce that it is not to be fooled by the fallacy of 'reciprocity,' will pull down commercial restrictions all over the world."—Vol. IV., p. 495. *Catechism on the Corn Laws.*

"When the draper buys bread, it may be very well if he can persuade the baker to buy clothes from him in turn. But if he cannot, it would be great folly to fancy he must be ruined unless he refuses to buy bread.

"The Americans make a foolish tariff by which they allow one half of their people to rob the other, with a general loss equal to the difference in question besides. But that is no reason why England should do an equally foolish thing in reply. If an American chooses to put out one of his eyes, there is no necessity for an Englishman's doing the same for reciprocity."—Vol. IV., p. 495. *Catechism on the Corn Laws.*

EXCHANGE.

"Two things are necessary to the completion of an act of commerce; first, that we should have what others want; secondly, that we should be at liberty to receive what they can afford to pay in, and it will be worth our while to take.

"A merchant in the actual state of things can afford to sell a piece of Leeds or Manchester goods in Prussia or Poland for a hundred crowns. If he could afford to take eighty, he might sell two pieces where he now sells one. If he was allowed to lay out the eighty crowns in corn, and bring it to England to a free market, he could sell the corn for as much as would give him a profit on the whole; and consequently he would accept the eighty crowns, and sell two pieces instead of one, and get two profits for himself, and give two profits to the manufacturers. He is restrained from selling the corn; and therefore he is restrained from doing all the rest.—Vol. IV., p. 523. *Catechism on the Corn Laws.*

"When a manufacturer produces goods and exchanges them abroad for corn, he may as truly be said to produce the corn, as if it came out of his loom or his flatting-mill. And if he is prohibited from doing this, it is *his* production that in reality is stopped."—Vol. IV., p. 481. *Catechism on the Corn Laws.*

HOME MARKET.—"I hold to my advice, to beware of talking nonsense about a 'home market.' The good market is the market that gives most. Get the value of twenty shillings for your Leeds cloth abroad, and you are directly to be asked, what you have done with the market that would have given you fifteen at home. If the home market is to be the best, let it prove it."—Vol. V., p. 20. *Leeds Times.*

## MACHINERY.

"On the subject of Machinery, it may be sufficient here to say, that if a prize had been proposed to the inventor of the surest, most constantly and universally acting encouragement to the multiplication of machinery, it must have been awarded to the man who devised the Corn Laws.

"Every master manufacturer who has a chance of selling his goods abroad, has a bale of his goods set before him and is told, 'You shall not compete with the foreigner, without paying a tax to the landlords first. If you grumble, *take it out of the wages of your operatives.* And when you cannot do that any longer, *sit down and invent machinery.*' Thus the landlords hold out a premium on machinery, and the operatives appear to like to have it so. The master manufacturer is driven into a corner between the loss of his trade, and inventing machinery to help to pay the demands of the landlords; and the operative is driven into a corner between starving, and making any improvement in the powers of machinery which he can get a few pounds or shillings by selling; and by the combination of the two, machinery is carried to the highest pitch that necessity, which is the mother of invention, can devise. Surely there wants no further asking, where machinery comes from; and small hope there is of its receiving any check, while the law is thus directed to force its employment, with the power of a perpetual screw, into every corner capable of receiving it.

"But the practical question for the operatives after all, appears to be, whether because they consider themselves injured by machinery, they will try to mend it by prohibiting the sale of the things made. Their complaint is, that too many things are made and too easily; if the demand could be caused to keep pace with the increase of things produced, they would be where they were, but it does not. The conclusion therefore come to is, that they will stop such demand as there is. Or if it is not this, it is the next thing to it; which is, that they will not bestir themselves to oppose."—Vol. VI., p. 57. *Leicestershire Mercury.*

"There would be no suffering from machinery, if the trade in food was free; but on the contrary great benefit. The cause of the suffering, therefore, is not machinery, but the refusal to allow the produce to be exchanged for food.

"That the use of machinery is detrimental in the long run to the manufacturing labourers, is an error which they ought to out-grow. Compare, for example, the extent of the stocking trade in the time of Queen Elizabeth,—when silk stockings were made with men's fingers, and sold for their weight in gold,—with its present state; and ask the five thousand labouring silk stocking weavers whether they would wish to see the trade reduced to what it was then. All the difference has been caused by machinery.

"Experience has proved, that when the production of any commodity is facilitated by machinery, the increase of consumption consequent on the reduction of price, in a state of freedom and under the existing circumstances of the world in respect of the desire to consume, is such as in the end to increase the demand for labour in the production *of that particular commodity.* If power looms could bring down the price of broad cloth to a shilling a yard, and the corn of foreigners might be taken from them in return,—so many people in different parts of the world would wear broad cloth who now do not, that there would be more employment for makers of broad cloth in the end than ever. If men cannot exchange the cloth because the agriculturists will not let them, the case is certainly altered. But then the fault is not in the machinery."—Vol. IV., p. 568. *Catechism on the Corn Laws.*

"The English manufacturer has a right to have the advantage of his machinery, and *all* the advantage. Instead of which, the agriculturist thinks he is doing a gracious act, if he leaves the manufacturer enough to place him on what the agriculturist is pleased to consider equal terms with foreigners, and puts the rest into his own pocket."—Vol. IV., p. 569. *Catechism on the Corn Laws.*

"Machinery, then, like the rain of heaven, is a present blessing to all concerned, provided it comes down by drops, and not by tons together; and anything which prevents its free and expanded operation, has an effect of the same kind as would be produced if the rain should be collected into water-spouts. It remains therefore to be seen, what laws and human institutions have done towards securing the free diffusion of the advantages derivable from God's gift of ingenuity to man. And here the first thing apparent in our own country is, that the aristocracy have made a law, that no use shall be derived from it at all. They have determined by Act of Parliament, that men may invent as many machines as they think proper, but shall not be allowed to sell the produce; or which comes to the same thing, shall not be allowed to sell for what is wanted in return. The whole misery about machinery,—every atom and fragment of suffering, alarm, and wretchedness directly or indirectly consequent thereon,—is the pure and necessary result of the gross fraud and half-witted idiotic cruelty perpetrated by the majority of the landlords upon the rest of their own order and of the community."—Vol. I., p. 356. *Westminster Review*, 1 *Jan.*, 1831.

Manufacturers.—"A common charge against manufacturers is, that they contract the faculties of the labourer. One equally useful when occasion suits is, that the manufacturing labourers are too knowing. The manufacturers are the Helotes of society; but their day will some time come." —Vol. II., p. 23. *W. R.*, 1 *Jan.*, 1832.

——"The sufferings of the manufacturers show themselves by fits, like an ague. But an ague may be a permanent evil, and have a permanent cause."—Vol. IV., p. 569. *Catechism on the Corn Laws.*

## MUTUAL DEPENDENCE.

"Does any mystery of nature conceal the fact, that different countries have been created under such circumstances as make it practically impossible, that a partial failure in the harvests of one should not be remediable by communication with the others, if man, in the wisdom of his absurdity, could be persuaded not to stand by to prevent? And is it not plain, that the suffering to one country, would be balanced by a corresponding profit to the other; and thus, as nature presented the cup of suffering and of profit to each by turns, the movement of the great machine would be kept up with the least practicable aggregate of human evil?"—Vol. II., p. 160. *W. R.*, 1 *April*, 1832.

"Experience proves, that it is not the improved and manufacturing nation, but the growers of rude produce, that are the dependents. Thus England can do without the trade with Russia, better than Russia without the trade with England. When the Czar attempted to stop the supply of naval stores, he was off his throne in an instant. And ten years afterwards, the inability of the Russian government to enforce the execution of a treaty in opposition to the commercial dependence of Russia upon England, was the cause of the ruin of Napoleon."—Vol. IV., p. 564. *Catechism on the Corn Laws.*

"There is no more evidence that nature intended every man to be fed by the land he lives on, when she has made provision for his being fed better by the produce of some other,—than that she intended every man to use no iron but what was dug in his own back garden. It is a baseless effort to cut men off from mutual assistance and the division of labour, for the advantage of a few monopolists."—Vol. IV., p. 574. *Catechism on the Corn Laws.*

## ROBBING ONE ANOTHER.

"What the landowners really say, is, 'Let us rob you all, and then you shall rob one another.' This is the bargain they offer; and the manufacturers swallow it openmouthed.

"Of all the petitioners upon this subject, the men of Stroud appear to be the wisest; for they petitioned that all the monopolies of the manufacturers might be taken away, on condition that the great monopoly of all went along with them. How the men of Stroud came by their wisdom, those who know them can best tell; but it is clear they are wise in their generation.

"The amusing part of the proposed fraud is, that we are all to get rich by robbing one another. The leader of the administration himself does not pretend to believe it. He knows full well, that the plan is as stupid as it would be to attempt to double the strength of an army by doubling each battalion in turn by drafts from the others. Nobody believes it but idiots. Rogues pretend to believe it, that they may feather their own nests."—Vol. IV., p. 436. *Catechism on the Corn Laws. (This part was written during the administration of the Duke of Wellington.)*

## THE CORN LAW A QUESTION OF RENT.

"The landlords, by the exercise of their power in the legislature, lay a tax to keep out foreign corn. Their undisguised object in this is to raise their rents; for whether there be reason in the various excuses they offer for it or not, they do not deny that they do it to raise their rents. And their rents are raised accordingly; that is to say, in the contracts which they offer to the competition of the farmers, the bidders, knowing that more money will come in, offer more for the contract. If the tolls on a given road were made twopence for a horse instead of a penny, and other things in proportion on the same principle, the turnpike-men would increase their biddings. The landlords then, having got out of the farmers by competition the highest biddings they can afford, next set the farmers to cry out, that they want nothing but what will enable them to pay. In the same manner, if there were a proposal for lowering the tolls on a turnpike-road, the turnpike-men might be set to cry out, that they wanted nothing but what would enable them to pay, and nobody could be so hard-hearted as to refuse the twopence for his horse.

"If the turnpike-men set up this plea, they would be told immediately they must go and amend their contracts;—that their having jobbed the road, might be a reason for giving them a fair time to renew, but if they should have been absurd enough to enter into contracts for seven years or for ninety-nine, this would form no reason why the tolls should go on without diminution to pleasure them. A case might even possibly arise, for legislative interference between the contractors and the lessors of the road; but the last thing any man could make out of the matter, would be a reason why the high tolls should be continued.

"In the same manner the farmers must not be allowed to be pushed forward, as the people whom we must support at the expense of paying a high price of corn because they bargained for it. Like the turnpike-men, they must go and bargain for less. Or if by their own incaution they have hampered themselves with leases, they must take it for their pains. Nobody has a right to lease out the public wrong, and expect the wrong to be continued in consequence of his contract. The landlord pockets all that the farmers can by competition be induced to spare; and he would do just the same, if the price were carried to any imaginable height. If the monopoly of corn were enforced and men multiplied, till they were glad to pay for growing corn upon flag-stones, and of course the rent upon all that was better than flag-stones was of enormous height,—the landlords would as much as ever be found sending the farmers round with the begging-box, on the plea that they wanted nothing but a remunerating price,—that is to say, the price which would pay them for growing corn upon flag-stones, they having at the same time bargained with the landowners for making over all the excess that should accrue upon the better lands, in the shape of rent. Rent is the difference between the total value of the produce of land, and what the farmer can cultivate it for with a living profit. If, therefore, there is land of all sorts of qualities, as in most countries is the case, the worst land cultivated will be that which will give the farmer's profit but no more, and in all the better lands the excess above this will be the rent. Hence the pretence that the farmer only wants what will pay him, is an ever-growing claim,—a claim which, if corn were raised to a guinea a peck, would be as strong as ever in favour of its being two,—a claim which, like the shoe to a waggon wheel, is dragged along with the wheel, and is just as much there as ever, whatever progress may have been made.

"The farmers are beginning to understand this, and to know that, with the exception of a portion of trouble they might have about their leases, they have no direct interest in keeping corn at a monopoly price; for the simple reason, that it is the landlords, and not they, that take the difference."—Vol. V., p. 413. *Suffolk Chronicle.*

---

## THE FAIR PRICE OF CORN.

"The price of corn ought to be, what men will voluntarily give for it in the absence of restrictions. No trader has a right to say his goods shall be bought from him at a certain price whether the buyer wants them or not. If one trader has the right, another has; and where would be the end?

"A fair remunerating price is what other men will voluntarily give. It is the dealer's business to see that the supply is accommodated to the demand; not to use violence to make the demand equal to the supply."—Vol. IV., p. 527. *Catechism on the Corn Laws.*

"The landlords' theory of remunerating price is a bottomless pit. When they talk of their barely obtaining a remunerating price, they mean *on the worst land on which the present price makes it practicable to grow corn.* Hence they would equally be found talking of a remunerating price, if corn had risen to its weight in gold.

"Since, then, in every imaginable state of the supply there must be some land or other that is paying a barely remunerating price, this proves nothing with respect to the market being plentifully supplied, or the propriety of prohibiting foreign corn.

"They want to be paid with a profit, for growing corn on the sand above high-water mark if it suits them; and to have an equal price for all they grow elsewhere besides."—Vol. IV., p. 526. *Catechism on the Corn Laws.*

**The Landlords' Case.**—"To say that the removal of restrictions would *reduce* the incomes of the landowners, is at most only saying it would take away from them what they ought never to have had. And there still remains the question, of whether they would be any real losers in the end. *Is this clear enough to them, to go to war with the rest of the community?* It may be very possible for them to draw money from the public loss, and be no gainers after all; just as a pond may draw water from another pond, and lose more at some other end than it takes in. And this other end is found in the impossibility of finding profitable employments for their sons, or marrying their daughters to the sons of other people who can do the same. A landlord is no gainer, though in spite of poor rates, he has £600 a year instead of £500, if the consequence is that he has eight sons and as many daughters to keep as miserable annuitants. This reason therefore applies to all except those who calculate on quartering their children on the public."—Vol. IV., p. 513. *Catechism on the Corn Laws.*

---

**The Farmers' Case.**—"The Corn Laws got up a spirit of prosperity for farmers at their neighbours' expense, in the same manner as a spirit of prosperity for linen drapers might be got up by an Act of Parliament that should prohibit the wearing of woollen coats. But that was seventeen years ago. The only consequence now left is, that there are perhaps five farmers where there would have been four, and that the five are much worse off than the four. If the five were as well off as the four, the farmers might plead that it would be all clear loss to go back again. But they are not; they suffer under all the difference that arises from the general state of the country being incomparably worse than formerly. Their children cannot all be farmers; and the Corn Laws have brought on a state of things where they can be nothing else. So sure as there is a Providence above, is it written that there shall be always ways in which those who wrong and defraud their neighbours shall in the end find out that they have made a rueful bargain."—Vol II., p. 319. *W. R.*, 1 *Oct.*, 1832.

---

**Farmers and Labourers.**—"The lamentable circumstance for the supporters of the corn law is, that little by little all their friends will be picked away from under them. The most feasible thing in the world, when information has taken a very few strides more, will be to convince the farmers and agricultural labourers, or an efficient portion of them, that they have at all events no urgent interest in the continuance of the public wrong. They gained for a season when the mischief was brought on, but their share in the general suffering has long since eaten up the benefits. By the converse of the case, it may be undeniable that the return to justice will be attended with some present exacerbation of their condition, but with the prospect of overpowering improvement at no very remote period. This is not the most favourable position imaginable to invite men to resort to; but it is a position which there is no reason to despair of inducing a great number of intelligent individuals to resort to in the end. There will be a desertion or at least a slackness, first among the farmers and agricultural labourers, next among those descriptions of landlords who are obliged to provide for their children in the world themselves, and have no hopes of quartering them on the public purse; and the end will be, that the remaining class of landlords with their few adherents, will have the honour of going to the bottom in a minority together."—Vol. II., p. 191. *W. R.*, 1 *July*, 1832.

---

**Mistakes of the Multitude.**—"Every man who chooses to run in the teeth of common justice and make himself the enemy of the multitudinous classes, must make up his mind to take the chance not only of what they may do right, but of what they may do wrong. There is no use in banditti being pathetic on the way in which they are sometimes treated when overpowered by the country side, and getting up a tragedy upon the sufferings of felons tied on their backs in carts, and considerably overtwitched about the wrists by the premature application of a halter. A humane *brigadier* will hinder it when he can; but he will not see in the possibility that he may not always be able to hinder it, the smallest reason why the country should be given up to the heroes with high crowns and cross garters. It is by no means certain that the oppressed classes in England *will* be moderate, if the concession of justice be put off till the hour when it can no longer be withheld. But their friends and leaders are not therefore the frank asses that should exhort them to sit down in sufferance for fear their enemies should be hurt. Let all sides take care of themselves; *our* business is to put you down, at all events till you show something like a flag of truce. That the operatives are at present not going right;—that they are going the way which threatens more evil than is necessary to their enemies, without accomplishing the good they desire to themselves;

—may be what any man has a right to hold, who is enough of an engineer to know that to try to scramble over the walls is not always the nearest way to take the town. But because the Lord's host is going wrong, is not a reason why a man should abandon the Lord's host; still less why it should be agreed and settled, that the good cause is a thing to be delivered up into the hands of its enemies."—Vol. III., p. 75. *W. R.*, 1 *April*, 1831.

NO COMPROMISE.—"No man ever got anything by giving up his just right where he had power to enforce it. To give up a part to save the rest, is a perfectly different question; but the people have no occasion to give up a tittle here. They have only to understand the thing, and use the means; and first or last, their enemies must be at their feet. And whenever that happens, they will overturn the most cruel, dishonest, and insulting structure of human wrong, that with the exception of the West Indian tyranny, has sullied the page of history. The landowners will call this setting one part of society against another. Is not the New Police setting one part of society against another? There is no use in mincing phrases; the people are trampled on by the rank and gross oppressions of an insolent order, who push their injustice to the cottage of the starving man and the bed-side of the dying, and feed their hounds on the blood and sinews of the industrious population. Two points are their law and their gospel; one, that they will not pay taxes and other people shall; the other, that fortunes shall be made for them at the expense of other people. All this they consider as their birth right; and they turn like hunted wild beasts upon anybody who talks of taking it from them. The people have the legal and parliamentary means of relieving themselves, if they have union and sense."—Vol. II., p. 399. W. *R.*, 1 *April*, 1833.

## HOW THE MONOPOLISTS BEHAVED FIVE YEARS AGO.

"On Thursday (18th March, 1837,) Mr. Clay brought on his motion for an alteration in the Corn Laws. As soon as Mr. Clay had finished speaking, an agricultural member (Mr. Cayley) rose with the seconder, and endeavoured to stop proceedings by counting out the House. The number was found above forty, and the seconder went on. Their first movement having thus failed, the landowners mustered kin and clan, and finally came down to the number of above two hundred. The ordinary routine of a-thousand-times-answered fallacies was put forward, and received as might be expected in an assembly where every man had made oath that he had a pecuniary interest in the question before him. At the instance of friends about me, I made repeated attempts to offer reply, as also to explain my reasons for not voting upon the actual question; but was unable to gain a hearing. Thank God, I have many better places! If I had been a jobber in a railroad or a dabbler in some monopoly, wishing to make a similar explanation, I should have been heard with reverential sympathy, to the extent that human organs could supply. Sir William Molesworth entered upon a demonstration of the mode of operation of the competition generated by the limitation of food, which was perfect in its way, but confined to a portion of the field. Mr. Hume was received with groans and hideous laughs when he attempted to open the case of that part of the community who have not three hundred pounds a year in land; and when he proceeded to connect the question with the New Poor Law, the sounds that issued from the landed benches had a touch of the New-Zealander.—Vol. VI., p. 227. *Letters of a Representative.*

## AN IMAGINARY PICTURE OF THE STATE OF A COUNTRY UNDER A CORN LAW, DRAWN IN 1827, AND SINCE REALISED IN ENGLAND.

"In such a country there would be seen crowds of youth of the middle classes, attempting to maintain themselves in credit by industry, and only dispersing the accumulation of their fathers by a fatality that nothing could ward off; families lamenting the ruin of their hopes, and men looking on the faces of their children as pledges of coming sorrow instead of aid. In such a country there would be campaigns against starving manufacturers; and men who had fought nations' quarrels, would be called upon to finish the sufferings of dying artizans. There would be a law to determine that every legislator should be a landowner, and a class of laws to make the poor die quietly, and without disturbing the higher orders by their efforts to escape. To be found houseless would be made a crime; because he that has parted with his house, has manifestly not starved when he ought. To be detected with horse-flesh in a bag, would be punished with fine or imprisonment; because a man who descends to such disgusting methods to save life, is evidently making efforts unfair upon his fellows. In such a country there would be troops of juvenile offenders in the towns; and regiments of poachers in the fields, living desperately on pheasant, because men are not permitted to buy bread. There would be 'distressed manufacturers,' and 'commercial crisis,' and 'a general glut,' and 'depravity of the lower orders,' and 'apprehensions for property,' and 'fears for establishments,' and 'danger to social order,' and every man asking his neighbour how these evils had arisen. On one side would be seen the rich few, enjoying with trembling; and on the other, industrious and able bodied men dying because working would not support existence as it ought to do; women and children trodden down in the mass of suffering, and retiring into corners to die without resistance, as is their nature; woe, and want, and wretchedness, and wrong; and all this that the squire's bitch hound might whelp in safety. If any legislators ever had a heavy responsibility, it would be those who tolerated such a state of things an hour after they had power to remove it. If any ever had a claim to the support of a grateful people, it would be those who ventured power and place by resisting the demands of the encroaching order, and putting themselves upon their country for their deliverance.—Vol. IV., p. 476. *Introduction to Catechism on the Corn Laws, first published in* 1827.

---

## THE NATURAL AND UNNATURAL SUFFERINGS OF THE PEOPLE.—DISTINCTION BETWEEN THEM.

"*To the Editors of the Sheffield Iris.*

"Sirs,—Too much can never be done to impress, in season and out of season, the images and feelings conveyed in the extract from your co-labourer of the *Leeds Times* in your paper of the 6th. But always weigh heaviest upon this point, that the distress, the agony, the woe are the results, not of the natural concomitants of human life, but of a distinct organization of law to that effect made and provided, as the means of placing a greater portion of the labour of the poor at the command of the sworn interested law-makers.

"When we view the spectacles of misery so forcibly described, let us always summon the reflection, that these are not the consequences of the primeval curse which destined man to toil or worse suffering during his residence on earth; nor are they contained in the most undeniable of all assumptions, that 'the poor we shall have always with us.' They bear precisely the relation to these facts which murder, wholesale or retail, does to the truth so gravely cited by Justice Shallow, that 'death is certain to all.' There is a natural suffering and there is an unnatural; there is one sorrow at the hands of Almighty God, and another sorrow of the landlords, and the proportions between the two are almost in the inverse ratio of the magnitude of the willers.

"To go over it again, we are not grieving over the fact, that every man, woman, and child must at some time or other be brought with pain and lamentation to the grave. We are not rending our garments nor our hearts, because among the chances and changes of this mortal life there must always be some who, either through defect of conduct or of fortune, will find themselves disappointed in their plans for honest success, and be bound to submit to the ills of poverty, or the still greater ones of dependence on the charity of their fellows. But we are bowed to the earth with the thought, that in this country so full of piety which is of no use, and of knowledge which settles the anise and cummin of Greek accents, and omits the weightier matters of the law, there should be a distinct organization by legislative enactment, regular, long-debated, premeditated, for raising and 'killing-off' a population of the poor, in order that, as they come in succession like the grains of coffee to the grinders in the coffee-mill, a pleasant flavour from their destruction, like that which saluted the nostrils of Jupiter from a sacrifice, may meet the organs of the tyrants of the soil in the shape of increased rents created out of the oppression of industry and commerce.

"It is not that such things are; it is that such things are done on purpose. It is that we have them done by regular human organization. God willed it not; the devil did not think of it, or at all events there are no traces of it in his history. The mixture of darkness and evil which made up the intermediate thing called man was the only hot-bed in which could be concocted such a fungus as a legislative assembly administering an oath to an interest against the public, and being quietly allowed in the possession of its prey."

"*London, April 10th*, 1841."

—Vol. VI., p. 287.

"As an old dealer in these subjects, I would suggest to the operatives at large, that the points on which clear views are most wanted among their class, and to which consequently their efforts should be directed, are the following:

"1. That whenever anything is bought at a dearer market, when it could have been bought at a cheaper, the difference of price is lost to the consumer as if it was thrown into the sea, and without any the smallest gain or increase of employment or wages to working-men in the aggregate. The workman who is employed in the home monopoly may gain; but he takes it all out of the pocket, not only of the consumer, but of some other workman besides, whom the consumer would have employed by the expenditure of the difference.

"2. That this principle tells with horrible effect, when the consumer is the *working man*, and the article to be consumed is what he cannot live without, food.

"3. That the consequence of such a system is that there must be a perpetual *killing-off* of the population of the working classes, from the moment their numbers have begun to press against the food produced at home. If only a certain number are allowed to be fed, all the rest must be brought to the grinder in succession, like the grains of coffee in a coffee-mill. And the New Poor Law will be that mill.

"4. That for wages not to decrease under such a system, is a thing impossible; and he that says so, ought only to be laughed at, for he in fact says, that many people shall be fed out of the same food that would keep a few. Still more ought he who should say, that to remove present prohibitions on food, would cause wages to fall; for it is saying that less shall be eaten out of much than out of a little.

"5. That the agricultural labourers are in the end brought to suffer, as much as the manufacturing. For as they have the same tendency to multiply, it is impossible they should not bid against each other for a limited quantity of food like the rest.

"6. That the mischief comes, by a process more or less roundabout, not only to all who are engaged in the various professions and occupations of life which have no immediately apparent connexion with either agriculture or manufactures, but to the farmers, and even to the owners of land, with the exception of such as either are to have no children, like the Fellows of Colleges, or who have some patent for keeping them out of the public stock.

"*London, April 17th*, 1841."

—Vol. VI., p. 301. *Sheffield Iris.*

## MERCHANTS OF HULL!

"Why are there bankruptcies and failures among you?

"Is it not because the trade to be divided is limited by law, while your numbers increase?

"The trade is to be limited to what can be carried on in exchange for a given quantity of corn. Hence merchants bid against one another for taking lower profits, as the operatives for taking lower wages; and the weakest go to the wall.

"The country may possess commercial capabilities for the maintenance of ten times the merchants, and ten times the population of every kind. But all shall be cut down to the tenth; the population in the poor-house, and the merchants in the *Gazette*.

"Suppose that in old time, Tyre, Venice, or Genoa, had declared they would eat no corn but what was grown in their own territory. Where would the "MERCHANT QUEENS" of the Mediterranean have been?

"You are told not to have trade, lest at some time it should be cut off. Would it not be as well not to have legs, for the same reason?

"*Hull, June* 23, 1841.

—Vol. VI., p. 386. *Election Proceedings.*

**Issued by the National Anti-Corn-Law League, Newall's-Buildings, Manchester.**

PRINTED BY J. GADSBY, NEWALL'S-BUILDINGS, MANCHESTER.

THE

# THREE PRIZE ESSAYS

ON

# AGRICULTURE

AND

# THE CORN LAW.

PUBLISHED BY THE

NATIONAL ANTI-CORN-LAW LEAGUE.

"A system from which the agricultural labourer is suffering more than any other part of the community."—*Earl Fitzwilliam's Address to the Landowners.*

"The painful confession must be made, that our own benefit is the true object for which this obnoxious code is established."—*Ibid.*

MANCHESTER:
J. GADSBY, NEWALL'S-BUILDINGS, MARKET-STREET.
LONDON:
LEAGUE OFFICE, 67, FLEET-STREET.
1843.
*Price Fourpence, the Three.*

THE COUNCIL

OF THE

# NATIONAL ANTI-CORN-LAW LEAGUE

TO THE

## FARMERS OF THE UNITED KINGDOM.

Fellow Countrymen,

We entreat you to read dispassionately and calmly the following pages, which are devoted exclusively to the consideration of your interests and the interests of your dependants.

Although we have been constantly told that the Corn Law is maintained for your benefit, the history of British agriculture, for the last twenty-five years, affords too much reason to believe that it has brought much suffering and loss upon both farmers and farm labourers. We ask you whether, since the passing of the famous Corn Law of 1815, with all your industry, intelligence, and frugality, you have found farming to be a thriving business? On the contrary, how many moderate capitals have since that time been swept away for rent—how many small holdings have been swallowed up by rich speculators, who now occupy vast breadths of land which formerly supported several homesteads? Cast your eyes around your various districts, tax the memories of your older neighbours, and reckon the number of tenants that have been ruined and sold up for rent since the Corn Law of 1815.

If the business of farming has not been prosperous during the last quarter of a century, we submit to you that the time is come when you ought to inquire whether the whole system of PROTECTION has not been contrived solely for the short-sighted gain of the landlords. This question is fully discussed by the authors of the following pages; and the writer of one of the Essays being a farmer, and therefore identified in interest with yourselves, you will, doubtless, give to his opinions all the attention due to a practical agriculturist. Again commending these pages to your candid consideration,

We are, fellow-countrymen, your well-wishers,

(On behalf of the Council of the League,)

GEORGE WILSON, Chairman.

# AGRICULTURE

AND

# THE CORN LAW.

## PRIZE ESSAY.

SHOWING THE

INJURIOUS EFFECTS OF THE CORN LAW

UPON

TENANT FARMERS AND FARM LABOURERS.

BY GEORGE HOPE,

TENANT FARMER.

MANCHESTER:
J. GADSBY, NEWALL'S-BUILDINGS, MARKET-STREET.
1843.

# AN ADDRESS ON THE CORN LAWS.

I have no intention to enter at any length into the question of Free Trade, except so far as it affects the tenant farmers and farm labourers of the kingdom. Free Trade has indeed been long recommended by those who have made political economy a study; and the last session of parliament, by the amended tariff and slightly modified corn bill, did homage to this principle; not so much by the extent of the alterations actually made, though they all pointed in one direction, as by the enunciation of the reasons and principles with which the head of a Conservative government advocated those changes. Arguments of a peculiar kind were used regarding the corn monopoly. High prices for grain were deprecated as an evil, but still it was urged that anything approaching to a free trade in corn would ruin the farmer, throw the land out of cultivation, starve the agricultural labourer, and finally ruin all classes. Now, what I wish to show, as a farmer, is simply this, that however necessary a corn bill may be to enable landlords to obtain high money rents, it is not at all requisite for the existence and well being of the tenant farmer, and still less for the agricultural labourer, but, on the contrary, that it is a positive evil to both.

I undertake to prove that it signifies but little to tenant farmers and agricultural labourers what the nominal price of their produce is, in comparison to steady markets and good customers; that the best, the only honest and true plan of fostering agriculture has yet to be tried, and that that method is, *cherishing the growth and securing the welfare of the largest possible number of consumers.* The landlords, who have hitherto governed this country, blinded by their own apparent interest, mistaking immediate profit to themselves as the best means of promoting the general well-being, have never hesitated to prevent the consumers buying their food at the cheapest market. If this odious monopoly of the first necessary of life must still be kept up, let it be distinctly understood by the country at large that it is solely for the benefit of the landlords. "Let," I say, "the saddle be put upon the right horse," for the tenants and labourers neither have, nor can they have any permanent interest in a system which directly lowers profits and wages, a system which restricts the energies of the people to the supply merely of the home market, necessarily of a limited character; or compels them to leave the home of their fathers and their affections, to seek a livelihood in distant colonies, and endure all the rigours and hardships of a first settlement in a wilderness.

A short review of some of the principal enactments regarding grain may not be uninteresting. At one period of the history of Britain the only law relating to grain was the prohibition to export it. The "wisdom of our ancestors" at *that time* did not imagine that a country could possibly be ruined by an over abundance in the supply of either corn, beef, or mutton. This discovery was reserved for later days. In the reign of Edward IV. the first act was passed prohibiting the importation of foreign grain, but only when the price of wheat did not exceed 6s. 8d. per quarter. It was said to be for the benefit of the "poor farmers," (this cant phrase is not of yesterday,) as they might be ruined from the plentifulness of the supply. Then, as yet, I suppose "poor landlords" had no interest in high prices, and the "poor buyers" could always shift for themselves. King William, in 1688, secured the firm alliance of the landed interest, by not only extending the acts prohibiting importation, but by granting bounties on grain exported. Millions sterling were thus expended, which both raised the prices at home and enabled foreigners to eat British food at least 20 per cent. lower than the resident native could do. The Corn Laws of 1773 and 1791 were improvements upon this barbarous policy, both allowing importation at nominal duties, the former when wheat reached 48s. per quarter and the latter at 50s. and 54s. per quarter. But the laws prohibiting importation were practically inoperative, principally from a deficiency in the machinery for ascertaining the averages until a short time previous to the year 1773. By the law of 1815, however, importation was wholly prohibited until wheat reached 80s. per quarter. This was done with the avowed purpose of bolstering up the price to something about that sum. Farmers were found, and brought from various parts of the kingdom, to state in evidence to Parliamentary Committees that unless they obtained 80s. or 90s. per quarter for wheat, the great bulk of the wheat-growing lands would be thrown out of cultivation, and the whole population might ultimately be starved, as the world could not supply us with a single month's provision. Fortunately, however, the result has since shown that high money rents were the only things incompatible with lower rates. The law of 1815 was the first that practically secured a monopoly of the home market to the British grower. It was then thought that, as we could not grow a sufficient quantity of food for our own population, the legislature had it in their power to fix the minimum price at which grain should be sold. We all know the bitter disappointment of those who entered into contracts and leases with that idea. A few years' experience made a solvent tenant almost a rarity. Notwithstanding these attempts to produce a continued artificial famine, a large importation of foreign grain taking place immediately previous to, and joined to the good crop of 1822, reduced prices one half, or wheat to 40s. per quarter. Then, again, we had Parliamentary Committees, but they could not report where the evil lay, because it did not happen to occur to them that rent had anything to do with the distress of the farmer. But I need not remind of this period those "poor farmers" who were obliged to sell their crop to pay a rent which they had agreed to give by calculating the price of grain at double what they could then obtain. Much persuasion surely cannot be required to satisfy them of both the danger and the folly of attempting to obtain famine prices in ordinary seasons. Neither shall I attempt to convince the wealthy, who could afford to store up their own crop, or buy that of their poorer neighbours, because I acknowledge at once that, for them, this system "*of a hunger and a burst*" wrought admirably, whatever wretchedness it produced to other members of society. The law of 1828 was a new plan to prevent importation by means of a sliding scale of duties; but as it has been confessed by all parties to have proved only beneficial to gambling speculators, it has been tinkered anew, and, as the bill of Sir Robert Peel, it has been again placed on the statute book during the last session of parliament. It is clear, however, that this supposed amendment was not meant to go to the root of the evil, (and indeed this was not even pretended by Sir Robert Peel,) but was intended to keep the price of wheat at 56s. per quarter, which has now been discovered to be a fair price, though we have seen that little more than twenty years ago farmers asserted that 80s., and some even 90s. per quarter was the lowest sum that wheat in this country could be raised for.

I have noticed only a few of the parliamentary enactments regarding grain, for there have been at least fifty during the last 200 years; but they all proceed upon the same short-sighted policy of endeavouring to extract the last penny from the buyers. Yet, notwithstanding all these laws, and the most complete monopoly of the home market that laws could give, how often have we heard of agricultural distress? distress which I know to have been no phantom of the imagination! *Parliament* has been besieged with petitions which should have been presented to the *landlords.* Committees have sat inquiring into the causes of the distress, but which only diverted the practical agriculturist from the right remedy which was at hand—the reduction of his rent. These artificial famine laws compe British farmers to occupy a singular position,—they are ruined, not by bad crops, but by the very richness of the blessings of a bountiful Providence. Such a startling fact at once begets suspicion in the mind that the position must be a false one. This may be converted into certainty by a perusal of the evidence given before the Agricultural Committee of 1836. There you will find that though for years no foreign grain had been in the market, yet that farmers paying money rents were distressed, while those whose rents were regulated by the price of grain had no cause of complaint. Corn bills, by raising prices in ordinary years, raise rents; but in years of superabundance, or after a large importation of the accumulated stocks of the continent, with even a moderate crop, these rates cannot be maintained; then high rents cannot be paid; and thus a money rent, which is only fair to a landlord in ordinary seasons, is so very hazardous to a tenant with a moderate capital.

As a tenant farmer, in an exclusively arable district of Scotland, paying a rent depending upon the price of grain, and averaging for several years past upwards of £1500 a year, for a farm possessing no peculiar advantages from vicinity to a market town, or anything of the kind; and upon a lease, originally of twenty-one years, of which there are a considerable number yet to run, and during which period repayment is confidently expected of large sums already expended in thorough draining with tiles more than five hundred acres, and otherwise improving and enriching the farm; thus situated, I should rejoice were the corn laws to be abolished whenever parliament meets, as I am satisfied that, *with a rent properly adjusted,* the skill and capital of the British farmer require no privilege that is unjust to the other classes of society; and I am by no means singular in holding these views. Many, whose hearts are with us, are silent from *prudential* motives; yet we know the sentiments of the Roxburghshire tenants, as testified by the gentleman (himself a farmer) who seconded the nomination of the Hon. J. Elliot in the last contest for that county; and also from what took place in the Haddington district of burghs, where almost all the farmers in the neighbourhood of North Berwick, who had votes, polled for the Free Trade candidate; and six or seven of these farmers each pay from £1000 to £1500 a year of rent. But it is unnecessary to extend examples; all farmers must know that what is so injurious to the other members of the community cannot possibly be ultimately beneficial to them; that, in fact, the success of agriculture depends wholly upon the prosperity of our manufactures; that it is this prosperity which makes agricultural produce of more value in Britain than in any other country in the world. But unless we are contented with the great natural advantages we possess in our proximity to the market, we shall assuredly starve to death "the goose that lays the golden eggs." It is matter of history that the farmers and gardeners in the neighbourhood of London keenly opposed in parliament bills that were introduced for the purpose of repairing and extending the public roads, because they said it would deprive them of their "natural monopoly" of the market of the metropolis; they said they paid much higher rents, and labour was much more expensive than what it was in the country,—precisely the arguments now used against the admission of foreign corn; but, fortunately for themselves, they were not listened to. London has grown and increased in size, and land and its productions have become of more value than ever. It is thus that the landlords themselves will be benefitted in the end; for may we not anticipate the same improvement and increase of population as has taken place in London for the kingdom at large, when the highway to it shall be cleared, not only of sliding scale bills, but of all turnpike charges for the exclusive benefit of any party whatever?

There is one reason often urged against the possibility of cultivating the soil and raising crops in this country without a monopoly of the home market, viz., *the expenses of cultivation.* I solicit the attention of my brother farmers to this question. It is admitted that the nominal price of labour is much lower on the continent than here, but when the quantity of work done is taken into account, this difference vanishes. In the principal wheat-growing countries, the labourer is at least four months in the year confined within doors, by the intense frost which seals up his rivers, and the snow which covers the ground; the burning heat of summer equally incapacitates him from the heavy labours of the field; whilst here both men and horses are actively employed on the farm every day in the year. And with perhaps the exception of America, where money wages are much higher and grain lower than here, there is no country in the world where the labourers bring the same spirit, activity, and intelligence to their work as they do in Britain; so that a far less proportion of produce is consumed by the labourers and cattle together, in raising any given quantity of grain, than what is required on the continent. But without insisting on this, I hold that, in farming operations in this country, the actual expenditure, in money, irrespective of the price of produce, is not by any means so large as to render necessary the present prohibitive system. I confess that, personally, I am but little acquainted with the methods of cultivation pursued in many parts of England; but I know well how matters are conducted in the best cultivated districts of Scotland, and I should imagine that what is found to answer well in this more northern region, would be found to be equally suitable on the richer soil, and with the more genial clime of England. In Scotland one man and a pair of horses are found amply sufficient to till properly sixty imperial acres, even under the six-course shift, or with one-sixth only in grass. The horses are, of course, kept entirely on the produce of the land, and it matters nothing to the farmer whether the food so consumed by them be either high or low in price. The ploughman himself never, in Scotland, receives his wages wholly in money, but he is oftener paid in full with the produce of the farm, having, besides different quantities of grain, his cow kept, &c. But admitting that his wages are wholly money, and call them 10s. per week, which is the hire for day labourers, who lose time by wet weather and other casualties, this does not amount to 9s. per acre on the sixty acres so managed. And I know, from practical experience, that over a farm under ordinary management, all the other outgoings payable in money, taking wrights', smiths', and saddlers' accounts, cash paid for clover seeds, public burdens, labourers' and harvest wages, need not exceed in amount 15s. per imperial acre; so that this, added to the ploughman's wages, if these are to be paid in cash, amounts to but twenty-five shillings the imperial acre, and which sum would be considerably reduced were there to be a permanent reduction in the price of food. You must consider also, that there are various modes of management, by some of which manual labour may be much more dispensed with than by the six-course shift, which, in Scotland, is reckoned the most expensive rotation. From anything, therefore, that appears, regarding the expenses of cultivation, it is not at all likely that any portion of land now cultivated will be thrown into pasture by any fall in the price of grain. That it may check the rendering waste land arable is conceded, but if it has been already improved, and at present yields sufficient to feed the men and horses employed upon it, and leaves a surplus as rent to the landlord, whatever the price of that surplus may be, it will still continue to do so. Nothing can prevent this except the labourer getting a greater share of the produce, which would be a most decisive proof of the national prosperity. But as beef and mutton always bear a relative proportion in their price to that of grain, so if, from the low price of the latter, land will not yield a rent, the proprietor can hardly expect it from raising the former. In the vicinity of large towns, or in densely populated countries, pasture grass for dairy purposes, and for the convenience of stock, will always command high rents. At present, in the immediate neighbourhood of Edinburgh, £8 to £10 per acre is a common rent for pasture fields, for which, if they were a few miles distant from the town, half those sums would be thought extravagant.

Perhaps you may have seen statements, by agricultural writers, of the expenses of cultivation and the value of the produce of a farm, and the difference exhibited between high and moderate prices, showing results apparently disastrous enough. If, however, you examine these statements narrowly, you will observe that an obvious fallacy pervades the whole, even where the different expenses appear to be fairly given. This consists in every thing being converted into money, such as expenses of keeping horses, cows, &c., and the price of seed, corn, &c., *whereas, were these and the landlord's rent deducted in grain, as they ought to be,* and if the tenant had, as his share, one hundred or two hundred quarters of wheat, or other grain, according to circumstances, it would then be seen that there was little if any cause of complaint.

I fearlessly appeal to you, my brother farmers throughout the kingdom, if there is not a mighty deal of humbug vented about the price necessary to remunerate the farmer, and about the expense of raising grain. You and I both know well that these depend almost, if not altogether, upon the *rent.* It is high money rents that make farmers sometimes think corn too cheap, and that is too often the cause of all their perplexing anxieties. When markets are high, farms are taken at such rents as if prices never could by any possibility fall lower, and then not seldom the tenant exists, as such, only by the generosity of his landlord, or bankruptcy and ruin follow. Free Trade would do away in part with that ruinous competition among farmers for land, by opening up other and more profitable investments for capital; while, by steadying the markets, which, by widening the range from whence the supplies are drawn, it would unquestionably do, it would enable us farmers to know something near what prices might be expected in ordinary seasons, and to frame our calculations accordingly. For it is those violent fluctuations that derange all our economy. No doubt if an individual occupies a farm on lease, at a money rent, it is his interest to obtain and keep up the price of grain as high as possible; but the moment his lease expires, a corresponding advance to the rise in the price of grain takes place in his rent, and justly too. But where the *rent* is regulated by the price of grain, which is by far the simplest and the safest measure of value, it is a matter of comparative indifference to the farmer what the price may be. In truth, it is then sometimes his interest to have that price very moderate. I allude to those years, (of which we have had several lately,) when we are unable, from deficient crops, to sell as much grain as we pay in rent to the landlord; whatever number of quarters we may want is still to be paid for; so the lower in price that it is calculated at, the better for us. Certainly, if we could get a high price with a good crop, we should make more money, but even in this country high prices and abundant crops rarely go together. It is only when we have little to sell that great prices are obtained. It must be obvious, then, that a corn bill that prevents the regular importation of grain into a country like Britain, must be a crying evil, even to farmers. A sliding scale of duties appears to be solely calculated to accumulate stores of grain, until, perhaps, immediately before the harvest, when the grain is almost wholly out of the hands of farmers; then only do prices reach that pitch to enable the importer to pay, or rather avoid paying, the duty, when the whole is thrown upon the market, just as we, the home growers, begin to dispose of our new crop. This has happened repeatedly; and what has taken place this season is a beautiful illustration of the working of such a measure. We had hardly got into security a most abundant crop of the finest quality, when the market was flooded by an accumulated stock of upwards of two millions of quarters of foreign wheat and about five hundred thousand cwts. of flour being suddenly thrown upon it. Had this wheat and flour been brought to market during the summer, as it was landed, (without noticing the advantage it would have been to our famishing population,) there cannot be a doubt but that now we should have been getting much higher prices for the crop we are disposing of. But it was kept in bond when we farmers had little or nothing to sell, and liberated just in time to forestall our market; so that in this instance the law, professedly framed for our advantage, has operated in a manner injurious to our interests. But a sliding scale will always have this effect, over and above attracting the attention of speculators exclusively to foreign corn, however low in price home produce may be. Men will take shares in lotteries. Besides, for every shilling grain rises, there is the additonal advantage of the *fall* in the duty, so that there is a profit two ways. If the prices rise and the duty falls to 12s. or 10s., it may still fall to 8s. or 6s., and then, if kept still longer out of the market, it may be got out of bond at the nominal duty. Of the 12,000,000 of quarters of foreign wheat which we have imported within the last five years, more than two-thirds of it have been entered for home consumption, either immediately before or during the time of harvest, so that the new crop and the foreign supply come to market together. But it is an invariable law of Providence that every attempt, whether through ignorance or design, to possess unjust advantages, recoils upon the heads of the offenders.

The uncertain nature of our demand for foreign grain causes the country to pay *higher* prices than would be the case with a regular trade; it also occasions heavy demands for specie, and compels the banks, for safety to themselves, to limit their circulation; it cramps trade and restricts the means of consumers; and in a short time it tells upon the agriculturist by a falling off in the demand in his market also. It is absurd to say that corn is the only article of trade that foreigners will not exchange unless for gold, especially when coupled with another common allegation, that they are so ready to sell it for such a small quantity indeed of the precious metals. Let the trade be regular, and grain will be grown for England; our manufactures will be readily taken in exchange, and our merchants will only require bills to enable them to square their accounts. But when we, as we now do, intercept the grain intended for others, according to all the laws of trade, *gold* can alone be taken in return for that grain.

Farmers without leases should have little cause to complain of free trade in grain, as they can have no difficulty in making new arrangements with their landlords, if such shall be found necessary. Those paying *grain rents*, we have shown, do not require any alteration. There remain however those tenants with leases, paying *money rents*, who may be entitled to relief so far by act of parliament, as that their money rents should be converted into grain at the average prices of the last five or six years, and be regulated for the future accordingly. Supposing that the said average price for wheat should be found to be £3 per quarter (less or more,) then for every £3 of rent now paid, the price of one quarter of wheat should be paid hereafter. Justice demands that this be done, and nothing more.

I may here allude to what is well understood as a fact, that, in many parts of England, *leases* are rarely granted by the landlords to their tenantry. Now, this I would consider "to be a heavy blow, and sore discouragement to agriculture." Landlords who refuse leases can have but an equivocal title to be ranked among "the farmers' friends." A lease, for a period of not less than nineteen or twenty-one years, is an absolute requisite to obtain correct or even economical management, or anything like the largest possible produce at the least possible expense. What tenant would for a moment think of expending on a farm £6 or £8 per acre, for draining, or of annually buying foreign manure, to cover, perhaps, the fourth of his farm, or even to erect a steam thrashing machine which so economises labour, while his rent was liable to be raised upon him the next year, or he himself be turned to the rightabout? Assuredly Scotsmen would hardly think any land worth occupying without a lease, unless at such a rent as would be little more than an acknowledgment of the landlord's superiority. It is these leases giving a temporary property in the soil, a property that is heritable, though not alienable, which has been the main spring in raising Scottish husbandry to the position it now holds.

There is one argument in favour of Free Trade, which will reach both the judgment and the feelings of every farmer who is a parent. What is to become of our sons and daughters, if the manufactures and commerce of the country cease to offer an opening for them? Farmers' sons cannot be all farmers, nor can their daughters all find settlements amongst their own class. We cannot, like the privileged orders, quarter our younger sons upon the State, or find them employment in the army, church, or colonies. They must push their fortunes in trade. A farmer with six children may probably keep a son and a daughter at home; but the other four will, in all probability, depend for their prospects in life upon the prosperity of trade and manufactures. In such a case, the family are more interested in trade than farming, in the proportion of two to one. With every parent, possessing natural affections, to whose heart his offsprings' welfare is dearer than his own, this view of the question will have great weight. Let it be remembered, at the same time, that if there is no opening for the younger members of the agricultural body in the towns, they will be forced back upon the soil, either to be supported out of the labour of others, or to bid against their neighbours for farms, and to raise rents and diminish profits. In fact, nothing can be more clear than that the trade of farming cannot long survive the ruin of manufactures and commerce.

I sometimes wonder that my brother farmers have never asked themselves this question—" Have we, as a class of capitalists, been more prosperous than other classes of traders?" Take, for instance, the grocers, linen drapers, or innkeepers, of your neighbouring market towns. Take the average of those engaged in any of these trades with a capital of say £2,000; then take the average of farmers, similarly circumstanced, and I ask you, which party, at the end of a dozen years, upon an average, has realized the most money? I know your answer will be in favour of the grocers, drapers, and innkeepers. How is this to be reconciled with the notion we have been taught to entertain by the landowners, that the farmers are especially protected? There have been no laws passed under the pretence of giving protection to drapers, grocers, or innkeepers; there are not a large number of landlords owning the grocers' shops in parliament professing to watch over *their* interests; and yet the retail grocers are more prosperous as a body than you. Surely this is enough to awaken your suspicions of the delusiveness (to use no harsher term) of all those promises which political landlords make to you at the hustings, or at agricultural dinners. But let me further ask, did you ever know the entire body of grocers, or any other trade, to be up in arms at the same time all over England complaining of distress? You may have known bankruptcies and losses to fall upon particular individuals, but did you ever know the whole body of any particular trade throughout the kingdom calling exclusively to Parliament at the same time to relieve them? No, such a thing never happened, and never can occur. Yet, we have known the farmers of England, in a body, five times complaining of *unparalleled* distress, since the passing of the famous law for their protection in 1815, and appealing to parliament for the relief of their sufferings, and this generally happened when trade and manufactures were comparatively prosperous! Will not such facts as these induce you to doubt whether the law which interferes with your trade, with no better result than these, had not better be totally and immediately repealed?

Upon this subject of protection, let me remind you that you have always secured to you the *natural* protection of the cost of bringing the corn from distant countries. Upon an average, I believe the freight and other charges, upon corn imported from the Baltic or America, amount to ten shillings a quarter. Now this, I say, is a *natural* protection, which nobody can deprive you of. Supposing you grow four quarters of wheat an acre, this protection of ten shillings a quarter is equal to two pounds an acre.

Let me offer an opinion as to the *mode* of repealing the Corn Law. It is apparent to every observing man that a tax upon bread will not be permanently borne in any shape. Neither fixed duties nor sliding scales will much longer be tolerated. Public opinion has decreed the overthrow of the entire system of miscalled protection, and the question now is one of *time* only. I have a strong conviction that nothing can be so unfavourable to your interests as the lingering death of the Corn Law. Whatever modifications take place short of total repeal, the burden will be thrown, if possible, under all sorts of pretences, upon the farmers. The experience of the late changes in the Tariff and the Corn Law has shown this pretty plainly. The landowners have laboured to convince you, at your recent agricultural gatherings, that the alterations in the late session have had little effect upon prices. They still try to assure you that *the law* will afford you ample protection. But, even if the lawdid protect you, (which it never did and never will,) what guarantee have you that the political landowners will not come to an agreement again in London next session, as they did in the last, with Sir Robert Peel, and consent to another alteration? Depend upon it, there is no chance of your coming to a satisfactory adjustment of rents and leases, *so long as you allow the intervention of politics in your bargains with the landowners.* Politics may be a winning game to those who have their own arrangements to make with the minister of the day, but I pity the case of the farmer who reckons any Corn Law for the value of a farthing, in making a bargain for his farm with his landlord. So long as the owners of your farms can point to *a law*, as a reason for obtaining a certain price for their produce, you will in no case be able to make a safe agreement for the use of their land. Get rid of all such interferences with your dealings at once. Let the Corn Laws be totally and immediately repealed, and then every tenant throughout the kingdom will at once be brought on fair terms to a settlement with his landlord. Public opinion and the necessities of the case will then force an equitable adjustment of rents and leases; and the dealings between landlord and tenant will thenceforth settle down into mere matters of business, with which politics will no longer interfere.

I now address myself to you—the farm labourers, for it is unblushingly declared that it is on your account, too, that we enjoy a Corn Bill. If you have attended to the preceding remarks, you will have observed what I think I have satisfactorily established, that, though the Bread Tax was abolished to-morrow, we should still possess the fertile soil of Britain, and that ploughing, sowing, and harrowing would go on much as usual. It has been said that, with low-priced food, a reduction in wages would immediately follow, but we see high-priced grain in Ireland, and wages from 8d. to 1s. a day, while the same quantity of labour, in America, with low-priced food, would earn a dollar, or 4s. 2d.; so that it must be an undoubted proposition that the wages of labour, like everything else, depend upon the supply and the demand. The only real connection between wages and the price of food is, simply, that the labourer's wages must be sufficient at least to keep soul and body together, while all past history proves that abundant seasons, or a plentiful supply of food, tend to raise both the real and nominal wages of labour. When the means of living is cheap, many labourers are tempted to leave their masters and become independent workmen. A large number of farm servants throughout the kingdom lodge and board with their masters, their board and lodging being usually esteemed equivalent to about half their wages; so that, when food is cheap, many farmers prefer (correctly for their own interest) taking on more hands, to sending the subsistence fund to market. This demand occasionally raises the money wages paid to the labourers. When provisions are easily obtained, labourers can afford to be occasionally idle; at least, they are not so readily obliged to agree to the terms offered by masters as in dear years, which so increase the difficulty of obtaining subsistence that workmen are glad to close with the first offer of employment. But it is not so long since 1836. You may remember the demand for labour, the rate of wages, and the price of grain at that time, and compare it with what you experienced last year. It has been found that, in every country, wages are high in proportion as the people are increasing in wealth; that however wealthy a nation may be, if that wealth be stationary, wages are very moderate; but when a nation retrogrades, the working classes die off from absolute starvation. Now, free and unrestricted commerce is the only means that can give Britain a chance to continue to progress; without it we must even go back. When it is recollected that millions in this country exist by manufacturing goods for foreign markets, which our own policy is constantly losing us, this will be at once conceded. Unless this policy is speedily changed, and we accept, as payment for our manufactures, American flour, Dantzic wheat, Baltic timber, and Brazilian sugar, an immense proportion of our population must inevitably be starved off through famine, which God forbid! or, what is almost equally to be deprecated, compete with you, the agricultural labourers, in your already over-stocked market. If there is one class more interested than another in this great question, it is you. With the impetus which every one admits Free Trade in food would give to our manufacturing body, I ask, is it too much to expect, that at least a portion of your number would be drawn off to that class, and thus leave a better remuneration to those who should remain? An additional demand for manufactures would raise the price of goods, and increase the profits of capital; workmen would be better paid, so that they and their families might enlarge their consumption of agricultural produce, to the benefit of all classes.

An intelligent farmer and shrewd writer,* at the close of last century, objected to Free Trade in corn on this ground amongst others, that it would raise the wages of agricultural labourers, while the farmer, by the admission of foreign corn, would be prevented remunerating himself by enhancing the price of his produce. Can there,

* Mackie's Supplement to Dirom on the Corn Laws. Edinburgh: William Creech. 1796.

then, be two ways of thinking, as to which side of the question your interest lies? Assuredly not.

After what has been stated, I call upon every *elector* especially, to dispassionately consider this question of questions, as well as the signs of the times. I am no alarmist. I have no dread of dependence on foreigners, even for food. The large importations we at present annually make show that we have come to that already, as well as for other things almost equally necessary. Neither am I afraid of war, knowing, as I do, that Free Trade is our best guarantee for peace; and that "were subjects wise, war is a game kings would not play at." But I do look with anxiety on the great and extended unions of the working classes, with the Chartist lecturer in every village, pointing to the palace of the wealthy and the wretched hovel of the workman. I am afraid of our institutions when he can say, "*You tell us we are unfit to govern ourselves, and you show your fitness to rule by robbing us with your bread tax.*" Property, whether in land or in accumulated capital, has unquestionably its rights; but is labour, the sole property of the masses, to be less sacredly regarded? Preventing tradesmen and mechanics from disposing of their labour in the best market, by refusing to allow them to take in exchange for it food, the staff of life, is certainly class legislation of the most odious description. With the world for our market, and wise and beneficial laws adjusting fairly to the shoulders of all the heavy weight of our grinding taxation, I have no fear, but a confident anticipation, that a long career of onward progress and prosperity still awaits our beloved land; that our population, increasing even now almost a thousand souls a day, may become so numerous and wealthy that even the cancelling of our untold debt may be readily accomplished. Suicidal madness alone prevents commerce in what is most essential of all, *food* for the millions of her people.

GEORGE HOPE.

Fenton Barns, by Haddington, N. B., 26th October, 1842.

*Printed by J. Gadsby, Newall's-Buildings, Market-Street, Manchester.*

# AGRICULTURE

AND

# THE CORN LAW.

## PRIZE ESSAY.

SHOWING THE

INJURIOUS EFFECTS OF THE CORN LAW

UPON

TENANT FARMERS AND FARM LABOURERS.

BY ARTHUR MORSE.

MANCHESTER:
J. GADSBY, NEWALL'S-BUILDINGS, MARKET-STREET.
1843.

# PRIZE ESSAY.

To protect and encourage agriculture has for many years been regarded by our legislators as the stepping-stone to prosperity, and the foundation of wealth and power; but whatever may have been the results of its supposed encouragement and protection, nothing can be more clear, than that though for a time the profits of tenant farmers may be raised by a law unduly raising the price of corn, yet that in the end the profits of farming must be regulated, not by the profits of that particular trade, but by the profits and well being of other trades generally. It is impossible to doubt, and indeed every man's experience would tell him, that if the profits of farming are large, and with a prospect of continuance, people from other trades whose profits were not so large, and even farmers themselves, would so bid against one another as speedily to bring the rent of land to its proper and actual value, according to the increased price of corn.

But it would be wrong to suppose that the profits of farming were always to be estimated by the amount of rent that is paid in any one year, or even series of years, for the history of the prices of corn shows us that it is one of the most variable of all articles of human consumption; and it also shows us that, independently of artificial causes, such as war, a derangement of the currency, or laws regulating the import and export of corn, it is affected by seasons frequently for many years together of a very abundant kind, and these followed again by many very deficient years. To say with any degree of certainty, therefore, what should be the amount of rent for any future year, must always be a matter of the greatest difficulty; but still it is obvious that a period of rising prices, when neither the landlord nor the farmer has calculated upon a rising rent, must be a season of prosperity to the farmer, and a period of falling prices, when a farmer is paying a rent calculated on high prices, must be equally a period of great loss to him.

The object of our corn laws, according to the avowed intentions of our legislators, professes to be to maintain a high and steady price of corn, and if they did accomplish this end there could be no shadow of doubt as to the benefit they would confer on the tenant farmer; but that they have succeeded in no one of these results, I think events have most fully proved.

The high prices of corn which were attained in this country at the close of the war, from the accumulated effects of bad seasons, the increase of wealth and population, and the formidable obstacles thrown in the way of importation by war, had led our farmers and legislators to form extravagant ideas of the price the country could afford to pay, and of the price at which corn could be afforded to be grown, and led to the passing of the act of parliament in 1815, by which wheat was not allowed to be imported for home consumption until the price had reached 80s. a quarter. For some time previous to this period, the home price had been so high as scarcely to be affected by the duty on importation.

The corn law of 1815, aided by deficient harvests, had certainly the effect of maintaining prices considerably above what they would otherwise have been; but still, during the whole period the act remained in force, from 1815 to 1822, the price of wheat averaged but 69s. a quarter, and in the last three of these years 1820, 1821, and 1822, the price was respectively 65s. 10d., 54s. 5d., and 43s. 3d. a quarter.

At this period we read of great distress among the farmers, public meetings held, and parliamentary committees appointed to inquire into the cause of the distress. The question why corn was low, and why it should not have been low, seems never to have entered into any one's head; the question always was, why was it not high, and why should not acts of parliament be made to keep up the price? It never appears to have occurred to farmers why rents and tithes, and the various outgoings upon a farm were high, nor do they ever appear to have entertained a doubt of the power of the legislature to maintain prices, as to make the trade of farming a better trade than other trades, which it must always be borne in mind is one of the necessary inferences of a corn law. With a view of allaying the fears of the agriculturist, and probably reflecting also that the importation of corn, at a time when it was needed, might in some degree be of benefit to the community, and indirectly to the farmer, a new law was framed upon a rather more liberal basis than the old, but still of such a restrictive nature as more than once to require the liberation of foreign corn as a temporary expedient.

The average price of wheat during the time this act remained in force, fron 1823 to 1828 inclusive, was 59s. a quarter.

In 1828 a new law was passed on a still more liberal basis than either of the two previous laws, and has been in force from that time to the present year. The years 1834, 1835, and 1836, were again periods of agricultural distress; and from the evidence taken before a committee of the House of Commons in 1836, it appears that, with the exception of the Scotch farmers who farmed upon corn rents, farmers generally were making no profits, and, in many instances, living upon their capital. On one point they generally agreed, that the agricultural labourer was never in more comfortable circumstances than he was at that time.

Since 1815 the farmer appears to have survived under prices, constantly falling from 69s., during the first period to 59s., in the second and under the third, from 1828 to 1839, of 57s. 7d.

Such is the history of the farming interest since the war, and it appears to corroborate what I before observed, that a period of falling prices must inevitably be a period of loss to the farmer.

While the hope has been held out to the farmer that the price of agricultural produce would be sustained, rent has fallen but little, and, in many instances, it has increased. Had the fall in agricultural produce been sudden, (like the fall of manufactured goods,) as undoubtedly it would at the close of the war had no protection been extended, there can be no doubt but that there would have been a great and sudden fall of rent. The loss would then have fallen on the landlord, which now has fallen almost entirely on the tenant. Farmers on a low rental, and with leases, would then have reaped all the advantage and profits to be derived from improved modes of cultivation, which, under the fancied security of the Corn Law, has now gone into the landlord's pocket in the shape of rent. There would then have been the probability to the farmer, instead of farming against a constantly falling price of corn, of having a constantly rising price. But it may be said, that, had all protection been withdrawn at the close of the war, the race of farmers existing at the time would have been swept from the land by so sudden a change. That it would have been a period of loss to the farmer I will not deny, but one which was unavoidable, and has since taken place to a greater extent. The high prices of the war had not been brought about by legislative interference, but by natural causes, over which Parliament had no control. It had been a period of great prosperity to landlords, and during which farmers had made large fortunes. It was to both a period of unmixed and gratuitous benefit, and they had not the slightest ground or pretence to ask of the nation to perpetuate such a state of things. They had derived all the profits from the high prices, and when the natural causes of the high prices no longer existed, it was but reasonable and just that high prices should cease. The war had left no taxes or burdens that were not more than shared by the rest of the community; and though some expenses of farming had risen with the high prices, yet most would speedily have fallen and adjusted themselves to low prices. Labour would not perhaps have fallen in the same ratio with corn, for reasons which I shall presently give; but horsekeeping, tithes, poor-rates, seed corn, and rents must all have fallen in a very near proportion to the price of corn. The farmer had not been encouraged by acts of Parliament to pay a high rent, nor could he have complained of Parliament not doing that which it had never promised to do. The men who had profited most by the high prices might not have been the identical men who were in occupation of their farms in 1815: but then it would have been as fair that the farmers of 1815 should have borne the loss as the farmers of 1822 or the farmers of 1835. But still the loss to the farmer was not a question as to time altogether, it was a question of amount also, for we have had lower prices occasionally since than we ever should have had with a free trade; and it is also unquestionable that the loss would have been largely shared by the landlord, had it taken place in the first instance.

It will hardly be disputed that the Corn Laws have not been successful in preventing very low prices of corn, or that they have not succeeded in maintaining a rising price, which, of all things, is of the most essential benefit to the farmer. That a free trade would operate powerfully in accomplishing these ends there are very good reasons to suppose. Upon a view of the situation of this country, as to the importation of corn, we find, that, in years of abundance, the prohibitory duties have so operated as to prevent any importation at all, and that the trade in corn has been of such a precarious nature and of so small an amount as not to form an article of regular and increasing supply from abroad; and in one year, since the passing of the law of 1828, we have actually been an exporting country. Now, the interest of the farmer is to maintain and encourage such an amount of importation as shall, from the increased wealth and population of the country, render it absolutely impossible that the home-growth could ever equal the demand. Let the quantity grown at home be ever so great, it is still the interest of the farmer that the consumption of the country should be greater. If with a free trade, instead of the present annual importation of one or two millions of quarters, we had five or six millions, it would be impossible that the low prices of 1821 and 1822 or 1835 and 1836, could ever again occur, for it would be impossible, under such circumstances, that we could be an exporting country. Nor would it be a small remuneration to the farmer if, instead of 39s. 4d., the price of wheat in 1835, it were 46s. or 48s., which would be at least the difference between an importing and an exporting price. It is not the interest of the farmer, as our pro-corn-law advocates tell us, to be independent of foreigners, and to grow enough for our own consumption, for it is not the interest of the farmer that prices should be the same here as abroad; and it must always be a protection to the farmer that the freights and expenses of sending corn to this country should be incurred by the foreigner, and that at no time we should cease to import corn. That corn would be at a high price under a free trade I do not think possible, or even desirable, but that it must gradually increase in price I think the situation and circumstances of this country render probable. Though there is still much waste land in the country capable of being cultivated, and much land already under cultivation capable of improvement, yet the importation required would be very great; and as soon as countries near to England had disposed of their surplus produce, we should have to go further for our supplies, and the more distant the ports from which we have to obtain them the higher must be the freights and expenses. The price of corn would thus be naturally enhanced to the producer in England; and, being paid for, as it must be, in manufactured goods of some kind or other, would not be felt as a burden or an injury by the rest of the community. It is not altogether a low price, but the power and liberty to exchange with other countries that we want. The price would then be yielded by willing wealth that is now wrung from poverty, and our landlords and farmers would find, to their surprise, that there are high prices of two kinds; one caused by deficiency in one particular article, and the other by general abundance of all useful articles. By the first of these two methods of obtaining high prices, they have attempted to benefit their own class, by keeping corn out of the country, and the result has been disappointment to themselves, and misery and suffering to others. By letting corn come into the country, other classes will be benefited and will live in ease and abundance; and from this ease and abundance will flow those remunerating and steady prices, and that prosperity, which have in vain been sought for in acts of Parliament.

That the prices of corn in this country should have been appealed to in support of the arguments that our corn laws have caused steadiness of price, is indeed strange, when prices in England have been more variable during the last thirty years than those of any country we are acquainted with; and when the variations that have taken place from the highest to the lowest price, under the law of 1815, amount to no less than 199½ per cent., and under the law of 1828, to 129 per cent. It may be said that the nature of this country would have given, under any circumstances, a more unsteady price than other countries; but upon examination I think we shall find there are abundant reasons for supposing the contrary to be the case.

It cannot be said that a narrow market is more steady than an extended one; nor can it be said that a country would have more steady prices were it excluded so entirely from the rest of the world as to have no importation of corn, whatever might be the wants of the inhabitants; nor can it be said that it is the nature of highly civilized and populous countries to be more variable in price than countries in a rude and barbarous state. The whole tendency of improved cultivation, and a higher and better kind of farming, is to make corn more steady in price, and if any country in the world should have been steady from this cause, it is England. From the maritime situation of England, and a great command of a variety of climates, and variety of markets, the argument is still stronger in favour of steady prices, for they are advantages in which respect few countries are similarly situated.

Though it is my opinion that prices would advance slowly under a free trade, yet, should prices remain stationary, there are many reasons to show why the trade of farming would improve under such circumstances. With low rents, low tithes, and low expenses, every improvement that is made in the implements of farming—every improvement that the farmer may himself make in the application or economy of labour, or the rearing or feeding of stock, would, in the first instance, redound to his own advantage; and not until a lease or tenantcy was expired could the landlord take advantage of the improvements, instead of, as at present, anticipating improvements in the rent. In the natural course of things, when improvements become general, and the price of food reduced in consequence of them, the public reap the benefit, and not the individual farmer making them. But then the farmer, as one of the public, and as a consumer himself, participates in the increased production, and so also the mechanic or manufacturer, and each and every class of the community who invents and increases the supply of articles useful or agreeable to man, in time surrenders his improvements to the public, and reserves to himself no more than the share necessary to his own individual consumption. In this, and in this way only, can increased production benefit the farmer; and if it can be shown that a steady and constantly increasing supply of corn, at a moderate and remunerating price, is the true interest of the public, there cannot be a doubt but that it is at the same time the true interest of the tenant farmer, and, ultimately, the landowner.

Though the advantage the FARM LABOURER would derive from the total and immediate repeal of the Corn Laws depends generally on the same principles that are necessary for the well-being of the farmer, yet there are other causes called into action which show that the labourer is more interested in a low price than the farmer.

The high price of corn in this country is a proof that in proportion to other articles it has a comparative scarcity, and in order to judge of the results, as affecting the wealth of the country in the particular article of corn, it is necessary to observe the mode in which the high price is brought about. Corn, being a necessary of life, has a greater tendency to variation, from a sudden addition or contraction, than a luxury; and a small quantity thrown into the market more than usual, either from the effects of abundant seasons, or increased importation, has a very great effect in lowering prices, and the subtraction of a small portion has also considerable effect in raising prices. Though no very accurate proportion between a deficiency of crop and a rise of price can be established, yet there is a rule, by an old author, who says, that a defect of one-tenth raises the price above the common rate three-tenths, and a deficiency of two-tenths raises the price eight-tenths, and so on, increasing very rapidly with each increased deficiency. But whatever the actual proportion may be, there is no doubt that the principle is correct. To keep corn higher than our neighbours, it is merely necessary for us to keep a portion of corn out of the market, and as we can seldom grow enough for ourselves, the end of raising the price is at once and easily accomplished by prohibiting importation. To say that the deficient quantity is made up by an increase of our home growth, is not the fact, nor ever can be the fact, as long as the price is higher here than in other countries, and no importation allowed. The very circumstance of a continued high price proves the existence of a continued deficiency; and it may fairly be inferred, that at least one or two millions of quarters of wheat are annually prevented by our Corn Law from coming into the country and being consumed. Whether this amount of corn was first produced, and then thrown into the sea, to raise the price of the remainder, or whether it is prohibited entering the country by law, is precisely the same thing.

It is not so much my object to prove that the money price of labour should be high, as that the actual condition of the labourer, with reference to his command over the necessaries of life, must increase with the increase of wealth in a country, and that with each increase of wealth the distribution will be more equal, by the labourer obtaining a larger share of the products of the earth for his own use than before.

The common sense and experience of mankind would tell us that cheap bread is better for a poor man than dear bread; and the first and most obvious answer to the question, why should it be so? is, because it is plentiful—its abundance is the cause of its cheapness. But it is asserted that the labourer's wages are generally reduced to such a price as to enable him to get but little more than the same amount of food at all times, with scarcely any increase in years of abundance. That this is very nearly the case in England is a lamentable fact, and partially but not wholly true. But it is not of what the condition of the labourer is, but of what it might be, that I have to speak. It is not that instances can be quoted which show that people in a state of political servitude and dependence may be constantly and permanently degraded in their situation, whatever may be the price of the necessaries of life. Of these there are unfortunately too many instances; but that, other circumstances being equal, the condition of the working man must be advanced by the increased production of any article of his daily consumption, it is impossible to deny; that wages rise with a falling price of corn is the rule,—that they fall is the exception to the rule.

With regard to the distribution of the particular article of corn, through the various classes of society, it may be observed, that there is not much more consumed in the houses of the wealthy in years of abundance than in years of scarcity. The corn over and above the quantity consumed by the farmer or the producer of corn, must be brought to market, and sold in course of time, for it would not keep without injury, and the interest of the money would always prevent corn being held for many years together. Now if it should happen that either from an abundant harvest, or increased importation from abroad, the quantity of corn produced should suddenly or permanently amount to a million or two of quarters more than before, it is clear that the relative quantity of corn compared with the quantity of labourers in existence for the time being is altered. Instead of there being 90 quarters of corn to 100 labourers, there are 100 quarters of corn to 100 labourers. The farmer is a seller of corn, and the labourer is a large buyer and consumer of corn. Here is a bargain to be made between the two parties as to the amount of corn to be given for a certain quantity of work, and the principle that comes into operation here is precisely the same as that of two men going into the market, each with something to sell. One has apples and the other has eggs to dispose of. If apples are abundant and eggs are scarce, the man wishing to obtain eggs for his apples, must give a larger quantity of apples than he would have done if apples had been scarce. This is the principle which regulates the exchange of all commodities, of which man has a surplus to dispose of that he cannot consume himself; and it is this principle which operates in the same way between two men dealing, the one for labour and the other for corn. If corn is abundant, and a man is able to earn as much in four days as will keep him for six, it is not likely that he will give his other two days' labour for nothing. Our Corn Laws alter the relative supply of labour and corn,—our Corn Laws make a provision that corn shall be less plentiful, but they make no provision that the number of the labourers should not increase; the relative supply of labour and corn is altered, and the consequence to the labourer is, that he gets less for his share of the produce of the soil than he otherwise would.

The irregularity of the price of corn has been of serious injury to the labourer in more than one respect, for it has induced the habit, on the part of the farmer, of lowering the wages of the labourer, and the habit, on the part of the labourer, of submitting to the reduction. A rise in the price of labour seldom takes place until some time after a rise in the price of corn, and during these periods, the habits and modes of living of the labourer are lowered, and many comforts are sacrificed. The condition and habits of the labourer thus reduced enable the farmer to take advantage of a fall in the price of corn; and, as is generally the case, the wages of the labourer are the first item in a farmer's expenses that the latter begins to curtail. Were the price of corn steady and the habits of the labourer improving, he would not submit to the reduction, and each improvement in agriculture which, under a free trade, would have the effect of lowering prices, would be participated in by the labourer, instead of being as at present entirely absorbed by the landlord and farmer. The labourer would then say, "Why should I continue to work and apply my labour to the land, without an increased share of the increased products, and why should the landlord and farmer, and tithe-owner, usurp all the increased production, and leave me in the same situation that I was in fifty years ago. Improvements in manufactures have made almost all kinds of clothing a third cheaper; we are better clad than our forefathers, why should we not be better fed also?" This would be a very fair argument for a labourer, and serves well to illustrate the effects of monopoly in corn, and free trade in clothing. How often do we hear people say that the working classes are dressing too fine, and above their situation? Why it only shows that articles of dress have become cheaper, and as a natural consequence the poor are better clad than they used to be. There has been no monopoly in manufacturing, and the consequence has been that the public have reaped the benefit. But with food the case is different. Of this there has been a monopoly, and the consequence has been that the people are not better fed than they used to be.

Though the money wages of agricultural labour have, in many instances, fallen with the price of corn during the last thirty years in England, yet they invariably form in cheap years a larger portion of the expenditure of a farmer than they do in dear years. In the out-goings of one farm with which I am acquainted, I find that the labour in a dear year formed 19 per cent. of the whole out-goings; and in years of comparative cheapness it formed 25 per cent. of the whole out-goings. Thus the labourer in the one case takes 25 per cent. of the produce for his share, and in the other case only 19. Though the proportion may not be the same upon all farms, still I believe the principle to be the same; and I have heard farmers say, that in some years of extraordinary cheapness it has taken nearly all their wheat crop to pay the labour. This has sometimes been made an objection among farmers to a repeal of the Corn Laws, that they cannot get the price of labour down to a level with the price of corn. It would thus be necessary if the price of corn were to fall much, that rent should fall in a greater ratio to compensate the farmer for the increased proportion of the produce taken off by the labourer. A better proof, perhaps, cannot be given of the poverty and stationary physical existence of the agricultural labourer of this country, than the fact of his having been so habituated to wages rising and falling with the price of provisions, as to be scarcely sensible of the advantage of a steady price of corn. Well did Mr. Burke say—"The squires of Norfolk had dined when they gave it as their opinion that wages ought to rise and fall with the price of provisions." If they really did so, it would involve the supposition that the rich alone should share the good things of this life, and that whatever may be the abundance in the land, the poor shall not partake.

The charitable feelings of some landlords and farmers, may at times keep the wages of labour higher than they might otherwise be, but this cannot exist everywhere, and if it did it would surely be better that the labourer should earn his bread by an honest independence than by the charity of the rich, and that he should obtain his wages as his right, and not as a favour bestowed by the patronage or caprice of the powerful.

America, perhaps, affords a better illustration of the principle that regulates the exchange of labour and food than is to be found in England. It is a very general opinion, that because America is a newly-settled country, the wages of labour are high merely on account of the vast quantity of fertile and uncultivated land, and that as the country becomes more densely peopled, the wages of labour will fall. The supposition usually is, that the reward of labour is highest in newly-settled countries, and that with the progress of civilization it usually diminishes. But as far as the history of America will guide us, the very contrary appears to be the case. Instead of the population approaching nearer to the limits of human subsistence, it appears that food has increased faster than the population. The habits of industry, the light taxation, the high intelligence and general education of the people, appear to have rendered their condition as a producing nation the most prosperous on the face of the earth. The price of flour, by which we may obtain a tolerably correct estimate of the costs of other agricultural products, appears to have gradually fallen in the last forty years. The price of a barrel of flour of 196lbs. appears to have been for the following periods:—

| | Dols. | Cts. |
|---|---|---|
| From 1795 to 1804 | 9 | 37 |
| „ 1805 to 1814 | 8 | 24 |
| „ 1815 to 1824 | 7 | 44 |
| „ 1825 to 1834 | 5 | 36 |

which would be in our money, per stone of fourteen pounds, for the different periods respectively, about 2s. 9d., 2s. 5d., 2s. 2d., and 1s. 7d.

With other articles of agricultural produce, proportionably cheap, people here who say that wages rise and fall with the price of provisions might imagine that wages were in America about 9s. a week, and that people would be very well satisfied and contented upon that sum. But so far from this being the case, the usual price of a day's labour is now a dollar (4s. 2d.), and this high price appears to have had no connection with the price of flour during the whole of these periods, but to have been constantly increasing while the price of flour has been constantly diminishing. As the result of a certain quantity of labour at given periods, Mr. Carey, of Philadelphia, gives the following. In 1699, as appears from the books of William Penn, according to the price of flour, and the price of a day's work at that time, it would have taken a man,—

| | |
|---|---|
| To earn a ton of flour | 137 days |
| In 1790, wages being about 3s. a day, and flour having fallen, it would have taken | 125 „ |
| And, in 1834, wages having risen to about 4s., and flour having fallen still further, it would have taken | 78 „ |

For an agricultural labourer in England, at the present day, with wages at 9s. a week, which would be about the average, and flour at 2s. a stone, it would require 213 days' labour to obtain a ton of flour.

There is also an absolute necessity for wages being high to enable people to purchase and consume large quantities of food, for if the increased food were not consumed by the working classes, it could not be consumed at all. Had the markets of England been open to the corn of America, there is no doubt but that the price of corn would have been lower in England, and more would have been consumed by the working classes. The proportion consumed by the working classes would have been larger, and the share of the capitalist less. It would have been a matter of difficulty for the wealthy classes to have kept down the price of labour, even had other circumstances been unfavourable to the labourer. The habits of a people are difficult to break through when once improved by increasing wealth and the enjoyment of new comforts, and it being the tendency of our nature rather to acquire fresh luxuries than to relinquish those already possessed, it is thus that the manners and customs of a people become every day more and more civilized.

The author of some corn tracts, writing in 1765, says—"Bread made of wheat is becoming more generally the food of the labouring people," and the cause of this happy change appears to have arisen from a comparatively low price of corn. There is, indeed, no other cause to which it can be reasonably ascribed. According to Arthur Young, the average price of wheat for 100 years previous to 1700, was 38s. 2d. a quarter, and the average wages of an agricultural labourer were 10½d. a day. For the sixty-six years ending in 1766, the price of wheat was 32s. 1d. a quarter, and the average wages of a labourer were a shilling a day. In the first instance, a man could earn but little more than a bushel of wheat for a week's work, and in the second instance, a bushel and a half. The steady fall in the price of corn appears to have operated favourably for the labourer, and to have done that which a sudden fall could not have effected, rapid changes in price being, as I have before observed, unfavourable to the labourer, inasmuch as, in dear years, he is deprived of comforts, and, in cheap years, neither his own wants nor the situation of the farmer will allow of the full advantage.

It may be said, that the demand for agricultural labour will be injured, in the event of a repeal of the corn laws, by land being thrown out of cultivation. No intelligent agriculturist, I think, can be found, at the present day, who believes that such would be the case. So long as land will pay any rent at all, it is almost needless to observe, it will never go out of cultivation. A vast quantity of the waste land, enclosed during the last sixty years, was enclosed when wheat was at 40s. a quarter, and there is no reason to suppose that the same land, which is now improved, will go out of cultivation with wheat at the same price; and, in order to make the poor or badly cultivated land of England grow more corn, a larger expenditure of labour, rather than a smaller, would be required. The Scotch farmers, who gave evidence before a committee of the House of Commons, in 1836, all agreed in saying, that they could do very well with the prices wheat had been at up to that period, viz., from 40s. to 48s. a quarter; and they also said, that there had been no distress among the farmers *paying corn rents.* Farmers paying money rents had done badly, and many of them ascribed their doing so to the circumstance of the Corn Laws raising expectations as to prices which were never fulfilled. A repeal of the Corn Laws might perhaps bring on a system of corn rents and long leases; but this would be beneficial, rather than otherwise, to the farming interest. Of the various items of expenses on a farm there are none, with but few exceptions, and these not amounting to 10s. an acre, that will not bear a strict reduction with the price of corn. Rent, tithes, poor-rates, and even taxes, would fall, and, in the receipts of a farmer, many kinds of produce would rise, such as wool, butter, and cheese, and milk and all articles which cannot be imported. The landlord would have no cause to complain, even if his rent did not bring in so much money as before. He would have his share of the produce of the soil, and in reason and in justice he can no more demand of the legislature to give his share a fictitious value than any other class in the community, and he would derive the same advantages that other classes would derive from lighter taxation, and from the daily improvements in the arts and sciences.

The same causes which led people in America to suppose that the opening of canals connecting the western with the frontier States would destroy the value of land in the old established States will affect England as they did the old States of America. By the increased trade that was gained by the old States, the value of land and the value of labour were advanced, and the increased consumption of agricultural produce prevented any material depreciation of price. In the same way would England, by opening her markets to the produce of the world, become the centre of civilization and wealth; and to suppose that, in the increase of her wealth, the very large classes, of whom I have more particularly been speaking, will not be participators, is to refuse the experience of history, and to doubt of the principles of human nature.

ARTHUR MORSE.

Swaffham, Norfolk, 25th Oct., 1842.

---

PRINTED BY J. GADSBY, NEWALL'S-BUILDINGS, MARKET-STREET, MANCHESTER.

# AGRICULTURE

AND

# THE CORN LAW.

## PRIZE ESSAY.

SHOWING THE

INJURIOUS EFFECTS OF THE CORN LAW

UPON

TENANT FARMERS AND FARM LABOURERS.

BY W. R. GREG.

MANCHESTER:
J. GADSBY, NEWALL'S-BUILDINGS, MARKET-STREET.
1843.

THE

# EFFECT OF THE CORN LAWS,

&c. &c.

---

The effect of our restrictive Corn Laws in hampering the commerce, depressing the manufactures, and famishing the people, of England, has been long known, and amply discussed. But that these laws are equally injurious to those classes for whose especial benefit they profess to be enacted, viz. farmers and farm-labourers, has not been so clearly made out, and is not so generally believed. The fact that any system of legislation should have the effect of diminishing the subsistence, and fettering the trade, of a great nation, ought, no doubt, to be sufficient to procure its immediate alteration. But unhappily it is not so; and in this country, as long as any numerous and powerful body of men believe, however erroneously, that their own interests are bound up in the continuance of unjust and partial enactments, so long will those enactments be maintained; or, if abolished, will be abolished only at the cost or the peril of a severe civil struggle.

The following pages, therefore, will be devoted to an examination of the real operation of our Corn Laws on the welfare of farm-tenants and farm-labourers; and if it shall appear, upon a dispassionate inquiry, that these classes have been, and are, *not gainers, but sufferers*, by these laws, we may hope that they will speedily join their commercial and manufacturing fellow-citizens in demanding their total abrogation. And first, as to their effect upon FARM-TENANTS.

I. At the very outset of the inquiry, it cannot fail to strike us as remarkable, *that the very classes, professedly to promote whose interests the principles of equal justice and commercial freedom have been trampled under foot, are, generally speaking*, in the majority of cases, and in the majority of years, *about the most depressed and unprosperous in the community.* If the system of legislative protection which has been so uniformly and unscrupulously followed were a sound one, the farmers ought to be the most thriving and fortunate of men; since for centuries back, but particularly for the last seven and twenty years, their prosperity has been professedly the especial care of Parliament; the agricultural interest has been the one to which all others have been at all times unsparingly sacrificed; and, if their measures have not answered, if their end has not been attained, it can only have been either because their object was not attainable, or because their measures were unwisely adapted to their end.

Now, what is the actual state of the case? None can answer this question so well as the farmers themselves. Since 1815 they have had almost every thing in their favour. Their customers, the consumers of agricultural produce, have multiplied with enormous rapidity; the wealth of these customers, and their consequent power of purchase, have increased with the extension of trade in a still more rapid ratio; the manufacturing and engineering enterprise of the country has absorbed immense numbers of labourers, who must otherwise have remained a heavy burden on the land; of late the remodelling of the poor laws has relieved them from a pressing and severe embarrassment; and taxes which bore exclusively upon the agricultural interest have been repealed to the extent of a million yearly.* Yet what has been the result? Is it not notorious, that, during this period, farmers have been in a state of frequent and deplorable depression? During this period, have there not been *three* several corn laws passed for their relief and encouragement alone? And, during this period, have their not been *five* parliamentary committees† sitting, to prove the existence, and inquire into the causes, of agricultural distress?

It is clear, then, that the object of our legislators has not been attained; not, we believe, because it is unattainable, but because the measures pursued have been unfitted to their aim. We are convinced (and, if we were not, the history of our corn-legislation would go far to produce the conviction,) that, in public as in private matters, selfishness, if too gross, generally defeats its own purposes; that unjust laws are always unwise ones; that the prosperity of any branch of industry can have no frailer basis, no more precarious tenure, than protective enactments; that the elevation of one class of the community cannot be permanently procured by the depression of the rest; and that an end which can only be obtained by oppression and injustice carries its own condemnation on its face.

The Corn Laws, then, so far from having insured success to the farmer, have not even secured him from frequent and severe distress. Thus far, all men will agree with us. Let us now inquire whether this distress may not be, in a great measure, traced to the operation of these very laws.

---

* The following table is taken from parliamentary returns, and the details may be found in the Companion to the Newspaper for 1836, p. 232:

| Years in which the reduction was made. | Agricultural Taxes repealed or reduced in that year. | Years since elapsed. | Total saving to Farmers by the reductions up to 1842. |
|---|---|---|---|
| 1816 | £281,695 | 26 | £7,321,070 |
| 1819 | 3,868 | 23 | 88,961 |
| 1822 | 470,108 | 20 | 9.402,160 |
| 1823 | 52,792 | 19 | 1,003,018 |
| 1824 | 6,876 | 18 | 123,768 |
| 1825 | 49,659 | 17 | 844,203 |
| 1832 | 8,710 | 10 | 87,100 |
| 1833 | 10,110 | 9 | 90,990 |
| 1834 | 102,000 | 8 | 816,000 |
| Total | £985,818 | | £19,780,303. |

† In 1816, 1821, 1822, 1833, 1836.

II. The case may be thus briefly stated. The existing Corn Laws profess to secure a certain price to the farmer for his wheat. On this price the landlords, the authors of these enactments, calculate and fix their rents; and on this price the farmers make *their* calculations, and contract to pay those rents. *But it turns out that the Corn Laws do not insure this price.* The rents have been adjusted on a fallacious supposition: the two contracting parties, therefore, cannot both be satisfied, and the weakest goes to the wall. The landlord exacts his rent, and the farmer is ruined. We appeal to the farmers themselves, whether this is not the true process in five cases out of six, in which they have been unfortunate.

The avowed object of all the Corn Laws that have ever been passed has been to fix and secure a price which would remunerate the grower; and the agriculturists generally, having a most religious conviction of the omnipotence of Parliament, have naturally concluded that the avowed object of any law would be effected by that law. The avowed purpose of the law of 1815 was to fix the price of wheat at 80s. a quarter. The language of the landed legislature was uniform upon this point. They declared that no lower price could be endured by the farmers; they told the farmers that such a price should be secured to them by law; and they arranged their rents accordingly. What has been the consequence? *In only two years* since that period has the annual average reached that price;* and those two were years of scarcity. The farmers, who had contracted to pay rents *which only a uniform price of 80s. would enable them to pay*, were, of course, impoverished or ruined.

In 1822 the average had fallen to 43s. 3d., and the deluded farmers were clamorous in their complaints. It was then declared, that the price of 70s. a quarter must be insured, in order to induce the farmer to keep a sufficient breadth of land under the plough; and a new Corn Law was passed to procure the desired result. Again the farmers were deceived, and lulled into fancied security; again rents were re-adjusted on the new assumption of a permanent average of 70s. *Yet in only one year† since that period*, and that one a year of scarcity, *has the price reached this point.* The rents, however, had to be paid. The landlord whistled, and the farmer paid the piper.

For some years subsequent to 1822, every one was dissatisfied. The consumers of corn thought they paid too much, and the growers of corn thought they received too little. Again, in 1828, a deliberate attempt was made to secure prices at once high and steady; such prices as would enable landlords to exact extreme rents, and farmers to pay them. *Sixty-four shillings* was now declared to be the remunerating price; and rents were calculated and settled on this basis. *Yet in only seven years out of the subsequent thirteen has this average been reached;*‡ and of those seven, five have been years of deficient harvests; and at least four years out of the thirteen have been years of severe agricultural distress.

In the spring of the present year a new law was passed, in the hope of fixing 56s. as the minimum price of wheat; yet, before the

---

*1817, 1818. † 1839. ‡ 1829, 30, 31, 38, 39, 40, 41.

harvest had been fully reaped, and before any wheat could be thrashed out and brought to market, viz., by September 10, *the average weekly return had fallen to* 51*s.* 6*d.*; and by November 5, it had dropped to 48s. 7d. Each successive Corn Law has, in fact, been a new and cruel deception to the unhappy farmer; yet to each has he looked with renewed confidence for his salvation:

> Cassandra's fate reversed is theirs;
> She, true, no faith could gain;
> They every passing hour deceive,
> Yet are believed again.

Our advice to him is to trust no more to such delusive protectors, to lean no more upon such broken reeds; but, after the experience he has had, to feel convinced that whatever prospects may in future be held out to him from the same quarter will be as faithless as the past have been.

> But do not thou the tale believe;
> They're sisters all, and all deceive.

The *first* evil, then, which the Corn Laws have inflicted upon the farmer has been this: *they have induced him to contract to pay rents which*, except in years of scarcity, *the price of wheat will not enable him to pay.*

III. The purpose of our restrictive Corn Laws is to secure high prices in this country by protecting the home grower against the competition of foreign produce; and by dint of looking always at the *intention*, and never at the *operation*, of legislative measures, a great number of our farmers have come to believe that low prices are the effect of foreign competition, and that high prices are the consequence of that competition being shut out. Now, how stands the fact? Why, that it is impossible to point to a single year of low prices in which there was any perceptible import of foreign produce; or to a single year of great foreign importation which was not also a year of high prices. The years 1834, 1835, and 1836 were years of low prices and of great distress and discontent among farmers, the average of wheat being under 45s. a quarter; yet the import of foreign wheat was only 122,175 qrs. The years 1838, 1839, and 1840 were years of high prices, and comparatively of farming prosperity, the average of wheat being 67s. 2d.; yet in those years we imported the enormous quantity of 7,858,500 qrs. Of this we say nothing more at present than that it undoubtedly establishes the fact, *that low prices of wheat in England are not, and have never been, the effect of foreign competition.* For five months at the close of 1835, and the commencement of 1836, the price of wheat ranged under 36s. a quarter; at which price no foreign wheat could have been imported from any country in the world, even had the corn trade been perfectly free, instead of being burdened as it was with a duty of 50s. a quarter. And in 1839, in spite of an importation of 2,681,400 qrs., prices never ranged so low as 66s. and averaged above 70s. The fact beyond all question is this, and it should be immoveably rooted in the understanding of every farmer, *that low prices are owing to abundant harvests, and not to the admission of foreign corn; and that high prices are owing to defective harvests, and not to the exclusion of foreign corn; since in the former case it is never admitted, and in the latter case it is never excluded.*

There is one case, and one case only, in which this rule will not altogether hold good. There is one case, and one case only in which harvests of extreme plenty will *not* bring prices of extreme depression; and that is, where the prosperity of trade, and the thriving condition of the whole community, enable the poor to live better and to eat more, and the rich to add to the number of their servants and their horses; and thus to increase the consumption till it keeps pace with the increased production. There is one case, and one case only, in which scanty harvests will not insure to the farmers prices extravagantly high; and that is, where the distress of trade and the impoverishment of all classes have produced a diminution in the demand for food equivalent to the diminution in its supply. Had the country been flourishing, and the people been in easy circumstances during the last two years, good wheat would have reached 100s. instead of 80s. Low prices may be produced by two causes; either by excess of production, or by diminished power of purchase on the part of the consumer. High prices may be produced by two causes; either by a deficient supply, or by a brisk and vigorous demand; and it is evident that they will be most profitable to the farmer when produced by the latter cause. Under the present system, high prices are only producible by deficient crops; so that when the farmer obtains the highest price, *then he has least to sell. If he is ever to profit equally by good harvests and by bad ones, it can only be by the community, who constitute his customers, being in a condition to buy largely in the former case, and to pay dearly in the latter.* If large crops and high prices are ever to go together, it can only be when manufactures are profitable, when industry is well remunerated, when all the people are well off.

In the production of this general prosperity, then, the farmer is as deeply and directly interested, as the merchant, the tradesman, or the labourer. *Yet to this general prosperity the Corn Laws are notoriously the greatest obstacle.* By the concurring evidence of the ablest men in every department; of practical merchants, of theoretical economists, of celebrated statesmen; the Corn Laws restrict our commerce, depress our trade, deprive our people of employment, and derange our friendly relations with foreign powers.

The *second* great mischief, then, which the Corn Laws inflict upon the farmer, is, *that they spoil his market, by impoverishing his customers.*

IV. We presume, that no doubt can exist in the mind of any one, that the *steadier* prices can be made, the better for the producer as well as for the consumer.* A trade in which the fluctu-

* "Fluctuations of price, whether they arise from alteration in the value of money, or from changes in the corn laws, cannot fail to produce evils in every branch of rural economy, which, independently of these disturbing causes, must

ations are excessive, partakes of the nature of gambling; and a gambling trade is in the long run always a losing one, and generally a ruinous one. The uncertainty which pervades prices prevents any thing like safe estimates, or accurate calculations. The farmer, being wholly unable to foresee whether he shall obtain 40s. or 80s. for his wheat, knows neither what rent he can afford to pay, nor in what style he can afford to live. If the price of corn were fixed, he would know pretty exactly what he had to expect, would be able to lay out his expenses before hand, and to calculate before hand on a certain, though it might be a moderate, amount of profit. This degree of uniformity, we know, is not attainable; but, the nearer we can approach it, the more desirable will become the condition of the farmer. Now nothing can be more certain than that our Corn Laws have increased fluctuations of price, *except that they were intended to prevent them.* One of the chief pleas for the perpetual legislative peddling on this subject has been, the necessity of preventing excessive variations in the price of so important an article as food. The far-famed sliding scale is the result of this alleged necessity; the offspring of previous variations; "the fruitful parent of a thousand more." It was a patent invention to produce uniformity of price. Yet the annexed table* will show how completely this, as well as all previous enactments, has failed in effecting even an approximation to its object; and Mr. Tooke, Sir Robert Peel's favourite authority, declares, (and, we doubt not, with perfect correctness,) that, under the sliding scale, prices *must* fluctuate *at least* from 36s. to 73s. a quarter, or more than 100 per cent.†

Here, then, we have three remarkable facts. *First,* we have a parliamentary declaration, that steadiness of price is the primary object, which must never be lost sight of, and which is perfectly essential to the welfare of the landlord, the farmer, and the labourer. *Secondly,* we have a law passed for the purpose of procuring this steadiness, which, nevertheless, has not prevented the most excessive

ever remain exposed to grievous vicissitudes from the uncertainty of seasons. These artificial fluctuations, however, only aggravate the natural evil; they render the income of the landlord precarious, *the fixed rent of the farmer a hazardous speculation,* and the wages of the labourer an uncertain remuneration. * * * *Steadiness of price,* which is conducive to settled habits, and forms the basis of all fixed engagements, *is the primary object never again to be overlooked.*"—"Report of Committee of House of Commons," 1833.

*

| Year in which the Corn Law was passed. | Lowest Price of Wheat under this Law. | Highest Price under this Law. | Fluctuation under this Law per cent. |
|---|---|---|---|
| 1670 | 35s. 6d. | 64s. 0d. | 80 |
| 1689 | 23 0 | 81 0 | 252 |
| 1773 | 35 7 | 59 0 | 67 |
| 1791 | 41 0 | 156 0 | 280 |
| 1804 | 49 6 | 155 0 | 213 |
| 1815 | 38 1 | 112 7 | 196 |
| 1822 | 40 0 | 69 0 | 72 |
| 1828 | 36 0 | 79 0 | 119 |

† Tooke on Prices, III. pp. 35, 38.

fluctuations. And, *thirdly*, we have it shown on the first authority, that this very law does and *must* aggravate these very fluctuations.* Surely a law passed with a definite object, and producing the exact opposite of that object, needs no further condemnation.

Moreover, it is perfectly evident, that steadiness of price is at least as important to the consumer as to the grower of corn. The grower, if he be a man of capital, may, to a certain extent, set a high-priced year against a low-priced year, and so make a decent average. But the poor bread-eater cannot do this. He cannot lay in a stock of flour at 36s., and keep it by him to consume when the price is 73s. He eats what he wants in the low-priced year; and when the high-priced year comes, he lives upon something else, or eats only half the quantity. Had the price been stationary at 50s., he would have been to the farmer a regular customer for a regular quantity; but, as it is, he is a customer at 36s., and he ceases to be a customer at 73s. This, therefore, brings us to the important principle, *that the country could afford to pay the farmer a better average price, if prices were steady, than if they are fluctuating.* What we complain of is, not so much that wheat should average 50s. a quarter, as that it should ever reach 80s.

The *third* great mischief, then, which the Corn Law inflicts upon the farmer is this: by aggravating fluctuations, it upsets all his calculations, and *prevents the country from paying him as high an average as, with steady prices, it would be able to afford.*†

V. From what has been already said, it appears pretty clear, that restrictive Corn Laws are decidedly injurious to the farmer. It remains to be seen, that, of all possible modifications of such laws, that which is known as the *sliding scale* is the most fraught with

---

* Under a fixed duty, or free trade, corn would come in just as it was wanted; the supply would meet the demand, and be proportionate to it, both in time and in amount. Under the sliding scale the price is rapidly and inordinately raised by the artificial withholding of the supply, till the lowest duty is attained, when it is as rapidly depressed by the sudden liberation of the whole quantity in bond.

† We apprehend that the farmers are very much deceived as to the actual average prices of wheat. The *apparent* average, from 1829—1841, as taken from the weekly returns, was 58s. 9d. a quarter; *but as by far the greater quantities are always sold in the low-priced years*, and generally *in the lowest-priced weeks of those years*, the real average paid to the farmers will be far lower, probably about 53s. On examining the quantity of wheat sold in 150 towns, from which returns were made to the corn inspectors, we find that in the *three dear years*, 1829, 30, 31, when the average price was 65s. 7d., the quantity sold reached only 8,515,000 qrs., while, in the *three cheap years*, 1834, 35, 36, when the price had fallen to 46s. 2d., the quantity sold reached 11,286,000 qrs. And in 1839, 40, 41, when the price had again risen to 67s. 1d., the quantity sold, notwithstanding a great increase of population, had fallen off to 10,938,000 qrs. In 1838, at 64s. 7d., 4,064,000 qrs. were sold. In 1839, *the price had risen to* 70s. 8d., *and only* 3,174,000 qrs. *were sold.* The same peculiarity appears if we compare different parts of the same year. In the two highest-priced months of 1835, viz., July and August, at the price of 40s. 9d., only 510,513 qrs. were sold. But in November and December, when prices had receded to 35s. 5d., 704,100 qrs. were sold.

Mr. Tooke has a similar remark (Prices, III. p. 40.) Between 1831 and 1839, the *apparent* average was 56s.; the *real* average obtained by the farmer he estimates at 50s.

mischief and delusion. It is, indeed, the very quintessence of evil. It is ruinous alike to the merchant, to the manufacturer, to the consumer; to the foreign producer, to the English farmer. If our legislators had sat down, in all diligence and good faith, to contrive a law which should be productive of a minimum of benefit to any class, and a maximum of injury to all, they could not possibly have devised one more exquisitely adapted to its end. Such are the singular errors into which even able men will ever be liable to fall, when they endeavour to counteract the operation of natural causes, when they commit themselves to an impotent struggle with the laws which govern the moral and material world.

Had the sliding scale been the exact converse of what it is; had it been made to slide in the opposite direction, the duty falling with the fall in price, and advancing with its advance; had the duty been nominal at 40s. and prohibitory at 73s., then, though in many respects more burthensome to the community, it would have afforded to the farmer a less delusive prospect than the present law; as he would in that case have reaped the full benefit of high-priced years. In one case, he would have been secured against foreign competition by low prices; in the other case, by the high duty. *His protection would have been proportioned to his danger.* "What," says Dr. Johnson, "is a patron? Is he not one who will see a man struggling in the waves, without stretching out a hand to his assistance, but who, as soon as he has reached the shore in safety, *encumbers* him with help?" Just such a patron has the sliding scale proved to the deceived and miserable farmer. When wheat is at 40s. a quarter, and no foreign corn can, in consequence, possibly come in, it mocks him with a needless protection of 50 per cent.; but when prices are rising, and prospects brightening around him, and he, unhappy dupe! is solacing his tantalized and thirsty soul with a golden vision of 73s. a quarter for his coming crop, the protection is suddenly withdrawn, and the deluge of foreign competition is let in upon him. Yet this is the law which farmers, in their darkness, have been strenuously struggling to save.

The sliding scale has yet a further operation which presses with peculiar severity upon the English agriculturist. *It depresses prices just when his stock of corn is largest, and when he is most anxious to realise; and raises them when he has none to sell.** This is not an accidental operation: it is inherent in the nature of a sliding scale. In five years out of six, prices are highest just before the harvest, because then the stock of wheat in the country is the lowest; and

* "The sudden admission of so large a quantity of foreign wheat in September, 1838, (1,513,113 qrs. in one week,) had the effect, notwithstanding the ascertained deficiency of our own growth, of depressing markets; so that the average price, which, on the 24th of August had been 77s., declined within the four following weeks to 61s. 10d.; so that whereas the previous rise to 77s. was for the benefit only of the wealthier farmers, who had been able to hold their stocks of the crops of 1837 to the last, the subsequent fall was to the detriment of the numerous class of small farmers, who, having by that time got their crops in everywhere south of the Humber, were threshing out, and, as usual, bringing the earliest supplies to market."—Tooke, III. p. 30.

they fall immediately after the harvest, from the opposite reason. We give in a note a table illustrative of this fact from 1829 to 1841,* showing that the average price has invariably fallen about harvest-time nearly 8 per cent., or from 60s. 4d. to 55s. 9d. a quarter. In the present year, this result has been still more remarkably brought out. The harvest was unusually early, and the stocks of farmers more than usually exhausted. On July 9th, the weekly average was 65s. 8d.; on September 10th, when the harvest was generally got in, and when farmers in the south were ready to bring their wheat to market, it had dropped to 51s. 6d., a fall of nearly 22 per cent.!

Now that this fall is to be attributed chiefly, though not altogether, to the operation of the sliding scale, is evident from the fact that it is equally observable in defective as in abundant years. *But* for the sliding scale, a rise in price would naturally be the immediate consequence of a deficient harvest. But the duty being always lowest when the price is highest, and prices having, as we have just seen, generally reached their maximum in August or September, the whole of the foreign corn in bond is certain to be liberated at that time, and is thrown upon the market so as to depress the price, just as the farmer (who, being rarely a man of capital, cannot wait till the reaction of the following summer, but must realise at once) is preparing to thrash out his wheat. The annexed table† will show, that, in every year of considerable foreign importation since the enactment of the sliding scale, (except 1831 and 1839,) the

*

| Year. | Average Price of July & Aug. | Average Price of Sept & Oct. | Year. | Average Price of July & Aug. | Average Price of Sept. & Oct. |
|---|---|---|---|---|---|
| 1829 | 64s. 5½d. | 59s. 0d. | 1836 | 48s. 0d. | 46s. 5d. |
| 1830 | 69 8 | 60 7½ | 1837 | 56 4 | 53 1 |
| 1831 | 62 5 | 59 8 | 1838 | 71 0 | 65 2 |
| 1832 | 60 10 | 53 4 | 1839 | 70 3 | 68 11 |
| 1833 | 53 3 | 51 5 | 1840 | 71 2 | 64 5 |
| 1834 | 46 10 | 41 3 | 1841 | 69 5 | 65 5 |
| 1835 | 40 8 | 36 5 | | | |

†

| Year. | Quarters of wheat, and wheat flour entered for home consumption in July, Aug., & Sep. | Quarters of wheat, and wheat flour entered in the other 9 months. |
|---|---|---|
| 1829 | 681,000 | 761,000 |
| 1830 | 1,435,700 | 294,000 |
| 1831 | 59,700 | 1,417,000 |
| 1832 | 278,300 | 98,400 |
| 1833 | 42,000 | 42,000 |
| 1834 | 23,000 | 41,900 |
| 1835 | 10,000 | 18,500 |
| 1836 | 12,200 | 17,900 |
| 1837 | 196,900 | 46,100 |
| 1838 | 1,538,500 | 409,500 |
| 1839 | 840,800 | 1,870,900 |
| 1840 | 1,587,600 | 813,500 |
| 1841 | 2,343,200 | 301,600 |
| 1842‡ | 2,580,000 | 320,000 |
| Total.... | 11,628,900 | 6,485,300 |

‡ Up to September 5.

chief portion has been poured into the market immediately before the harvest, and the lowest point of duty has almost always been reached in August or September.

The experience of the last fourteen years, then, and more especially of the present year, must, we think, have convinced the farmer, *that the inevitable operation of the sliding scale is to expose him to the overwhelming competition of a sudden influx of foreign corn, just at the period when he has most to sell, when he is most anxious to sell, and when, consequently, such competition will be most severely felt.* Is this the effect which he looked for from it? Is it an effect which he is desirous to perpetuate? Does it not convince him that the sliding scale, to which he trusted for protection, has been, in truth, his greatest enemy?

But it has a still further, and still more hostile, operation on the poor farmer. *It exposes him to the depressing competition of a larger quantity of foreign corn than is actually wanted, or would otherwise come in.* When it becomes evident that our harvests are likely to be deficient, orders are sent abroad for large quantities of wheat, which continue to come in long after the deficiency is supplied, and when prices are receding to a moderate level. Under ordinary circumstances, this extra quantity would not be called for till it was actually wanted; but as, under the sliding scale, the duty is rapidly rising, and will soon become prohibitory, the importer is obliged to enter it at once, and bring it upon a market where it is not required, and which, consequently, it must tend unduly to depress.

Moreover, this happy invention, the sliding scale, not only exposes the farmer to the risk of more foreign wheat coming in than is required, *but of much coming in when none at all is required.* The corn merchant is obliged to act beforehand in an estimate of probabilities. If he conceives that the harvests are likely to be deficient, he does not wait, as under a free trade he would be able to do, till the deficiency is ascertained, but he sends out his orders for foreign corn to come in at the period when the duty is usually the lowest, and the price the highest, viz., just before the harvest. But it sometimes chances, that he is mistaken in his anticipations, that the crop turns out a fair average, and that importations are not needed. But his orders are executed, and the foreign corn comes pouring in. He dares not wait for the chance of the duty rising to a point which shall make his speculation overwhelmingly ruinous: he must liberate his corn on the best terms he can, and bring it to market as early as he can, whether wanted or not, before the full effect of the harvest in depressing prices has had time to operate.

This, then, is the *fourth* count of the farmer's indictment against the Corn Laws; that *they introduce foreign corn at the worst possible moment;* that *they introduce more than is wanted*; *and* that *they introduce it when not wanted at all.*

VI. Thus far we have considered the effect of the Corn Laws on the interests of the farmer, considered merely in his capacity of a producer;* and as a producer, we have shown them to be in every way injurious to him. Either they raise the average price of corn, or they do not. If they do not, it is clear that neither he nor his landlord has any interest in maintaining them. If they do, we have seen that his landlord reaps the benefit, because he calculates his rent accordingly. *But the farmer is a consumer as well as a producer, an eater of corn as well as a grower of it; and, in this capacity, low prices, and not high prices, are desirable for him.* Nay, more; he is a consumer to a greater extent than any other individual in the community; for to his own consumption must be added the far larger quantity required for seed-corn, and for feeding his cattle. High prices, therefore, not only add materially to his household expenses; they increase his cost of production, and thereby diminish the profits of his occupation. This point is too clear to need any further elucidation. As consumers, we repeat, farmers are more interested in low prices than any other class of men in the country.

But farmers are consumers in another point of view. They have to feed the poor. In the agricultural districts they are the chief rate-payers. Now, the Corn Laws augment the poor-rates by a double operation. They increase the number of paupers, by depressing trade and manufactures; and they add to the cost of their maintenance, by raising the price of corn. The latter effect may be judged of from the annexed table,† from which it appears, that, in five agricultural counties alone, the difference of pauper expenditure between a cheap year, and a dear one, was £78,131 under the old system, and £71,913 under the amended law. The former effect, though equally certain, it is not so easy to show by tabular statements; but it is notorious that the manufacturing districts, when prosperous, draft off, and provide employment for many thousands of labourers from the agricultural counties who would otherwise have to be supported by the rates of their native parishes;‡ that, if these labourers had remained, or were now to be returned upon their native parishes,

* It should be borne in mind, that the farmer is a producer of other articles besides corn: he is a producer of meat, of milk, of cheese, of butter; and in proportion as the price of corn rises, must the people's consumption of the other articles be reduced. But our limits prevent us from dwelling upon this point at present.

†SUMS EXPENDED FOR THE RELIEF OF THE POOR.

| COUNTIES. | Under the old Poor Law. | | Under the New Poor Law. | |
|---|---|---|---|---|
| | 1829. | 1833. | 1837. | 1839. |
| | £ | £ | £ | £ |
| Bucks ............ | 135,239 | 124,200 | 61,634 | 72,367 |
| Bedford ............ | 84,513 | 77,819 | 37,447 | 39,889 |
| Essex ............ | 282,132 | 239,946 | 149,356 | 165,340 |
| Devon ............ | 222,381 | 210,825 | 169,449 | 194,361 |
| Dorset ............ | 90,949 | 84,293 | 63,531 | 81,373 |
| Total ........ | £815,214 | £737,083 | £481,417 | £553,330 |
| Average Price of Wheat. | 66s. 3d. | 52s. 11d. | 55s. 10d. | 70s. 8d. |

‡ "We do not know the exact amount of migration from rural to industrial districts, but we know that it must have been immense; for while the *natural* increase of the population, (*i.e.* the excess of births above deaths,) during the last ten years, has been much the greatest in the former, the *actual* increase has

the consequent augmentation of the rates would bring ruin upon every farmer in the country; that this re-emigration will assuredly take place, if the present depression of trade and manufactures should unhappily continue; and that continue it assuredly will unless those restrictive Corn Laws, which press so heavily both upon our foreign commerce and our home demand, shall be speedily removed. *The repeal of the Corn Laws is therefore necessary to save the farmer himself from ultimate and entire ruin.*

---

Let us now consider the effect of the Corn Laws upon the FARM LABOURER. The effect may be stated in two words: *they raise the price of the commodity he has to buy, and lower the price of the commodity he has to sell.* They enhance the cost of provisions, and depress the wages of labour.

I. Like all consumers, the agricultural labourer has a paramount interest in cheap food. It is calculated, that, in ordinary years, one-half his whole expenditure is laid out in bread. In years of scarcity, however, he must expend much more than this, and yet obtain much less. When the price of corn is low, he has, therefore, a far greater command of the comforts and necessaries of life than when it is high. This requires no elaborate demonstration. The labourer knows it to be the case. A very slight consideration will show that it must be so. Uniform experience has shown that it is so.

Some persons, however, have ventured to assert, that this operation is counteracted by an alteration in the rate of wages; that the wages of the labourer rise and fall according to the price of corn, and in proportion to the price of corn; and that his command of the necessaries of life, in consequence, always remains the same. The falsehood of this statement is obvious from the following considerations. Years of high price are always years of scanty crops, and are so merely *because* they are years of scanty crops. To affirm, therefore, that, when corn is dear, the labourer is enabled to purchase as much bread as when corn is cheap, *is to affirm that*

been much the greatest in the latter. A careful examination of the table given below, coupled with the annual increase of the population, will leave little room for doubt, that since 1836, the manufacturing districts have found employment and subsistence for at least 400,000 additional persons.

| AGRICULTURAL COUNTIES. | Increase per cent. in the Population from 1831 to 1841. | Births to Population in 1830. | Deaths to Population in 1840. | MANUFACTURING COUNTIES. | Increase per cent. of Population from 1831 to 1841. | Births to Population in 1830. | Deaths to Population in 1840. |
|---|---|---|---|---|---|---|---|
| | | one in | one in | | | one in | one in |
| Hereford ........ | 2.9 | 37 | 63 | Lancaster ...... | 25 | 38 | 32 |
| Cumberland ..... | 4.8 | 36 | 51 | Durham ......... | 27 | 35 | 43 |
| Norfolk ........ | 5.7 | 33 | 51 | Warwick ........ | 19 | 36 | 45 |
| Oxford .......... | 6.1 | 32 | 50 | Stafford ........ | 24 | 32 | 51 |
| Suffolk .......... | 6.3 | 37 | 52 | York, W. R. .... | 18 | 38 | 45 |
| Buckingham .... | 6.4 | 36 | 52 | Chester ........ | 19 | 43 | 42 |
| Average .... | 5.4 | 35 | 52 | Average .... | 22 | 37 | 43 |

N.B. The year 1830 is the last for which we have any calculation of the births."

"*Not Overproduction,*" &c., by W. R. Greg, p. 16.

*he can obtain a larger proportion of a scanty crop than he can of an abundant one*, which is manifestly both an untruth and an absurdity. In years of scarcity, it is obvious that *some classes* must consume much less bread than they do in years of plenty; because there is much less to be consumed. *What are these classes?* Are they the rich, or are they the poor? Are they the higher and middle classes, or are they the labouring classes? We know that the former rarely alter at all, and never alter materially, their rate of consumption: we know, therefore, that the consumption of the latter must fall off in a more than proportionate degree. When the rich are compelled to retrench, they retrench in luxuries, not in food. When the pressure of scarcity compels the poor man to retrench, he has no luxuries to lay down, and his retrenchment, therefore, falls almost immediately upon his daily bread.

It is, no doubt, the case in many parts of England, perhaps in all, that the wages of the farm labourer do vary to a certain extent in years of great diversity: that is to say, that, when the price of provisions is so high as to make it impossible for the labourer to maintain his family on his ordinary wages, those wages are advanced, though in an inadequate degree; otherwise he would be obliged to seek assistance from the parish; and the farmer knows, that whether he pays the advance in the form of wages or of poor-rate is a matter of comparatively little moment. In like manner, when the price of provisions is unusually low, wages are commonly reduced, because the general redundance of labour in the agricultural districts enables the farmer, in the great majority of instances, to procure hands at the lowest rate of earnings that will afford a bare subsistence. But is there a single agricultural labourer in the country who will affirm that his wages go as far when wheat is at 60s. as when it stands at 40s.? We believe not.

In 1835 and 1836 the prices of all kinds of farming produce were unusually low; and, in the spring of the latter year a committee of the House of Commons was, of course, appointed to inquire into the causes of the existing agricultural distress. Great numbers of witnesses from all parts of the country were examined, the chief portion of whom were farmers. Of thirty-eight of these, who were particularly questioned as to the comparative condition of the labourer at that time, in order to ascertain whether or not he had benefited as he ought to have done by the low price of food, only eight spoke doubtfully or negatively; the remaining thirty declared, with one consent, that, although wages were unquestionably low, the labourers were, in general, fully employed, *and had never within their memory been in so comfortable a condition, or able to procure so large a supply of the decencies and necessaries of life.** A similar committee, which had sat in 1833, at which period also prices were moderate, and produce was abundant, reported to the same effect in the following words:

> "Amidst the numerous difficulties to which agriculture in this country is exposed, and amidst the distress which unhappily exists, it is a consolation to find that the general condition of the agricultural labourer in full employment *is*

* First, Second, and Third Reports of the Committee of 1836, especially p. 353.

*better now than at any former period; his money wages giving him a greater command over the necessaries and conveniences of life."*

In 1836, when the committee made their report, wheat was under 40s. a quarter. Within three years of this period, the price had reached 73s., or nearly double. Was the labourer as comfortably off in 1839* as he had been in 1836? Could he procure any thing like the same amount of wholesome and nutritious food? Could he expend as much in clothing? Had his wages advanced in any thing like a corresponding proportion? *If they had*, why was the home trade so bad? Why were the poor-rates so much heavier in the latter year?† Why had the consumption of exciseable articles so greatly fallen off?‡ And why had the duties on malt, tea, and sugar, been so singularly diminished?§ *If they had not*, what becomes of the assertion that the high price of wheat is no injury to the farm labourer?

II. But the wages of the labourer are not only *not raised* in proportion to the price of corn; it admits of certain demonstration, that in the long run they are actually lowered by the operation of the Corn Laws. That these laws have the effect of curtailing *both the foreign and the home demand*, for the products of manufacturing industry, we shall take for granted, because it has been so repeatedly proved, and is now so generally acknowledged, that all reasoning upon the subject here would be superfluous. In proportion as they have this effect, they limit the extension of manufactures, and the employment of the people therein. They limit the demand for labour, and consequently lessen its remuneration.

The number of individuals occupied in the cultivation of the soil

* "The state of prices of provisions, and of the rate of wages in the last two years, (1838, 1839,) strikingly confirms the deductions from previous experience of the little tendency which exists in wages to follow a fall or rise in the prices of provisions, except at long intervals, and then only in a degree far short of such fall or rise.....In a few instances, the wages of agricultural labourers have been raised, but in a very trifling proportion to the rise of necessaries; and in cases where an advance has been granted, it has rather been from motives of fear or humanity on the part of the employer than as a legitimate consequence of an improved demand relatively to the supply of labour."—*Tooke on Prices*, III., p. 52.

† In spite of the increased economy brought about by the progressive introduction of the amended law, the total amount expended for the relief of the poor had risen from £3,800,000 in 1836 to £4,310,000 in 1839. And the *increase had taken place in every county in England*, except Lincoln, Shropshire, and Southampton.

‡ The excise duties collected in 1836 were £16,587,992, and in 1839 they had fallen off to £15,488,000, instead of having risen to £17,088,000, which they would have done had they kept pace with the population.

| § Duties on | 1836. | 1839. | Would have been in 1839 had it kept pace with the Population. | |
|---|---|---|---|---|
| | £ | £ | | |
| Malt...... | 5,776,094 | 4,853,992 | | |
| Tea ...... | 4,255,949 | 3,222,571 | | |
| Sugar ..... | 4,348,609 | 4,224,595 | | |
| Total .. | £14,380,652 | £12,301,169 | £14,812,560 | Diminution, two millions and a half. |

has not increased, and will not increase, with the extension of that cultivation. On the contrary, it has diminished, and we have no doubt will continue to diminish, unless some such change should take place in our system of agriculture as shall approach to garden cultivation. In the ten years ending with 1830, we know that tillage had been much extended, and that large additional quantities of land had been brought under the plough. The number of enclosure bills passed during that period was 205; yet, during that period, the number of families engaged in agriculture had *decreased* from 978,500 to 961,000; while 170,000 families had been added to our total population. The returns of the last ten years, from 1831 to 1841, have not yet been published; but we will venture to predict, that, when published, they will show a similar result. From this we draw two conclusions, which admit of no denial; *first*, that the economy of labour by the introduction of improved modes of culture more than counterbalances the demand for labour by fresh land being brought under the plough; and consequently, *in the second place*, that it is not to any advance in agriculture that our increasing population must look for employment and support. We believe that our soil now employs its maximum of labourers, though it certainly does not yield its maximum of produce.

But the population of Great Britain multiplies at the rate of 200,000 annually, of whom three-fourths, or 150,000, must be estimated to belong to the working classes, who must either starve, or live upon charity, or subsist by the labour of their hands. Employment must be found for 150,000 additional pair of hands every year. As long as trade and commerce prosper, they will find this employment in manufacturing pursuits, and the subsidiary crafts; when trade and commerce are depressed and blighted, they will be thrown back upon the land, either to live in idleness upon its fruits, *or by competition to depress the wages of the farming labourer*. Hitherto the course of events has happily followed the former alternative; but the time for the latter is fast approaching, nay has actually commenced; and, unless the Corn Laws are speedily removed, it can no longer be arrested. Now, we have seen that no additional hands are required for the cultivation of the soil; in fact, their numbers are already redundant. What, then, must be the effect of the annual influx of 150,000 additional labourers into a market already overstocked? What, but *ruinously to depress the wages of labour, the price of the only commodity the poor man has to sell!* The conclusion is as certain as any in arithmetic, that *such a check to the advance of manufactures as the Corn Laws are fast bringing about will infallibly reduce the earnings of the agricultural labourer to the very lowest point at which even the most uncomfortable life can be sustained, far below even their present pitiful amount.*

As to what the Corn Law *has* effected, some controversy may arise. As to what it has *not* effected, there can be no controversy whatever, since it must be evident to the dullest understanding, that what has not been effected at all cannot have been effected by the Corn Law. The Corn Laws, then, have *not* made farmers prosperous, have *not* made prices steady, have *not* raised nor maintained the wages of the labourer. Yet these were the *avowed* objects for which they were enacted. The object they *have* effected was one which was not avowed, viz., to raise the rents of the landlords; and this they have effected at the expense of undermining that national prosperity by the continuance of which alone can high rents be permanently secured. With the blind unthrift which is the usual companion and corrective of rapacity, they have killed the goose which laid their golden eggs.

W. R. GREG.

*Caton, Lancaster*, 30*th October*, 1842.

DAWN ISLAND
A Tale
BY HARRIET MARTINEAU.
Written for the National
Anti Corn Law Bazaar
May 1845.

*Harriet Martineau (1802–76)*, friend and correspondent of Richard Cobden[1] wrote *Dawn Island* for the Anti-Corn Law League bazaar held in Covent Garden Theatre, 12–27 May 1845. In her *The History of England during the Thirty Years' Peace: 1816–1846* she described the League's campaign as having

> approached more nearly to a genuine National Education than any scheme elsewhere at work. By the Anti-corn-law League the people at large were better trained to thought and its communication, to the recognition of principles, the obtaining of facts, and the application of the same faculties and the same interest to their public private affairs, than by any methods of intellectual development yet tried under the name of Education.[2]

In reflecting on the significance of the repeal of the corn law Martineau sided with the free trade radicals who regarded repeal as merely a step in the direction of much more sweeping constitutional reforms.

> It was quite true that there was a popular disposition 'not to agitate questions that are at the foundation of our institutions.' The great reform of policy – of procedure which had now taken place had excluded all present thoughts of organic change from the mind of the people. Inferior in importance as the late enterprise was to that of Reform of Parliament – inferior in its order, and in its import – it was yet great enough to absorb for the time the political energy of the nation. . . . It does not follow, however, that organic change may not arise from an inferior order of reform; and in this case it was clear to those who were aware of the facts that the power under the Reform Bill [of adding registered voters in the counties by the organised purchase of qualifying property] discovered by Mr. Cobden of renovating constituencies must, sooner or later, bring forth vast political results.[3]

[1] She had been instrumental in bringing about a reconciliation between Cobden and Peel in 1846 shortly before the corn law was repealed, see Nicholas C. Edsall, *Richard Cobden Independent Radical*, Cambridge, Mass., and London: Harvard University Press, 1986, pp. 162–3.

[2] Harriet Martineau, *The History of England during the Thirty Years' Peace: 1816–1846* volume II. 1830–46, London: Charles Knight, 1850, p. 416.

# DAWN ISLAND.

## A Tale.

BY HARRIET MARTINEAU.

MANCHESTER:
J. GADSBY, NEWALL'S-BUILDINGS.
1845.

# CONTENTS.

# PREFACE.

This Tale, written for the purpose, is my offering to the Bazaar of the National Anti-Corn-Law League.

However small its value, this contribution is made by me without hesitation, because I think that earnestness of conviction on the principle of Free Trade,—as on any principle whatever,—is most effectually evinced and employed by every one working in his own way for the cause. The separate gifts of a thousand of us contributors may be of insignificant value in themselves; but, as evidence that a thousand minds, and a thousand pairs of hands have been at work on the ground of a common conviction, the testimony is not unimportant. For my share, therefore, I have written this Tale; and I shall be gratified by its being granted a place among a myriad of other avowals of interest in the cause of Free Trade.

H. MARTINEAU.

Birmingham, April, 1845.

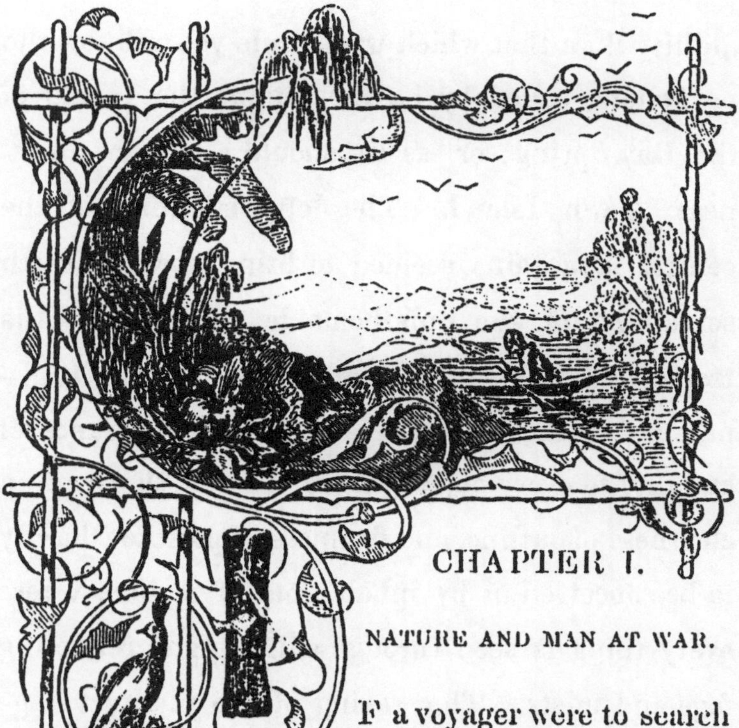

# CHAPTER I.

## NATURE AND MAN AT WAR.

IF a voyager were to search through the world for an abode of peace, he would probably choose, for its outward aspect, one of the small tropical islands of the Pacific; and of the whole Archipelago, no one could present a more enticing appearance of tranquillity than that which was, while yet unknown to navigators, called by its inhabitants the Island of the Day Spring; or, as we should call it for shortness, Dawn Island. The lofty summits of the central mountains seemed to bring down to earth something of the unfathomable quietness of the tropical skies which overarched them. The transparency of the atmosphere gave an appearance of stability to every object within reach of the eye,—a clearness of outline, and firmness of position, hardly to be conceived of by inhabitants of regions where every thing is seen through shifting and refracting fogs and mists. The waving of the plumy foliage of the cocoa-nut grove, and the leap and gush of the mountain streams, rather lulled than disturbed the senses of the observer; and if he turned his gaze to the shores, he could not but think that the space between them and the coral reef which surrounded the island contained the stillest waters he had ever seen. The coral reef extended to various distances from the shore, now stretching out so as to enclose a lake-like expanse of two miles in breadth, and then bending inwards so as to leave no more room than for two canoes to pass. To any gazer, looking down into the clear depths of these waters, all appeared even calmer than on the surface. Fathoms deep, he saw an apparent foliage and fruitage, delicate as vegetation itself—fragile-looking as the slenderest weeds, but giving way to no lapse of waters, and not stirred by the gliding of a throng of fishes, as the boughs of trees are by the flitting of birds. These many-coloured corals, sprouting and branching out from the sandy bottom, gave the idea of a luxuriant garden suddenly overflowed, and petrified by the deluge. The stillness of the land and waters within the reef was made more striking by the chafing of the ocean beyond. The long breakers rolled in, rising in height and force as if they would surmount the barrier, but clear and lovely as opal; and on the first encounter with the reef, their white crests were dispersed in showers of spray, which merely dimpled the smooth waters within, and sent a solemn sea music resounding through the nearer inland groves.

While such was the peaceful aspect of Dawn Island in ordinary times, there was one day in the history of its inhabitants when all was disturbance, through its length and breadth. Wars were indeed frequent,—aggressive or defensive wars with the people of another island, or conflicts arising from rebellion at home. On the present occasion, an expedition, with the king for its leader, was going forth to put down an insurrection on the opposite point of the island, where a dismissed minister had gathered round him all the discontented, and was putting forth a claim to the regency of the island, on the deposition of the king,—the heir being still a child.

On the king's side, the preparations had been going forward for some days. The weapons were cleaned and pointed, and their handles smeared with resinous gum, to make them fast in the warriors' grasp; the god Oro was brought out from his temple, and a red feather solemnly taken from the image by the priests, and borne hither and thither with the army, as a symbol of Oro's presence and sanction; the fleet of canoes was assembled in the lagoon, and the altars were dressed in those which were to convey the symbols and sacrifices of the gods. While the priests were preparing for the final ceremonial, and the king was holding a council under the deep shade of a bread-fruit tree, the orators were working up themselves and their hearers of the army into a state of high excitement, bidding the warriors to dart upon their enemies like a sheaf of lightning bolting from the clouds, to fasten upon them as barbed arrows on the flesh of the thigh, to overwhelm them as a waterspout advancing upon a fishing fleet, and finally to come home in triumph, to devour their chief foe as the shark swallows the strong man, when most secure in his strength. Some of the hearers were transported with the fervour of the oratory, casting glances of fire on their comrades, and uttering shouts of triumph. Of these comrades, however, some were of a different temperament, and others had their sobriety of mind preserved by the sight of their wives, who were hanging on the rear of the assemblage; or of their houses, which peeped out from the groves, or nestled in the meadows; and these remembered that the triumph was premature, and that, till the disposition of Oro was fully ascertained, no man could say with any assurance on which side would be the victory, and on which the devastation. Among some of these soldiers arose a rumour of "Where is Miava? Who has seen Miava, on this day when he should have been seen by every one?" And this muttered inquiry was taken up and loudly echoed by the women, whose excited imaginations immediately caught the alarm. A panic spread lest old Miava should have gone over to the rebels, and carried Oro's favour with him. In haste and trepidation, numbers ran to see whether the presents brought for the priest were sufficient—whether the mats and the cloth were of a handsome quality, and so arranged as to please the old man's eye, and stimulate his zeal in propitiating the god. All was found satisfactory enough,—at least in the eyes of the priest next in rank, who gave notice that Miava had merely retired to the woods, for peace and quiet, till the war should be over. He was now weary of the wars of which he had seen so many; and he left it to younger men to deal expressly with the gods, and receive the reward of their prayers and watchings. As the fatigues and anxieties were left to his juniors, so were the mats and the cloth, and even the canoe which he had heard was intended for him if he obtained a good response on the present occasion.

No one ventured to say a word in disparagement of the junior priests; but all were cast down by the absence of old Miava, who had for many years offered with his own hand the last human sacrifice, slain while the warriors stood, ready to start, with their arms in their hands. The king, who kept an eye on all that passed, from his station in the shade, marked the discouragement which fell upon the forces, and the cooling down of the orators, as their hearers turned their heads another way. He gravely observed to his council, "Miava must be brought down from the woods. By sunset, he must have his hand on the stem of the sacred tree."

"But if he will not come?" objected the chief minister.

"Then the war cannot proceed; and which of you will suffer that? Miava must come."

## CHAPTER II.

### PUERILE MAN AND HIS GODS.

At sunrise of this, as of every day, Miava had come out, to spend his hours in the wood or on the rocks. There was nothing in the abodes of any of the inhabitants of the island to tempt them to stay within,—no coolness, nor cleanliness, nor comfort. Holes in the roof let in the rain and mosquitoes; hollows in the earthen floor held stagnant water; the long grass with which the floor was strewed was never changed, and the food and drink dropped upon it rotted and fermented; so that the litter was presently fit only for a stye. There was no separate sleeping place; only the drier parts of the floor were chosen,—the parts near the walls, and there the mats were spread, and a low block of wood was placed for each head that desired the luxury of a pillow. Those who had pigs let them wallow in the midst; and those who had fowls let them perch where they would. No wonder that Miava was out early, exchanging the grunt and cluck of his domestic stock for pleasanter out-door sounds, for the fall of the broad bright cascade which leaped the rocks near his hut, for the rustle and clatter of the long stiff leaves and light leaflets of the cocoa-nut trees which sprang from the crevices of the precipice at hand, and for the distant murmur of the sea.

As he came out, he glanced at the smaller hut which stood a little way behind his own. Women, being regarded as an inferior race, were provided with a sort of kennel, where they might eat their coarser and poorer food, and wait the bidding of the men of the family. They were required to cook for their masters at the superior oven provided for the better abode, to carry in the baskets of food and wait on the eaters, and at night to sleep in the most comfortless corner of the larger dwelling; but further than this they were not indulged. They must eat only when others had done, must not touch anything particularly good nor complain of anything particularly bad, must always be within call, and wait standing, must not lie down at night till all the animals were asleep, and must, without fail, be busy at the oven before their masters awoke in the morning. So Miava glanced round at his daughter's kennel and at the ovens, and, not seeing her, ought, according to rule, to have been very angry.

But Miava was not wont to be angry; and least of all with Idya. Idya was not his own daughter; but had been adopted under circumstances which endeared her to him as much as if she were. She had been deserted in her early childhood,—her parents being both slain in war, and no one caring to nourish a helpless little creature of a sex not worthy to be offered in sacrifice, and of an age not ripe for cooking and beating fibre-cloth. So she would have perished on some rock or in some recess of the meadows, if Miava, who was of such dignity as to brave public opinion without detriment, had not connived at her continued existence, and tacitly taken some measures to secure it. He threw her some of the inferior sorts of fish which were brought to him in tribute, and did not inquire where she broiled them. She once found in her sleeping hole a mallet for beating cloth,—a mallet which was not too heavy for her strength,—a clear permission to learn to make cloth, if she could induce any women to teach her. It was even reported that not only had some one provided her with a bark foot-sling, for climbing cocoa-nut trees, but that Miava himself was once caught showing her how to use it, and taking care that she did not fall in her first attempt. By some imperceptible means, Idya grew up to be useful, like other girls, and to be indulged as few other girls were. When, as on this morning, she was not abroad before her proprietor, he did not beat or scold her, but said to himself that he was probably astir earlier than usual, or that Idya looked prettier and pleasanter when she was awakened by the first sun ray or the early breeze, than when scared out of her sleep by a kick or a growl.

He first repaired to his morning station, a point of rock whence he could overlook in privacy the valley beneath, and a wide range of shore. There he forgot everything in the interest of watching the gathering of the forces, and the reception of the king and his council. He was thankful to be on his quiet perch, rather than amidst the preparations,—for other reasons than he could freely avow. His mind was troubled by so much strife, and far more deeply troubled by being made, through his office, the abettor of strife. He had only followed custom and tradition in what he had done; but of late these had failed to sustain him completely,—to steel his heart against the cries of dying men, and to make him glory, for the sake of the gods, in sending the victim's right eye on a leaf for the king to pretend to eat. The slightest qualm of doubt as to the correctness of such proceedings spoiled all the complacency of them; and then again, there was the fear that any such qualm was an offence against the gods. He was glad that years and long service now afforded him an excuse before Oro and the king for being out of the affair altogether. And with this sense of relief he looked down this morning on the moving multitude.

As he watched, absorbed in thought, he was startled by a rustling in the bushes near, and next by the appearance of a woman whom he knew as the inhabitant of one of the best abodes in the valley below. Her face was now convulsed with fear, and her dress was torn, as if with scrambling through the thickets. She strove to speak, in vain.

"Feito," said the priest, "your son is now a man; and he must go out with men to the battle. When he was dying under the sorcerer's curse, and you fetched me to save him, was it not your wish to see him a man among men on such a day as this?"

"It is my wish now," replied the sobbing mother; "but the best hope for him now is that he may be as a beast among the mountains."

"Is he tabooed?" quickly inquired Miava.

"He is,—and in him all of us. Many months since, he sent to the king only half the bread-fruit that was expected, though we kept too little for ourselves. Since then, I have lived in fear. My children said to me still when the new moon appeared, 'We are safe;' but they will say so no more. The chief of our valley received the token to find a victim last night. He accepted it. There is no other than my son fit for the sacrifice. We have fled thus far. Tell us where further to fly."

"Where is Motuaro? Gone up the mountain before you?"

"How could he pass the threshold of Idya?" said the mother, with a melancholy smile.

Miava sighed, as he quickly turned homewards, followed by Feito and her young daughter. He had seen with satisfaction, for some time past, that Motuaro loved Idya. He had hoped to see Idya the young man's wife: but now, if the family must leave their bread-fruit tree and their fishing boat, and be outcasts in the mountains, what could he wish?

As he expected, he found Idya in tears, yet not listening to her lover, but rather hastening from him to meet his mother, to whom she rushed with a wail of grief, as soon as she saw her. The young man, who was following closely and sadly, now turned back, saying,

"She does not love me. I will go and be the sacrifice, for no one else is so miserable."

"You will go to the mountain," said Miava, with a tone of authority. "You are young; the king will soon be old, and the taboo may be buried in his grave."

"The taboo is everywhere now," cried the mother in despair.

"I can show you a place where it cannot hurt you," said Miava, wrapping his garment about him, as if preparing to guide the fugitives.

During the moment of waiting, the ears of the mother, quickened by terror, caught the sound of voices from amidst the wood below. At a sign from her, all listened. It was certain that men were approaching. Not an instant was to be lost. Miava whispered to Idya,

"Lead Feito and her son up by the path of the torrent to the sorcerer's den. They must enter it without fear; but you must not set foot in it. You must at once return,—and by the other path. No one is in the cave, and nothing shall hurt them. They will find food there till I can show them how to find more."

At a sign from his hand, the party were gone.

Miava did not return to his station; for he desired to intercept the party who were ascending through the wood. As he leaned against the door-post of his hut, awaiting them, the thought that more and more haunted his life settled down gloomily on his mind.

"'The forest-tree shall grow; the coral shall spread and branch out; but man shall cease.' If prophecy is true, this is the truest. My father walked through thirty peopled valleys; and his father through fifty. Of those fifty I have seen thirty desolate. Our young men die childless outcasts in the dens of the mountain; and our strong warriors go out and never return. Yes, the tree grows as lofty as ever; and the coral spreads in the sea as the convolvulus on the earth;"—and he looked from side to side, and could see no space between the trees where its bell-flowers did not sprinkle the grass;—"but man is fast dwindling, and will soon cease from our world. Too true is prophecy; and some fearful prophecies remain."

Here his meditation was interrupted by the messengers from the king, who came to beseech or require him to officiate in the sacrifice below. For some time he resisted. But when it appeared that the greater number of the party were on the point of being despatched in pursuit of a victim for sacrifice on the mountain, his concern for Motuaro and his mother, and his immediate power of saving them prevailed. He agreed to go on certain conditions;—that the deputation should, to a man, attend him, with such observances as he should prescribe; that he should select the victim; and that he should be the watcher in the temple at night for the response of Oro.

It was with a heavy heart that Miava slowly descended to the shore. The herald blew the trumpet-shell before him,—its harsh blast startling the birds from their hiding places in the trees; and a young priest in the rear beat the sacred drum, whose dreary sound spread fear of the taboo wherever it was heard.

"I had hoped," thought Miava, "never again to have spread fear through a race already doomed to cease. But by waiting on the god this once more, I may save a man. Yet, is it saving a man, when another must be chosen?" He put down this painful question by the remembrance, "This, however, is not my affair. It was within the memory of my fathers when the gods first required, by a dream, that the highest gift—man himself—should be offered. I am glad I was not the dreamer; but there can be no doubt of the will of the gods. And it is good to be able to choose the sacrifice, and turn aside the vengeance of the king. And it may be that Oro will give no response to-night; and then the war must not proceed, and many will be spared. How the people fly from the trumpet and drum! But the gods must be served, or man will cease at once. Oro perhaps chooses one to save a multitude. At all events, we must entice him from going over to the rebels. And Motuaro is safe for this time."

# CHAPTER III.

## THE PRIEST AND THE ORACLE.

As soon as the assemblage on the shore perceived that the priest had come to the sacrifice, shouts of joy rent the air. The king did not conceal his exultation; and at his command, more presents were brought, and laid on the pile of the priests' offerings. Miava's heart was somewhat lightened. He unconsciously felt the reality that there must be in any observances which so deeply involved men's passions of hope and fear; and he was aware of the dignity there was in being the medium between them and the unseen powers. He approached the Aoa,—the sacred tree which none but priests could pass without trembling,—and looked up among its wilderness of boughs with a tranquil gaze. There hung two human bodies,—the sacrifices offered at the beginning of the war-gathering. These he ordered down, and caused to be enclosed in baskets of cocoa-nut leaves, and slung up to the rafters of the temple, to leave the tree clear for the one remaining victim.

This tree, much resembling the banian, was as good an illustration as the vegetable world could furnish of the continuous being and self-diffusion of the deities worshipped in Dawn Island. Every branch sending down roots to the ground, and the sources of life being thus multiplied perpetually, it seemed as if the tree must live for ever. No man could ever learn from his fathers when this grove-like tree was a sapling; and it was now a firm and universal belief that a bird had brought some seeds from the moon, and had dropped one on Dawn Island in his flight.

While Miava, in examining the interior of the Aoa, retired out of sight beneath its pillar-like stems, the gazers little knew that he met his attendants under the shadow, to give orders fatal to one of themselves. He named the victim,—and in a few moments more the man was felled by a blow on the back of the head, as he stood on the outskirts of the crowd, jesting with a comrade. He was a young man of turbulent temper and vicious habits, who could be spared better than most; yet his heavy fall, and the shrieks of his flying family, penetrated with horror all who saw and heard. Such spectacles might increase their awe and dread of the gods, and certainly lessened their feeling for the sufferings of men; but the natural anguish of the moment could not be extinguished by custom and familiarity.

The rites now went forward with order and speed. The chief victim was suspended from the tree; the hogs were slain and baked,—their heads placed upon the altars, and their flesh partly eaten by the priests. The messengers of the gods, rising in the shape of birds from out of the tree, on a burst of harsh music, were dismissed to the place of abode of the deities, somewhere near the foundation of the world, to announce and invite, in the usual terms:—"There is war in the world. Come up to the place of light, and help your worshippers."

Before evening, the red feathers, taken from Oro's very image, were deposited in the sacred canoes; and all was ready for starting at daybreak, if only the response of the god in the night should be favourable. For its announcement, many waited with anxiety. The king himself lay on his mat before the gate of the temple; and his council watched on the steps which, on three sides, surrounded the inclosure. Miava was within,—he alone; and his station was in the innermost court. There stood the image of the god Oro, under a sort of wooden canopy. The rest of the court was open to the sky, but so walled round as that no eye could pry into the transactions of the priest and the oracle.

Miava was intently on the watch for a sign from the god. How it would come, he knew not; whether in the sighing of the breeze, or the piping of the night bird becoming articulate, or in a louder murmur of the waves, or by shooting stars flashing across the sky, (as meteors do in that climate,) or in a dream. After listening till his senses became confused, he lay down before the image, and looked up into the heavens, in order not to miss any token that might be manifested there. His sight was so dimmed by age that even the steady blazing stars of the tropical sky were to him blent in one hazy light; but if Oro wished to communicate with him, he would send a flaming meteor sufficiently near to the earth. The uncertain waiting for such a sign, however, wearied his eyes, and he slept,—a broken and anxious sleep. He dreamed, or fancied, that a voice whispered to him,—he knew not whence,—"The forest-tree shall grow; the coral shall spread; but man shall cease." Anxious to be assured, he cried, "Again!" But his own voice roused him. He started up. Nothing seemed changed. The hideous image of Oro stared, immoveable as ever, and the sounds of the night were all that was heard.

Miava's heart interpreted the prophecy, recurring at such a moment, as a token that there must be more slaughter,—that the war must proceed. But he would not conclude hastily. The night was not half spent. If Oro, or a messenger spirit from him, had really entered the image, there would be something done to preclude doubt. For hours he waited. The breeze had died away; the piping bird had gone to roost; the heavens were calm. There was no further sign.

As the dawn broke, and objects within the court became more clear, he perceived that something hung from the neck of the idol which was not wont to be there,—the singing-shell used by sorcerers in their divinations. These shells, being never known to refuse to answer, were carefully monopolized by those who had a right to intercourse with the demon which each contained. Miava saw at once that Oro had sent his messenger to speak to him through this shell.

Reverently and anxiously he lifted the shell to his ear. It sang, of course;—and to Miava the murmur appeared to be an incessant repetition of the plaint, "Man shall cease." The shell dropped from his hand. He could no longer question the response. He took a red feather from the image, and held it aloft as he issued from the inner court. The first golden spark of the sun was just rising from the brim of the ocean when he came forth. The king started to his feet. The council all arose, and each man uncovered his head and shoulders, in devout expectation.

"The war must proceed," said Miava.

"Oro is with us?" inquired the king.

"He is not against us, for he has replied," said Miava, mournfully.

"A multitude will return home?" asked the king, struck by his tone.

"Many will not return," replied Miava, speaking to the royal ear alone. "All else is made to flourish, but man to war and perish. Forests arise, and see how the corals spread! But man must cease."

The king's heart sank as he heard the old prophecy,—now confirmed on the threshold of Oro's abode. He looked wistfully in the face of the priest, and walked in silence down to the shore where his canoe led the war-fleet.

## CHAPTER IV.

### MORE HUMAN SACRIFICE.

The war proceeded. Many indeed of those who went out never returned; but the destruction of the rebels was the most complete. Except the few who escaped to the recesses of the mountains, and a very few more who got off to sea through a perilous passage in the reef, none survived. Of the first, some soon perished from want, while others became in course of time wild men, forgetting language and such arts of life as they knew, and actually sinking lower than many brutes. Of the fugitives by sea, a small number reached Evening Island,—the only land visible from Dawn Island, and so far distant on the western horizon, that no one thought of reaching it, except in a struggle for life. The lot of the prisoners taken alive was the worst. They saw first the destruction of their forces and their cause. They saw their huts burned—the women and children slain—their bread-fruit trees felled—the tops of their cocoa-nut trees cut off—total ruin overspreading their settlement. But, more than this, they had eaten their enemies after battle, and they knew that their own time was come. Theirs were not the feelings of disgust with which civilized men regard the act; but rather of a humiliation scarcely to be conceived of by any but a savage; for civilized men can never be absolute slaves to circumstance and event. They knew the passion of triumphant revenge under which they had swallowed the flesh of foes, and the exultation with which they had boasted of sharing with Oro his favourite feast. Now, they were to suffer, not only death by torture, but the contempt and malice of gods and men,—each in solitary despair.

The festival was indescribable. To Miava it was as tolerable in aspect as it could be to any one; for, as he saw in the idol Oro not a hideous image cut in wood, but a chosen form into which the war-god descended at will, so he saw in cannibalism a divine rite permitted to valiant men. The spirits of men were believed to be absorbed or imbibed by the disembodied deities, to whom in consequence had ever belonged the title of "Man-eaters." When human sacrifices were offered, there was no doubt in the mind of a believing priest that the spirit of the victim was drawn out and appropriated by the god, as the plantain from its rind, or the milk of the cocoa-nut from the shell; and, as spirits thus fed upon spirits, it seemed a sharing of the privilege for body to devour body. Thus, even such an one as Miava had calmly taken his share of the feast of victory, and was able to meditate on the act on his way up through the woods to his home.

At home, he found a very different kind of entertainment going forward. Motuaro was there, pursuing his courtship of Idya in defiance of personal danger, and of the discouragement of Idya herself, and in neglect of the mother and sister he had left in the wilds. He could not keep out of sight of the poor girl, who wished him far away. He followed her wherever she went, put jessamine blossoms in her hair, and declared his love in words of passion; but the customs of his country and tribe rendered his courtship as laborious and irksome to

Idya, as it was unacceptable for other reasons. He never dreamed of not being waited on and provided for by her, as men always were by women. She had to go down to the shore for shell-fish, and even to cast a net for salmon. The leaves in which his food was to be baked must be plucked by her, the stones heated, the plantains gathered; and she must attend upon him during the meal. They were thus engaged,—Motuaro supping in the middle of the floor of the dwelling, and Idya attending on him, when Miava appeared in the door-way.

Idya sprang to meet him, telling him what was at the moment uppermost in her mind,—that she had been wishing that he had been home, that she longed to wait on *him* at his meal.

"Yet," he replied, "you cannot long serve me. As Motuaro's wife, you must soon serve him."

Motuaro sprang up in joy at hearing these words. But Idya replied,

"No,—I do not wish to be Motuaro's wife. I wish to live as we have lived; if only Motuaro would not leave his place of safety to follow me, when I do not desire to see him."

"I will find a place of safety for him and you," replied the priest. "I see that he will neither be safe, nor provide for his wants, nor give food to his mother in the mountain, while he follows you in vain. You must be his wife, Idya;—it is best; and you must."

Idya made no reply. The tears ran down her face the whole time she continued to serve the meal; and when it was done, she disappeared.

Miava then told the young man of the utter devastation of the other side of the island, and the undisturbed possession he might take of any spot there, while the district was supposed to be haunted by the demons who delight in such places. An incantation, such as Miava could supply, would protect any retreat from these demons; and a safe and thriving home might thus be secured for the family, in the very midst of a desolation which would forbid the approach of any one else. Miava promised to go himself in search of a place of abode, if the young man would immediately depart to his retreat in the mountains, and not return till the new moon, when he should receive his bride. Motuaro, all joy and thanksgiving, engaged not to molest Idya by his presence before the marriage-day, and forthwith set out for the mountain, without attempting to take leave of the poor girl whom he now considered securely his own.

When Idya came, at her guardian's call, to hear the arrangement made, she turned away her face from him, that he might not see in the moonlight the traces of tears.

After relating to her the plans laid, Miava told her that she ought to rejoice in a prospect of married happiness so much more promising than was at all common. Not only did her lover woo her with a passion which was indisputable, but, from their mode of life, it was improbable that he would have more wives,—at least for a long time to come; and before that time, she might, by devotedness and prudence, have obtained an influence over him which would secure her a considerable amount of dignity and authority in the women's house, whoever might afterwards be the favourite.

Idya could at first only weep: but she soon timidly asked why she must marry, when she wished to stay and serve her guardian.

"You are growing old," she said. "If I go, you will grow cold and hungry, more and more;—and I——"

"That is the very reason," replied the priest. "I could not long give you a home. The cold and weary season of my perishing is at hand; and the young should be about their business and their pleasures. I had my time of youth and strength. Now my turn with the old men is come; and I must grow more weak and poor and comfortless, till I can live no longer. And your turn is come to be the young man's wife."

Idya did not dream of disputing this,—so fixed was the idea in all minds that the helpless, whether from age, sickness, or desertion, had arrived at their turn to perish. She therefore offered only a plea for herself. She represented that there might be some time yet before the feebleness of age came on; that Miava was not imperious and requiring as young men were; that she was now free from ill-usage and hardship; and that she had rather not bind herself to such toils and sufferings as a husband would inflict on her. She preferred the kind voice and contented temper of her guardian to Motuaro's present love; and if he ceased to love her, he might be very tyrannical.

This was true, Miava admitted: but matters would be made worse by delay. To be a first wife was an opportunity not to be lost; and she must make no further objection.

Idya did make no further objection. At the next new moon, she was married to Motuaro, with such celebrations as the priest's influence could provide, without the affair coming to the knowledge of the king, or other enemies of the bridegroom, and without danger of the young people being tracked to their new and unsuspected home.

## CHAPTER V.

### VITAL TRIBUTE.

The home of the new-married pair was in a spot which united safety and beauty with healthy influences. Wherever, through the whole circumference of the island, a stream descended along a valley to the shore, there was an opening in the reef opposite the mouth of the valley and river, affording access to the open sea just where fresh water was in abundance. Where such openings occur may commonly be found islets at the point of the reef,—the soil brought down by the river, and the weed and drift wood washed up by the sea, being accumulated against the barrier, and rising at last to the height of some feet above the water, affording a favourable spot for seeds to germinate, for roots to bind the soil, and at length for trees and shrubs to supply a covert for birds and game. Such an islet was chosen by Miava for the abode of the young people,

—removed so far from the scene of battle as to be out of sight and reach of its effects, and yet so decidedly in the district of desolation as to be safe from the intrusion of any person on the other side of the island. The little green platform was not more than half a mile round. Three cocoa-nut trees rose in the midst; and a good deal of shrubbery afforded fuel at once, and promise of concealment in case of need.

In the dead of night, Motuaro ventured to the little cove, near his former home, where his canoe lay, and brought it round in the smooth water. It was not long before Idya had obtained enough of the fibres of the cocoa-nut tree to make nets, wherewith she procured fish for their support. Their abode was merely a hut of poles, set up between the three trees, wattled with twigs, thatched with cocoa-nut leaves, and the earthern floor strewn with dry grass. Their only luxuries were the beauties of the air, earth, and sea. These Motuaro continued to enjoy a good deal of; as he did little but bask on the shore, or bathe in the inlet. But Idya had no time or thought to spare from the business of living,—poor as was the living obtained by her utmost care and industry. For months after her marriage, she rarely had news of her guardian. He was hardly strong enough now to make so distant an excursion;—she could not be spared from home; and she did not dream of asking her husband to take so long a walk to satisfy any anxiety of hers.

A season was at length approaching, in the prospect of which Idya earnestly desired to see the friend whom she loved best in the world. One evening, her husband found her resting on the ground,—apparently playing with the blossoms of the white convolvulus, which spread over the grass and the coral sands, down to the very edge of the water. Motuaro expected to find her at the oven, baking his supper; and he was not quite pleased. He asked her what she was thinking of, to be lying there. She replied, as she slowly rose, that she was wondering whether Miava knew that a child would soon be born to her.

Her husband asked if she felt afraid of being alone with him. If this had been a fourth child, which was to live, it would be necessary to have some one with them, to take care of it. But he knew how to dispose of it, and ——

Idya said it was about that that she wished to see Miava. She supposed, however, that no mother would be right in preserving her first child.

"No; nor the second," her husband replied. Of course, she could have no time to attend to it, in their present way of life;—that was what *he* had to say about it. Miava had other reasons to give, he believed, which would show it to be very irreligious and shocking to preserve a first child. Nobody did it, as she well knew.

Idya had lived so much in the woods, alone with her guardian, that she did not know much of what was done in society. She wished she had asked Miava about it; for, she now would like to hear the reasons why her heart ought not to feel so sad.

Motuaro told her that he thought he would go up to the priest's dwelling, this very night. He had a reason. He had found a fine turtle; and a turtle could not be eaten by any man without the sanction or participation of a priest. He would try to persuade Miava to come down, and eat the turtle with him. She must immediately supply him with food to support him on the way; and, as soon as he was gone, she must bury the turtle in the sand, to await his return.

Idya obeyed with alacrity. She had no interest in the turtle,—no woman being permitted to taste food so much more worthy of men: but she would have undertaken any task for the chance of seeing Miava.

She saw him the next evening. When the meal of turtle was finished, and Motuaro dropped asleep, and she stood behind the priest on the moon-lit shore, she spoke with a beating heart the question that lay so heavily there. She supposed that Motuaro must destroy their infant, as soon as it should be born.

"Certainly," replied Miava. "Can you doubt it?"

Idya was silent.

"Motuaro said something to me of your having feelings different from other women," continued the old priest: "and you have lived very much out of their way. But, besides the custom, there are the reasons for the custom."

"What are they?" cried Idya eagerly. "Could I not carry my child on my shoulder while I am baking and making cloth, and let it lie in the canoe while I am fishing?"

"No," replied Miava. "Motuaro would not like it. But it would also be a disrespect to the gods. The brothers of Oro were bound to celibacy. Their followers were bidden to live and die childless. They could not let their children live. It is necessary that some of our children should be reared: but respect for the gods forbids that many should live; and among these, there must be no first-born."

Idya had nothing to say to this. It was some relief to her to hear that there were reasons extending beyond her husband and herself. Looking forward without hope, she felt but little grief at the time. She never heard the cry of her child, and did not know the moment when its new breath was stopped. The first time she raised her head from her mat, Miava showed her the exact place in the earthen floor where the infant had been trodden down, a few inches below the surface. Some fresh grass was strewed over it; and on the precise spot did Motuaro many a day afterwards sit, to take his meals.

Miava thought he perceived that Idya, when she soon arose from her mat in order to bathe, avoided treading on that spot; and Idya thought she perceived that Miava watched, to see whether she did so or not.

She might be right; for Miava's mind was far from being at rest while haunted by the old prophecy. As he sat alone in the canoe that evening, apparently enjoying the lulling motion given by the ebb and flow of the waves through the opening in the reef, his meditations were not altogether as serene as his position and the scene before his eyes.

"The shark is a horrid foe," thought he; "and no year passes but a shriek is heard from the shore, and blood is seen upon the waters, because the shark is there.—The water-spout is very fearful; and in the stormy months, we know that some canoe or fleet is doomed to be engulphed, and the rowers to be seen no more.—War is more fatal than ten water-spouts or a hundred sharks.—But for ten warriors there die a hundred infants. Those who are born should be more than those who die; but if every man has one or two living children, and many more dead, how are our valleys to be peopled again? and will not rather the twenty peopled valleys become two?" He looked up the valley, and marked the clumps and groves that bordered the stream. He then gazed down into the clear depths of the inlet, and sighed forth the too familiar words, "The forest-tree shall grow,—the coral shall spread,—but man shall cease."

## CHAPTER VI.

### THE PRIEST AND THE ADVENT.

When Idya bathed, she did it with all the energy and enjoyment of the women of her tribe, who, having few other pleasures and much fatigue, revel in this mode of refreshment. It was her delight to dive to the deepest hollow of the white sands, for any tempting object she perceived there; and to swim out through the opening in the reef, to sport with the breakers beyond.—One day, before the old priest had returned to his home, and when he was sleeping away among the shrubs the hottest hour of the day, Idya had thus gone out some way into the open sea, for the pleasure of being brought back by the tide, when, rising from a dive, she saw something more wonderful than all that the coral caves contained.

On wakening Miava, and as she stood beside him with dripping hair and her garment hastily wrapped round her, she told him that she had seen a floating island, carried along by wings. At first she had thought it a very large bird, sent from the moon; but on looking again, she doubted about its being alive.

As she spoke, Miava looked extremely grave. He observed that there was an old prophecy which his father had desired him never to forget, or permit to be forgotten,—that some day a canoe without an out-rigger* would arrive from another world, and would be the cause of great changes.

"But this is not a canoe," objected Idya.

"Not like a canoe a hundred times larger than ours?"

"No. And besides, no canoe could hold men, or swim for a moment without an out-rigger."

"So said the people to the prophet, at the time. But he launched his wooden dish on a pool, and it floated; and he said it was thus that the great canoe would come."

---

* An out-rigger is an appendage to a single canoe whereby its balance is preserved, and it is prevented from sinking when loaded.

"Let us climb the tree," said Idya, "and see whether the swimming island is in sight.—O! cannot you climb at all?—I will tell you what I see; but you will not believe me."

From the loftiest of the three trees, she saw very well what she wanted. But, after a while, she slid rapidly down the stem, being unable to endure the vision any longer. The vessel was coming nearer and nearer; and she had perceived that there were living and moving beings on board.

In silent consternation, she and Miava sat watching just within the verge of the shade. At length, Idya uttered a loud shriek, and even Miava hid his face in the grass for a minute, as an awful spectacle presented itself. A large and strange boat appeared in the opening, and it had no out-rigger! This boat held ten personages, who were rowing somewhat as men paddle; but Miava could not think they were men, from their appearance. At all events, they were not inhabitants of the world, as he told Idya,—imploring her not to shriek again, but to let the apparition pass by. The shriek had, however, been heard. The strange boat did not immediately stop, but proceeded to the shore; but one of the rowers pointed out to his comrades something on the islet. Of course, the cowering pair thought they were perceived; and they shook in every fibre of their frames; but it might be only the roof of the hut, or the cocoa-nuts on the trees that were observed by the stranger.

"It is true;—the day is come!" exclaimed the old priest, as soon as he dared speak. "We have seen the out-riggerless canoe; and these visitors are people from behind the sky."

"They have faces," said Idya, whose eyes were better than the old man's. "They have faces; but they are almost as white as the sand; and in nothing else are they like men.—What shall we do? Shall we drown ourselves?"

"Not yet," said Miava. "We can still do that, if they prove too dreadful. And they may be messengers from the foundation of the world. We must wait."

They were nearly sick with waiting and expectation, when Motuaro appeared. He popped up his head from the smooth water, scrambled on shore, and threw himself down beside the priest and Idya.

He had seen them,—seen more of the strangers than any one else yet. He had been fishing,—an exercise which he had had the grace to undertake while his wife was recovering her full strength. He was coming home with a good supply of fish,—singing at the top of his voice, and not looking behind him as he paddled, trusting to the accustomed solitude of the region, when he heard a shout from the shore. What a sight he beheld! There were several pale man-like beings splashing about in the shallow part of the stream, while two or three were on their knees higher up, drinking greedily. He rubbed his eyes; but the vision remained; and the appeal to his ears left no doubt. The strangers beckoned him to approach; and their gestures were so distinct that he dared not disobey. He slowly paddled towards them; but his terror was so great when two of the beings ran into the water to meet him, laid white hands on his canoe, and shouted at sight of the fish, that he threw himself over the stern, dived to the lowest depths, swam for home, and left his property as a sacrifice to the people from behind the sky.

These strange people, meantime, when they had satisfied their thirst by bathing and drinking in the stream, looked about for fruit and other fresh food; but, within the range of their view, all was desolate. Nothing but rank and barren vegetation overspread the scene of the late war. The voyagers turned from the bare stems of the cocoa-nut trees, and the prostrate bread-fruit trunks, and from the naked rafters where fowls had once roosted, to look at the islet whence they had heard the shriek. Presently, their boat was nearing its little beach; and then Miava appeared from the shade, approaching to meet them. No other idea had entered his mind than that they were messengers of evil,—all the changes he had known in his life being for the worse. He therefore confronted them first,—partly that he might be their immediate victim, if necessary, rather than his young companions; and partly that he might try the power of spells upon personages so strange.

When he came near, he found that they were not

all white. One man, though in all other respects like the rest of the party, was of a complexion nearly as brown as Motuaro's. This man not only made signs of amity to the priest, but spoke so that his words were for the most part understood. He said that the white men came from another country, far away.

"From another world,—from behind the sky," replied Miava. "Have they a sun? or do they live in a region of night? They have the skins of those who live in darkness, but they have eyes given them for our sun."

"They live in our world, and our sun shines upon them when it leaves us," said the interpreter.

Miava looked to the east, and from that horizon to Evening Island he gazed slowly round, and shook his head.

"There are other islands, besides these two," declared the interpreter. "I come from one further towards the sunset than yonder island, and yet the sun sets still far to the west. The foundations of the world are further off than you know of; and these men live between you and those regions of night. They not only live in the light of our sun, but they eat food as we do,—hogs, and fowls, and fruit."

The Europeans heard the familiar names of these last articles, and, supposing the conference had reached a practical point, now advanced, and holding out some unknown curiosities, repeated the words denoting hogs, fowls, fruit.

Miava looked from one to another in bewilderment. The sailors were not disposed to wait his time. One threw sticks at the cocoa-nuts on the trees, and brought down ripe and unripe at random. One cut a stalk of sugar-cane, and found it so delicious that others joined him. Two caught a hog, and put it into a sack, and then into the boat. They trusted to their commander's paying for what they took; but when he perceived how unused Miava was to barter, how unaware of the value of the articles produced, he stopped the proceedings.

First, he caused all the cocoa-nuts to be piled in one heap, and offered, through the interpreter, that Miava should select from his goods what he thought would pay for them. As it now indeed appeared that the visitors were not messengers of evil, the priest was anxious to relieve his companions from their terror; and Motuaro and Idya came at his cheerful call. Of many articles offered, they could not at once perceive the value; but there were some which they coveted on the instant,—even before Miava could satisfy himself that they were not unhallowed. Above all, Idya, who spent many a weary hour in kindling and watching the fire of the oven, was struck and charmed by a little box whose contents would make fire in a moment. She considered it worth more than a whole grove of cocoa-nuts. But her husband thought quite as well of a pewter spoon, with which he saw a sailor helping himself to the juice out of a sugar-cane. Motuaro at once saw the use of this, and how it would aid him in his favourite occupation of feeding. The captain accommodated matters by giving the spoon in exchange for the canes. The hog then remained to be paid for.

Miava eagerly insisted on the choice of an equivalent being his: and it was granted on a cry of delight and admiration escaping from one usually so composed. The captain had observed that the old man's sight had failed a good deal; and he placed first on his own nose, to show that they were harmless, and then on Miava's, a pair of spectacles. As soon as he could be persuaded to open his eyes, how great was his amazement! He saw distinctly the faces of all around him, and the leaves of distant trees, and the crests of the waves beyond the reef, and the blossoms of plants growing within the wood. He gazed around him, uttering new exclamations at every discovery of some long-lost object of sight, and then hurried away alone into the shrubbery, in the fear that some accident or quarrel might deprive him of his new treasure.

But what he saw during the daylight hours did not affect him nearly so much as the revelations of the night. When Idya had, with a beating heart, lighted a match to kindle the fuel of the oven, and Motuaro had supped, using his spoon for every mouthful, they were glad to sleep after the fatigues of so exciting a day. But the re-awakened sense of the old man would not permit sleep to approach him. As he cast his eyes upwards, trying whether he could see anything at midnight, he saw, through a hole in the roof, a shining star. A starry night was one of the fairest pictures in his memory. Now it occurred to him that by this magic power he might enjoy it again. He rose hastily from his mat, and went out, escaping from the canopy of the trees to the open shore. There he remained for the succeeding hours,—hours which made him young again, not only in sensation, but in emotion and thought.

"Nothing is settled," thought he, "even to the oldest, to whom the young come as to oracles. News may arrive, even to our latest day; and what we knew and had forgotten comes again like news. No one could better tell once where particular stars were to be looked for than I; but there had so long been to me only a misty shine in the sky in summer nights that I had almost forgotten the sights that were behind it. And now the little yellow fires burn clearly,—so many that the gods themselves can hardly count them. What would Teoro think of them; he who has always been dim-eyed? I will seek him out, and try to make him see them. But I know something of what he will feel, for I have this day been shown some wonderful things, about which I have been dim-eyed from my birth. I thought there had been no men but those like ourselves, all living in the islands of this wide sea; but I am told, and I must believe it, that very different men live somewhere in the world, —knowing our sun, being able to float and fish in our sea, and to drink water and eat flesh and fruit as we do. They must be men, because they did not draw out and devour our spirits, but chose rather to eat fish and a hog. Yet they must have to do with the gods, because they have magical powers, and can give them to us,—causing fire to come in a moment where there was none before, and making dim eyes old and young by turns. If there are such different kinds of men, how can I tell how many sorts there may be? And if there should be many kinds, how much longer will it take for man to cease? At first, before I knew these strangers to be men, I feared that they were sent to bring men to an end quickly; but now, if the world is so very large, and the same sun shines on so many tribes, the end must be a good way off. The forest tree may raise its head till it reaches the cloud that hides the mountain-top,—the coral may spread out till it binds together all the islands of the sea, before man ceases altogether. Ah! but," pondered the old man, sinking from his mood of exultation to despondency, "though this may be true about the race altogether, may not our part of it be near perishing? Have I not seen it dwindle mournfully in my day? And who knows but these strangers may come to hasten the destruction! Yet no!" he considered, brightening again. "The strangers who were to arrive in an out-riggerless canoe were to cause remarkable changes; and it would be no change, but a sad continuation, if men were to dwindle till they cease. These predictions seem to contradict each other, as that about the wonderful canoe contradicted the knowledge of all men. Yet that one became clear. And these may become clear. If these pale strangers should ever appear again, I will ask whether men become fewer in other parts of the great world, and whether their trees grow tall and their corals spread wide. But I can think of all this to-morrow; and to-morrow the stars will not be seen, and no one can look at the sun till evening. Ah ha! the moon is near the brim of the sea! Can she have waned so much? She looks as if she had but five nights left; but her light is strong on the waves, and I see them heave and sparkle as I never do when she is roundest. Can she be made young as my eyes are?"

This point might have been settled in a moment by Miava's looking at the vanishing moon under ordinary conditions; and this, of course, he was well aware of. But it was hard to part with his new enjoyment for a moment; and while he was considering about it, the moon dropped beneath the waves.

## CHAPTER VII.

### A HIGHER DISCLOSURE.

After this night of wondrous enjoyment, misfortune was in store for the old man. Having seen some of the beautiful things in which he had once delighted, he had a mind for more. He desired Idya to take him in the canoe to the clearest and smoothest part of the inlet, that he might gaze down, and once more see the branching corallines. In the midst of his pleasure, the spectacles fell from his nose into the water, and sank fathoms deep. Miava covered his face with a corner of his garment; for he was sorely grieved. Idya presently leaped into the water, and dived again and again; but it was some time before she could find the spectacles; and when she did, one glass was gone, and the other broken. Idya wept abundantly; and there were tears on the old man's cheeks as they drew to the shore.

There they found a fearful sort of consolation. The white men were come again; at least, their boat was riding in the cove. No one was visible but two men who had been left in charge of the boat, and who had found a pine-apple, a little way off, which they were busily eating,—supposing they had the beach all to themselves. Idya made a sign of silence to the priest, pushed her canoe behind some bushes, entered the water again, and swam to the ship's boat, whence she soon returned with a pair of spectacles, a spoon, and a box of matches.

Miava stroked her head, in sign of approbation of her skill, and, drawing back a good way from the water, put on his new spectacles. But where was the beneficent power gone? All objects were dim and confused,—worse than when he used only his own eyes.

He could not recover from his mortification and perplexity,—with which was mingled a fear of the displeasure of the god to whom he ought to have promised an offering before Idya did the deed,—Hiro, the god of thieves.

The Europeans landed, wholly unaware of the

loss of their property. They came prepared for barter on a somewhat larger scale, as well as to fill their water-casks from the springs on the shore. The captain was surprised at the depression of the old man, whom he had seen so dignified and self-possessed the day before; but Motuaro, who presented himself in a trice, was as energetic a customer as could be desired. The difficulty was that the islanders had scarcely any thing to exchange for the many articles they wished to have. The captain first, to their great joy, offered to pay them for the fish the sailors had taken the day before. For this, he gave Idya a piece of cloth which looked to her very curious and pretty. She wrapped it round her, and found it much lighter and easier than that which she herself had, with hard and protracted toil, beaten out of the fibres of trees. Motuaro saw at once the use of an axe, for which he gave a hog,—his last hog,—saying to himself that Idya must catch more fish, and he would try and find turtle. There were knives and scissors; and the young people saw how useful such things might be made; but they had nothing to give for them.

They promised to collect fruits and fowls, and to make some mats, if allowed a few days; but in their own minds they resolved to take what they wanted, in some sly way, from the boat.

When the whites were about to depart, Miava roused himself to use his present opportunity, and, approaching the interpreter, begged him to win over the captain to put the magic again into his spectacles, that he might once more see beautiful things with them.

The captain examined the spectacles, consulted with one of the sailors, and then bade the interpreter ask Miava how long he could see beautiful things with that instrument. He told eloquently what he had beheld yesterday and during the night, adding that he had lost his treasure in the sea this morning, and Idya had gone to the bottom to recover it.

"The lie and the theft may be the woman's," observed the captain to his men. "These are Dr. Symons's spectacles,—unfit for old eyes. He must have them back, of course; and we must come to an understanding with these people. Get the old man to sit down, Turoa," he added to the interpreter, "and be sure you make him understand what I say."

The captain and Miava sat down opposite to one another on the grass, and the interpreter stood beside them,—the sailors being ordered to fall back out of hearing, and look well to the goods and the boat.

"You are a priest, Turoa tells me," the captain began; "and therefore you must be thought wiser than your neighbours."

Miava looked grave, and said that messengers came and went between the gods and the priests.

"And do not the gods permit men to make themselves comfortable by exchanging things with one another, as we have been doing to-day?"

"We grow fruit, and rear fowls and hogs, and catch fish, each for ourselves," replied Miava, "and when we send out warriors to plunder from our enemies, and bring home wealth, the god Hiro goes with them,—if we, the priests, can induce him."

"And then some of the wealth is brought to the priests?"

"Certainly. They have toil in praying and watching."

"And what does Hiro say when you take plunder from one another?"

Miava looked shocked, and said that was a crime for which men and women were sometimes punished with death. Against such, guard was kept. Large pieces of cloth were drawn up to the roof, where thieves could not get them; and small ones were laid beside the pillow every night; and the fowls and hogs were housed within the dwellings; and every body was against thieves, and they were always punished, when they could be caught.

"And if a pair of spectacles, like those, were stolen from my boat, would the thief be put to death?"

"Certainly not," replied Miava. "They would be taken from strangers; and there is no harm in that."

"The old fellow is in earnest," observed the captain, aside to a comrade: "but I must make him a little wiser, priest as he is.—Did your young friend there find his canoe safe, after we were gone yesterday?" he inquired of Miava.

"Yes."

"And is he satisfied with what my men gave him for his fish?"

"Ask him."

"Why do you suppose we did not take the canoe and the fish without troubling ourselves to give any thing in return? We are strong men,—strong enough to carry away by force all that we wish for from this island."

"There are many warriors on the other side," declared Miava.

"Yes; but warriors cannot stand against thunderbolts; and we can blow thunder and lightning upon your people till they lie dead upon the ground, thicker than the skeletons we saw heaped together yonder."

"And," interposed Turoa, "they are struck dead by these thunderbolts before they have time to throw a spear. And, besides, the whites can do this from such a distance that no spear can reach them."

"Is this true?" asked Miava, bewildered.

"Quite true," said the captain: "but we do not wish to blow our thunder here,—unless you would like to see it."

Miava was quite satisfied with hearing of it.

"Well; why do you suppose we do not take all you have by force?"

"We might hide our things, and go away into the mountains in the night."

"Just so. We should not get what we want if we frightened you away, and spoiled your property. We wish to be friends with you; and for several reasons. We like to see people look cheerful and glad when we come among them. We like to supply you with things which make you comfortable and pleased; and we like to be able to come to your island, and get fresh water when we are thirsty, without putting any body into a fright, or having to hurt any one. But if you hurt us, we shall be angry perhaps; and if not, we must go and give our useful and wonderful things to some other people."

"We cannot hurt people who blow thunderbolts," humbly observed Miava.

"Yes, you can, though you cannot kill us. A wise man who is my friend cannot see the small plants on the ground, nor the leaves on the tall trees to-day, because you have got his spectacles,"—pointing to the pair held by Miava. The old man, in indistinct shame at the detection, and in an equally vague fear of seeing a thunderbolt issue from some one's mouth, hastened to surrender the spectacles. No one would receive them, as they belonged to no one present; but Dr. Symons was within hail, and he came gladly to recover his property.

"Now try these," said the captain to Miava, tendering him a pair like those of the day before. Again the old man's delight burst all his restraints of shyness and fear. He produced the frame of the unlucky pair brought up from among the corallines.

"Why did not you show me these before?" asked the captain. "You see I can help you. Now—what will you give me for these new ones?" Observing a glance pass between one of his comrades and another, he observed, "Ay, I would give him spectacles, and any thing else he had a mind to, with all my heart; but don't you see, the best kindness I can do him and the people of the island is to teach them to trade,—and honestly? A few sugar-canes and hogs are cheap payment for the best lesson any one ever taught them."

The sailors agreed in this; but one could not resist adding to the value of the article by tying the spectacles on the old man's head with a piece of black ribbon out of his own private store. Miava promised any thing and every thing in his power, as the price of this purchase. In consideration of the accident by which he lost the first pair, a turtle, duly consecrated by him, was accepted in payment.

The captain then opened to the awakened mind of the old man a view of the comforts which would be at the command of the islanders, if they could trade. He showed him axes enough for half the householders in the region. He showed him clasp-knives, tin-bowls, looking-glasses, hammers, and nails, and promised to prove to him at night that he could make his dwelling light in the inside, while all was dark without. But he explained that many men had worked hard to make these wonderful things, and that something that was wanted must be given in return, or there would be no encouragement to bring them. Both promised to consider well what the islanders could offer, or learn to provide, in exchange for such beneficial supplies.

For hours did Miava ponder this conversation. One of the practical conclusions he drew was of some importance.

"When neighbours in a valley can exchange things so as to please one another, there is cheerfulness, and none of the anger and danger that there are when men snatch or steal what they wish for, without considering whether the owner likes to part with the property. If these neighbours were always to consider each what he himself would like to be done to him, and do so to the other, there would be continual peace between them. And if all in the valley were to do the same, there would be peace from end to end. And if," he continued, brightening, "it were so through the whole island, there would be no more war. And if other kinds of men and ourselves were to do the same, there would be no terror, nor blowing of thunderbolts, and we should have their wonderful gifts, and they would have our fresh fruits when they are thirsty, and our mats for a shade at noon. If every where men could so please one another as they would be pleased themselves, and there was peace, man would not cease for a long time yet. But then—" and his heart sank—"how could it be about the sacrificing of men to the gods? for no man likes to be sacrificed to Oro; and yet somebody must be devoted by the priests. I must think about this."

# CHAPTER VIII.

## SPIRITUAL TRIBUTE.

The strongest desire was excited in the minds of Miava and his companions to obtain more of the precious articles brought by the strangers. All the rest of that day, they consulted about raising the means of purchase. Idya was to work harder than she had ever done in her life before, and Motuaro himself promised to go fishing. Idya prepared to go to a marshy place at the foot of the mountains, to catch wild ducks,—a delicate process, about which she was very clever,—swimming softly and slowly, her head covered with a calabash, and thus approaching the birds unseen, and then pulling them quickly under the water by the feet, before they could give notice to their companions. She was also to take her sling, and bring down some wood pigeons. On receiving this last order, she looked grave.

Miava observed that these were all things to eat

and drink,—things that would soon disappear, and leave no trace for the foreigners to remember them by. If the strangers could carry something to their own country which people there would admire or could use, the captain might return, and bring more wonderful gifts to the island. Idya must go through the whole thicket, and see how many cotton shrubs there were, and what prospect of seed there was, that she might plant some, and raise cotton,—as the interpreter said was done in his island. And she might mark the sandal-wood trees for the captain to look at. Some of his men had talked of bringing axes on shore, Turoa had declared, to fell and carry away sandal-wood.

Idya made no reply but by a shudder till her husband had gone out,—which he presently did when there was talk of real work to be done. She then entreated Miava not to send her alone into the bushes, for she was afraid,—not of any man,—not of the gods,—but of her own babe. On the lagoon or the shore, she could look around her and fear nothing; but in the thickets, the spirit of her child appeared to be every where,—she could not escape from the spectacle of it; and into the bushes she really dared not go.

Miava attempted to console her by saying that in this vision there was nothing uncommon. He named several women whom he knew to be thus haunted by their lost babes, till some of their offspring were allowed to live, when the liability usually ceased. A sinful thought here crossed his mind,—so shocking that he put it down,—that it was ungrateful and unkind of the gods to torment thus the mothers who showed respect to their celibacy, while, if the same women indulged their own natural affections, they would not be afraid in the thickets, or any where else.

Miava's compassion for his young daughter made him wish, as he said, that Motuaro would undertake that part of their business which she shrank from; but, while thieving from strangers was considered an innocent act, there was no chance of men being roused from their indolence to honest industry. Motuaro was now swimming off to the ship, hoping to bring away some booty from the boat, or by a sly and adventurous visit on board.

He swam round once, unperceived, and he found something so desirable in the course of that circuit, that he had no immediate wish to look further. The ship's flag was hanging so low as to touch the water. Its gay colours and wonderful fabric attracted Motuaro's cupidity, and he seized it, and had nearly cut away half of it when a shout from on board warned him to retreat. He had, of course, no idea of the sacredness of a flag. The captain knew this, and thought the present a proper opportunity for duly impressing the islanders with a sense of it. He ordered guns to be fired after the swimmer,—taking care that the aim should not be at him, but at the cocoa-nut trees which overshadowed his dwelling.

The middle tree rocked and fell with a crash which terrified Miava and Idya as thoroughly as the captain intended. Idya could see the men on board stoop to the guns, as they took aim, and then send forth flame, noise, and destruction.

"They are blowing thunderbolts!" she and Miava exclaimed at the same moment.

They next saw that Motuaro was swimming

homewards at his utmost speed, and for a moment they wondered that he had been spared. But it was only for a moment. He shrieked out, "The shark!"—leaped half out of the water with a cry of agony, and then disappeared amidst the wide stain of his own blood, which dyed the breakers and the lagoon to the very shore.

The captain was concerned,—not doubting that a shot had unintentionally reached the thief. He sent out a boat to pick up the victim, whose mangled remains showed at a glance what had been the manner of his death.

That night, the captain stood, with Miava and the interpreter, beside the bier, on which the dead man was placed in a sitting posture, his ghastly face appearing above the coverings which hid the rest of the body. No countenance and manner could be less formidable to most people than those of the captain; but Miava regarded him with a painful awe. One cause of this was that the captain had fulfilled his promise of making a dwelling light within, while all was darkness without. He had caused the shed (to which one end of the dwelling was now reduced by the fall of the tree) to be lighted up with lamps,—a spectacle perfectly new in the island. The unwholesome floor had also been swept out, and strewn thick with white coral sand, which seemed to glitter in the lamp light.

"Tell me," said Miava, solemnly, "are the sharks your messengers? The blue sharks are the messengers of our gods; and you come from near their region of night. If the sharks are your servants, tell me so."

"They are not," replied the captain, with a convincing seriousness. "I did not desire this man's death. If I had, I could have struck him dead in a moment, as I knocked down your tall tree. I wished him to live, and remember that he must not steal from foreigners,—and particularly that he must not touch their sacred things."

Turoa here conveyed to the priest some idea of how and why national flags were tabooed; and Miava promised to teach the king and his subjects so distinctly that there could be no mistake, that no one of them could lay hands on this token of world-wide citizenship, and hope to live. When Miava heard that no men on earth need ever hope to buy it,—that no captain would ever sell it for the wealth of the whole world, he was so deeply impressed as to wonder no longer that the gods had taken up the cause of the white men, and had sent a shark to destroy Motuaro.

He timidly inquired whether, in the country of the flag, Motuaro's widow and family would be tabooed. He was relieved and surprised by the answer that individuals were answerable for their own sins, and that Idya would be pitied and aided, —she being innocent of all offence.

"Then," he exclaimed, "you will not cause her to be tabooed here."

"Certainly not. Show me how I can serve her, and I will prove to you how we think on these matters. Where and how will she live?"

"Where and how would you wish her to live?" asked Miava submissively,—affording an opportunity for a lesson which the captain did not throw away.

"What person in the world does she love best?"

"She loves no one but me."

"What? has she no child?"

That sad story was soon told; and the mournful impression it made on the captain struck Miava forcibly.

"Did she love her husband?"

"No," replied Miava tranquilly. "It was necessary that she should marry him; but she loved only me, her father."

"Then we need not be so sorry for her, after all," said the captain, "except indeed about her babe. If that infant had lived, she would have had some one to love besides you,—some one to care for after you are dead. And you would have had that little one to play about your knees as you sit in the shade, and lead you about when you grow more blind. And you let that child be murdered!"

"You are displeased now," pleaded Miava; "and the gods, and the priests, and the king, would have been angry if the child had lived."

"How do you know that your gods would have been angry?"

"They would have sent misfortunes on Idya and all of us, if we had let a first-born child live?"

"Have you ever tried? I will answer for it there are many mothers willing to try whether it is really so, if you would let them have their way. Would not Idya herself, if you had not overborne her?"

"She would. But to show this disrespect to the gods!—who could dare to permit it?"

The captain quietly said that he doubted whether the gods were satisfied with things as they were. He would show respect to them in a different way.

With extreme eagerness, Miava inquired his meaning, saying,

"You come from near the foundations of the world. You may know more of these things than we do. How may we best show respect to the gods?"

"Do they show your people any lasting favour now?" asked the captain. "If I saw yonder valley full of happy families, I should think you had found a way to please your gods; but I see it desolate and spread with skeletons. I look for husbands and wives who love each other, and carry their infants in their arms; and here I find a widow who cannot mourn that her husband is dead in his prime, and who dares not go among the bushes lest she should be haunted by the murdered child who ought now to be asleep upon her bosom. What is plainer than that she is punished by the gods for some dreadful mistake? If such is the state of things on the other side of your island, I should say that the gods are so displeased that it would be wise in you to try a new and a better way."

"There is an old prophecy which sounds in my mind in every place at all times," said Miava. And he mournfully repeated the familiar words.

"Why, there is a plain warning for you!" exclaimed the captain. "Your men must cease while you have wars, and murders at the altars and at the birth of infants. If the forest-tree and the coral are not good enough to offer to the gods, and man alone is so, surely he is too good to perish out of the world while forest-trees and corals are growing.—Ah! I see your difficulty. You think the gods must have the best of created things devoted to them; and so do I."

"You do?"

"Yes; but in a very different way from yours. If

you knew the gods to have one wish stronger than any other, would you not think it most respectful to observe it? Well! all that we know the gods to have made and done shows to my mind that they intend men to grow and ripen, like the fruit on the trees, and not to fall till it is fully ripe. If you planted a tree, and children and foolish people plucked and threw away the fruit,—some as soon as it showed itself, and the rest before it was ripe,—would you not be displeased, and leave the tree to perish?"

"I would taboo the fruit," observed Miava.

"That is right," said the captain. "I wish you would taboo men's lives. That would be the best respect to the gods, who made men live."

The priest covered his face in the agitation caused by this suggestion of a vast idea. The captain quietly left him, beckoning to Turoa to follow him.

"Taboo the life of man!" thought Miava, as he stood alone beside the bier. "What then would be the tribute paid to the gods? Would it not still be the spirits of men,—of living instead of dead men? If the gods had rather that the spirits of men should ripen and multiply, and be full of wisdom and joy before they go to them in the region of night, no wonder they are displeased at the number of immature and unhappy wretches that we have offered to them! No wonder priests are haunted by the warning that man shall cease! My spirit is heavy and sad; for their displeasure is terrible. But if we can learn a better way, the anger and the curse may be withdrawn, and man may again increase. True was the prophecy, that the out-rigger-less canoe should bring about great changes in our world!"

# CHAPTER IX.

## NATURE AND MAN AT PEACE.

The captain was not sorry that it suited his purposes to move round to the peopled side of the island, for he saw how the germs of civilization which he and his traffic had planted in this new soil might be fostered by his appearing before the king and his subjects as the friend of the influential old priest. The funeral of Motuaro taking place necessarily the next day, the body was conveyed round by the widow and Miava in their canoe, a short time before the ship left her station.

A great number of eager inquirers were assembled round the body, and the king had assured himself that his tabooed subject was beyond the reach of his wrath, when the attention of all was called away by the spectacle of the vessel, so many times larger than any they had ever seen, coming round the point. Miava's explanations of this vessel being the one indicated in the old prophecy fell upon excited minds; and all who heard were ready to obey his directions to prepare for barter.

The exchanges of food and foreign goods were carried on with more order than is usual on the first occasion of a newly-discovered people being one of the parties; and when even the most fortunate sellers found that, much as they had gained, there were many other desirable things which they could not have till they could offer commodities less perishable and more valuable than food, it was not difficult to bring them to a purpose of preparation for a better traffic, if the Europeans would promise to come again. Those who had axes engaged to furnish sandal-wood; and others, enamoured of cotton and linen cloths, and being assured that they, by industry, could produce the cotton and flax needed for such fabrics, began to inquire how they could be instructed in the art of growing them. Matting and cordage they could soon supply, to a small amount; and tortoise-shell could be added, when its European value was known. It was only the comprehensive mind of the old priest which could grasp at once all these details, and take in the prospect opened by the advent of Commerce in his world. For him it was almost too much. His breast heaved, as he put the question to the captain,

"What shall I offer to our gods when I send messengers to tell them that the out-riggerless canoe has come?"

"Lay before them," said the captain seriously, "an axe, and a knife, and a looking-glass, and a garment of cotton. These good things come out of the spirits of men; and they will please the gods till they themselves send natural death to bring the spirits of men to them, when all the work is done that they can do in your world."

The king understood Turoa's words of interpretation, and looked confounded.

"No more sacrifices of men!" he cried.

"No more," said the captain emphatically, "unless you wish to offend the gods who send you, by that vessel, the changes foretold long ago."

"But how shall I deal with my disobedient subjects?" asked the king, innocently, "if I cannot rid myself of them, and keep them in fear by the sacrifice?"

"The gods will show favour very soon, and make your world happier, and your subjects more contented, and better able to pay tribute than ever before; so that there will be less need to make them afraid. And men will increase; and the more men the more tribute."

"Men will increase?"

"Yes; as surely as the forest-tree rises, and as fast as the coral branches out over the sands of the sea. But not unless you make one great change which you have never yet been told."

"Tell us now," cried the king and priest in a breath.

"I have told you that the gods will henceforth have what the spirits of men can make and do, rather than the spirits themselves; men's works and men's thoughts, rather than their bodies in sacrifice. Do you hear me?"

"Yes. Tell us the other great change."

"No one knows when the spirits of men begin to work, or when they leave off; or whether they work best when their bodies are weak, or when they are strong. Every human creature that has a spirit in him must therefore be taken care of, and kept alive as long as possible, that his spirit may do all it can in the world."

"How many spirits have we sent away too early!" exclaimed Miava.

"That was before these changes," said the captain. "When you try the new ways that are now to begin, you will find how the spirits of old men speak wise things, and how the spirits of little children promise what they will do as men,—just as the day-spring promises what the noon will be. And then your old men, and your blind and sick people will not be left to perish because they are weak; and no more infants will be destroyed."

"But what can our women do, with so many children?"

"In our country," the captain began——

"That is near the foundation of the world;—he comes from nearer the gods than we are," the priest solemnly reminded the king.

"In my country," pursued the captain, "we men

do differently from you, because we love our children, and do whatever we are permitted to keep them alive. We ourselves get food and build houses and obtain clothes. Our women make the clothes, and keep the houses clean, and cook the food, and take care of the children."

"And must we do as you do?"

"You will do it because you like it, when once you let your infants live to show that they have spirits. If a husband and a wife smile, like those people there,"—pointing to a man and woman who were amused at their child's gambols,—"if one child makes them smile so, think how their spirits would laugh if all that they have destroyed were at play beside them! When every dwelling has such laughter in it, you will know that the gods are favourable, and that man will not cease."

His hearers being absorbed in the contemplation of these wondrous changes, their instructor, whom they now regarded as a messenger from the gods, gravely asked,

"Where is the mother of that dead man?"

Miava looked doubtfully at the king.

"Speak," said the king.

"But the taboo!"

"She must not be hurt," declared the captain. "The taboo is to be buried in her son's grave."

"Then Motuaro's dwelling, yonder, in the valley ——" said the priest.

"Is for her and for Idya to live in, and for you, Miava, if you will, that all may see that the taboo is taken off, and that the old and the feeble are to be taken care of, for their spirits' sake. If you are willing," he continued, turning to the king, "I will fix a sign on the house which shall make all men know and remember."

The king having nothing to object, a white flag was presently fixed on the roof of Motuaro's dwelling, marking it at once for safety, and as the abode of the old priest.

That done, the captain and his people took leave of the king and priest with parting presents, and promises of further intercourse, either in their own persons or by other messengers from the uttermost parts of the world.

Groups were assembled on every headland, and

the tallest trees were occupied by men to watch the sailing away of the mighty vessel.

"It has left behind the will of the gods," thought Miava, "and great gifts from them. I too, whose eyes were so dim, can see it depart as the young men do. We know now of such changes as were never told to men before since our world was made; and when these messengers come again, they will perhaps show us more. But they have told us the greatest news,—that man shall not now cease. That curse is taken off."

"You were like a preacher or a prophet to these poor people," observed Dr. Symons to the captain, as they stood on deck, watching the receding shores of the beautiful island. "Were my spectacles your text? If so, they are highly honoured."

"Every thing is honoured, be it what it may," replied the captain, "which is an instrument for introducing the principles and incitements of civilization among a puerile people. Yes,—I was their preacher and prophet just now;—and without affectation,—without any hypocrisy. I thought of nothing less, when I landed, than giving such a discourse; but it warmed my heart and filled my head to see how these children of nature were clearly destined to be carried on some way towards becoming men and Christians by my bringing Commerce to their shores."

THE END.

MANCHESTER:
PRINTED BY J. GADSBY, NEWALL'S-BUILDINGS.

# HOW WILL FREE TRADE

# IN CORN

# AFFECT THE FARMER?

BEING

AN EXAMINATION OF THE EFFECTS

OF

CORN LAWS UPON BRITISH AGRICULTURE.

BY

RICHARD GRIFFITHS WELFORD, ESQ.,

MEMBER OF THE ROYAL AGRICULTURAL SOCIETY OF ENGLAND.

---

LONDON:

JAMES RIDGWAY, PICCADILLY.

1843.

*Richard Griffiths Welford (1804–72)*

Works by Welford include:

*How will Free Trade in Corn affect the Farmer? Being an Examination of the effects of Corn Laws upon British Agriculture*, London, 1843.

*Courts of Law and Equity* [Reports] New Practice Cases, etc. (Reporters. Lord Chancellor's Court – Easter Term, 1844, to Hilary Term, 1847 – R. G. Welford) 1847.

*Courts of Law and Equity* [Reports] Reports of Cases in the Law of Real Property and Conveyancing, etc. (Reporters. Lord Chancellor's Court – R. G. Welford), 1846.

'The Influences of the Game Laws', being classified extracts from the evidence taken before a select Committee of the House of Commons on the Game Laws, and some introductory remarks. . . . With an appendix, and an address to the tenant farmers of Great Britain, by John Bright. London, 1846.

'Laws of Real Property as affecting Agriculture'. See *Practice with Science*, vol. 2, 1867.

'On Leases, etc.' [Two Lectures], see *Practice with Science*, vol. 1, 1867.

*A Practical Treatise on Equity Pleadings, with observations on the new Orders of 1841, and an appendix containing those Orders*, London, 1842.

'The impolicy of the present high duties on tobacco; and their injurious effects on the trade and morals of the country . . .' London, J. Gadsby, 1848.

# CONTENTS.

# PREFACE.

It is not now necessary to preface such an inquiry, as that I propose to institute into the operation of the Corn Laws on Agriculture, by any preliminary dissertation on the principles of free trade. Since 1820, when the merchants of London presented by their organ, Mr. Alexander Baring (now Lord Ashburton), their memorable petition in favour of free trade, those principles have, with more or less of timidity and reservation, been acted upon by every successive administration. The late ministry, that of Lord Melbourne, in the last days of its political existence, gave in its unqualified adhesion to the doctrines of free trade; and the same doctrines have been subsequently propounded, with great distinctness and ability, by Sir Robert Peel and Mr. Gladstone, as the general rule which must henceforth regulate our commercial legislation.

Such, then, being the rule, the advocates of the corn laws must make out special and peculiar grounds for excepting corn from the ordinary law: whether they have established such grounds is one of the objects of the following pages to inquire.

I also propose to inquire, whether the owners or occupiers of land have really obtained the advantages they expected from a system of restriction, confessedly injurious to all other classes of the community.

The conclusion, in favour of an entirely free trade in corn, at which I have arrived, is the result of no bias towards commercial as distinguished from agricultural occupations, for early training and present tastes lead me altogether to sympathise with agricultural pursuits. Neither have my opportunities of observation been scanty; first, in the office of my father, who as a country attorney was also extensively employed as a land-agent; and subsequently, during several years of experience acquired by my own practice in the same professions, previously to my being called to the bar, I have seen the effects of some of the great fluctuations of price upon the interests of both landlords and farmers.

Hence, many years ago, I became firmly convinced of the injurious operation of the corn laws; and amongst the numerous landowners and agriculturists, whom business connections, family ties, and personal intimacies, rendered for several years almost exclusively my associates, I never hesitated to avow and defend my opinions in favour of free trade, or to point out the absurdities and the wrongs occasioned by the corn laws. I have thus been constantly subject to that sort of authoritative refutation, which practical farmers once thought so conclusive, and that by arguments and calculations very similar to those in favour of restriction, which are profusely scattered through the evidence offered to the various committees on agricultural distress, and which I have now attempted to sift. These arguments may be all resolved into statements of isolated facts, only accurate under the actually existing circumstances; or, into an assumed necessity for continuing a system, which had grown out of the extraordinary period of the late war, after things had reverted to a more natural condition. This naturally led to a close scrutiny of one's own views, and a strict examination of the facts and circumstances so confidently urged to prove them untenable. In every case the efficacy of corn laws to secure high prices was assumed to be incontestible, while the most ridiculous exaggerations of the cheapness and abundance of corn in the north of Europe were treated as incapable of disproof. For the *bread-eaters* there was then little pretence of sympathy.

At present, also, I have, as a practical farmer, a direct and lively interest in the prosperity of English agriculture. Therefore, although study and observation, resulting from a practical acquaintance of some years standing with the management of landed property, and with the ordinary relations of landlord and tenant, have convinced me of the impolicy of *all* restrictions on the trade in foreign corn, and of the absolute futility of all the arguments, by which the advocates of the corn laws have endeavoured to justify those restrictions, I cannot be suspected of entering upon the present examination with any bias adverse to the agricultural interest.

R. G. W.

Northaw, Herts, March, 1843.

# HOW WILL FREE TRADE IN CORN AFFECT THE FARMER?

## SECTION I.

### AGRICULTURE AND THE CORN TRADE, PREVIOUS TO 1814.

ALTHOUGH the present corn laws originated in 1814, and their merits or demerits must be tried solely with reference to the state of things which has existed since that period, the opinions and circumstances, which led to such a system of restriction, will be but imperfectly understood without a brief retrospect of the state of agriculture and the corn trade in the preceding century.

From the commencement of the eighteenth century to about the year 1765 there had been in this country an almost uninterrupted succession of abundant seasons, and thus the prices of corn and provisions were low, whilst the trade of the nation was progressively increasing. The average price of wheat, from 1701 up to 1766, has been estimated at 32*s.* 1*d.*, which is lower, by some sixteen per cent., than the average price of the preceding century. The population, during that time, steadily increased; the number of inhabitants in England and Wales having advanced from 5,475,000 in 1700, to upwards of six millions in 1740, and 6,737,000 in 1760. In 1770 the population was 7,428,000. And not only had the English population increased in numbers during the first sixty-six years of the eighteenth century, but the material prosperity of the mass of the nation had increased in even a greater ratio. Adam Smith, in his "Wealth of Nations," which was published in 1776, says, referring to this period, "the most decisive mark of prosperity of any country is the increase "of the number of its inhabitants*;" but adds, that in "Great Britain, and most other European countries, they "are not supposed to double in less than five hundred "years." The same writer states, that the real recompense of labour—the real quantities of the necessaries and conveniencies of life given to the labourer—had increased considerably during the eighteenth century. And another writer on Political Economy, the late Mr. Malthus, observed, that "during the last "forty years of the seventeenth century, and the first "twenty of the eighteenth, the average price of corn "was such as, compared with the wages of labour, "would enable the labourer to purchase with a day's "earnings two-thirds of a peck of wheat. From 1720 "to 1750 the price of wheat had so fallen, while wages "had risen, that instead of two-thirds, the labourer "could purchase the whole of a peck of wheat with "a day's labour." These advanced wages led to a "marked improvement of the quality of the food consumed" by the labouring classes, "and a decided "elevation in the standard of their comforts and conve-

* To the reader, who recollects the coincidence of a rapid increase of population in Ireland with the most appalling poverty, it will naturally occur that this remark must be taken with some qualification.

" niences." Although cultivation was greatly extended during this period, as is proved by the increased number of inclosure bills — being 16 only in the reign of George I, 226 in that of George II, and advancing to 734 in the first fifteen years of the reign of George III, *viz.* from 1760 to 1775 — but little rise in the value of landed property, similar to that which has been observed during the last fifty years, had then occurred. The mercantile classes were gradually acquiring wealth, and those accumulations of capital, which soon afterwards gave such an impetus to trading enterprise and so greatly increased the value of land, were silently going on. Arthur Young, alluding to the value of landed property in 1770, says, " a neighbour of mine in " Suffolk, who inherited a considerable landed property, " informed me, that, in various conversations he had " between 1770 and 1780 with a relation far advanced " in years, much surprise was expressed at the rise " of rents which then began to take place. Through " the long period of his relation's experience no rise " was ever thought of; and lease after lease in long " succession was signed, without a word passing on " the question of rent: that was an object considered " fixed; and grandfather, father, and son succeeded " without a thought of any rise: in many cases land- " lords were much more apprehensive of losing a " tenant at the old rent, than having the smallest " conception of raising it to a new one *."

The agriculture of Scotland, which was much behind that of England, began, about the same period, to feel the vivifying influence which commercial wealth

---

* Inquiry into the Progressive Value of Money, p. 102.

imparts to a nation. The following extract, descriptive of Scotch agriculture at this time, is taken from an Essay*, which obtained the "Highland Society's" prize a few years ago.

"Agriculture in Scotland, as having been at this time much farther behind, partook even to a greater degree of this improvement; and it is between 1765 and 1775, that we trace the opening of a better system, which had begun to be introduced at the commencement of this epoch. Still, however, husbandry, as generally practised in Scotland, continued in a comparatively rude state; and, notwithstanding the very laudable exertions of many patriotic landed proprietors in various parts of the country, to introduce, by example, a better order of things, no great progress appears to have been made — excepting in some favoured districts — in exciting the tenantry to depart from the long-trodden path pursued by them. It would appear, at this period, a great proportion of the arable land in Scotland was still very partially enclosed, so that even contiguous farms under tillage were not separated by any distinct fence. The antient practice almost universally prevailed — excepting in the neighbourhood of towns, and in those favoured districts alluded to — of occupying farms as "*In-field*" and "*Out-field*," as it was called. By this mode of management, the land near the steading, or farm-offices, received all the manure collected and prepared there, and thus an attempt was made to keep those lands for many successive years under a corn-crop, consisting of wheat, or more commonly of oats, beans or barley, and peas; and, although an occasional imperfect fallowing was introduced at the close of each rotation of six or eight years, the constant succession of corn-crops kept the soil in a continually impoverished condition. The out-field land, which formed the bulk of the possession, was made to grow a succession of oat-crops, generally three, until, exhausted in strength and overrun with weeds, it was suffered, under the dominion of this new possessor — and without any attempt being made to assist the herbage by the introduction of seeds — to rest, until the caprice of the occupier should deem it prepared to undergo the renewed attempt to produce another series of scanty crops. The only manure ap-

* Account of Improvements in the Agriculture of Scotland, by Mr. John Dudgeon, of Skylaw, near Kelso — republished in the first vol. of the Journal of the English Agricultural Society (1839).

plied to this division of the farm was effected by occasionally folding the few live stock then kept upon detached portions of it; after which, in this case, it was expected to yield four or five corn-crops in place of three. Very little wheat was at this time grown in Scotland, and, even upon soils adapted for the successful culture of this grain, the short-sighted cupidity of many landlords prevented its more extensive cultivation, as being of an exhausting nature to the soil. The drill system of husbandry, especially during the early part of this period, was little practised in any part of Scotland, and the culture of turnips in this form, which at this time had its origin in this part of the island, entered only partially into the rotation of a few of the best farms. Potatoes were then only beginning to be cultivated in the fields, and the introduction of grass-seeds had not made any extensive progress beyond the *in-fields* of the best districts. Improvements, however, made very rapid progress towards the close of the period under consideration; and the system of leases having come more extensively into use—since the restrictions in entails affecting their extent was abolished by the act of 1770—encouragement was afforded to tenants to expend more liberally, and to embark further in a species of speculation, which now gave promise of considerable success. Hence, we find rents rose very considerably about this time, and many proprietors, who had expended largely in the improvements lately introduced, found themselves amply remunerated by an increase of rent, in some cases to nearly treble their value twenty years before."

Many passages are also found in the histories of this period, indicating the activity of British commerce, which has been since so prodigiously developed. Smollett mentions, that in 1750, "the subjects "of his Britannic majesty imported more iron and "steel than all the other countries in Europe;" and the contradictory petitions for and against the measure then passed for admitting American iron into the United Kingdom, prove, incidentally, the extent and importance to which the smelting of iron and manufactures in metal had attained. Every session of Parliament now began to be occupied with bills for the improvement or protection of some branch of commerce, which, absurd and unsound in principle as some of them were, plainly demonstrated the transition of the nation from the condition of an agricultural to that of a commercial people. Bounties were profusely given to favoured trades, whilst more rational means of encouragement to the silk and cotton manufactures were adopted, in the reduction of the duties on China and Persian raw silk, and the absolute exemption from all duty of cotton and silk, the produce of Georgia and Carolina. Indeed, during the thirty years of abundance which preceded 1750, the nation had been so remarkably aggrandised by her growing manufactures and commerce, as to become an object at once of envy and increased respect to the rest of Europe.

The winter of 1755-6 was remarkable for its severity, and the consequent failure of the following harvest, and a great dearth of provisions. The public voice was loud in denunciation of the "villanous "schemes of forestallers and engrossers," and the legislature was called upon to visit upon the heads of millers and bakers, in the shape of penal laws and stringent regulations, punishment for a scarcity the effect of the seasons. But, as this country then constantly exported grain, the prohibition of exportation, combined with considerable importations of corn, aided more effectually by an abundant harvest in the following year, dissipated for the time such economical chimeras. But it must not be supposed that a legislature then, as now, containing a preponderant landed interest, left a trade in which they were so much concerned as that of corn, unfettered by statutable regulations. A bounty on the exportation of grain (5*s*. a quarter on wheat, and 2*s*. 6*d* on barley or malt) was given, although, in ordinary seasons, the produce of the country seems to have afforded, without such a stimulus, an ample surplus beyond the wants of its inhabitants, accompanied by a prohibition of the import of foreign grain. The ten years, however, from 1765 to 1775, seem to have contained many in which the crops were deficient, and the prices of corn tended to a permanently higher range, so much so, that a new era in the history of the corn trade began. From 1765 our consumption of grain was beyond the native growth, and thenceforth, with one or two accidental exceptions, the nation constantly imported in deficient seasons a part of its supply of corn. Up to 1773 permission to import corn had been conceded, under the pressure of scarcity, and for temporary exigencies; but in that year the opponents of a prohibitory corn law succeeded in carrying a fresh act, which allowed importation of wheat at a duty of 6*d*. per quarter, when the price was at or above 48*s*.; and the bounty and exportation were to cease together, when the price was at or above 44*s*. a quarter. From this time to 1792, the average price of wheat in England was about 50*s*. a quarter, rising occasionally, as in 1775, to 59*s*., and falling again to 43*s*., and once, in the abundant year of 1779, to 36*s*. per quarter; the corn law, therefore, had but little effect either in preventing importation in bad seasons, or promoting exportation in good ones. In 1791, the landed interest, not satisfied with the advantages secured to the owners of the soil by the act of 1773, procured a law preventing importation, except when wheat in our markets should reach or exceed the price of 54*s*. a quarter, while the bounty on exportation, when the price fell to 44*s*., was still continued. The duty and bounty on other grain bore the usual proportion to wheat.

It has been shown most conclusively by Mr. Tooke, in his masterly work, the "History of Prices," that, though the vast development of our manufacturing and commercial industry enabled the people of Great Britain to consume, at prices so much enhanced, the greatly increased quantities of corn which they required in the latter half of the eighteenth century, yet that the rise in prices of produce was mainly the effect of a series of irregular seasons and the frequent recurrence of defective crops. Every examination into the details of seasons, either of scarcity or great abundance, serves to show, that prices have always varied in a ratio much beyond the utmost computation of differences of quantity in the crops of grain. This fully accounts for the fact, that periods of partial deficiency have generally produced temporary agricultural prosperity; while, on the other hand, every occasion of transition from dearth to abundance has been marked by complaints of agricultural distress *.

This tendency of prices to rise beyond the degree of the deficiency — especially in the case of corn— must be kept constantly in view when considering the events which occurred in this country between 1792 and 1814, and the extraordinary prosperity enjoyed by the farmers and landlords during that pe-

* To those who require a full elucidation of the effect of the variations in seasons upon prices, I recommend Mr. Tooke's History of Prices, above referred to, where the subject is treated with a fulness of detail and closeness of argument, which leave no room for questioning the positions of the author.

riod. It is from omitting this primary and obvious cause for the extravagant prices to which agricultural produce attained during the war, when foreign supplies were obstructed, that so many persons seek for explanations of the phenomenon amongst the other circumstances of the times, which only contributed to those high prices in a subordinate and secondary degree. War demand, and the profuse government expenditure in one year of large sums raised by loans, furnish, with many respectable reasoners, the solution of all difficulties; but a little consideration will satisfy us, that although the demand of the government for warlike stores and munitions may attract more attention than the ordinary and steady demands of commerce, yet that all the industry and all the capital attracted to the trades which supply the war demand must have been drawn from other, and probably far more productive employment; and the men, who as soldiers and sailors, were diverted from the peaceful occupations of commerce, manufactures, or agriculture, consumed but little more of agricultural produce than they would have done had they remained engaged in creating wealth instead of being occupied in the destruction of their fellow-men. Upon this subject of war-demand, Mr. Tooke remarks, that "the fallacy of the doctrine, "which represents a general elevation of prices, both of "commodities and labour, to be a necessary consequence "of a state of war, proceeds (and cannot otherwise than "so proceed) on the supposition that the money expended by the government consists of funds distinct "from, and over and above any that before existed; "whereas it is perfectly demonstrable, that an expen"diture by government, whether defrayed by immediate "taxes to the whole amount, or by loan on the antici-"pation of taxes to be levied, is *nothing but a change in* "*laying out the same sum of money*; and that what is ex-"pended by government would and must have been laid "out by individuals upon objects of consumption, pro-"ductive or unproductive." Those who attribute the high prices of corn during the late war, to what is called war-demand, overlook the historical fact, that in the previous century war and a large government expenditure, defrayed by loans, existed at several periods, during which the prices of grain were considerably lower than in previous and subsequent periods of profound peace. Amongst the numerous evils of war the increased consumption and waste of food is often overrated, but the way in which war acts upon the prices of such commodities is plainly by obstructing or diminishing supply. From the following state of the Windsor prices of wheat, kept at Eton College, it will be evident, that in the case of the agricultural produce of this country, there was, for upwards of a hundred years previous to 1793, as low a range of prices during the periods of war as during intervals of peace:—

| | | | | £. | s. | d. |
|---|---|---|---|---|---|---|
| 1688 | to | 1697 | 10 years of war | 2 | 2 | 6¼ |
| 1698 | ... | 1701 | 4 years of peace | 2 | 6 | 0 |
| 1702 | ... | 1712 | 11 years of war | 2 | 2 | 0 |
| 1713 | ... | 1739 | 27 years of peace | 1 | 15 | 10¾ |
| 1740 | ... | 1748 | 9 years of war | 1 | 11 | 6½ |
| 1749 | ... | 1754 | 6 years of peace | 1 | 13 | 11½ |
| 1755 | .. | 1762 | 8 years of war | 1 | 17 | 1¾ |
| 1763 | ... | 1774 | 12 years of peace | 2 | 8 | 11½ |
| 1775 | ... | 1782 | 8 years of war | 2 | 6 | 6½ |
| 1783 | ... | 1792 | 10 years of peace | 2 | 10 | 2½ [*] |

[*] Tooke's History of Prices, vol. i, p. 97.

That the late war, from its extent, and in the latter part of it from its very anti-commercial character, operated most seriously upon the prices of corn in this country by obstructing all foreign importation during a period when, from the frequent recurrence of deficient crops, coincided with a constant increase of population, and rapid improvement of our manufactures, such an extraneous supply was required, will be presently made plain enough. Again, a small band of very pertinacious theorists insist that the high prices of corn, and all the agricultural prosperity of the war, arose from a depreciated currency; but the fallacy of their reasoning has been so frequently shown, and their nostrum so completely rejected by the good sense of the nation, that it would be a mere waste of time to bestow much space upon the doctrines of the "Currency doctors." That the depreciation of the currency during the war formed an addition to the many evils the people endured from a long protracted state of aggravated hostilities cannot be denied, but so far as that depreciation—a depreciation distinctly marked by the difference between the value of paper money and gold coin—affected prices, it was to produce a general rise of prices; whereas the gains then made by the agriculturists and the landowners arose from the enhancement of their peculiar commodities in a proportion far beyond the general rise of prices.

In 1792, at the commencement of the French war, the nation had fully recovered from the depression consequent upon the American war of Independence, and was beginning to reap the fruits of the grand inventions in science and art as applicable to manufactures and the rapid progress of our cotton manufactures, in the steady increase of population, and no less steady improvement in the condition of all classes of the people. The population of England and Wales had increased from 7,953,000, in 1780, to 8,675,000 in 1790, whilst every branch of trade and agriculture was advancing with a steady progression. The writer of the Essay upon the Agriculture of Scotland, to which I have before referred, commenting upon the period from 1783 to 1795, observes, "Besides the unprecedented increase of population which took place at this time, and which created "a great additional demand for the ordinary descriptions "of food, the improved habits of the people at large, and "a more full and substantial mode of living, gave rise "to a much more extended use of wheaten bread and "butchers' meat: the increased luxury of the higher "classes, in servants and horses, also operated as a "new demand; and new markets so near home being "established in the increasing towns and villages "throughout the country, imparted a spirit to the "energies of the farmer, which were principally ap- "plied to the further reclaiming of those lands which "had not hitherto been under the influence of the "plough." So much had rents advanced, that it has been calculated that the total rental of Scotland, which, at the close of the American war, in 1783, did not amount to more than £. 1,500,000, in 1795 exceeded £. 2,000,000. And the advance of agriculture and rise in rents was even more conspicuous in England at the same epoch.

The harvest of 1792 was wet, and much grain injured: the following spring was a very dry one, and although the crops of wheat proved moderate, the Lent corn was generally deficient. In 1794 a very hot and dry summer produced a crop of wheat scanty in amount of produce though of good quality, while the spring corn and leguminous crops were so parched in many parts of England as "scarcely to have re-"turned the seed committed to the ground for them." The winter of 1794-5 set in early, and proved to be so inclement and severe, that injury to the growing crops was much apprehended. This, in addition to the increased consumption which always occurs in severe winters, excited very general alarm. Wheat rose from 55*s.* 7*d.* a quarter, on the 1st of January, 1795, to 77*s.* 2*d.*, on the first of July in the same year. Government had adopted extraordinary measures of precaution to meet the expected dearth, by the seizure of all neutral ships bound with corn to France, and the employment of agents to buy corn in the Baltic ports. But the scarcity of corn was at least as great on the continent of Europe, as well as in America, as with us; and the competition of the French government in the corn markets of Europe raised prices so much, that the quantity of wheat imported in the whole of the year 1795 did not quite reach three hundred thousand quarters. Under such threatening circumstances the average price of wheat in this country reached in the month of August the enormous height of 108*s.* 4*d.* a quarter. In the latter part of August the weather cleared, and the harvest proved fine, so that by October the average price of wheat had fallen again to 76*s.* 9*d.* the quarter.

It was in November, 1795, that Mr. Burke wrote his letter, entitled "Thoughts and Details on Scarcity," wherein he says, "It must be remembered, that this

" year of produce (the year 1794), short, but excellent, " followed a year, 1793, which was not extraordinary " in production, nor of a superior quality, and left but " little in store. At first this was not felt, because the " harvest came in unusually early—earlier than com- " mon by a full month. The winter at the end of 1794 " and 1795 was more than usually unfavourable both to " corn and grass, owing to the sudden relaxation of very " rigorous frosts, followed by rains, which were again " rapidly succeeded by frosts of still greater rigour than " the first. Much wheat was utterly destroyed. The " clover grass suffered in many places. What I never " observed before, the rye grass or coarsebent, suffered " more than the clover. Even the meadow grass in " some places was killed to the very root." In the spring the crops partially recovered, but were subsequently much blighted and injured by the effects of cold East winds at the time of blooming. Mr. Burke then proceeds to say, " On thrashing, I found things as " I expected—the ears not filled, some of the cap- " sules quite empty, and several others containing only " withered hungry grain, inferior to the appearance of " rye. My best ears and grains were not fine; never " had I grain of so low a quality, yet I sold one load " for 21*l*. Since then the price has risen, and I have " sold two loads of the same sort for 23*l*." But not only was wheat and other corn thus dear, but meat and dairy produce rose equally in price from the scarcity of fodder; for instance, Mr. Burke says, "The store- " swine, from the failure of subsistence last year, are " now at an extravagant price. Pigs, at our fairs have " sold lately for fifty shillings, which two years ago "would not have brought more than twenty." "In "many places a full fourth of the sheep or lambs "were lost; and what remained of the lambs were "poor and ill-fed, the ewes having no milk." This last loss arose from the failure of the turnip crop of 1794. As usual there was a cry raised against the "monopoly of farms," "forestalling," and "regrating," and a general disposition existed to account for the high price of provisions by any but the true and simple cause, the visitation of two unproductive seasons. Lord Kenyon, in charging the Grand Jury at the Shropshire assizes, talked of "a report that a set of in-"dividuals are plundering at the expense of public "happiness, by endeavouring, in this county, in this "most abundant county, to purchase the grain now "growing upon the soil. For the sake of common "humanity I trust this is untrue. Gentlemen, 'tis "your duty as justices to see justice done to the coun-"try;" and much more to the same effect. All this is sufficiently ridiculous, but it shows the serious apprehensions of scarcity which were then generally entertained.

Now began that interference with the wages of agricultural labour, which afterwards expanded into the allowance system, and has inflicted so much mischief upon English husbandry and so many miseries upon the English peasant. It is due to the manly sense of Mr. Burke to mention the protest he made, in the work from which I have before quoted, against the unsound principle of interfering between employer and employed.

"It is not true," says Mr. Burke, "that the rate of wages

has not increased with the nominal price of provisions. I allow that it has not fluctuated with the price, nor ought it, and the squires of Norfolk had dined when they gave it as their opinion, that it might or ought to rise and fall with the market of provisions. The rate of wages in truth has no *direct* relation to that price. Labour is a commodity like every other, and rises or falls according to the demand. Wages have been twice raised in my time, and they bear a full proportion — on corn a greater than formerly — to the medium of provision during the last bad cycle of twenty years."

After showing that all above what the interest of employer would induce him to give is a *tax*, and, if left to the will of another, an *arbitrary tax*, he says,

"The tax proposed on the farming interest of this kingdom, is to be levied at what is called the discretion of the justices of the peace."

And, in allusion to the same subject, he incidentally gives the following picture of what had up to that time been the ordinary condition of farmers.

"It is a perilous thing to try experiments with the farmer. The farmer's capital (except in a very few persons, and in a very few places) is far more feeble than is commonly imagined. The trade is a very poor trade, and subject to great risks and losses. The capital, such as it is, is turned but once in the year; in some branches it requires three years before the money is paid. A greater or more ruinous mistake cannot be fallen into, than that the trades of agriculture and grazing can be conducted upon any other than the common principles of commerce; namely, that the producer should be permitted, and even expected, to look for all possible profit, which, without fraud or violence, he can make; to turn plenty or scarcity to the best advantage he can; to keep back or bring forward his commodities at his pleasure; to account to no one for his stock or his gains. It is very rarely that the most prosperous farmer, counting the value of his quick and dead stock, the interest of the money he turns, together with his own wages as bailiff or overseer, ever does make twelve or fifteen per cent. by the year of his capital. I speak of the prosperous. In most parts of England I have rarely known a farmer, who to his own trade has not added some other employment or traffic, that, after a course of most unremitting parsimony and labours (such for the greater part is theirs), and persevering in his business for a long course of years, died worth more than paid his debts, leaving his posterity to continue in nearly the same equal conflict between industry and want, in which his last predecessor, and long line of predecessors before him, lived and died."

Some advance was however made in wages, but it was far from being adequate (even with the allowance) to meet the increased price of the necessaries of life.

The war was then very generally thought to have had great influence in the rise of prices, and, inasmuch as military operations of the French and other continental nations interfered with the supply of foreign grain, which but for the war would have prevented such an unprecedented advance in the cost of provisions in this country, that opinion was in a sense correct. Some measure, both of the extent of the deficiency and of the public apprehension of the danger of dearth, may be found in the statement of Lord Sheffield in the House of Commons in December, 1795, who said the crops were deficient from one-seventh to one-third, that there was no old stock, and no prospect of any adequate supply from abroad; and in the remedies proposed and adopted to encourage importation. A bounty on importation, varying from 16*s.* to 20*s.* a quarter according to the quality was granted on wheat, and 6*s.* per cwt. on flour, from the south of Europe, till the quantity should amount to four hundred thousand quarters; and from America, till it should amount to five hundred thousand quarters; and one of 12*s.* to 15*s.* from any other part of Europe, till it should amount to five hundred thousand quarters; and from 8*s.* to 10*s.* after it exceeded that quantity. These bounties were to continue till the 30th of September, 1796. Members of the two Houses of Parliament bound themselves to reduce the consumption of bread in their own households by one-third, and to promote such a reduction wheresoever their influence extended. Then was the absurd fashion of wearing hair-powder put down, by a tax imposed with a view to prevent such an unprofitable application of wheat flour.

The dearness of food produced many riots and disturbances amongst the agricultural population, and the distress of the working classes in general was most severe. The privations endured by all persons who depended upon limited money incomes, and by those a little above the working classes, were also extreme. In the spring of 1796, the average price of wheat again reached 100*s.* a quarter. That in such a state of things the fears of the public should have exaggerated the dangers of the times — great as they were — requires little proof; and the effect of the stimulus afforded by such prices upon the owners and occupiers of land in promoting the extension of tillage and the application of capital to land, is matter of history. From this period of actual or anticipated famine, this time of suffering to the bulk of the community, is dated the great prosperity of the landed interest. Farmers, who had leases, realised enormous profits; and landlords, whose farms were not under lease, obtained on every new letting increases of rent hitherto unparallelled. The following extract, from an article by Arthur Young, in the Annals of Agriculture for 1796, affords a practical illustration of the effect of a deficiency in advancing prices in a ratio beyond the amount of the defect, which was the great source of profit to the farmers of that day.

"The average price of wheat for the twelve months, from May, 1795, to April, 1796, has been, on an average, in England and Wales, 10*s.* 7*d.* per bushel, and that of barley 4*s.* 9*d.* Now, the price for twelve years ending 1794, was for wheat 5*s.* 10*d.* and for barley 3*s.* 3*d.* For the year above described, therefore, the price has exceeded that average 4*s.* 9*d.* per bushel for wheat, and 1*s.* 6*d.* for barley. Let us suppose the annual consumption of wheat to be 8,701,875 quarters, and that of barley 10,545,000 quarters, and further, that the deficiency of the crop, on the average of the two years, so far as they affect the period in question, has amounted, in wheat, to one-fifth; and that the barley has, on an average of the two crops, been a medium: in this case there would have been consumed

| | |
|---|---|
| Of wheat 6,961,500 qrs., the extra price on which, at 4*s.* 9*d.* the bushel, or 38*s.* the quarter, is ...... | £. 13,226,840 |
| Of barley 10,545,000 qrs., at 1*s.* 6*d.* per bushel, or 12*s.* a quarter. ........................................ | 6,327,000 |
| | £.19,553,849 |

" If, therefore, these data are just, and they are ventured merely as calculation on uncertain foundations, the farmers have received in these two articles only, near 20,000,000 sterling beyond the deficiency of the crop, supposing the deficiency to be one-fifth, which is a very great one, and without adding a word on the price of meat or any other article."—Vol. xxvi, p. 469.

Here we see, that a far larger sum was distributed among the growers of corn than could be derived from medium or abundant crops; a profit derived through the alarm and distress of the times at the expense of the rest of the community.

The harvest of 1796 was abundant and well secured, which, combined with the importation of eight hundred thousand quarters of wheat, under the influence of the bounties I have mentioned, gradually reduced its price, until in December, 1796, the average was 57*s.* 3*d.* the quarter. The fall continued until the summer of the following year, when the price varied between 49*s.* and 50*s.* a quarter. The harvest of 1797 was wet and stormy, and the price of wheat advanced to 60*s.* in October of that year, receding again after the harvest of 1798, which was moderately productive, to 48*s.* in the month of November. In January of 1799 the average price of wheat was 49*s.* 6*d.*, which is as low as the average of several years previous to 1793. The autumn of 1798 had been wet and unfavourable for wheat sowing, and the succeeding winter was long and rigorous, much snow fell late in the spring, and the season was altogether untoward; the crops having an unpromising appearance the average price of wheat rose, in May, 1799, to 61*s.* 8*d.*, all other agricultural productions rising in the same proportion. The summer and autumn were wet, and the crops were much injured, so that at the close of the year the price of wheat was 94*s.* 2*d.* a quarter.

In the beginning of 1800, the deficiency of grain again engaged the attention of Parliament, when the defect of the late crop was estimated at one-third, and the high prices then current in the corn growing countries of the Continent were alluded to as an obstacle to a foreign supply. Again were various devices for limiting the consumption of grain resorted to, and bounties offered on importation. No great importation however took place, and the unfavourable appearance of the crops of 1800 caused the average price of wheat to rise in June to 134*s.* 5*d.* per quarter, whilst barley was 69*s.* 1*d.*, and oats 51*s.* 1*d.* Butchers' meat was also very high. With what unction have I heard some of my friends, who were farmers in that day, refer to these prices, and talk of the "glorious times for "farmers," apparently forgetting that there were others of the community, not farmers, to whom "these "glorious times" were seasons of unmitigated suffering.

The summer of 1800, up to the third week of August, was hot and dry, and a considerable quantity of corn in the earlier districts was well got in: some importation was also taking place; and the markets for wheat suddenly declined, in August, to 96*s.* 2*d.* a quarter. On the 19th of August, however, incessant rains set in, and a large proportion of the wheat crop being still in the field was sprouted and much injured. In Scotland the crops suffered more than in England; and no less than 1,242,507 quarters of foreign corn were imported, yet notwithstanding that supply the average rose, in December, 1800, to 133*s.* a quarter. The events of the war were at this time peculiarly adverse to the procuring a foreign supply: Russia, under French influence, had laid an embargo on British shipping; Denmark was hostile, and Prussia had in the previous July imposed a duty of 10*s.* a quarter on the exportation of wheat, a measure aimed expressly at this country. In the following season, as had been foreseen, the Baltic was entirely closed against us. Dearth produced its usual consequences of tumult and riotous proceedings, and it is alleged that the peace of the metropolis was with difficulty preserved. Prices continued to rise until March, 1801, when the average of wheat was 156*s.* 2*d.* per quarter!! Nearly all other articles of European raw produce advanced simultaneous, partly in consequence of the inclemency of the seasons, and partly from the extraordinary obstacles to importation caused by the war. The increased weight of taxation, also, on all necessaries, such as salt, soap, candles, leather, malt, beer, sugar, tea, tobacco, and spirits, had rendered all such articles of consumption inordinately dear.

None suffered more from this dearth than the working classes; the very lowest class of labourers could with difficulty obtain the means requisite to sustain themselves and their families, whilst, notwithstanding a rise of wages in most branches of industry, the classes above the lowest, and many skilled workmen, could do little more than provide themselves with the barest food, clothing, and shelter. Statements were at this time put forth, amongst other classes of artizans, by the journeymen tailors and the printers' compositors, from the former of which it appeared that their wages from 1777 to 1795 had been 1*l.* 1*s.* 9*d.* per week, which, at the then average price of 7½*d.* for the quartern loaf, would purchase 36 loaves, while the utmost advance of wages they had obtained was, in 1795, to 25*s.*, and, in 1801, to 27*s.* per week, which would purchase only 18½ loaves in the last named year. The compositors, whose wages had advanced from 24*s.* to 27*s.* in 1795, and to 30*s.* in 1801, showed an equal disproportion between the advances of wages and the increased prices of necessaries. Nor were the agricultural labourers better off, though in some districts a considerable increase of wages, or rather, of wages and parish allowance together, had been conceded. Arthur Young, in his Annals of Agriculture for 1801*, says, that "a person now living in the vicinity of Bury, Suffolk, "who, when he laboured for 5*s.* a week, could purchase "with that sum a bushel of wheat, a bushel of malt, a "pound of butter, a pound of cheese, and a pennyworth "of tobacco; while the same articles, in 1801, cost "1*l.* 6*s.* 9*d.*; and, supposing his wages in the last "named year to be 9*s.*, and his parish allowance from "the rates 6*s.* a week, making together 15*s.*, it would "require 11*s.* 5*d.* more than his wages and allowance

* P. 265.

" together to purchase the same quantities of consum-
" able commodities he procured when his wages were
" 5s. a week." The following comparative estimate of prices of necessaries at four different periods, by an inhabitant of Bury St. Edmonds, is extracted from the Appendix to a Report of a Committee of the House of Commons in 1800:—

| | 1773. | | | 1793. | | | 1799. | | | 1800. | | |
|---|---|---|---|---|---|---|---|---|---|---|---|---|
| | £. | s. | d. | £. | s. | d. | £. | s. | d. | £. | s. | d. |
| Coomb of Malt ...... | 0 | 12 | 0 | 1 | 3 | 0 | 1 | 3 | 0 | 2 | 0 | 6 |
| Chaldron of Coals ... | 1 | 11 | 6 | 2 | 0 | 6 | 2 | 6 | 0 | 2 | 11 | 0 |
| Coomb of Oats ...... | 0 | 5 | 0 | 0 | 13 | 0 | 0 | 16 | 0 | 1 | 1 | 0 |
| Load of Hay ......... | 2 | 2 | 0 | 4 | 10 | 0 | 5 | 5 | 0 | 7 | 0 | 0 |
| Meat ......... ........ | 0 | 0 | 4 | 0 | 0 | 5 | 0 | 0 | 7 | 0 | 0 | 9 |
| Butter .............. | 0 | 0 | 6 | 0 | 0 | 11 | 0 | 0 | 11 | 0 | 1 | 4 |
| Sugar (Loaf)........ | 0 | 0 | 8 | 0 | 1 | 0 | 0 | 1 | 3 | 0 | 1 | 4 |
| Soap ................ | 0 | 0 | 6 | 0 | 0 | 8 | 0 | 0 | 9¼ | 0 | 0 | 10 |
| Window Lights (30) | 3 | 10 | 0 | 7 | 10 | 0 | 12 | 12 | 0 | 12 | 12 | 0 |
| Candles ........... ... | 0 | 0 | 6 | 0 | 0 | 8 | 0 | 0 | 9½ | 0 | 0 | 10¼ |
| Poor Rates, per Qr. | 0 | 1 | 0 | 0 | 2 | 6 | 0 | 3 | 0 | 0 | 5 | 0 |
| £. | 8 | 4 | 0 | 16 | 2 | 8 | 22 | 9 | 4 | 25 | 14 | 1¼ |

Of this period Mr. Tooke observes, "But simple
" and obvious as were the causes of the great advance
" of prices, there were persons who denied, or pro-
" fessed to doubt, the existence of scarcity to account
" for the high prices, as there have been persons who,
" in more recent times, have denied the existence of
" abundance as accounting for a fall of prices*." And this time of suffering and dearth formed the great epoch of agricultural prosperity. I cannot cite more unexceptionable evidence to that effect than the Prize Essay of the Highland Society before mentioned,

* History of Prices, vol. i, p. 229.

wherein, having disposed of the period anterior to 1795, the writer says—

"But we hasten to go on to the next period, as infinitely more marked and conspicuous in the bright career of Scotch agriculture. The epoch from 1795 to 1814 exhibits, indeed, an era unexampled in the history of improvement in any other country. Many favourable circumstances operated to produce this result, and that these events, equally applicable to the sister kingdom, did not produce so striking an effect in England, can be accounted for in part from the circumstance that she previously occupied a more elevated position in the scale of improvement. But the want of leases there, perhaps, more than any other cause, contributed to her having been outstripped in this laudable struggle. Great Britain was now engaged in the heat of the war occasioned by the French revolution; and, without going into the abstract question as to the general effect of war upon prices, there is no doubt that the peculiar character of that contest tended materially to affect the price of agricultural produce, both in this country and throughout Europe. The extensive military operations carried on over a great part of the Continent could not fail to interfere seriously with the productiveness of those countries where such distractions existed; while the obstructions to commercial intercourse enhanced materially the value of our supplies from abroad, which, at one time, indeed, were nearly cut off by the peculiar tactics of the enemy. These causes induced a greater attention to be devoted to agriculture here. But, above all, the great rise in price, chiefly attributable to the frequent recurrence of bad seasons at this time, tended to give an extraordinary impetus to agricultural energy. The average price of wheat, which had been under 50*s.* per quarter during the twenty years immediately preceding 1795, rose in that year to the average of 81*s.* 6*d.*, and in the subsequent year, at one time, reached 96*s.* The price, however, recurred to the average of 54*s.* in 1798, owing to the favourable seasons of 1796 and 1797; but a series of excessively high prices followed*, which was attended by a great degree of prosperity to all persons engaged in agriculture. No doubt this great rise of price was occasioned chiefly, as we have noticed, by a cause which operated also to lessen considerably the

* Of the twenty years, from 1794 to 1814, the average price of wheat was 89*s.* 7*d.*—Eton Tables.

disposable quantity of farm produce; but it has been demonstrated*; that the effect of a deficient crop is to raise the price of the produce of the land greatly beyond the ratio of the defect, and, consequently, that a larger sum, in ordinary cases, is distributed among the growers, after a year of deficiency, than is derived from medium or abundant crops. Besides, higher prices, from whatever cause, act in enhancing the estimation of the profits of that pursuit from which they are derived. Hence the profits obtained from agriculture came to attract attention, and a liberal application of capital ensued. Those engaged in the cultivation of the soil eagerly sought after information in their profession — more anxiously observed and copied the improvements of their intelligent neighbours — and a praiseworthy spirit of rivalry generally obtained.

"A combination of so many favourable circumstances soon became evident in the rapidly improved face of the country. The liberal returns from agriculture gave rise to an increased application of capital to the soil, to an extent indeed, in many instances, which, as matters turned out, in the end frustrated the accomplishment of individual reward. A spirit of intelligence prevailed more generally among those engaged in husbandry, and more judicious and correct principles came to be applied in the chief operations of the farm. A further improvement took place in the system of rotations; clovers were now extensively cultivated; a great breadth of land which had been managed by an imperfect fallow was applied further to turnips; and it came to be the universal rule that clover, or some description of fallow crop, was interposed between every two culmiferous crops. But the order in which cropping was pursued was beginning to be regulated, not so much by any fixed rule of rotation as by the application of correct general principles, varied often according to results."

The consumption of butchers' meat is also said to have increased, estimated by the numbers of cattle alone, 30 per cent.; but the increased weight rendered the increase still greater. This is attributed to the better condition and increased luxuries of the people.

"But what, above all others, is indicative of the astonishing degree of improvement which accrued during this period, is the unprecedented rapidity with which the rent of land got up. There

* Young's Annals of Agriculture for 1796, vol. xxvi, p. 469.

is every reason to believe that the estimate, which states the rise of the arable portion of the land in Scotland to have amounted to considerably upwards of 100 per cent., is nearly correct. We have seen that, in 1795, the rental has been given as amounting to 2,000,000*l.* In 1815, the total rental of Scotland, exclusive of houses, amounted to 5,278,685*l.*"

Again let me remind the agricultural reader of the deep shade the privations of the community afforded to this glowing picture. The spring of 1801 was genial; and the preceding winter had been less rigorous than the two former ones; while the death of the emperor Paul, and the peace with Denmark, which followed the battle of Copenhagen, rendered the aspect of political affairs more promising. The Baltic had again become open to British shipping, and all the apprehensions, which the absolute obstruction of supplies from that quarter had caused, were removed. The enormous price of corn had also occasioned a greatly increased breadth of cultivation, which, as the seed time both for wheat and spring corn, had been favourable, improved the prospects of a home supply in the next year. Prices of wheat, under these circumstances, rapidly declined to 129*s.* 8*d.* in June, and to 75*s.* 6*d.* by the end of the year. The importations of wheat in this year amounted to 1,424,766 quarters, and about half that quantity of barley and oats. The harvest proved to be one of moderate abundance.

That temporary cessation of hostilities with France, known as the peace of Amiens, occurred in 1802; and the harvests of that year and of 1803 being of about an average production, the price of wheat went gradually down to 57*s.* 1*d.* a quarter, at the close of the former year; and further declined, notwithstanding the renewal of the war early in the latter year, to 52*s.* 3*d.* at its end. For the first three months of 1804 prices still subsided, so that the average of wheat for March was 49*s.* 6*d.*, or, as nearly as possible, to the level of 1792. And this occurred, be it remembered, after twelve years of war, and eight years after the suspension of cash payments. This fall in prices too had taken place in the face of the increased cost of production; the wages of labour and the expense of all kinds of implements used in husbandry having, as I have shown, risen from the frequent recurrence of scarcity during the previous twelve years. The government loans, also, had raised the rate of interest, and taxation had become more burthensome. On the other hand, tillage had been greatly extended, and there is no doubt that the native produce of corn was larger, on an average crop, in proportion to the ordinary consumption, than in 1792. The cost of a foreign supply had been increased by the renewal of the war, which had added from 5*s.* to 10*s.* per quarter to the usual rate of freight and insurance of corn. Such a fall of price, however, was not submitted to by the landed interest without an effort for further protection, and petitions to that effect poured in upon Parliament. The committee of the House of Commons, to whom these petitions were referred, appear to have fully understood the causes of the foregoing fluctuations, for they reported that—"It appears to "your committee that the price of corn, from 1791 to "the harvest of 1803, has been very irregular; but, "upon an average, increased in a great degree by the "years of scarcity, has, in general, yielded a fair profit "to the grower. The casual high prices, however, "have had the effect of stimulating industry [appli-

" cable to agriculture], and bringing into cultivation " large tracts of waste land, which, combined with the " two last productive seasons, and other causes, have " occasioned such a depression in the value of grain, " as, it is feared, *will greatly tend to the discouragement* " *of agriculture, unless maintained by the support of* " *Parliament*." Upon this, a bill was brought in by Mr. (now Lord) Western, imposing a duty of 24*s*. 3*d*. a quarter on wheat, when the price should be under 63*s*.; 2*s*. 6*d*. a quarter when between that price and 66*s*.; and 6*d*. when above 66*s*., which was afterwards passed into an act. This law proved practically inoperative, for the harvest of 1804, especially the wheat crop was very deficient, not only in this country but on the continent of Europe generally, and, in consequence, the price advanced in December to 86*s*. 2*d*. the quarter. The quality of the wheat too was very inferior, so that the average price scarcely exhibits the full extent of the rise; in October, 1804, fine white wheat was quoted, in Mark Lane, 90*s*. to 92*s*., and in January, 1805, white Dantzic at 100*s*., 120*s*., and 126*s*. a quarter. On this recurrence of dearth, various strikes and combinations to advance wages took place among the manufacturers, and an advance of wages was pretty generally established by the working classes, though by no means adequate to the increased cost of provisions.

The weather, previous to the harvest of 1805, was unsettled, and the average price of wheat rose to 98*s*. 4*d*. in the month of August; but the weather then taking up, and the crops having been well secured, and proving better than was expected, a fall of 20*s*. a quarter occurred by the end of the year. It was in this year that a new coalition was formed by the governments of this country, and those of Austria and Prussia, against France, which resulted in the following year in the complete subjugation of Prussia by Napoleon. The Prussian government had, in March 1806, prohibited British ships from entering into any of its ports or rivers, a measure which threatened to cut off all supply of corn from the Baltic, and the appearance of the crops being unpromising, the price of wheat rose again to 84*s*. in June. The harvest, however, having been about an average, and the promise of the succeeding year favourable, the price again declined in the summer of 1806 to 73*s*. 5*d*., and continued to fall till after the harvest of 1807, which was but moderately productive. The price of wheat was in November, 1807, 66*s*. In the beginning of 1808, the scantiness of the preceding crop was apparent, and under the effect of political events*, on which it is no part of my purpose to comment, the Baltic was completely closed against the British flag. The farmers, too, who under the influence of recent fluctuations had become speculators in grain, very generally withheld their stocks from market in anticipation of higher prices, it being then computed that an average crop did not suffice for the nation's consumption without the aid of importation. Hence prices immediately began to rise, distillation from grain was prohibited, and all the then usual preparations for an apprehended scarcity were made. The

---

* It may save the trouble of reference to mention, that the Berlin decree followed the battle of Jena in the autumn of 1806. The British orders in council were issued in 1807, and the bombardment of Copenhagen, and the Russian embargo on British shipping, occurred in the autumn of the same year. The nonintercourse act of America, consequent on the orders in council, was passed in 1808.

harvest of 1808 was deficient; no foreign supply was obtainable, and there was, in fact, a small balance of exports of about 15,000 quarters of wheat to Spain and Portugal. Wheat rose to 81*s.* 1*d.* in July, 1808, and to 92*s.* at the close of the year. Yet such were the obstructions to importation, that no foreign supply was forthcoming. In March, 1809, the average price of wheat reached 95*s.*; but the crops promised well, and in July the price got down to 86*s.* 6*d.* The harvest season turned out so exceedingly wet, that scarcely any part of the crops was secured in good order, and, besides, the quantity of wheat proved to be below an average. The average price, therefore, rose in December to 102*s.* 6*d.*, though the best samples were worth 125*s.* a quarter. Some 400,000 quarters of corn were imported from France and the Netherlands during the year under licenses from the British and French governments.

The spring of 1810 was cold and ungenial, and the crops were generally very backward, circumstances which, with the known deficiency of the stock in hand, raised wheat to the average of 116*s.* in August. At this time the expenses of freight, insurances, and licenses on wheat amounted to the enormous sum of from 38*s.* to 50*s.* per quarter; yet the importation in 1810 amounted to about 1,500,000 quarters of wheat and flour, and 600,000 quarters of other grain and meal. About the middle of August the weather cleared up, and the whole of the crops were secured in good order. Wheat at once declined, and was at the price of 97*s.* 1*d.* by the close of the year. The corn dealers, who are stated to have speculated largely upon the unpropitious appearances of the early season of the year were severe sufferers, and many of them became bankrupt.

The price continued to fall till June, 1811, when it was 86*s.* 11*d.* In August a reaction occurred, and the price advanced till the eve of the harvest of 1812, when the *average* price was 155*s.* 1*d.* In Mark Lane, the best Dantzic wheat fetched 180*s.*; and oats were sold as high as 84*s.* a quarter!! The crop of 1811 had been deficient, but not so strikingly so as to attract particular attention; and though the weather, during the harvest of 1812, was unsettled, it was not so decidedly bad as to injure the crops; and opinions varied as to the probable yield. Of foreign supply, from the vast expenses of importation, there was no prospect. In this year the dealers seldom showed a sample, the corn was always bespoken—a fact, which, to those who know aught of the details of corn dealing, indicates, perhaps more than any other circumstance, the insufficiency of the supply. At this period farmers and landlords had the fullest conviction that the high range of prices of the previous three years would be permanent; and accordingly this was the time when rents experienced the greatest rise, and speculations in land became most general. All purchases of land made before 1811 turned out profitable, if sold during the years 1812 and 1813. I have often heard a relation of my own, who began farming some fifty years ago, and who confessed to having put by 3000*l.* (beyond his housekeeping expenses) from the occupation of about 1200 acres, in more than one year of the "good times," say, that he had made far more money by the purchase and resale of land than by farming. This gentleman commenced life with a large sum of money, and his purchases of land have been only such as his ample means justified; but I suspect that not a few of the landowners, who most strenuously clamour for protection, are to a certain extent in the condition of the speculator, who some years ago petitioned Parliament for relief, representing that he had in the years 1811 and 1812 "laid out "150,000*l.*, partly his own and partly borrowed, in the "purchase of land, which had since so much fallen in "value that he was ruined by the loss." After such a precedent, speculators, who have been ruined by the purchase of foreign *securities*, must be persons of exemplary modesty not to have preferred their complaints to the legislature.

In the autumn of 1812, the price of wheat fell to 113*s.* 6*d.*, at about which average it stood till the month of August, 1813, when, the harvest having proved very abundant, the price again declined to 73*s.* 6*d.* in December. The fall in corn was accelerated by the events of the war, which seemed to promise that at no distant time the whole of the continent of Europe would be again open to the British merchant. In evidence that the high price of 1812 mainly arose from scarcity, it may be mentioned that in France, Italy, Germany, Spain, and Portugal, a nearly corresponding rise of prices occurred. By the July of 1814, wheat was at 66*s.* the quarter, and would probably have been lower but for the severity of the previous winter and the backward and unpromising character of the season; and, in the event, the crop of that year was injured to a considerable extent, though the great breadth of cultivation, and the superabundant produce of 1813, together with an importation of 800,000 quarters, brought down the market price of wheat (after a temporary rise of 10*s.* a quarter), to 65*s.* 8*d.* per quarter, at the termination of the year.

## SECTION II.

### STATE OF AGRICULTURE AND THE CORN TRADE FROM 1814 TO 1828.

It has been necessary in the preceding section to trace somewhat minutely the fluctuations in the price of corn, which occurred during the war, in order to show what was the origin of those variations, as well as of the almost famine prices of corn in certain years. But though the oscillations of price were great, the general average of the period was extremely high, wheat being from 1794 to 1814 no less than 89*s.* 7*d.* a quarter.

It is most essential to a due estimate of the operation of the corn laws since 1814, that the real causes of the previous high prices of provisions should be thoroughly understood; for we find men writing and talking vaguely of the "prosperity" of the country during the war, and seeking to reproduce that state of things which was the combined result of dearth and obstructed foreign trade. As I have briefly shown—and further researches into the records of those times will more completely confirm my views—that, with the exception of the landed interest and (from causes presently to be noticed) those engaged in manufacturing enterprises, all classes suffered most severely during the earlier years of the contest, and it was only towards 1809 and 1810, when high prices had assumed the appearance of permanence, that wages, salaries, and professional remuneration were raised in any proportion to the increased expenses of living. It was the vast extension of our manufactures, especially those connected with the cotton trade, which enabled this country to make the progress it did during the war, in spite of the obstacles and difficulties imposed by the obstructions of the contest, and to grow so much in wealth and power as to consume yearly increasing quantities of corn and other necessaries at such prodigious prices. No-one can doubt that but for the burthens of the war—amongst which, it cannot be too often repeated, must be reckoned the high price of corn from obstructions to foreign supplies in years of scarcity—the accessions to the wealth, and power, and population of the nation, for which it is so largely indebted to manufactures, would have been infinitely greater than those which actually accrued. The sudden gains obtained by the owners and tillers of the soil formed, during the high prices of the war, a deduction from the general means of the nation; and the claim of the landed interest to be exempted by legislative enactment, at the expense of the rest of the community, from the effects of restored abundance, after having profited so largely by a rise of prices far beyond the ratio of deficiency, seems upon every consideration of principle and policy to be so unjust and unwise, that a very strong case of necessity for such exemption ought to be made. Whether such a case has been made out remains to be seen.

At all events, no sooner had the price of corn fallen in 1814, than loud and general demands from the agriculturists were made on the legislature for protection against foreign competition. Then commenced that struggle, that hitherto fruitless struggle (which is still continued on the part of the landowners), to obtain for their commodities, in seasons of abundance, the prices of scarcity and dearth. Accordingly, committees of the Houses of

Lords and Commons were appointed to inquire into the allegations of agricultural distress, both of which examined numerous witnesses—landlords, farmers, surveyors, and corn-dealers;—and the Commons' Committee presented a report, which formed the basis of our corn law legislation. Before I address myself to that report, as showing the objects and opinions of those who prevailed in founding a prohibitory system with respect to foreign corn, I will just stop to notice that the law of 1804, which imposed a duty of 24*s.* 3*d.* a quarter on wheat when the average price did not exceed 63*s.*, never came into operation at all, inasmuch as up to 1814, the average price was constantly above the importation limit, and our ports therefore continued always open to the reception of foreign corn *when it could be obtained.* The committee in their report proposed to consider the subject referred to them under three heads.—1st. As it related to the then "recent extension and improvement of agriculture;" 2ndly. As to the then "present expense of cultivation, *including the rent;*" 3dly. "The price necessary to remunerate the grower." The report then stated that all the witnesses ascribed "the great increase which had taken place in the annual produce of our soil, and the late rapid extension of the improved system of our husbandry" to the stimulus afforded by the high prices of the previous twenty years—a conclusion there is no reason to question. The report then added, "The great source of "encouragement is to be traced to the increasing "population and growing opulence of the United "Kingdom; but it is also not to be concealed, that "these causes, which they trust will be of a permanent and progressive nature, *have been incidentally* "*but considerably aided by those events, which, during*

" *the continuance of the war, operated to check the im-*
" *portation of foreign corn.*" Here is a distinct explanation of the real origin of the high prices; the committee made no mistake as to the cause of the lower prices then complained of by the landed interest, and as I shall presently show, the active partizans of that interest out of doors used a very thin veil to cover the real object—the maintenance of high rents. This they imagined might be effected by substituting high import duties on grain in lieu of the impediments caused by the war.

The report went on to say, " *The sudden removal of*
" *these impediments* appears to have created among the
" *occupiers* of land a certain degree of alarm, which, if
" not allayed, would tend to prevent the inclosure and
" cultivation of great tracts of land still lying waste
" and unproductive, but also to counteract the spirit of
" improvement in other quarters, and to check its pro-
" gress on lands already under tillage." Now, the proverb that "gold may be bought too dear" applies with great force to the observation of the committee about waste and unproductive land; and that the progress of tillage would not be so rapid under moderate prices, as when wheat might be run up to 7*l.* 15*s.* a quarter under apprehensions of deficiency is so plain, that the statement is a mere truism. The question which ought then to have been fairly considered was, what, under the altered state of circumstances, would have been the safest foundation for agriculture. The committee stated, that money rent had been doubled within the previous twenty years, but that the landlord's share of the gross produce, which used to be one-third, was at that time not more than from one-fourth to one-fifth, and that the expenses of stocking and cul-

tivating a farm had been likewise doubled. When it is considered that the rent of land can only be that portion of the produce which remains after payment of the expenses of cultivation, and the lowest rate of remuneration for which farmers will consent to expend their capital and labour in husbandry; and that every fresh application of capital to cultivated land, and every resort to inferior land—the "waste and unproductive tracts" of the committee—is attended with a less return in proportion to the outlay; and when it is known, nay, stated by the committee, that the supply of corn during the war was drawn from our own soils by means of extended tillage and improved systems of husbandry, it does betray a tendency to hasty conclusions on the part of the committee to complain, that rents (though admittedly double in amount), formed a smaller proportion of the "gross produce" of the land, than they did in former times of lower prices and less extended cultivation.

It is so all-important to the elucidation of the corn law question, that the nature and origin of rent should be precisely defined, that I shall borrow from Colonel Thompsons's "True Theory of Rent*" a few clear statements upon that point.

"It is easy to imagine the existence of a country in which the land should be of a uniform and high quality, and where, from the great facility of procuring crops, and the consequent non-improvement of agricultural science, the cultivators should, for ages together, have no idea of the processes by which an European farmer forces

* *Exercises Political and Others*, by Lieut. Col. T. Perronet Thompson, vol. iv, p. 404: a work, which, from the extent and variety of its contents no less than from its logical and accurate argument, forms the most complete manual of political economy extant.

an increased crop through the expenditure of an increased quantity of capital upon the land. The whole of the cultivated portion of Egypt, and great part of India, present specimens of such a state of things, yet in both these countries a heavy rent is paid to the great landlord, which is the government. The simple cause of rent in such countries, and everywhere else, is, in reality, nothing but what Adam Smith pointed out long ago.- It is the same that gives rise to the rent of the vineyard that produces Tokay. It is *the limited quantity of the land, in comparison with the competitors for its produce;* or, as it is sometimes termed, the monopoly."

And the author here explains that

"When the term monopoly is thus applied to land, it does not necessarily mean a monopoly arising from any immediate act of the owner; for a monopoly in the sense here meant, will arise to a certain extent under any system that can be imagined. There must always be a monopoly of the best land, the nearest land, and that which is most favourably situated for the consumption of its produce; and this monopoly must cause such land to yield a rent."

And he illustrates his definition thus:—

"Let the case be supposed of a small number of settlers taking possession of a large and fertile island; and let the soil be so good, and their habits of agricultural energy so limited, that a slight scratching of the ground and throwing in the seed shall be all the cultivation they at first think of bestowing, as for ages together has been a picture of the agriculture of many tropical countries. If the land was unappropriated, and every man might occupy at will, it is plain that in the commencement no man would pay another any rent, either for leave to cultivate, or for the grass, wood, &c., which might be the spontaneous produce. Or if instead of the land being entirely unappropriated, the right of property in it was vested in a number of owners, but who were without the means of bringing the land into immediate cultivation, it would be equally plain that the competition would in the commencement reduce the rent which any of them could obtain to the lowest possible magnitude, which is, in fact, no magnitude at all. In such an establishment, the degree of each man's wealth, supposing him to possess the brief capital required for setting his industry in motion, would be in proportion to the exertions of himself or of his family. He that by his activity could raise or collect much corn, fruit, sheep, furs, or whatever else were the objects of industry within his reach, would be comparatively rich."

And such is very much the condition of a new and fertile colony.

"But when population and cultivation had increased so as to begin to press against the limits of the soil contained in the whole island, and there was no longer new land to be had for asking, a very different scene would begin to arise. All the population which was not employed in agricultural labour, or supported without labour upon some kind of previous accumulation, must apply itself to manufacturing industry. And as the number of persons so employed increased, a competition would arise among them for the products of agriculture upon which they must live; and this competition would oblige them to give a greater portion of the results of their own labour, in return for a smaller and less luxurious quantity of agricultural produce than they had been accustomed to receive. It is true that the land must finally find food for all that live on it, as the vineyard finds wine for all that finally drink Tokay; but it does not therefore follow, that many of those who live on it, may not, when their numbers have increased, live much less abundantly than they used to do, and give a much greater quantity of the results of their own labour in return for a given quantity of the produce. It is proved by the experience of all countries, that moderately good land is capable of producing food for many times the number of hands required for its cultivation; so that all these numbers may be called into being to assist in the demand. Hence, if the exchange of commodities was conducted by the intervention of a circulating medium, the money price of agricultural produce must rise in comparison with the money prices of other commodities. *The landowners would then begin to get rich, through the simple fact of their being landowners, and there being no more land to own.*"

Now, this is an exact description of the position of the owners of land during the period from 1794 to 1814, stripped of its accessory and subordinate circumstances. Again,—

"If it should be found some day that a contiguous island had sprung up of the same nature with the first, their prospect of increased wealth would drop at once; and every thing would go on as it did at the commencement, till the new island had been peopled and cultivated like the other. But if this does not happen, the lucky landowners will incontinently begin to swell into men of landed wealth. If they keep their land in their own hands, they will rise into what are termed gentlemen-farmers, or men who unite in their own persons the characters of landlord and cultivator. But as soon as what they obtain by the sale of their produce, is sufficiently greater than the amount for which they can hire one of their less fortunate neighbours, who is heir to his own industry and no land beside, the greater part of them will hire a farming-man or overseer with part of the produce, and sit down in the enjoyment of the *otium cum dignitate* of landed gentlemen with the remainder. And from this step of the farming-man, they will soon proceed to the further one, of finding a farming-man who will advance his own capital, making an adequate deduction out of the produce in return; or, in other words, a farmer or tenant. The reason of this further step will be, their desire to get more completely rid of the trouble of superintending the employment of the capital; for a tenant has his own interest at stake in watching it with the utmost exactness, while a farming-man, having no such interest, must still be superintended in a considerable degree. And all the *residuum* left after delivering to the tenant the portion of the proceeds which the competition among individuals of his class obliges him to accept, will be rent. And what the tenant will be obliged to accept, will be such a part of the price of the produce, as will return him the capital he must lay out, with the lowest rate of profit for which men under the existing habits of the society will consent to lay out farming capital and superintend its employment. But of the existence of this *residuum*, the primary cause is manifestly the increased price of corn."

Now, from the scheme which the landowners hit upon of prohibiting the importation of corn into this "island" until the average price reached 80*s*. the quarter, it is clear they were quite aware that "the primary cause of this *residuum*," or rent, was the increased price of corn; at all events, that the cent. per cent. they had obtained within the twenty years previous to 1814, was mainly brought into existence by the high prices. The termination of the war, by putting an end to the obstructions to importation, acted upon the interests of the owners of land in this country, to some extent, like the springing up of the "new island" of Colonel Thompson's illustration. They had immediately a less close monopoly; they were exposed to the competition of the continental growers of corn, and, in the absence of prohibitory law, would have lost, in the first instance, all that portion of their increased rental which had been occasioned by a succession of indifferent seasons when no extraneous aid could be obtained; but they would have retained all that portion which accrued to them from their monopoly of "the best land, and the nearest land, and that which is most favourably situated for the consumption of its produce." All that increase of rent, which was the natural result of the "increasing population and growing opulence" of the nation must have, and, in fact, has been retained by those who own its soil. That the landowners would not have been without ample compensation for the loss of even that portion of their gains, which was derived from national misfortunes, will appear in the progress of this examination; their natural "monopoly" would have secured to them all the increase of rent consequent upon the national progress in wealth and civilization, although a somewhat reduced breadth of tillage (an occurrence by no means likely) had been the result of leaving the corn trade and the farming trade to their natural channels.

Some measure of the proportion of the actual war rents, which the landowners would have naturally retained after the obstructions of the war had ceased, may be found in the following extract from the evi dence of Professor Low given in 1833, which shows, that even after twenty years of unsuccessful struggle against the laws of supply and demand, and the mischievous fluctuations thereby caused, the average rent of land *in Scotland* was nearly double what it had been previous to the year 1794. The following is his description of the effects of the rise of prices upon the Scotch tenantry :—

"Rents began to increase in Scotland with the commencement of the war, and the ratio of the increase increased after the scarcities of 1799 and 1800. From 1800 to 1804, the situation of the agriculture of Scotland was highly favourable ; during that period, rent had not become excessive, or charges so oppressive as they afterwards became. Many farmers held old leases, and by realising capital, *were enabled to extend their concerns, or establish their sons in farms*. Those circumstances, added to the increasing *demand for farm produce of all kinds, gave a great stimulus to rents*, which continued to operate till the year 1814. Comparing the period from the year 1781 to 1794, with the period from 1800 to 1804, I think the average rise of rents in Scotland was about 86 per cent. ; and comparing the same period, 1781 to 1794, with that from 1804 to the end of the war, I think there was a rise of about 150 per cent. on a medium."

And he afterwards said, that on comparing the average rate of rent in Scotland from 1781 to 1794 with that of the present day, it was then (1833) about 90 per cent. higher than before the war.

This is a practical comment upon Colonel Thompson's accurate and scientific definitions of rent; and will be usefully kept in view when we come to see how ill the attempt of the landowners, to secure the famine portion of their war rents through the creation of an artificial scarcity by the law of 1815, succeeded.

It is true that the scientific examinations of economical questions, with which most persons of ordinary information are now familiar, had not then obtained such general currency as at present, and that a real apprehension of possible impediments to the future supplies of foreign grain did to some extent exist ; but a reference to the arguments and assertions by which the committee's recommendation of a protecting duty on wheat of 80*s*. a quarter was supported by persons of repute and ability, will convince the most incredulous that the assumption of rent to be a fixed quantity was not altogether the result of ignorance. Besides, many of the evils which have been since caused by the corn laws, were clearly pointed out in 1815 by the parliamentary opponents of those laws. The committee of 1814 considered and inquired with great diligence as to "the present expense of cultivation, *including the* "*rent*," an arbitrary classification, which plainly implied a Canute-like determination to say, "happen what may, rents shall not fall." Circumstances, however, have proved too strong for landlords or legislators. The advocates of protection in Parliament then used very little of that reserve, now almost universal amongst them, in asserting their main object—the maintenance of rents. In a tract written by Mr. Jacob, and published in 1814, entitled, "Considerations on the Protection required by British Agriculture," broadly asserts the same argument. He says (p. 82), "Among "many we frequently hear the landed proprietors cen-"sured for having raised the rent of their lands, and "such persons exclaim, 'the rents must be lowered;' "this, therefore, requires some consideration. A con-"siderable class in the country, possessors of estates "derived from their ancestors, important to the com-"munity by their rank, by their education, and their "virtues, from which has hitherto been drawn the far "greater portion of our statesmen, our magistrates, our "clergy, and the officers of our army and navy, have "been compelled by the increased expense of every "article, both of necessity and luxury, to follow the "march of circumstances, and increase their revenues, "not by any force, but by voluntary conventions with "their tenants, who, on their part, have cheerfully "agreed to give an increased income, the advance on "their productions enabling them to do so without in-"juring themselves. *Now, without any abatement in "the cost of those articles, which are indispensable in "their rank*, without any reduction on the imposts, "which bear with peculiar pressure on them, these re-"spectable members of the community are expected to "reduce their incomes.'.... 'Must the newly-acquired "proprietors of land, who have invested their capital "in purchases, which produce much less annuity than "they could have obtained from other modes of invest-"ment, see their incomes reduced to a still lower "standard, *and that whilst the stockholder is to suffer "no reduction?*"

Now, this language betrays an ignorance or neglect of first principles, not a little astonishing in so acute a writer as Mr. Jacob; but it plainly marks the objects avowed, and the manner in which they were supported, by the protectionists in that day. Yet Mr. Jacob does not trust to such arguments to prejudice, as I have extracted, for in earlier passages he had very elaborately endeavoured to show: First,—That no more than about a month's consumption of corn in this country could be, under any circumstances, imported from abroad, and that, therefore, habitually to rely upon a foreign supply would be highly impolitic. This seems an odd way of addressing those who were in an agony of alarm at an expected influx of cheap foreign corn. In the position of Mr. Jacob, that the quantity of wheat which could be profitably imported into this country under the most unlimited freedom of trade, has been at all times greatly exaggerated, I entirely agree, as well as in his observations that "there is great reason to apprehend, that "ignorance of the relative quantity of grain which is "produced at home, to that which is imported from "other countries, has been the cause of the greatest "fluctuations;" and that "both in 1805 and 1812, "the prices of corn were raised far beyond what the "deficiency in the quantity grown could have justified." Having shown that no great proportion of our whole consumption of grain could be drawn from abroad, he argues, secondly, that it was desirable to "hope for a "return of the circumstances which, till the year 1766, "had long existed in this country, when we had not only "sufficient for our own consumption, but had usually "a surplus quantity of corn for that of other coun-"tries;" that this was only to be effected "by giving "such encouragement to agriculture as will convince "the most cautious that, in embarking their property "in such operations, they shall be secured, *as far as* "*legislative enactments can secure them*, from any risks "but such as arise from their own negligence, or from "unfruitful seasons; and as the dread of competition "with those, who, from various causes, can raise corn "cheaper than the British husbandman, acts as a check "on our cultivation, the rendering such a competition "impossible, would give the strongest stimulus to those "who have property to embark in agriculture." He then cites the opinions of the witnesses examined before the parliamentary committees of that year, to prove that wheat *could* not be produced under 80*s*., and proposes a protecting duty of 88*s*. a quarter.

This evidence is not a little curious, and for the sake of contrasting the agricultural calculations of 1814 with those of subsequent periods, I must briefly refer to the statements of some of the witnesses.

Mr. Buxton, from Essex, laid before the Lords' committee a variety of calculations to show that wheat should sell at from 95*s.* to 100*s.* per quarter, barley 45*s.*, and oats 35*s.*, to pay the expense of the farmer. Mr. Driver, the land-surveyor, thought 5*l.* a quarter for wheat was the price necessary for the protection of the grower: this gentleman's evidence, as to the manner of valuing land, is instructive, as showing how utterly at sea land-valuers are, and must be, under such an artificial system of prices as that occasioned by the corn laws. He at one time thought 5*l.* a quarter the natural price of wheat in England, afterwards lowered his estimate to 90*s.*, and finally settled at 80*s.*, the then act of Parliament price. Mr. Lake, from Kent, "proved most clearly," that wheat at 84*s.*, beans at 42*s.*, and barley at 32*s.* per quarter, would create a loss to the farmer of 7*s.* 4*d.* per acre! The Scotch farmers in those days thought they could live at the prices which were to ruin the husbandmen of Kent. Mr. Benett, from Wiltshire (now one of the members for South Wilts), produced a very detailed statement of the expenses and produce of a farm of 945 acres in that county: taking the price of wheat at 96*s.*, barley at 48*s.* a quarter, there was, according to Mr. Benett's calculations, a yearly loss sustained of 66*l.* I well remember this gentleman s first contest for the representation of Wilts, when none of his supporters could show themselves without being saluted with "no barley bannock," "no oat cake," and divers similar cries, which sufficiently indicated the popular estimate of his evidence amongst *bread-eaters* and the labouring classes of that county. The only witness, who thought a less price than 80*s.* sufficient, was Mr. Mant, who—provided the property tax was taken off and labour reduced—fixed 72*s.* for wheat, an opinion then deemed an agricultural heresy of the worst sort, for which he was taken to task by Mr. Jacob without mercy. In all these calculations rent was assumed to be an immutable portion of the expenses.

Such were the opinions which prevailed in the legislature in 1814, and which, in the following year, ripened into a corn law, prohibiting importation of grain until the average price of wheat reached 80*s.* a quarter, and barley and oats in that proportion. And what was the result? The agriculturist was assured of high prices, "as far as legislative enactment could secure them," and foreign competition had been "rendered impossible," except in a time of famine, yet (the previous harvest having been propitious) in December, 1815, the *average price of wheat was 53s. 7d. a quarter, barley* 25*s.* 11*d.*, *and oats* 19*s.* 9*d.*; and, in January, 1816, the averages were still lower, being for wheat 52*s.* 6*d.*, barley 24*s.* 8*d.*, oats 18*s.* 7*d.*, a lower point of depression in the prices of corn than had occurred since 1804! This was enough to have shaken the faith of the farmer, who was promised 85*s.* to 90*s.* for his wheat, and *whose burthens were calculated on such data*, in legislative protection. It is remarkable, that during those low prices a foreign demand for British wheat arose in the south of Europe; but a severe frost and heavy fall of snow in February of 1816, together with accounts of scarcity and rising prices in France and Germany, caused the price to advance, so that in May the average for wheat was 74*s.* It is scarcely necessary to remind the reader that the summer of 1816 was the most inclement, and the harvest the most disastrous which had occurred in this country since 1799. The crop of grain was both deficient in quantity and inferior in quality, and the average price of wheat rose in December to 103*s.*

The season was even worse on the Continent than in this country, so that only 100,000 quarters were imported during the year, though the ports were open from the month of August. The continental prices, in fact, exceeded those of this country: at Vienna, Munich, and Stuttgard, in September, 1816, wheat was 116*s*. 10*d*., 127*s*. 2*d*., and 127*s*. 1*d*. respectively; and advanced, by September of 1817, at the two latter places to 141*s*. 2*d*. and 138*s*. 7*d*. a quarter. In France, wheat was in June, 1817, as high as 137*s*. 6*d*. a quarter. During that year no less than 300,000 quarters were shipped thither from this country. Under these circumstances the price of wheat reached in June, 1817, 117*s*. a quarter. This revived the hopes of the landed interest, who began to imagine their former "prosperity" was returning. That such an enormous rise in price would more than compensate the growers of corn for the badness of the season will be evident to all who know the details of rural affairs. Though the great bulk of the crop was injured, it was not absolutely spoiled, and most farmers would have saved some small portion in tolerable condition, which, selling for much more than the average price, would make their total receipts very considerable.

It is certain, that in seasons of general deficiency or injury to the crops, the growers of corn are fully compensated, upon the principle I have before adverted to, *viz*. that the ratio of increase in price is greater than the actual deficiency; if, therefore, the farmer can be secured from all fluctuations, except those caused by the seasons, and have his burthens calculated according to a steady average price of years of ordinary fertility, he will be effectually insured against bad seasons by the rise of price which is certain in such seasons to occur.

Up to June of 1817 the weather was unpromising, and the average of wheat of that month was 111*s*. 6*d*. a quarter; then, however, the season became finer, and the crops, though not very abundant, were in part secured in moderately good order. The average fell in October to 77*s*., and the ports remained closed till February of the following year, the average having then been for some time upwards of 84*s*. The summer of 1818 was as remarkable for heat and drought as that of 1816 had been for wet, and considerable apprehensions of scarcity were entertained. Hay rose to 9*l*. and 10*l*. a load, and beans, peas, turnips, and potatoes were believed to have completely failed. Hay was, in this year, imported from New York. Upwards of 1,500,000 quarters of wheat had been imported, and, as is always the case in dry seasons, the yield of wheat turned out better than from the smallness of the quantity of straw had been expected; the average for wheat fell in December, 1818, to 78*s*. 10*d*. per quarter. From the peculiar character of the season other grain was much dearer, beans and peas being worth nearly as much as wheat. The produce of the harvest of 1819 * was an average one, and the price of wheat for the year was 72*s*. The winter of 1819-20 was severe, and the spring cold until June, when some fine weather occurred, becoming again unsettled until August, when it cleared, and the crops were well ripened and got in. The price of wheat fluctuated with

* I have not made any especial reference to the resumption of cash payments, because, even if there was any thing in the arguments of those "who have bewildered themselves in the mazes of the currency theory," its effect would have been to depress the prices of corn and other commodities in an equal proportion.

the weather between 65*s*. and 72*s*. a quarter. The bulk and yield of the crop exceeded expectation, and the average of wheat got down to 54*s*. in December; falling again, by July of 1821, to 51*s*. a quarter. The produce of this abundant harvest was estimated at full one-third above an average crop, taking into consideration the greatly extended breadth which had been cultivated under the influence of the temporary rise of 1817 and 1818. 1820-21 was a mild winter, but the spring was cold, the summer and harvest time showery; and, though the bulk of corn was large, its condition was not good. A speculative rise in the price of wheat to 62*s*. took place in September, 1821, falling again to 50*s*. at the end of the year; and further, by August, 1822, to the low average of 42*s*. a quarter. It must be remarked, however, that the inferior quality of the wheat of 1821 had a considerable share in producing so low an average price. 1822 was fine, and the crop secured in excellent order.

Again a loud cry of agricultural distress was raised, and a committee was appointed by the House of Commons, which sat in April, 1821. This committee examined a great number of witnesses, and made a report, which is in many respects remarkable, and in none more so than in the indications it affords that experience was surely, though slowly, teaching the more intelligent of the agriculturists, by hard and stern lessons, the futility of legislative protection. It required, however, some fifteen years more ere the full effect of that teaching was made manifest before the committee of 1836.

The period just past under review, *viz*. from 1814 to 1821, is one of the most eventful in the history of British commerce. It was a time of transition from the high prices and speculation in exorbitant fluctuations, which, from their long continuance, appeared to the majority of traders necessary incidents to commercial undertakings,—to the ordinary current of peaceful commerce. That to the agricultural interest—meaning thereby farmers and landlords—it was undoubtedly a time of anxiety and suffering has never been denied. During the war, from the causes before adverted to, the occupation of agriculture, which in all ages has been one of slow and steady progress, a pursuit wherein attention to minute details and frugal industry could alone secure competence, had become the field for the most reckless and daring speculations. Whilst prices were continually rising from year to year, as, with a few temporary exceptions, was the case throughout the war, and corn, no matter at what expense raised, was certain to be sold with great profit, men would be certain to be crowding hap-hazard into the business of husbandry. Persons, without any capital of their own, undertook farms in the confident expectation that after one or two crops, sold at increasing prices, they would be enabled to maintain their ground. Others extended their concerns beyond the limits a sober estimate of their means could have justified, in full reliance upon permanently high prices and a rising market. Tradesmen left their own occupations to become farmers, and so great had become the competition for farms, more especially in the latter part of the war, that landlords, instead of being active agents in advancing rents, had only to select their tenant from a host of candidates. This state of excitement naturally led to speculative purchases of land by mere jobbers, as well as by already existing landowners.

All these operations were greatly assisted by the facility with which landowners and farmers obtained accommodation from country bankers, who were as eager to extend the circulation of their paper promises to pay, as the agriculturists were to use them, and with as full a belief in an unlimited and indefinite rise of prices. The same sort of thing was going on in the trading world under the influence of the Bank of England issues. The result of these conjoint operations was to depreciate the whole currency, and in the year 1814—the time of the greatest depreciation—to the extent of 25*l.* 2*s.* 6*d.* per cent.; in fact, that which in that year was, by courtesy, called a one pound note, was worth a fraction less than 15*s.* So far as regarded the landed interest, the whole of this flimsy structure, this air-blown bubble of "prosperity," was dependent upon a continuance of the high prices of scarcity, and the existing obstructions to the importation of grain.

It is not a little amusing to observe, in the examinations of the committee of 1836, the innocent simplicity with which Mr. Cayley refers, as to a kind of elysian age, to the time when the farmer, with no other security than a growing crop of grain, could obtain from the country bankers advances to enable him to carry on the cultivation of his farm and gather in the crop, from the price of which the advances were expected to be repaid. That such ticklish operations were performed, and in many instances with temporary success, must be admitted; but like those venturous gentlemen, who, speculating in *rouge et noir*, came off winners for a time, the successful performance of one such transaction induced, nay necessitated another, and, as in both cases, constant success could only happen if *all the chances turned out in favour of the speculator*. "The pitcher goes too often to the well."

The year 1814 brought peace and plenty. I can recollect the exuberant rejoicings of that time, the transparencies of "Peace and Plenty," and the illuminated cornucopias with which the inhabitants of my native district (one entirely agricultural) celebrated the nation's deliverance from a twenty years' war, though I little thought how busily our representatives were then engaged in devising an artificial scarcity. The conditions upon which these reckless agricultural speculations could alone succeed having altogether failed, the failures amongst farmers and land speculators became very numerous, and many of the country bankers, who had been in effect co-speculators with them, failed also. This occasioned some reduction in the amount of the currency, which, therefore, rapidly increased in value: in 1817 and 1818, the depreciation of the circulating medium was only 2*l.* 13*s.* 2*d.* per cent.; in 1819, when cash payments were resumed, the depreciation was 4*l.* 9*s.* per cent., and in 1821, the real and nominal value of the currency became identical. From analogous causes a great fall in the prices of all other commodities between 1814 and 1817. The shipping interest was depressed, because the impediments arising out of the war being removed, the same amount of tonnage was equal to extended service; much shipping had been discharged from the transport service; and the reduced price of timber had naturally lessened the value of existing shipping. House property, also, declined in value from the greater cheapness of building materials. Of that fall, previous to 1818, Mr. Tooke says (vol. ii, p. 12), "Of that great "and memorable fall of prices, the principal part be-

" yond that which was the effect of the seasons, and a " recoil from extravagant speculations in exportable " commodities, is clearly attributable to the transition " from war to peace; not from war, as having caused " an extra demand, but as having obstructed the " supply, and increased the cost of production; nor " to peace, as having been attended with diminished " consumption, but as having extended the sources of " supply, and reduced the cost of production." It is certain, however, that notwithstanding the sufferings of particular classes, and the temporary want of employment in some trades, that the mass of the community greatly benefited by the return of peace and abundance. From that time the real wages of workmen became much higher by reason of the cheapness of all the necessaries of life; and it is only necessary to glance at the progress of trade, in the interval between 1814 and 1821, to find there is no reason to regret the times of scarcity and high prices.

In 1814 the merchant shipping of the United Kingdom consisted of 8,975 vessels, of 1,209,248 tons, manned by 83,793 seamen, which had increased in 1817 to 11,255 ships, of 1,625,121 tons, and 97,273 seamen. In 1818 a great extension of import trade occurred, and the shipping was 13,006 vessels, of 1,886,394 tons, and 111,880 men: from this there was a reaction, but by 1822 the shipping employed was about equal in number, tonnage, and seamen that of 1817. Wool, silk, and cotton were also imported in largely increasing, and as it proved for a time, in excessive quantities. Still, though loss was incurred by speculations in those articles in 1819, the quantities of them since imported and consumed have steadily and largely increased. The state of the revenue of 1821—particularly of the excise and customs—proves also the increased prosperity enjoyed by the mass of the people. The increase of our population had been coincident with our great advance in manufacturing industry, and a very considerable part of that increase up to 1821, was the result of the extraordinary diminution that had taken place in the rate of mortality. In 1780 the rate of mortality in England and Wales was in the ratio of 1 in 40; that, in fact, one-fortieth part of the whole population died annually; in 1790 the rate was reduced to 1 in 45; in 1801 the rate of mortality from the scarcity of that year was much increased, but on an average of the four or five preceding years it was 1 in 47; in 1811 the mortality was 1 in 52; in 1821, only 1 in 58, marking a regular progression in the comforts obtained by the numerous classes.

Let us now look at the state of the agricultural interest in 1821, as disclosed by the report of the committee of the House of Commons in that year. This committee was expressly appointed to consider "the "petitions complaining of the depressed state of agri-"culture:" and they reported in substance—That the then present prices of corn, appeared by no means adequate to the charge of raising it, the tenant having to pay from his capital a considerable portion of his outgoings. That notwithstanding this pressure on the farmer must have affected the retail shopkeepers in country towns, official documents proved that the consumption of articles, the subjects of excise and customs' duties, had increased in 1820, when compared with an average of the three preceding years. That our principal manufactures had also increased. Rents had hitherto been paid without arrear, except in particular districts, "*a punctuality affording a hope that the te-*" *nantry possess resources which will enable them to sur-*" *mount their difficulties,*" and that landlords had, in many instances, lowered their rents, not only on new leases but on subsisting contracts. That revulsions of the same nature, if not in the same degree, had occurred in different periods of our history, particularly in 1804 and 1814. That the statements and opinions then given on the ruinous operation of low prices, strikingly conformed with those contained in the evidence annexed to the report. That the fears of those who reasoned on the continuance of low prices, were naturally dissipated by the natural course of seasons and events. That in agriculture, and in all pursuits in which capital and industry are embarked, there had been and would be periods of reaction, a reaction proportioned to the previous prosperity of the pursuit, and the degree of personal exertion and investment of capital, prompted by that prosperity. That *there exists in the distribution of capital and labour a natural tendency to remedy such disorders, and any interference on the part of the legislature had often operated to prolong them.*

That the increase of rent during the war was owing to the diminished value of the currency, and *the extensive investment of capital in land;* but the proportion to be ascribed to either cause could not be accurately defined. That to the restoration of the currency the committee ascribed a part of the depression of prices, but expressed a belief, that the *ultimate effect on rent, of a resumption of cash payments,* would fall far short of some of the predictions suggested by the present alarm. That the diminution of rent, from this cause, could not, in the end, exceed that part of the increase which grew out of the depreciation, perhaps it might not go so far.

That commodities had fallen in other countries, in at least an equal proportion to the fall of corn in England, and that such derangements were produced by the convulsions of the past thirty years, and which would not *cease until the habits and dealings of individuals, as well as the intercourse of nations, should have become adjusted to that state likely to become again the permanent condition of society.* That the then depression of the corn market was the result, not of the large importations of 1817 and 1818, but of the abundant crops at home in 1819, 1820; and that the supply of wheat from Ireland had greatly increased since 1806, when free import was "so judiciously" permitted. The report then took an historical view of the corn laws and corn trade in this country, which concludes with the opinion, "*that the only solid foundation of agricultural prosperity is laid in abstaining as much as possible from interfering, either by protection or prohibition, with any branch of industry.*" The report distinct y suggests, "that if we should create, by artificial means, too great a difference between the cost of subsistence in this and in other countries, it might have the effect of driving capital abroad, *and of leaving our unpaid population to be maintained by the landed interest with diminished resources.*"

The disadvantages of the law of 1815 appeared to the committee to be, that it prompted the grower to extend the home cultivation, by the hope of a monopoly price, while its occasional interruption might deprive him of it when most wanted. To the consumer and dealer it baffled all calculation. At one time, it exposed our market to be occasionally overloaded with foreign corn; at another, in the event of a considerable deficiency in our own harvest, it created a competition on the Continent, by the effect of which prices were rapidly raised against us. Who can venture to deny that the above is an accurate account of the operation, not only of the corn law of 1815, but of every other corn law since enacted? The report also refers to the fluctuations in the price of corn as dependent on our own seasons, and says, that as favourable or unfavourable seasons occur, not at short intervals, but at rather long cycles, and irregularly, *the situation of the grower of corn is rendered hazardous in a country in which the lowest price accounted necessary to afford him a remuneration considerably exceeds the prices of the rest of the world.* And the committee finally recommended a "repeal of the then present law, and to lay open our "trade in corn with all nations, subject only to such a "duty as might compensate to the British grower the "loss of the encouragement arising from the high "freight and other import charges during the war." No particular amount of duty was recommended by the committee. This is an able document, and indicates great progress, on the part of the members of the committee, in a knowledge of the true position and future prospects of the agricultural interest; but they do not seem to have adverted, either in their report or in their examinations, to that which will, in the end, be found the only solution to agricultural difficulties, *viz.* the decreased cost of producing corn in periods of permanently low prices, and the practicability of vastly increasing the productiveness of lands already under tillage, by the application of more capital and labour, and the adoption of improved husbandry.

The report, however, fell still born; it was too much in advance of the sentiment of the House of Commons, and no practical conclusion was founded upon it. Another committee was appointed in 1822, upon whose report an act was passed, by which the limit of total prohibition was nominally reduced from 80*s*. to 70*s*. a quarter for wheat; but then, an import duty of 12*s*. a quarter was imposed, if the price was under 80*s*., *and a further duty of* 5*s*. *for the first three months* after the price should have been between 70*s*. and 80*s*. At a price above 80*s*. and under 85*s*. the duty was to be 5*s*., and an additional duty for the first three months. This law would have been more injurious than that of 1815, but it was not to come into operation until the ports became open, by the average price reaching 80*s*., and as that never occurred previously to the passing of the new act of 1828, it thereby became extinct, without ever having been called into effect. But, valuable as is the report of the committee of 1821, as a testimony of the impolicy of the then corn law, and for its assertion of the general principle of freedom and non-interference, it is in the evidence of the witnesses, in their commonly unconscious testimony *against* protective laws, that, in the present state of the question, the most important matter will be found.

In looking at that evidence, it must also be recollected, that nearly every witness had been marshalled by Mr. Webb Hall's committee of ultra-protectionists, and came forward under the firmest conviction that nothing but an absolute monopoly of the British market could save the agricultural interest from utter ruin.

I mention these circumstances merely to show that the testimony afforded by their evidence *against* protection, has all the value attributable to the testimony of unconscious or unwilling witnesses. I do not complain that their statements were overcharged, and their pictures of distress too highly coloured ; but I assert, that the very facts they mention to prove the necessity for protection, are completely condemnatory of restriction.

Mr. R. C. Harvey, a miller and farmer, from Norfolk, on the borders of Suffolk, largely engaged in the meal trade, and occupying land to the extent of 1,400 acres, partly his own and partly rented, and which he valued altogether at a rental of 1,500*l.*, gave a detailed account of the value, in money, of the produce of his farm. The yearly average for the three years ending in 1813, was 5,538*l.*; for the three years ending in 1816, 3,984*l.*; and for the three years ending in 1819, 6,860*l.* For 1820, his gross receipts were 4,099*l.*, and for that of 1821, he expected when his crops were sold his receipts would be nearly 30 per cent. less. This gentleman was not prepared with an account of his expenditure, though he admitted there had been a "good profit" upon the first and third series of three years, but alleged there had been a loss upon the three years in the second series. He had made no alteration in the mode of cultivating his farm in consequence of the state of the times, and said, that he had in his employ upon the farm *fifty* persons, men, women, and boys—a number admitted to be beyond that which was necessary; but they were employed to keep them off the parish. The farm was stated to be in high condition, and that one-half was in corn, or a fourth of the whole wheat, and another fourth barley. Now, when we find this gentleman with such a superabundance of labour, and farming without any change of system whatever, and that he had made, upon the average of the ten years, rather more than three rents and a half yearly, it does appear to have been a little chivalrous on his part to come and testify to the indispensable necessity of the price of 80*s.* a quarter for wheat, to enable the farmers of England to continue the cultivation of the soil. Any one who knows aught of husbandry will be aware, that with a very little alteration of system Mr. Harvey's farm might have been made highly profitable, notwithstanding a low price of corn. Besides, had he not been chiefly his own landlord, he would probably have thought some abatement in rent, from the scale of 1812, no more than reasonable. So much for this gentleman's direct evidence; incidentally he told the committee that rents in his district had not been generally reduced since 1814, and that the husbandry was in consequence degenerating, farmers having been obliged to pay their stipulated rents out of their capital. This had led to a reduction in their stock, to growing less turnips, and to much double cropping; that though there was no land gone out of cultivation, " there was a great proportion very fast approaching " bad management; farmers were catching at a straw, " and desirous of growing all they could in a year." His own crops had been best when other people's were worst, which he attributed to the high condition of his land; and he said, that fatting bullocks had paid the farmer just at the time, it appeared, the farmers were unable to buy or keep any bullocks to fat. Now, does not all this point most directly to the cause of the evil, *viz.* contracts by farmers to pay rents, calculated on the expectation that the price of wheat would never be lower than 10*s*. a bushel, whereas it scarcely averaged 7*s*.? I will presently show how they dealt with this matter in Scotland, and what has been the result. Mr. Harvey admitted that the farmer would be glad of low prices, permanently low prices, if he could reap equal profits, because he would employ less capital. As regarded the labourers, they were well off when in regular employ, and where they had not been pauperised by magisterial interference. He also stated that his flour trade had increased, and that he sold, on an average, seventy sacks a week more among men he had served for years. This speaks volumes as to the condition of the mass of the people. He was himself then giving his men 1*s*. 9*d*. a day, and had never given more than 2*s*. 6*d*.

Another witness was Mr. Hanning, a considerable landed proprietor in Somerset and Devon. In the former county his property consisted of rich grazing and dairy (permanent grass) land, the "arable a rich "friable sandy loam, capable of being worked at little "comparative expense, and of growing crops of any "description." He had reduced his rents since 1814, taking one with another about 20 per cent.; but the reductions to different tenants were made in very different proportions; some had had more than 30 per cent., and Mr. Hanning had found, that, which I am surprised all landlords do not sooner discover, "assist-"ing poor tenants by deductions of rent was of no use," and he had in consequence adopted the plan of paying for manures, digging, &c., actually applied to the farm. Now, though this was unquestionably wise, if Mr. Hanning thought fit to retain tenants so deficient in the necessary capital, yet what a picture of husbandry in the rich vales of Somerset does this evidence present. In North Devon this gentleman possessed some poor clay land, which twelve years before (1809) had been let at a rent of 500*l.* to a tenant who then possessed 2,000*l.* of capital; that rent had been recently reduced to 300*l.*, but the tenant was then two years in arrear, his capital was all gone, and if a distress had been then made upon him it would not have produced 200*l.* Surely in this case it would have been better, both for landlord and tenant, to have put an end to the holding. Here the tenant's capital had been obviously sunk in the fruitless struggle to keep up rents. It is not surprising that Mr. Hanning granted no leases, and the tenants desired none. His rents, after all his reductions, had considerably advanced since 1792.

What misery and turmoil were here inflicted upon landlord and tenants, through miscalculations sanctioned by act of Parliament!

Mr. Ellman, from Sussex, gave a very similar account of the state of farmers in his district. His own farm had been taken on lease in 1790 at 680*l.* rent, retaken in 1811 at 1,200*l.*, and reduced in 1815 to 1,000*l.*, at which it then continued. Mr. Ellman was a great and successful sheep breeder, and did not assert that his own occupation was not profitable. But he was agent for a large estate, whereon the abatements had been from 20 to 25 per cent., and even as much as 35 per cent. then very lately, on farms taken during the highest prices. The greatest sufferers were on the heavy tillage land. He thought the farmers could pay no rent, except on down farms *where they keep more stock*; that farmers who had commenced within ten years, *with little capital*, must give up their farms. That green crops were getting less, and, for want of capital, farmers were falling back upon the antiquated system of naked fallows. And Mr. Ellman cited a particular case which tells the same story. On one farm of a property he managed, the rent of which was 220*l.*, the tenant, four years before, "kept four or "six oxen, six or eight young growing up stock that he "bred to come into work, and generally four cows. I "found," said Mr. E., "the other day, all the young "stock gone, all the oxen gone, and he had only three "cows; and had taken in four or five horses, which I "saw in the yard treading down the straw, instead of "the oxen and young stock." Can such be the benefits the legislature promised to the agriculturists in giving them, on paper, a close monopoly? Mr. Ellman showed, though with a different purpose, that the then corn law—and every subsequent corn law has done the same—induced the speculator in corn to prefer foreign grain to native, thereby preventing operations, which, in a natural state of trade, would somewhat counteract the depression of price in very abundant seasons. He being asked, "A man buying bonded "corn at 46*s.* has no probability of selling it till it rises "to 80*s.*; but another person buying free corn at 50*s.* "or 60*s.* may sell it whenever he pleases?" replied— "The *precariousness of the seasons in this country is* "*such, that we usually have, once in about three or four* "*years, a very defective crop*, when, if the price does "not rise to nearly or quite 80*s.* a quarter, it is totally "impossible that a farmer, under those circumstances, "can be remunerated: so the speculators in corn "(those who have got money at command) will not "purchase, under those circumstances, British corn at "60*s.* if they can buy foreign corn, though under bond, "at 40*s.*, though the one is free, and the other under "bond at the time." As regards the last forty-five years Mr. Ellman's remark upon the seasons is perfectly just, and the effect of any system, by which the price of corn in this country is kept permanently above the continental level, must have the effect he stated of attracting speculation in cheap years to foreign in preference to British grain. And, in a different part of his evidence, he has stated as a fact, that a part of the then heaviness of the country markets was occasioned by the dealers buying "less for storing up," although they were buying more for consumption. In further confirmation of the improved condition of the labouring many, Mr. Ellman stated, that he was giving his own men 2*s.* 2*d.* a day, notwithstanding the low price of corn.

Another witness, Mr. Rodwell, a farmer and land-agent in Suffolk, gave a similar account of the deterioration which had been going on in the husbandry of that county since 1814. He said there was not then a tenth part of the beasts fattening upon corn and oil-cake there had been a few years before; a fact, which to the farmer is in itself a history of misfortune. The rents were, in many instances, two years in arrear, and "*no abatements of rent would enable many of the then* "*present tenants to go on.*" This is an exemplification of what Mr. Hanning found on the western side of England, *viz.* "that it was of no use to make abate-"ments of rent to poor tenants." Witness after witness stated, that the poverty of the tenants arose either from having originally taken their land without the necessary capital, speculating upon exorbitant prices, or from their capital having been absorbed in payments of rent calculated on a *minimum* price for wheat of 10*s.* a bushel. And, be it observed, no change of system had been adopted by the tenants to meet the alteration of times, except in those numerous cases where they were lessening their green crops, selling their oxen and young stock, and abandoning the fattening of beasts; changes which at once indicated and accelerated approaching ruin. Neither landlord nor tenant seemed to have a conception that rent was to be made in any way but by the accustomed growth of corn, and a great breadth of grain culture, which, though it might have answered under the high prices of 1811 and 1812, *and for a brief period*, could never be permanently sustained. And in such a state of things reductions of rents were literally useless, for in a great portion of the inferior soils the landlord might have given up *all* his rent, and the tenant sunk the whole of his capital in the hopeless attempt to farm under a fallacious system of ideal monopoly. A great many calculations were delivered in by various witnesses, intended to prove, that at the then low price *wheat could not be grown at a profit, even if no rent was paid.* Most of these calculations came from the occupiers of heavy tillage land, or poor clay soils, and they all assumed, as the basis of their estimates, the actual system and the accustomed expenses: where they did grow fallow crops at all, they looked at them with a half grudging eye as an expensive preparation for a grain crop; and, in some instances, where admission was made of a return from the sheep, no other account of it was given than a small price per acre put upon the turnips. Where, however, such calculations were most confidently made, few if any turnips were grown; fallow, wheat, clover, wheat and beans, being the ordinary rotation adopted. Experience has now clearly shown, that except in extraordinary circumstances such a course cannot pay.

The statements made of the rents actually paid, showed that, as compared with 1792, the amount of rent still marked the advanced value of land, though in a few instances loose statements were offered of rents which had been one-third higher in 1814, as compared with 1792, and that a full third had since been abated. Such accounts were in general vaguely given, and invariably referred to poor clay land, to which the observations on the necessity for a change of system, with altered prices, most forcibly apply. When figures were given, a great increase was always the result. For instance, besides those alluded to in the foregoing evidence, Mr. Rodwell mentioned, that in 1796 he had taken the farm on which he resided, on a fourteen years' lease at 300*l.* — the previous occupier having paid at the rate of about 160*l.* — that he renewed his lease in 1811, when the rent was advanced to 500*l.*; and he observed, that at its expiration, which would be Michaelmas, 1822, "there ought to be" an abatement of 25 per cent. Now, though I will answer for it Mr. Rodwell renewed his lease in 1822 with a far less abatement than 25 per cent., yet taking it at that rate, there would still remain a rent of 375*l.* to be compared with 160*l.* in 1792. And one fact stated by Mr. Rodwell, and indeed by several other witnesses, has a most important bearing upon the amount of rent, which was, that in 1821, 2,000*l.* was as good a capital for stocking a farm, as 3,000*l.* would have been in the dear year of 1817. The smaller the amount of capital which can be employed upon a farm for its advantageous cultivation, the larger in general will be the rent certainly the larger proportional rent paid to the landlord, besides affording a greater number of competitors. This is fully borne out by the comparatively high rent paid for permanent pasture land, which requires less capital than an arable farm; and again, by the enormous price paid for hay-farms within reach of the metropolis, which are well and profitably managed with a less outlay of capital than any other description of land *.

Mr. Custance, a London land-agent largely employed, spoke of two particular farms under his care; one of which had been let on lease in 1796, at 248*l.* a year, relet in 1810, at 339*l.*, and again in 1817, at 522*l.*; but great improvements in the last interval had been made, by or with the aid of the lessor. The farm was still (in 1821) held at the same price. The other was let also in 1796, at 341*l.*; relet in 1812 (the year of highest prices), at 768*l.*; and relet again in 1819, at the reduced rent of 674*l.* Now this I apprehend to have been very much such an alteration of rent, as would represent the average reduction upon well tenanted farms throughout England.

Before quitting the evidence of 1821, I must refer to the testimony of Mr. Maugham, a gentleman much engaged as a land-agent in Wales, which strikingly

* I make this remark, taking the state of English agriculture as I find it disclosed by the committees of 1821 and 1833, the general accuracy of which my own personal observation has confirmed, and without reference to the question whether or not the system of convertible husbandry, which has been so successfully in operation in Scotland, is the best course for both landlord and tenant in England. To that part of the subject I shall address myself, after tracing the actual operations of the corn laws on agriculture down to the present day.

confirms my observation with respect to the higher rent of permanent pasture; he said, that rents were very well paid in Wales, and had been but little reduced, which he attributed to the less extent of tillage in Wales, and to the tenants, generally men of small capital, looking to the breeding of stock upon permanent pasture for the means of payment of rent. Now, whatever might have been done by an instructed farmer with large means and the experience of the last twenty-five years, there can be no doubt that the Welch tenant, with Welch means and appliances only, was able to pay a higher rent to his landlord during the period from 1814 to 1821, from his farm having remained chiefly in permanent pasture, than he could have done, had it been converted *by him* into tillage under the stimulus of the prices of 1812.

That an early and prompt adjustment of rents to the altered circumstances of the times was felt, in 1821, by some of the most observant and intelligent persons conversant with landed property to be the true interest of the owner no less than the tenant of the soil, appears by a letter from Mr. Loch to Sir John Sinclair, dated in May of that year, from which I extract the following pertinent passages.

"The present distress* of the agricultural interest " *is permanent*, and one which, in as far as tenants " are concerned, can only be met by a reduction " on the part of the landlords, in such proportion as " the amount of their respective rents may require.

* The writer seems here to have used the word "distress" as synonimous with low prices, and at that time those terms were almost universally deemed identical.

" I am fully aware that such a measure is one which " will not be generally agreeable to the great body of " landlords, and to many it may not be possible. Of " this, however, there can be no doubt, that the sooner " they adopt the resolution the better will it be for " themselves, their tenants, and the country. If they " delay it the tenants will exhaust their capital, *already* " *nearly gone, by the payment of the last years' rents.* " How can it be expected, *but that under the pressure* " *of such circumstances, that they will not bear heavy on* " *their farms.* The result must be the ruin of the " tenantry and the land. The sooner, therefore, the " landlord can make up his mind to this measure, *the* " *richer he will ultimately be in securing a respectable* " *tenantry and preserving the condition of his land.* " And to a certain extent, the effect of this measure " would be less serious to the landlord than at first " sight it appears to be, for the amount of his income " will in a certain degree remain the same, though the " nominal amount be altered, as he can now purchase " most articles of food and raiment much cheaper than " he did*. One class of losses to which the farmer " was subjected is at an end, his having been obliged " to sell cheap what he bought dear, and generally at " a loss. Every thing having now fallen, he may buy " at such a rate as to give him a fair profit, *provided* " *his* rent is *such as* not to run away with it."

To very much the same purpose writes the late Mr. T. G. Bramston, at one time member for the county of Essex, and father, I believe, of the gentleman of that

* How much more strongly does this observation apply in this year 1843 to clothing and other articles of domestic and personal convenience.

name who now sits for South Essex, in a tract published in 1822, and to which my attention was directed by a friend well known in that county*; it is entitled "A practical inquiry into the Nature and Extent of the "present Agricultural Distress, and the means of re-"lieving it." He says, "Parliament may administer "palliations; but the landed interest must place its "chief dependence upon itself; upon the combined "efforts of landlord and tenant; upon their cordial "co-operation with each other." What was the currency question, the extent of its former depreciation, or the proper time of its restoration, to the farmer. "The deed is done, and ought not to be recalled; the "measure is pregnant with future good; but let the "farmer live to see it; let him not be overwhelmed with "present evils; he is as willing to pay, and as well pre-"pared to pay *in produce* as ever." Mr. Bramston then alludes to the imperative obligation to sell upon any terms which an arrear of rent, or a high money rent, imposed on the farmer, as one of the causes of the great depression of prices. This is a cause frequently mentioned by the witnesses of 1821, and it shows how much the occupier is injured by those fluctuations of price which derange the value of land, and set at nought all power of calculating rent. He then puts the "case of an occu-"pier at a rent of 100*l*., set under the supposition that "wheat was to maintain the price of 80*s*. per quarter,"

* D. W. Harvey, Esq. The pamphlet alluded to is a very sensible one, and though I differ from the conclusions of the writer who advocated protection, I was never more convinced, than when reading it, of the impolicy of that line of free trade advocacy, which would mix it up with party politics. The late Mr. Bramston was a supporter of Mr. Canning.

whose "gross receipts were to be equal to four "rents, or 400*l.* The reduction of price from 80*s.* to "54*s.* (the price of 1821) must at once subtract 32¼ "per cent. from the gross returns of his farm, reducing "them to 270*l.*;" and this probably, *the mode of cultivation remaining the same*, is not very far from the practical operation of the law of 1815; for we have seen, that the gross receipts of Mr. R. C. Harvey*, in Norfolk, were upon an average of three years ending in 1819, during which time the price of wheat approached the nominal parliamentary *minimum* of 80*s.* a quarter, amounted yearly to 6,860*l.*, while the average yearly receipts of the three low priced years, ending in 1816, was only 3,984*l.*

The action of such a system on the small farmer is described with full knowledge of the class. "A farmer "of this class possesses no property but the stock upon "his farm; he makes no calculations, he sets apart no "specific portion of the produce for payment of "interest of the sum invested on his farm, or for the "maintenance of himself and his family; but he lives "hard, and the means of a hard subsistence are neces-"sarily taken from the produce of the farm as they are "wanted; for they can by possibility be derived from "no other source." And the protecting duty would leave this man, *even if no rent was paid*, 130*l.* in debt. Then the larger farmer, though he may have made money in the time of high prices, was, in truth, in little better position. Admitting some of such farmers were to be met with, Mr. Bramston says, "And even, in these "cases, if the investigation were to be pursued, it

* Ante, p. 60.

"would probably be found, that the accumulations of "better days are at this time rarely available. They "have been devoted perhaps to the education and ad- "vancement of a son to a higher walk in life; to the "establishment of sons in business, or daughters in "marriage; to the purchase of a farm, or the erection "of a house." By some, such gains were expended in the improvement of the farm, by others in more "costly "diet, clothes, and furniture, and in a more free enjoy- "ment of the amusements and pleasures of life." This is strictly true. I have often heard observations from landlords and agents upon the mode and style in which their tenants had lived, who came, during the low prices of 1822 and 1832, to ask for abatements in rent, and sometimes there was doubtless much justice in such remarks; but it must be remembered that farmers only increased their expenditure during the war, in common with all others, who were benefiting as they were from high prices.

As an illustration of the power of accumulation within the reach of non-speculating farmers, during the high prices from 1793 to 1814, I would instance three gentlemen, brothers, each of whom occupied as tenant, during the whole of that period, a large upland farm—perhaps of 1500 or 2000 acres—in that wide, open district of Wiltshire, known as Salisbury Plain. Each started in life with about sufficient capital for advantageously carrying on his business; but, I believe, without other property. They all lived respectably and quietly, occupying the rank and having the establishments of gentlemen; but they entered into no speculations, they bought no land, I am not aware that either of them ever added to his occupation any other land than the farm or farms with which he originally commenced, and they regularly invested their savings in public securities. They all acted rigidly upon Shakspeare's precept, "Neither a lender "nor a borrower be." Two of them are now dead, and they both left behind them very large fortunes, very far beyond the amount which those who had known the even tenor of their way had thought possible, though they were always believed to be men of considerable wealth. The other is still living, and there is every reason for thinking him no less wealthy than his deceased brothers. It is true, the farms these gentlemen occupied must have required considerable capitals; consisting of light soil, which will grow heavy crops of wheat and barley, provided it is kept in good condition, and which, in that district, is effected by means of large breeding flocks of sheep, for whose sustenance good turnips are indispensable. In this district, the adage of the Flemish farmer, "No corn without manure, no manure without cattle, no cattle without roots," with the substitution of sheep for cattle, has always been an article of agricultural faith.

Tó return to Mr. Bramston's tract, where he says the landlord ought to make an abatement to the tenant in strict conformity to the difference between the real price of wheat and that promised by the corn law. Whatever may have been the case then, I do not think that any such scale will meet the necessity of the present day; but rents must, to use an expression of Mr. Bramston's, "undergo the process of recomposition." Rent must be calculated upon a reasonable estimate of the whole produce of the farm. Tenants have suffered enough, and landlords also, though in a less degree, from the law which induces the farmer (to use a common proverb) "to place all his eggs in one basket." In 1822, the price of cattle, as well as the price of corn, was so low as to furnish an additional cause of agricultural distress. The evidence of the witnesses of 1821 showed, that under the pressure of high rents and other unadjusted burthens, the farmers were rapidly decreasing their stock of cattle, in oxen and young stock as stated in Sussex, and in fat bullocks in Norfolk, Suffolk, and Cambridge, and thus the markets became overdone. It appears that the number of neat cattle sold in each of the two years (1821 and 1822) exceeded by nearly ten thousand the number sold in the years 1819 and 1820 respectively, and the excess of sheep in the two latter years was in even a greater proportion. The same comparative increase occurred at Liverpool, Hull, and other great markets in England. This would sufficiently account for the low price of meat, and mark the deteriorating influence upon agriculture of the law then in operation. Though not within the immediate scope of this tract, I may mention that, under the influence of a section of the agriculturists, the government of the day was, in 1822, induced to consent to a measure for issuing four millions of exchequer bills in loans to parishes, and for the promotion of public works, and to a postponement of the abolition of the small notes' circulation. Both were intended by those who urged them to cause a nominal rise of prices by increasing the currency, and both failed in effecting the intended object.

Throughout the year 1822, prices of grain continued to fall lower than in the preceding year; so much so, that the average price of wheat in the last three months of that year was only a fraction above 38*s*. a quarter; not half the *minimum* price promised by the corn law! This low average was, however, in a considerable degree, attributable to the very inferior quality of the wheat of 1821. That of 1822 was of good quality, and, in the beginning of the year 1823, it began to raise the average, which, in January, was 40*s*. 8*d*.; and from thenceforth, chiefly from the unpromising weather, wheat continued to rise, until in June the average was 62*s*. 5*d*. Though the harvest was wet, the price declined to 46*s*. 5*d*. in October, rising again to 50*s*. 8*d*. in December. The fluctuations of this year were entirely to be ascribed to varying expectations entertained of the harvest, and calculations of the stocks in hand. In January, 1824, it was found, that the crop of the previous harvest had been deficient in quantity and of bad quality; hence the average price rose to 59*s*. 8*d*., and in the next month to 65*s*. 10*d*. This advance in price brought forward larger quantities than were expected; so that the market price of wheat dropped to 55*s*. 4*d*. in September of 1824. The harvest of that year was wet; the average rose in December 63*s*. 6*d*., and the stock in hand becoming reduced, a further advance to 67*s*. 6*d*. occurred in the spring of 1825. Now the feeling of indignation against the corn law ripened into a decisive agitation, and it was sufficiently strong to induce the government to admit, in April, 1825, 525,231 quarters of foreign wheat for home consumption, at a duty of 10*s*. a quarter. Yet this only prevented a rise; for the average price of wheat remained at about 68*s*. the quarter until the commencement of harvest, which proving productive, the average declined, though slowly, to 63*s*. in December, 1825.

This was the autumn of the well-remembered panic, the result of previous extravagant speculations, and wheat, possibly partaking of the universal depression of the period, fell from an average of 60*s*. in January, to 55*s*. 6*d*. in March, 1826. Part of this fall might have happened from the belief that the government would again liberate bonded wheat; for, on a declaration having been made by ministers in Parliament, that there was no intention of admitting the wheat then in bond, the average rose again in April to 60*s*.

Public opinion was, however, too strong to permit the government to persist in that course; for the manufacturing population was in great distress, and from the aspect of the weather and the appearance of the crops, a further advance was apprehended, so that in May, 1826, all the corn then in bond was released. Ministers also proposed to be invested with the power of admitting 500,000 quarters more during the recess in the event of a deficient harvest, and at the same time an alteration of the corn laws, involving some relaxation of the prohibitory part of the system, was announced for the next session. The summer of this year was remarkably dry, and the crops were secured early and in good condition; all, however, except the wheat crop, being greatly deficient. Under an order in council, in September, foreign oats were admitted at a duty of 2*s*. a quarter, and rye, beans, and peas at 3*s*. 6*d*. The average for wheat in December, 1826, was 58*s*. 1*d*. In July, 1827, the price again rose to 60*s*. The wheat crop was a full average, but the grain not of first rate quality; and soon after harvest, 572,733 quarters of wheat and flour were admitted at a 20*s*. duty. The average then fell to 49*s*. the quarter by the end of the year. This brings me to the corn law of 1828, a most important change of system, under which the trade in grain was regulated up to Sir Robert Peel's act of 1842. It will have been seen, from the foregoing survey of the state of the corn markets since 1822, that, notwithstanding the complaints of agricultural distress, a distress sufficiently real, and notwithstanding the vast influence of the landed interest in Parliament, after the fearful years of 1816 and 1817, government never dared to permit the rigid enforcement of the corn law, when the state of the home crops would have given the agriculturist the prices promised by that law. The admission of foreign grain into consumption, which took place in 1825, 1826, and 1827, was a virtual abrogation of the law of 1815; a tacit confession that the monopoly thereby promised could not be enforced.

It was in contemplation of the alteration of the corn law proposed by Mr. Canning in 1827, and afterwards in preparation for the act of 1828, that the two missions of Mr. Jacob to the corn growing countries of Europe, in 1825 and 1827, were undertaken, and which produced his valuable reports on the trade in corn and the agriculture of the North of Europe of 1826 and 1828. It would swell this tract too much to go into any detailed examination of those reports, but it is necessary to state the general effect of them, for the purpose of correcting the extravagant and exaggerated estimates of the quantity of corn which, under a free trade in grain, might be drawn from those countries, and of the low price at which it could there be produced. With the exception of part of Poland, immediately in the neighbourhood of Cracow, the soil of the vast districts of Northern Europe, which we are accustomed to consider corn growing countries, is by no means of such high natural fertility as has been represented; and it has everywhere been cropped to the fullest extent the capital of its inhabitants will permit. Indeed, all the land in these countries has been over-cropped, and the owners have not the capital which would be necessary to restore it by keeping stock. Besides, the climate effectually prevents that system of green cropping which is so successful in all the improved districts of Britain. The winters are extremely long and severe, so much so that winter tares cannot be grown; and the summers, again, are usually so hot and dry, that turnips as often fail as succeed, and spring tares do not produce enough green food to make them worth growing. Mr. Jacob mentions a noble proprietor in Mecklenburg, of great intelligence, who resided for some time in the best cultivated districts of Scotland, for the express purpose of learning the most approved system of husbandry, in the belief that the Scotch farming would be peculiarly applicable to the soil and climate of his own estate. He adopted all the Scotch plans, and persevered for many years with great energy; but, though he obtained a larger produce than his neighbours, the green crops, upon which he necessarily depended to keep the large stock of cattle improved husbandry requires, so frequently failed, either from the severity of winter or the heat and drought of summer, that he finally let his estate according to ordinary terms of the country. Here the climate seems to limit the produce most effectually, for if even the cultivators had the capital (which they have not) wanted to restore to the land the amount of manure that would completely renovate it, the climate would interfere with their operations. The most improved course of cropping in use, is first a year's fallow followed by three crops of corn in succession; then grass, mown one year and pastured for two; in general the rotation is far more scourging than this. The acreable return under such a system is necessarily very small: for instance, in the Prussian dominions it is calculated, that the average increase of the four kinds of grain, *viz.* wheat, rye, barley, and oats, taken together, is not more than four times the seed sown, and not one-fourth of the neat stock and sheep to the same extent of land is kept, as will be found in this country, which fully accounts for the very low standard of fertility. Nor is the circumstance immaterial that Poland, the country upon the whole of the greatest natural fertility, has for nearly two centuries largely exported grain, whilst nothing deserving of notice has been imported which could be converted into nutriment to the soil. Mr. Jacob observes, "the " system of rotation by which two crops of corn are " raised in succession, and nothing is administered to " refresh the land but a fallow (and that is the Polish " system), would exhaust the best soil with which we " are acquainted. In every part of my journey through " Poland, the impression communicated, in looking at " the fields, whether with growing crops, in stubble, or " under the operations of the plough, was, that they " were approaching to a state of exhaustion from " excessive cropping." And this was confirmed by the statistical facts. In the eleven years, ending with 1805, the annual average exports of wheat, from the mouths of the Vistula, were 438,263 quarters; in the eleven years, ending with 1825, the exports from the same ports were only 151,729 quarters a year.

Many parts of the North of Africa, and of Asia Minor, which formerly supplied large quantities of corn to Europe, have since become deserts; and, as the first report justly remarks, "one of the chief causes "of the progress we have made in agriculture, and of "the superior productiveness of our fields, has arisen "from our exporting but few, and importing many of "those articles which are capable, when decomposed, "of becoming manure."

In his second report, Mr. Jacob fully confirms the opinions he expressed in his first. One serious impediment to profitable exportation of corn from Hanover, Mecklenburg, Pomerania, Holstein, and the rest of the Danish provinces, and, in fact, throughout the corn countries of the Continent, is to be found in the state of their roads, which are completely in a state of nature, impassable in wet weather, and rough, heavy, and difficult at all times. Some of the best wheat lands are forty and fifty miles from their shipping port, and much of the wheat at Hamburgh is sent there sixty miles by land carriage. The following statement of marketing expenses would surprise an English farmer, who sends a load of wheat, weighing 4,800lbs., with two or three, or at most four horses. In Mecklenburg, a most intelligent proprietor stated, that he sent his corn twenty-four miles to Rostock by a four-horse waggon, which, from the badness of the roads, can only draw 2,400lbs. in weight, or half an English load; and from this he must subtract 180lbs., the weight of three and a half bushels of corn, carried for the subsistence of the cattle on the journey. Forty-one and a half bushels of wheat only are sent at once, and selling at 3*s*. a bushel will produce the sum of 124*s*. 6*d*., from which, after 4*s*. 8*d*. money expenses, and 10s. 6*d*. horse provender, making together 15*s*. 2*d*., shall have been deducted, will leave the sum of 109*s.* 4*d.* only as the net produce of a waggon-load of wheat. At a distance of forty-eight miles, only thirty-eight bushels could be sent, besides the cattle provender, which would cause an expense of 30*s.* 4*d.* to be deducted from the gross sale of 114*s.*, leaving only 84*s.* 8*d.* net. On rye the expense of carriage is 13 per cent. I remember a friend in the west of England, whose farm was twelve or thirteen miles from his market town, though the road was an excellent turnpike, complaining of the distance for sending his corn as a serious drawback on the value of his property. How would he like to farm on the shores of the Baltic? Mr. Jacob, after mentioning that the English demand for oats, which I have mentioned as having occurred in the autumn of 1826, had quite cleared the Continent of that grain, so much so that the price, in the summer of 1827, was doubled, says, that it is "only when export has been repressed by "restrictions that any quantity has ever been furnished "deserving of notice." And, in reference to Friesland, the land of oats, he says, "From the circumstances of "the yeomanry many can keep their corn in years of "low price, and most feel a pride in doing so; and "though in small portions in the hands of individuals, "yet when it has been pent up by our restrictive laws "for several years, they can pour in such a quantity as "is large for so small a country, though but a mere "trifle in comparison with our regular consumption." And the remark applies with equal force to wheat, which is produced almost exclusively for exportation; the occasional opening of the English market, and the *consequently sudden and high-priced demand* being the prize for which the foreign corn merchant is constantly watching. Now, the testimony of Mr. Jacob's reports and the internal evidence of their accuracy is most satisfactory, completely negatives the possibility of any greatly increased produce of wheat in Northern Europe, except at such an increased cost of production as would put all competition with wheat of our own growth out of the question. But, admitting some increase might take place, yet if it could be brought month by month into our market, in the ordinary course of commercial dealings, without accumulating in such quantities, its effect on our own prices would be comparatively trifling, whilst the consumer would buy corn at a lower rate than under our restrictive system. It would injure the British grower less and benefit the British consumer more than the large quantity of foreign wheat now occasionally introduced in a mass.

The idea, that we exclude foreign wheat by our corn laws, is a mere delusion : we do receive it, and we receive as much, probably more, under the sort of periodical panic in which the importation occurs, as would be imported under a permanently open trade.

Mr. Jacob, in his second report, says, " At the then " present harvest of 1827 it is doubtful if ten days' " consumption of wheat could have been drawn from the " whole Continent, even at an advance of 100 per cent. " on the prices of the period." The reader will remember, that at the period of his visit, which was in the summer of 1827, the continental markets had been cleared by our admissions of foreign wheat in 1825, 1826, and 1827.

Independently of exaggerated statements of the productivenes of the corn growing countries of Europe, made by the friends to a protective system in this country, the appearance of the homestead about a continental farm is such as to give casual observers an erroneous idea of its produce. The house and buildings are enormously large, from the necessity which exists of boarding a great many of the peasants in the farmer's dwelling, and of housing, during a long winter varying from five to seven months, all the cattle, sheep, and live stock of every kind kept on the farm. So indispensable are these buildings, that without them the land itself would be of no value whatever; and, of the whole value of a property, full one-third consists of its buildings. These are, moreover, very expensive to keep up, and the annual outlay for that purpose forms an important item in the cost of production. This expense is incident to the climate; and, perhaps, many readers will remember, that in the account of an agricultural tour in Canada and the United States, made not long ago by that eminent agriculturist Colonel Barclay Allardyce, the want of buildings to shelter the cattle, and the difficulty of growing green crops, where the alternations from cold to heat were so extreme, are mentioned as the chief obstacles to improved husbandry in those countries. There, the as yet unexhausted vegetable soil, the accumulation of innumerable ages, and the illimitable outlet of the "far west," prevent agricultural improvements from being of absolute necessity. Not so on the continent of Europe, where the exhausting process has been going on for centuries, and any large addition to the growth of corn must be had at an increased ratio of cost, which a demand, fifty times as intense as any this country could occasion, would never repay. Though corn might, to some extent, under a constantly open trade, be brought to England from other countries, wherein the soil and the climate render its cost of production far less than in the north of Europe, yet the expense of transporting so bulky an article as corn, and its liability to be heated and impaired in a voyage of any duration would be fully equivalent to the smaller cost price. That cause will ever make the prices of European markets for grain those which will regulate our own. Mr. Tooke, who has always traded largely in the products of the north of Europe, also stated in evidence before the committee of 1821, that very exaggerated views of the cheapness of corn upon the Continent were entertained from casual and temporary circumstances: and he mentioned, that the harvests in Germany, the Netherlands, and the north of France, of 1818 and 1819, were even more abundant than those of the same years in this country. Indeed, all accounts of the foreign corn trade, upon which any reliance can be placed, tend to prove, that the *annual* amount of surplus corn which can be profitably brought to this country is comparatively small, and that all the statements which have been made to the contrary, as for instance, that of Lord Stanley, that 38,000,000 of quarters of wheat could be grown in the Russian province of Tamboff, originated in misapprehension or mistake.

## SECTION III.

### STATE OF AGRICULTURE AND THE CORN TRADE FROM 1828 TO 1842.

FROM 1828 a new era in our corn law legislation commences; absolute monopoly was professedly abandoned by the landed interest, and, in lieu thereof, a shifting scale of duties was adopted, which, according to the declared intentions of its framers, was to secure to the British grower a price ranging between 65*s.* and 70*s.* a quarter for wheat, and other grain in the same proportion, and to protect the British consumer from the effect of any scarcity which should raise the price of wheat beyond about 72*s.* a quarter. In passing I must remark, that the *average* price of wheat has never attained to 72*s.* a quarter in this country, except when the crops of grain here have been exceedingly deficient, and no relief by foreign supply, arising either from peculiar circumstances or prohibitory law, could be obtained. However, the declared object of the promoters of the late corn law was, to strike what they designated a fair balance between protection to the British grower, and dearth to the consumer of corn in this country. The mode of carrying out their object was this: weekly returns of the corn sold were directed to be made from all the principal corn markets of England and Wales, from which a weekly average was to be made up, and at the end of every six weeks an average of the prices of the whole preceding period was again to be made up and published; which six weeks' average regulated the import duties on grain *. When the average price of wheat, ascertained as above mentioned, should be 62*s.* and under 63*s.* a quarter, the import duty was declared to be 24*s.* 8*d.*; and for every shilling the average price fell below 62*s.* a quarter, the duty increased 1*s.* also: thus, when the average price should be 40*s.* a quarter — which had happened before, and has occurred since, the passing of the law now under review — the import duty on a quarter of foreign wheat amounted to 46*s.* 8*d.* Now, as a duty of 24*s.* 8*d.* on wheat at 62*s.* a quarter was clearly a prohibitory one, it is impossible not to coincide with the Lincolnshire member of Parliament, an ardent advocate of protection, who on a recent occasion said, "the landed interest incurred a great deal "of superfluous odium through this scale of duties." On the other hand I must say, they assumed to themselves, and perhaps for a time received, a very superabundant measure of credit for tenderness towards the consumer, as having, by the act of 1828, substantially relaxed the system of restriction enacted by the law of 1815: and, as the average price ascended 1*s.* the quarter, the duty descended at the same rate, until the price

* I have not loaded this Tract with references to other corn than wheat, unless where there happened to be any peculiar circumstances applicable to other kinds of grain; both because I assume, from the ample discussions which have taken place in the last two years upon the corn law question, and from the very accessible forms in which the chief statistics on that subject have been published, that there are very few readers unacquainted with the provisions of the act of 1828.

was 67*s*., and then the duty came down two shillings for every shilling the average price rose; then again, at the average of 69*s*. the duty was 13*s*. 8*d*.; at 70*s*. the duty was 10*s*. 8*d*.; at 71*s*. price, a fall to 6*s*. 8*d*. took place in the duty; at the price of 72*s*. duty fell again to 2*s*. 8*d*., and at 73*s*. to a 1*s*. duty.

It is plain from an inspection of this scale, that its framers intended the duty to be absolutely prohibitory until the average price reached 70*s*. a quarter, and in that respect their calculations have proved accurate, for no imports—none I mean in a commercial sense, as possibly a few accidental parcels may have paid the higher duties—have occurred at duties averaging altogether in any one year so high as 10*s*. 8*d*.; and in only one year, since 1828, has the average rate of duty paid amounted to 6*s*. 8*d*. The effect, also, of the manner in which the averages were taken under the act of 1828, was to produce a somewhat lower, though perhaps statistically a more accurate average than was obtained under the former law, several smaller and more remote market towns being included in the list of places from whence returns were directed; and the requirement of a high *average* price during six weeks to regulate the duty necessarily implies a considerable period of previous high prices. The average, as taken under the law of 1828, is estimated to be 5*s*. a quarter of wheat lower than under the former plan.

The difficulties this sliding scale of duties imposed upon the importing merchant, by introducing a new element of uncertainty into the corn trade, are obvious. Thus it has been said, " Suppose a merchant commis-
" sions a cargo of wheat when the price is at 71*s*. a
" quarter, in the event of the price declining only 3*s*.

"or to 68*s*., the duty will rise from 6*s*. 8*d*. to 16*s*. 8*d*.; "so that if the merchant brings the grain to market, he "will realise 13*s*. 8*d*. a quarter less than he expected, "and 10*s*. less than he would have done had there "been no duty*." On the other hand, if the average price had risen and the duty fallen, the importer would reap a profit beyond his calculations. Inasmuch as the merchant usually calculates on a fair profit, the increased chances of hazard or gain were likely only to lead to reckless and over speculation in the corn trade in seasons of apprehended scarcity. And such has been the invariable operation of the sliding duties. Again, the scale offered irresistible inducement to the speculators in corn to withhold their supplies until the last moment, in the hope of catching the lowest outlet in the "trap," and as this was sure to happen just on the eve of harvest, when the stocks in farmers' hands being most reduced the price is highest, a large supply of foreign corn, as might be expected, always came upon the market in a mass, and entered into competition with the new crop of the home grower, when from the quantity of British corn on sale the market is weakest. The imports thus suddenly made are seldom nicely calculated to the wants of the consumers, being generally in excess, and the necessities of a great body of farmers compelling them to come into the market, let the price be high or low, an unnatural fall of prices is occasioned, to the serious detriment of a large portion of the agriculturalists: and it is notorious that the consumer never benefits by such temporary falls in prices as are thus occasioned. Such were the impressions

* M'Culloch's Commercial Dictionary—article, Corn Laws and Corn Trade, p. 426.

entertained of the effect of this scheme from the first by all who reasoned upon general principles, and every succeeding season has since served to bring it more and more into disfavour with practical men.

The harvest of 1828 was of a varied character; being wet in the earlier portion of the time, the grain in the more forward districts of the east and south of England was carried in bad condition, but the weather having cleared up about the middle of August, all the corn of the northern parts of the island was secured in good condition. The markets quickly rose after harvest, so that the ports became open to foreign wheat at the lowest duty of 1*s.* a quarter, the average price in November having reached 75*s.* 3*d.* The quantity of foreign wheat then imported was 842,000 quarters, which paid the average duty of 1*s.* 9¼*d.* per quarter. There was at the same time a great increase of the imports from Ireland, being 157,349 quarters of wheat and 279,938 cwt. of flour, beyond the importation of the year 1827; the crops too proved less deficient than was anticipated, the surplus of the old stock was larger than had been calculated on, and the foreign importation above mentioned had occurred. These things operating together produced a fall in the average to 64*s.* 7*d.* in July of 1829, and the crops of that year were deficient and badly got in. The farmers, fearful as to the operation of the new law, hurried their damp and inferior corn to market, which depressed the average price at the close of the year to 55*s.* Throughout January and February of 1830, the major part of the British corn brought to market sold under 50*s.* a quarter, but the small portion which came in dry condition fetched from 70*s.* to 75*s.*, whilst fine foreign was worth 80*s.* a quarter. This was a time of severe distress to the occupiers of heavy clay lands, the crops of which were not only deficient in quantity and of low quality, but had been got in at a very heavy expense. The total quantity of foreign wheat imported in 1829 was 1,364,000 quarters, which paid the average duty of 9*s.* 2¾*d.* per quarter.

The winter of 1829-30 was severe, and in the spring so manifest had become the deficiency of the previous harvest, that about 300,000 quarters of foreign wheat were entered for consumption at the high duty of 20*s.* 8*d.* a quarter. This importation was in some measure rendered necessary from the dampness of the home-grown wheat requiring a large admixture of better grain before it could be made into flour; for since 1816 there had been no crop so low in quality as that of 1828. The summer of 1830 proved unsettled, and produced as its usual consequence a good deal of speculation upon the forthcoming harvest; prices rose so much, that in August the average reached 72*s.*, and all the wheat and flour that was in bond or had newly arrived, amounting altogether to 1,400,000 quarters, was entered for home consumption at the low duty of 2*s.* 8*d.* a quarter. This immediately lowered the market to 61*s.* 7*d.* in October; but an opinion having prevailed that the crop of 1830 was decidedly below an average, the average rose again by March of 1831, to 73*s.* 5*d.* The total quantity of wheat imported in 1830 amounted to 1,702,000 quarters, at the average duty of 6*s.* 4¼*d.*

It was in the autumn of 1830 and the succeeding winter, that very alarming riots broke out in the agricultural districts, which were in part occasioned by abuses of the poor law, as administered amongst the rural population of the south and west of England, and were aggravated by the high prices of provisions, and the consequent complaints of insufficiency of wages. The errors and abuses which had existed in the poor law administration from the year 1794, the first rise of which is noted by Burke*, had, since 1814, increased with a fearful rapidity, and their injurious operation upon agriculture formed no inconsiderable part of the inquiries of the committee of 1821. The effects of the allowance system in deteriorating the condition, moral and physical, of the agricultural labourer, and its tendency to stimulate an unnatural increase of the rural population, had become more generally conspicuous in the interval between 1821 and 1831†. A systematic effort has since been made for the removal of these evils, which has been undoubtedly to a considerable extent successful; but the old poor law has left habits and feelings, both amongst the occupiers of land and the peasantry, which have had an evil influence upon English agriculture, and will require time for correction.

The winter of 1830-31 was variable, but the spring was remarkably cold, and it turned out at harvest

---

* Quoted ante, p. 15, 16.

† No one acquainted with the districts, where the allowance system prevailed, can doubt the effect of that system in stimulating a great proportionate increase of the rural population. I remember being present at a petty sessions in the west of England, when a labouring man brought in his son, a mere boy in appearance and manners, and on his behalf applied *for an allowance from the parish for the son's two children*. The magistrates, accustomed as they were to such things, could not forbear expressing their surprise at the youthful appearance of the young father of a family, and asked his age; his father replied, he was *nearly* nineteen, and had been married almost two years.

that the wheat crops had suffered from mildew and other diseases incident to a wet and cold summer. In Essex, and the heavy wheat soils near the metropolis, there was a general deficiency. No less than 1,491,000 quarters of foreign wheat had been admitted into consumption in the spring of this year, at an average duty of 4*s.* 8*d.*, under the speculative opinion that there would be a very general failure of the then growing crops. But the crops of the more distant districts not being so defective as had been anticipated, and the foreign importations having exceeded the effective demands of the market at the previous high rate, the average price went down by December, 1831, to 60*s.* 5*d.* In this year, as in the three preceding years, the average price by no means represented the real effect of the seasons upon the subsistence of the community, inasmuch as the averages were greatly reduced by the large portion of inferior grain which made its appearance in the markets.

The winter of 1831-32 was mild, and the spring not remarkably forward; but the summer was somewhat unsettled, which, in July and August, 1832, raised the average to 63*s.* August, however, was fine, and most of the crops of wheat south of Yorkshire were secured in good order. Some injury was afterwards caused by heavy rains, attended with a warm atmosphere; but, upon the whole, the harvest was well secured, and the yield generally abundant. Prices immediately fell, and the average in December, 1832, was as low as 53*s.* 7*d.* The average price of wheat during the five years ending in 1832 was 61*s.* 2*d.* per quarter, and in that period no less than 5,725,221 quarters of foreign and colonial wheat had been imported into this country. It is not therefore surprising that the committee of the

House of Commons, to whose report I shall presently refer, arrived somewhat unwillingly at the conclusion, that, to a certain extent, this country was habitually dependent upon importations for its supply of corn. In reference to this last cycle of five years, Mr. Tooke remarks, that the average deficiency of produce in this country was such, that had the same obstacles to importation existed, as prevailed during the five years ending in 1813, and if the 44*s.* a quarter, which those obstacles caused, had been added to the price of wheat during the war, the average, instead of 61*s.* 2*d.*, would have amounted to 105*s.* 2*d.*; or, taking the difference caused by the new plan of taking the averages at 5*s.* a quarter, to 110*s.* 2*d.* It must be also recollected that by 1832 the population had greatly increased. At the same time, it is probable there had been some increase of average productiveness caused by improved husbandry; for, as I shall have occasion to show, that notwithstanding the complaints of agricultural distress, which have been so regularly coincident with a good harvest since 1813, the practice of agriculture has been, upon the whole, steadily progressive since the peace.

The year 1833 was one of comparatively low prices (the average of wheat varying from about 51*s.* to 54*s.*), and its commencement was marked by a transition on the part of the bulk of the community from comparative dearth and stagnation to a condition of activity and abundance, and by loud complaints of agricultural distress. The distressed state of agriculture was alluded to in the speech upon the opening of Parliament, and a select committee was in consequence appointed to inquire into the subject.

I now come to the report of the select committee of the House of Commons in 1833, which plainly proves what, in the opinion of the landed interest, was the condition of the agriculture of the kingdom at that period. After referring to the statements of the committee of 1821, that a considerable portion of the outgoings of the occupiers of arable farms could only be paid out of the capitals, and not from the profits of the tenantry, and "that the returns of farming capital were "at that time considerably below the ordinary rate of "profit," the report says, "and no evidence adduced "before your committee of diminished outgoings, contrasted with the change of prices in the interval, "would warrant, at this moment, a different conclusion." The average price of wheat in 1821 was 54*s.* 5*d.* per quarter; the average price of 1833 was stated at 53*s.* 1*d.* per quarter, and, "although some of the "charges connected with general taxation had been "reduced since 1821, the local burthens, such as poor-"rate and county-rate had been grievously augmented." The report then expressed a fear that the difficulties of the occupiers alone remained unchanged, but that their savings, arising from high prices previous to 1821, and which were alluded to by the committee of that date, were "either gone or greatly diminished." The report of 1821 had assumed, that the annual growth of corn in the United Kingdom was, upon an average crop, about equal to the annual consumption; but the committee of 1833 were "satisfied, by the "strongest concurrent testimony from different parts of "Great Britain, that the occupiers of inferior soils, "*especially of heavy clay-land, have of late expended* "*less labour and capital in their cultivation.* This "*neglect*," observes the report, "arising *from low* "*profit and prices inadequate to the cost of production*,

" *combined with a series of wet seasons, peculiarly disad-*
" *vantageous to land of this description,* has caused a " diminution in the gross amount of produce, and the " discontinuance of the use of artificial manures, to- " gether with a system of over-cropping, has *impaired* " *the productive power of these inferior soils;* and in " some cases, where the poor-rate is heavy, their culti- " vation has been entirely abandoned. Moreover, it is " not unworthy of observation, *that these clay-lands are,* " *in many instances, proved to be ancient corn land on* " *which wheat has been grown from time immemorial.*" It was stated that there had been great diminution of the stock of grain on hand, as compared with 1816, when, according to the evidence of Mr. Jacob, there was, previously to the harvest of that year of scarcity, six months' supply of wheat in the hands of the farmers and dealers; and the accuracy of that gentleman's general view was stated to have been confirmed by the local experience of occupying farmers throughout England. Mr. Jacob's evidence on this point is very striking. He says, "I did suppose, at one time, when " we had a harvest in 1816, which was so very defi- " cient, we had then six months consumption in the " country. I do not think there has been a month's " consumption in the country at the time of harvest " since 1829."

**" Q. 64.—Can you form any opinion of what was the cause of the reduced stock in the hands of the farmers ?—A. I suppose, in some measure, the reduction of capital; *they have been paying a good deal of rent out of their capital.*"**

**" Q. 51.—You say that in 1816, preceding the bad harvest of that year, you think there were six months' consumption in store, and recently not more than one month; supposing the harvest of 1816 were to come over again, from whence do you contemplate the**

supply?—A. It could not be supplied from all the world. My opinion is, that if we were to diminish the growth of English wheat by one-tenth of that now produced, we should not be in a safe state in case of a deficient harvest; for all the world could not make up the deficiency. We are now about four weeks in the year deficient in our growth on an average; last year the harvest was one month earlier than the year previous, so that we were enabled to get to the end of the year. The harvest of 1832 ought to supply thirteen months, and I dare say it will do so; but if we have a deficient harvest, and the next harvest gives us but eleven months' supply, and owing to bad weather it be deficient one-tenth more, there would be such a deficiency as all the world could not easily supply at any price; *for wheat is not the food of man in any other country to the same extent as in England.* In France even, where wheat is much more used than in the north and east of Europe, Chaptal states that there are only about 17,000,000 of quarters grown, of which near 3,000,000 is wanted for seed, and that for a population of 30,000,000 persons, whilst we require nearly as much for half that number of persons; yet the French are supposed to be a nation of bread-eaters."

This, and similar evidence, established to the satisfaction of the committee, that the capital of the farmers had diminished, and inferentially proved (as they thought) the hazard of depending to any large extent upon a foreign supply of grain.

The report then went on to say, that the committee had formed a decided opinion that the stocks of home grown wheat in the hands of the farmer and dealer had gradually diminished; *that the produce of Great Britain was on an average of years unequal to the consumption;* that the increased supply from Ireland did not cover the deficiency; and, that in the (then) present state of agriculture, the United Kingdom was, in years of ordinary production, partially dependent on the supply of wheat from foreign countries. The increase of the poor rate, county and highway rates, *as a burthen upon the farmer*, were specially referred to by the report; but the committee, in reference to rent, said, "those outgoings, however, which the "law does not impose, are placed beyond the control "of the legislature, are private bargains open from "time to time and regulated by competition. Who "are to judge what profit, rent, and wages ought to "be? Certainly no legislative authority; for these are "matters of convention, dictated by the reciprocal "convenience of the parties, and silently indeed, but "surely, adjusted to their reciprocal necessities."

The improved condition of the labourer was distinctly recognised. On this subject the report says, "Amidst "the numerous difficulties to which the agriculture in "this country is exposed, and amidst the distress which "unhappily exists, it is a consolation to your com- "mittee to find that the general condition of the agri- "cultural labourer, in full employment, is better now "than at any former period, his money wages giving "him a greater command over the necessaries and "conveniences of life." And a contrast is exhibited between the condition of a Somersetshire labourer, as described before the committee of 1821, and that of the same peasant in 1833. The instance taken from a particular county was declared to be no unfair sample of the improved condition of the labourer in full employment throughout the country *.

* It must not be supposed, because I have only incidentally alluded to this part of the subject, that, from the sources whence I have derived the facts and reasonings of my text, I could not have adduced most abundant evidence of the immense advantages low prices of food bring to the agricultural labourer; but my main object being to show, that the owners and occupiers of land, and

The committee stated, that the Scotch farmer had suffered less from the fall of prices than the English; having been protected by the corn rents, then lately come into general use in Scotland, from the effects of a falling market. In Ireland, as far as the then growing demand of the English market extended, agriculture was improving, and the growth of wheat and other produce rapidly increasing.

The report emphatically adverts to the importance of steadiness of price, and the injury inflicted upon every branch of rural economy by fluctuations in prices. The uncertainty of seasons must frequently cause grievous vicissitudes to all engaged in the cultivation of land; but "artificial fluctuations, whether they arise "from alternations in the value of money, or from "changes in the corn laws, only aggravate the evil; "they *render the income of the landlord precarious*, "*the fixed rent of the farmer a hazardous speculation*, "and the wages of the labourer an uncertain remu-"neration. *Steadiness of price, which is conducive to* "*settled habits and forms the basis of all fixed en-*"*gagements, is the primary object never to be again* "*overlooked.*" The conclusion the committee drew from these premises was, that the then existing corn law, that of 1828, had produced steadiness of price, and that any change in that law was to be deprecated. The report adds, that rents were then rapidly approximating to the level of existing prices, and that

---

especially the latter, have been injured and not benefited by the corn laws — that too being the only ground upon which the protectionists now make any serious stand — I have thought it better not to encumber the principal argument with any collateral topics, however important in themselves.

" the hopes of melioration in the condition of the " landed interest rest rather on the cautious forbear- " ance, than on the active interposition of Parliament."

When the objects for which the appointment of this committee was promoted, and the spirit in which its examinations were conducted—clearly evincing extreme views of the necessity of protection—the report becomes important evidence that restriction had *not* secured to the agricultural interest that kind of prosperity its advocates so vainly sought for. Though some of the members of the committee might have dreamed of altering the law of 1828, by the adoption of a more stringent monopoly, all that was passing around them so clearly demonstrated the impossibility of effecting such a change, and a public opinion of the impolicy of corn laws had been so constantly growing, that the efforts of the friends of " protection to agriculture" were directed rather to preserve the then corn law from alteration, than to increase its restrictive provisions. In obtaining a defensive report, the success of the advocates of the corn law was complete; but the assertion that farming capital was diminishing (with the exception of a few limited districts), is directly contradicted by nearly all cotemporary evidence. The witnesses who were examined generally came with a strong, lingering feeling for the high prices of the war, and their instances of retrograde cultivation were invariably confined to clay soils, a description of land which had been particularly obnoxious to injury from preceding four or five years of redundant moisture. Many intelligent agriculturists had, in 1833, arrived at the conclusion that a somewhat different system of cultivation would become necessary, if the prices of grain continued at a permanently low range; but so completely had the existing generation of farmers been educated to look for profit chiefly from their grain crop, and to base their calculations upon high prices, that it required the experience of another series of variations to make them understand how fallacious such expectations must prove.

That the corn laws, which successively promised a *minimum* price of 80*s*. and 70*s*., mainly contributed to prevent the agriculturists from appreciating their actual condition there is no doubt; and it is equally certain that the only object the framers of those laws had was to keep up money rents. Under certain circumstances, it was apparently the common interest of both farmers and landlords to maintain high prices, and for a long time both classes were satisfied to co-operate with each other, for the procurement of that desideratum, so far as legislative enactment could secure it. But there was also a conflict of interests between landlords and tenants, which, though overlooked while the struggle to visit the consumer with artificial scarcity appeared temporarily successful, became fully apparent when an abundant harvest had cheapened corn below the average level of the European market, by mere competition amongst the home growers. Then tenants began to see, that though they could " pay in produce," that is, though they could deliver to their landlords so much grain, at the prices of corn when they made their bargains as would make up their rents, they could not, when prices had fallen perhaps a third or a fourth, make up their money rents without selling for that purpose such a proportion of their whole produce as was absolutely ruinous. This truth was more apprehended in Scotland than in England, and led in the former country, about 1822, to a very general conversion of the money rents, stipulated for in 1814, into corn rents; and nothing but the fluctuations in price caused by the corn law, prevented its perception throughout the kingdom. Farmers began to perceive, that the existing competition for farms would enable landlords to obtain the largest share of the produce, calculated at prices artificially enhanced by the corn laws, which farmers, when obtaining such prices, could possibly offer, while, if in fact these prices were not constantly sustained, the contract for a farm became merely a catching bargain, which placed the farmer at his landlord's mercy.

Very many sacrifices of capital were undoubtedly made by tenants in the interval between 1821 and 1833, and they fell most heavily upon the occupiers of clay lands from two causes; first, the extreme wetness of the years 1827, 1828, and 1829 had been peculiarly injurious to such soils; and secondly, the farmers on "heavy clay land" had always been in the habit of looking exclusively to wheat, in a greater degree than any other farmers. From the wet seasons, too, the heavy land farmers in many of the most fertile English counties, had been severe losers from the rot amongst their flocks, which prevailed so extensively during these years as to become an important national calamity. The observation of the committee, that the deterioration, which they had reported as having occurred on "heavy clay land," had happened on land "in many "instances proved to be ancient corn land, on which "wheat had been grown from time immemorial," shows that they were imperfectly acquainted with, or were unwilling to admit, the changes which had taken place in wheat cultivation. Nearly all specific instances of loss, proved before the committee of 1833, went to show, either that the landlord had insisted too rigidly upon the letter of engagements made under a mistaken estimate of the prices of produce; or the tenant had expended his capital on land peculiarly fitted for wheat, and with too exclusive a reference to the production of that grain; or some grievous loss, as from the rot, had been suffered from the wetness of the few previous years. It was proved in evidence, that surveyors, in making their valuations, take only the actual prices of the day; and it is plain, that so long as the farmer's rent is fixed on a calculation of prices having a continual tendency to fall, he must inevitably be a loser, if his landlord insists upon the full amount of rent.

I shall not dwell long upon the evidence of 1833, inasmuch as the witnesses examined before the committee of 1836 spoke to the same period of time, with the advantage of an experience derived from three additional years of most exuberant abundance. Some part of the testimony of Professor Low, is however so much in point, in reference to what I have said upon the subject of heavy land, that it ought not to be passed over. Professor Low, who had through life been a surveyor extensively employed in Scotland, to the question, " If you were to be asked as to the value of a farm this " year, to enter at Martinmas next for nineteen years, " and you were directed to be cautious not to mislead " the employer in asking too large a rent, but to put " such a value on the land. as, presuming the corn law " to remain the law, the tenant could afford to pay;

" from your experience of that law, what price would " you put upon the quarter of wheat as between land- " lord and tenant?" replied, " I should have great " difficulty in determining that point. *Valuers of land* " *have generally only occasion to consider the letting rate* " *of land at the time.* I have occasion to know that the " farmers themselves have been recently calculating " pretty much upon the following prices; wheat from " 56*s.* to 60*s.* per quarter, average 58*s.*; barley, 32*s.*; " oats, 24*s.*; and at those rates I conceive, with ave- " rage crops and a good price, a fair price for butchers " meat, the rents now in the course of being stipulated " for could be paid."

Again he says, " In one highly cultivated district in " East Lothian, where the farmers have trusted to " tillage rather than live stock, there has been very " great distress, and a greater fall of rents than in any " other part of Scotland. Here the system has been " to have their lands under a course of constant crops; " the tenants have expended capital largely upon it, and " trusted to larger returns of produce perhaps than in " any other part of Scotland. The district has suffered " from deficiency of its staple produce, wheat, during " three successive years, 1826, 1827, and 1828. In " this district 25 per cent. reduction on the rent has " not been sufficient to save the tenant's capital."

The whole of Scotland had diminished its growth of wheat upon the aggregate, but, with the exception of the district in the Lothians (strong clay land), before-mentioned *not acreably.*

So the evidence of Mr. William Ruddle Brown, of Broad Hinton, near Marlborough in Wiltshire, not only offers a fair specimen of the evidence on which the report was founded; but, as I am well acquainted with the district in which his farm is situated, and, I believe, with the farm itself, I will endeavour to illustrate the testimony by particulars which do not appear in the appendix to the report.

Mr. Brown stated, that he occupied a farm of 1,800 acres, which he entered in 1812, taking to the latter end of a lease which expired in 1817; that on his new taking (for ten years) the rent was reduced "about 10 per cent.," and he continued to hold his farm at the same rent until 1833, when he was about to give it up, "because he found farming unprofitable." The total amount of rent was not mentioned, but the farm was stated not to have been highly rented, in comparison with other land in the neighbourhood. The quality of the soil was very various, some part chalk, and other parts strong clay; the one description of land being so intermixed with the other, that both were frequently found in different parts of the same field. Subsequently, Mr. Brown said, the best of his land was rented at about 30*s.* the acre, with a tithe composition of 7*s.*; and this land produced, on an average, 24 bushels of wheat an acre: the rent of his inferior land was about 20*s.*, and tithe 5*s.* 1*d.* an acre, and its produce per acre of wheat was, on an average, 18 bushels. A large flock of sheep, amounting to 1,400, was kept, and a small dairy. From 1812 to 1830 the sheep answered best, yet they appeared to have been subject to some considerable casualties. In 1821 his flock was infected with the rot from the wetness of the season, and in 1830 no less than 500 sheep died from that disease in four months, and 400 more were sold at 3*s.* 8*d.* a piece. Mr. Brown estimated his loss, in that year, at 4,000*l*. He also stated, that his losses in 1822, when he sold great quantities of damaged wheat at 3*s*. a bushel, had been very serious. The amount of capital originally invested on the farm in 1812 was 8,000*l*., and Mr. Brown expected to realise only 6,000*l*., though he had not sold his last crop, which was then growing; and he believed, that the result of his 20 years' occupation would be the loss of 2,000*l*. the difference in the money value of his stock on entering, and its (presumed) produce on going off. Mr. Brown's account of the prospects of agriculturists was somewhat desponding, and he is one of those who seemed to think cultivation on the clay soils had been deteriorating. He said, that about 15 per cent. had been the average abatement from the war rents in North Wiltshire, but that 30 per cent. must be abated if the then prices of corn continued. Mr. Brown stated, that he employed more labourers than he actually wanted, to keep them off the parish rates; and expressly noticed, that the labourers had never been so well off as at that time. Indeed, the report of the committee as to the improved condition of agricultural labourers sets at rest for ever any question — if such question could ever have been fairly raised — as to the benefits conferred upon farming labourers by low prices of farm produce. The poor rate on this farm amounted to 4*s*. in the pound upon the rack rental. Thus the rent, tithe, and poor rate upon the best land, producing 24 bushels of wheat, would amount together to 41*s*. per acre; and on the inferior, producing 18 bushels, to 29*s*. 6*d*. per acre.

Now it is impossible to read this evidence without being struck with the fact, that no question on the subject of draining was asked by the committee, nor was any allusion thereto made by Mr. Brown, yet he had suffered severely from the rot in his flock in 1821; and, though this loss was so obviously caused by the wetness of the land, yet nothing in the shape of a remedy appeared to have been thought of for nine years, when, from the same cause, a second loss of 4,000*l*., amounting to one-half of the total value of the capital engaged on the farm, was sustained. My own impression is, that no draining was done in that particular district in which Mr. Brown's farm is situated during that interval; and I believe few weeks passed at that time in which I did not ride by or over some part of it. The farm lies upon the shoulder of land between the abrupt termination of the north-western extremity of the Wiltshire chalk hills, and consists principally of strong, deep, and heavy, but not infertile clay, on the chalk marle formation: the southern extremity of the farm must be on the chalk hills, while the north stretches down into the pasture district of North Wilts*. Broad Hinton lies open to the north, and had the reputation of backward land, but I was much surprised to read the small *acreable* produce of wheat stated by Mr. Brown to have been his average crop. The whole of this district is capable of being easily drained, having a gentle inclination throughout its breadth towards the great

* Mr. Ellman, of Glynde, Sussex, whose farm appears to occupy, geologically, a site precisely analagous to that of Mr. Brown's farm in Wiltshire, *viz.* partly on the chalk hills and partly on the deep clay of the chalk marle below the chalk, particularly stated, in reference to the rotting of sheep, that the springy land at the foot of the chalk, *if not most carefully drained*, was very apt to produce the rot amongst sheep.

vale which lies beneath it; and the immediate vicinity of the chalk would render the extensive use of lime of ready attainment, though I believe draining alone to be necessary to render this soil, which is a clay-marle, extremely productive. I am convinced that a too exclusive cultivation of wheat and beans was the great cause of the complaints of such farmers as Mr. Brown in North Wilts.

But taking his own account of his farming, does it bear such a decisive character of loss as to induce an intelligent farmer to withdraw from the pursuit? I think not. Mr. Brown admitted he had made money by his farm, when his losses in 1821, and 1830 by sheep, and in 1822 by a bad wheat harvest, cut down his profit; but even then his loss was confined to the estimated difference of his stock sold off at a period of agricultural depression, having been bought in at the very zenith of the high prices.

No change of system had been made in consequence of the alteration of times, nor had any of those enterprising outlays, in the shape of drainage and liming, by which the Scotch agriculturists met the low price of grain; and concurrently with several bad seasons for the crops on strong land, there was the tremendous loss, by rot, on sheep. This case can scarcely be cited as evidence that the cultivation of strong land was in a "state of progressive deterioration." Mr. Brown was a man of ample means, and I have no doubt he withdrew from farming under feelings of disgust at the loss he had sustained in 1830; besides, he about that time obtained a lucrative land-agency, which rendered a residence in another part of the country more convenient.

Mr. Robert Hughes, another witness examined in 1833, and who had long been much employed as a surveyor and land-agent in Wiltshire, expressly stated, that no land had gone out of cultivation in that county, and that neither the capital employed, the produce of wheat, or the stocks of old corn, had diminished. Yet he was several times led into a *general statement*, that the farmers' capital in Wiltshire had deteriorated, an apparent inconsistency, which a perusal of his evidence shows to have arisen from the fact, that he called the lessened money-value of farming stock a deterioration of capital; a circumstance likely to be strongly impressed upon this gentleman's mind from his having relinquished farming about three years previously, and probably converted his stock into money at prices far below its original cost. Mr. Hughes had held 2,000 acres upon the same stratum of land as Mr. Brown, *viz.* on the chalk marle, and not many miles from Broad Hinton; and probably a comparison of his ingoing during the war, and his outgoing about 1830, presented a difference in figures of considerable magnitude. Such a loss, however, if loss it can be called, is most improperly termed a deterioration of capital; as the stock would have been as effective as ever for carrying on the business of farming. The same thing would happen, on selling off, in almost any business on the stock being realised; and indeed might easily occur, and often has occurred, upon an investment in the funds. Though Mr. Hughes was evidently an ardent protectionist, the whole effect of his evidence is adverse to the views he advocated, and made strongly against the conclusion of the committee, that agriculture was declining. He stated, that within a year or two the rents of as many as 200 farms had been settled by his valuations, and that upon an average the reduction of rents from those of 1814 scarcely amounted to 10 per cent., that he generally fixed the rent without being made aware of the former rental, and his valuation very often exceeded the old rent. The basis upon which he valued was to calculate wheat at 56*s.* a quarter, and barley and oats in proportion: in 1814, and for some time afterwards, he had been accustomed to assume that the price of wheat would be 80*s.* a quarter; and he expressly stated, that the fluctuations of these recent years, together with the uncertainty whether the corn laws could be maintained, rendered it very difficult to make *any* satisfactory calculations. Mr. Hughes, like most of the other witnesses, represented the strong wheat lands as those on which the tenants had suffered most from the low price of wheat, and the three successive wet seasons.

But a period of low prices was then commencing, which no legislative enactments could correct, and which, in three years, taught the agriculturists the absolute futility of protection. The crop of 1832 was an average one; and the summer of 1833 having been dry and warm, the wheat crops, though reported thin on the ground, were found to yield well and to be of good quality. The wheat crop of 1834 was the most productive ever remembered in this country, and, with partial exceptions in limited districts, was secured in good order. This, with the stock on hand, reduced the average price, at the close of the year, to 40*s.* 6*d.* a quarter. The produce of 1835 was little less luxuriant than that of 1834, but the bulk of straw being unusually great, some heavy rains in the last few days of June, accompanied by high winds, laid the crops more extensively than was ever known to have occurred in the same space of time; the wheat never entirely recovered, and the yield was inferior to that of the preceding year, though the harvest was fine, and the new corn came early to market in good condition. The average price, in December, 1835, was as low as 36*s*. the imperial quarter!! Though nobody attempted to attribute the low prices to any thing but the exuberance of three successive harvests, the usual cry of agricultural distress was so loudly raised, that select committees of both Houses of Parliament were appointed to inquire into the nature and causes of the alleged distress. And although neither committee could agree upon a report, the evidence offered to the Commons' committee (which for extent, variety, and importance exceeded that of any former inquiry) left no doubt upon the minds of all unprejudiced persons that the protection, promised to the agriculturists by the corn laws, was entirely illusory; and that little or no compensation was obtained, even by the landed interest, for the mischiefs those laws occasioned to the community at large. It is impossible to read that evidence without being convinced that the cheapness of 1834 and 1835 resulted from plentiful harvests and improved cultivation, which had become partially and silently adopted by a large proportion of the most intelligent agriculturists. And now it appeared that the occupiers of the clay lands had obtained the largest share of nature's bounty, the dry warm summers having been peculiarly favourable to the heavy soils.

Mr. John Ellman, of Glynde, Sussex, said, that "upon clay lands the produce of wheat in the last "three years had been most extraordinary;" and that the increase in quantity upon such soils was quite sufficient to account for the low prices. So favourable were the dry summers to the growth of wheat upon strong land, that Mr. Ellman said the clay soils which usually produced about twenty bushels to the acre, in the two last years had averaged in Sussex thirty bushels, being an increase of one-third. Besides, the fine seed time of those years had occasioned a great additional breadth to be sown. This was spoken to by many of the witnesses.

Mr. Robert Hope, of Haddington, gave a more precise measure of the increase per acre of the wheat crop on his farm in 1832, 1833, 1834, and 1835, as compared with that of 1828, 1829, 1830, and 1831; in the first named years the average yearly produce was 657 quarters of wheat on 175 acres; while, in the four preceding years, the yearly average upon the same quantity of land was only 385 quarters, being an excess of 272 quarters a year upon 175 acres, in each of the good years; and this, though in a small degree the effect of improvement of his farm, arose chiefly from the favourable season. Wheat had not been so low in this country since 1780, which sufficiently proved, that, notwithstanding the vastly increased consumption of modern times, such had been the advances made in the art of husbandry that the produce of the United Kingdom, *in favourable seasons*, was fully sufficient for the increased population.

Some variations of opinion have prevailed at different times as to the sufficiency of the home-growth of corn for the supply of the community. The committee of 1821 said, "our growth is probably equal on an average to our consumption," while that of 1833 thought that the produce of Great Britain was, on an average of years, unequal to the consumption, and that in years of ordinary production the United Kingdom was partially dependent on a supply of wheat from foreign countries. Mr. Jacob was then also of opinion, that, upon an average, 1,500,000 quarters of foreign wheat, or, at his estimate about a month's consumption, was yearly required in aid of our native produce. In 1836 again, the general inclination of the opinions given was, that in ordinary years our production was sufficient for our consumption; and it was shown beyond all question, that in years of such abundant produce as 1833, 1834, and 1835, our growth of wheat was fully equal to the consumption of the United Kingdom, then at its very highest point from the activity existing in all branches of commerce and manufactures. Since 1836, there has been a large yearly importation of corn, and prices, up to the harvest of last year, indicated a considerable degree of scarcity. The question, however, seems not to be very material; because it is clear that in seasons of deficiency, which for the last fifty years have recurred every three or four years, and commonly in periods of several years in succession, notwithstanding the stimulus to grain growing apparently given by the corn laws, some considerable supply of corn must be derived from foreign countries. Every obstacle to importation, therefore, which is interposed, whether by the actual amount of duties levied, or through the jugglery of a sliding scale, must greatly aggravate the sufferings of the community under a bad season. No practicable scheme can secure to the British agriculturist the absolute monopoly of the British market, and all the attempts to secure a partial monopoly have resulted in alternate distress to the consuming public and the agricultural interest; a state from which there will be no relief until the natural laws of supply and demand are left to their unimpeded course.

Few persons, not practically acquainted with agriculture, are aware of the great variations which occur in the productiveness of different years. I have before alluded to the great acreable increase of wheat grown by Mr. Hope in Haddingtonshire, in the four abundant years preceding 1836, over the antecedent four years of comparative deficiency, and Mr. A. Howden adduces similar facts. His wheat crop on one hundred acres of land was—

| | | |
|---|---|---|
| In 1829 ... ... ... .. | 664 | sacks. |
| 1830 ... ... ... ... | 476 | do. |
| 1831 ... ... ... ... | 520 | do. |
| Total of three deficient years | 1660 | sacks. |
| In 1832 ... ... ... ... | 845 | sacks. |
| 1833 ... ... ... ... | 1078 | do. |
| 1834 ... ... ... ... | 800 | do. |
| Total of three productive years | 2723 | sacks. |

Difference in favour of the productive years 1,063 sacks, or an average annual excess of 177 quarters of wheat upon one hundred acres of land. Again, Mr. Arnall, the inspector of corn returns at Boston, Lincolnshire, which is the market for the grain of a wide district, says, that in 1829, 72,964 quarters of wheat were sold in Boston, and in 1834, 131,370 quarters, showing a difference in the produce of that one district of no less than 58,406 quarters of wheat. The variations in price, between the seasons of dearth and those of abundance, may be put in juxta-position with these differences of quantity: the average of wheat for 1829 was 66*s.* 3*d.* a quarter, and for 1836, after three years of abundance, it was 48*s.* 6*d.*; the average of the three preceding years having been only 46*s.* a quarter. Such differences in the quantities of home grown wheat are wholly caused by the effect of the seasons, while the breadth of wheat sown always varies with the seasons, increasing after a year or two of deficiency and high price, and diminishing again after years of cheapness and abundance.

Some of the witnesses in 1836 estimated the difference of the breadth of wheat in different years as high as one-fourth or one-fifth; but a much smaller variation in wheat culture would account for an immense oscillation in price. Nearly all the fluctuations of price, derived from the latter cause, are to be attributed to the corn laws, which have introduced speculation on the price of wheat so largely into the business of the British farmer, who has been too apt to vary his breadth of wheat with the variations of the sliding scale rather than according to deliberately pre-arranged rotations.

Though it is certain that some part of our supply of corn must, occasionally at all events, be obtained from abroad, still the amount required is so small, when compared with our total consumption, and the advantages of the British grower, in his nearness to the market and the goodness of his roads, in his command of capital, and the superiority, upon the whole, of his climate and soil, in his improved and improving knowledge and means of culture over his continental competitor, are so numerous and decided, that it is wonderful the landed interest think their occasional and temporary monopoly—stripped, as the subject has been of many of its exaggerations—worth the struggle and the losses, the heartburnings and distresses, the maintenance of the corn laws has caused, and possibly may for some little time continue to cause, to the British nation. No corn laws could protect the landed interest against low prices caused by the abundance of home grown grain, and from the period of 1836, when that was generally understood, the abandonment of the corn laws became merely a question of time with the more intelligent agriculturists.

The following review of the agriculture of Scotland since 1814, which I have extracted from the prize essay before referred to, and which was written in 1837, bespoke the more healthy tone of self-reliance which had been growing amongst the agriculturists, especially those of North Britain, for some years:—

"But while the progress of improvement in agriculture has gone pretty steadily on to this result, its success has not been, as during the former period, so uniformly great; and its history in this respect displays a more chequered aspect. The great fall of prices, which took place about the close of the war, created a reaction, which soon told with severity upon a numerous class of agriculturists. Rents, which had attained an unnatural elevation, from the confidence inspired by so long a continuance of high prices, occasioned a great embarrassment to the majority of tenants. Hence a period of severe agricultural distress early began to manifest itself. The price of wheat, which for the previous five years had averaged upwards of 108*s.* per quarter, fell in 1815 to 53*s.* 7*d.*, and in the January of the following year to 52*s.* 6*d.*; and although there was a revival of prices to a considerable extent, owing to the deficient harvests of 1816 and 1817, Scotland did not participate much in this improvement, as that deficiency arose from a cause—the lateness of the seasons—which materially influenced the productiveness of the crops in this part of the kingdom. The crop of the following year proved, indeed, productive, but a different result being early anticipated, and alarm being easily excited, from the previous short supplies, an unprecedentedly large importation, amounting to upwards of 1,500,000 quarters in this year, depressed prices again beyond the fair ratio, and occasioned such an accumulation as operated to keep grain under a remunerating price for many years. A severe check was thus given to agricultural energy in many places, generally felt in those districts where operations had been carried on to such perfection as to induce a freer recourse to corn crops than was consistent with the ultimate preservation of the soil in good heart. In East Lothian, for example, at this time, much distress prevailed, until the high rents prevalent there were adjusted according to a principle having reference to the comparative value of grain at this time with that which existed at the entry to the farms. In other cases, leases entered upon during the prevalence of high rents were fast lapsing; and under a more equitable adjustment of rents, a fresh spirit of enterprise ensued, which, favoured by the very difficulties which now presented themselves, excited to new exertions, and gave rise to new modes of management, which proved successful, to mitigate the threatened distress, and ultimately tended to the advantage of both the occupier and the land. We allude to a more extensive system of grazing, which now became prevalent in some of those districts hitherto entirely, and perhaps under any circumstances too exclusively, devoted to the production of corn crops. The agriculturists of Scotland partook also of the depression which characterised the state of the other industrial classes of the kingdom in 1824-5; but since that period, though certainly not at all times in a flourishing condition as respects their finances, they have gone on in a steady progressive state of improvement, and have added, by their economy, ingenuity, and intelligence, greatly to the increased resources of the country. It is by this greater productiveness that they have been enabled so well, in spite of a much lower range of price, compared with rents, to bear up against a course of circumstances which otherwise must have overwhelmed them; and we need no other proof of the further improvement in Scotch agriculture, since the period of the war, than a comparison of the rents during the war and subsequently, with the now decreased value of agricultural produce. It is to be regretted that we have no means, with perfect precision, accurately to know the comparative amount of these rents, but it seems very generally to be allowed that the decline which took place in the first ten years of this period, has been very materially made up by the rise which has since occurred; so that the rental of Scotland, it is confidently assumed, may now be held equal to what it was in 1810*. The rents being then the

* M'Culloch's Statistical Account, vol. i, p. 539.

same in 1810 and 1837, we find the average price of wheat and barley for ten years previous to these years respectively to stand thus:—

| | Wheat. | Barley. |
|---|---|---|
| From 1800 to 1810 ... | 81*s.* 2*d.* per qr. | 41*s.* 5*d.* per qr. |
| " 1826 to 1837 ... | 55*s.* 8*d.* | 31*s.* 4*d.* |

Butchers' meat and wool, we have reason to believe, were also considerably higher during the former period; so that, assuming agricultural capital to have yielded an equal return at the two periods, we are compelled to the conclusion, that in productiveness our fields have nearly doubled since the beginning of the century. Now we know, that though this preliminary assumption is far from the truth, it would be much more incorrect to suppose that the whole apparent difference which this article of price exhibits found its way into the pocket of the farmer of the former period: on the contrary, we believe that the great proportion of this difference of price is made up to the farmer of the present day by increased productiveness, perhaps to the amount at least of 70 per cent. This result, it is confidently presumed, has been chiefly brought about during the period under consideration, and has been mainly effected by the judicious intermixture of the feeding and grazing of live stock with arable culture; by which, not only has the soil been brought to a greater fertility when under culmiferous crops, but to produce all the additional live stock now kept as clear disposable gain. To increase the amount of this live stock has been the chief care of the successful farmer, and has led to many of the greatest improvements in the husbandry of modern days. The great extent to which draining, for instance, has been carried, in a great measure is owing to the desire to produce an additional breadth of turnips, that more live stock may be maintained. Foreign manures have also been introduced, and liberally employed with a like end; and even the climate has acquired great amelioration from the extensive plantations, which have been executed chiefly with a view to afford shelter for sheep."

Both in 1834 and 1835, the hot weather, which was so advantageous to the wheat crops, occasioned some deficiency of barley and oats, and beans and peas; and wheat of the lower kinds was largely substituted for other corn in feeding cattle and swine, and in the distilleries. The immediate effect of the low price of wheat was to diminish the quantity sown in the autumn of 1835, as stated by some of the witnesses before the Commons' committee, to the extent of from one-fifth to one-fourth; and in the spring of 1836 the appearance of the crop was unfavourable. The harvest in the south of Britain, however, was good; but in Scotland and the north of England the crops were so backward, and the weather so cold and wet, that much of the grain never ripened at all, and considerable quantities of wheat were shipped from London and the eastern counties to the north. The crops had also failed in America, and supplies were sent to that country from Europe; and these circumstances co-operating with the diminished breadth of wheat, raised the average, in the autumn of 1836, to 61*s.* 9*d.* The autumn was remarkably wet; much land intended for wheat was left unsown in the northern districts, and the winter set in early with every appearance of rigour. The winter proved cold, the spring of 1837 ungenial, and the crops backward, under which influences wheat, which had again fallen to 53*s.* at the close of 1836, rose in June, 1837, to 56*s.* 2*d.* The weather during harvest having been somewhat unsettled, the average rose in August to 60*s.* 1*d.*; but eventually the crops were secured in tolerable condition throughout the island, and the markets gave way. Some speculators in foreign corn, who had anticipated a low duty, now entered for consumption about 150,000 quarters of wheat at a high rate of duty. This had been the only importation worth naming since 1831; in 1835 and 1836 there was a small balance of exports. The quality of much of the wheat of 1837 was inferior, and the spring of 1838 being cold, the summer stormy and dripping, the average of England rose in August to 72*s.* 11*d.* a quarter. The weather on the Continent was not more favourable than in this country, and though 1,715,771 quarters of foreign wheat were admitted into consumption in that year, at the average duty of 1*s.* 7*d.* per quarter, and 311,914 cwt. of foreign flour at 6*d.* per cwt., the price of grain continued to rise, so that at the close of the year the average price of wheat was 76*s.* 1*d.*

The year 1839 was unusually wet, and the average in January and February advanced as high as 79*s.* 8*d.*, and from thence gradually declined, with occasional fluctuations, to 65*s.* 10*d.* by the end of December. No less than 2,500,045 quarters of foreign wheat at a duty of 1*s.* 11*d.*, and 590,117 of wheaten flour at 1*s.* 9*d.* duty, were entered for home consumption in 1839.

The average price, throughout the winter and spring of 1840 ranged between 60*s.* and 70*s.*, being in March, 1840, 67*s.* 7*d.*, and continued at about that sum up to the beginning of July. Now, up to the summer of 1840, the averages were greatly depressed by the badness of the corn, so that these average prices gave no idea of the extent of the deficiency in the crops. In a letter, addressed by Lord Fitzwilliam to the clergy of England, upon the subject of the corn laws, which is dated 29th of March, 1840, his Lordship observes (after stating that the legal averages do not always afford the true criterion of the price of human subsistence), " that the last harvest " was, in most parts of England, and the whole of " Scotland and Ireland, so unfavourable to the preser- " vation of the crop, that a large portion of the corn

" hitherto brought to market has been totally unfit for " use. The averages therefore have been moderate, " not because it is *plentiful* but because it is *bad.*"

Although the spring of 1840 was cold and harsh, it was dry, as was the great part of the summer. As the harvest approached unfavourable opinions of the crops began to prevail, and a speculative rise in prices occurred, which drove the average for wheat, on the 3d of September, up to 72*s.* 8*d.*, and the large quantity of 1,217,860 quarters of foreign wheat was entered for home consumption in one week, at the duty of 2*s.* 8*d.*: from that time to the end of the year the average quickly declined to 59*s.* 10*d.*, which was the price in the last week of December. In 1840 the total amount of foreign wheat retained for home consumption was 2,011,774 quarters, and the average duty paid was 7*s.* 2*d.*, while no less than 925,722 cwt. of flour at a duty of 3*s.* 7*d.* per cwt. were supplied from abroad. Wetness was again the predominant character of the autumn of 1840, and of the whole year of 1841; and the averages began to rise from the commencement of the latter year until the 10th of September, when the average being 73*s.* 2*d.*, 1,852,619 quarters of wheat were admitted at the lowest duty of 1*s.* From that point the average declined to 63*s.* 9*d.* at the end of the year. In this year 2,236,152 quarters of foreign wheat were imported for home consumption at the average duty of 3*s.* 5*d.*, as well as 531,752 cwt. of foreign flour at the duty of 9*d.* per cwt. Thus, in the four years from 1838 to 1841, no less than 8,463,733 quarters of foreign wheat, and 2,359,805 cwt. of foreign flour had been imported, the chief part at duties so low that the protection thereby afforded to the home grower can only be called nominal. During these four years the manufacturing and commercial classes of the kingdom have been suffering from distress, want of employment, and privation,which for extent, duration, and intensity, have had no parallel in our history; and it is probable that the diminution in the consumption of provisions has, during those years, been greater than even in the high prices of 1812 and 1816: so severe and increasing has been the destitution of the artizan population. This unexampled distress, which has been distinctly traced to the falling off, if not permanent decay, of our foreign trade, has naturally excited a deep and wide-spread feeling of indignation against the corn laws; as those laws have done more, from time to time, to divert and destroy our foreign trade, and to encourage the establishment of rival manufactures in other countries, than all the rest of our restrictive laws put together; yet they are neither few nor innocuous.

But the landed interests have not shown the slightest sign of abating one jot of their cherished protection, and a proposal by the late administration to substitute fixed duties on grain for the sliding scale, led to a dissolution of Parliament, in August, 1841, when free trade, or the maintenance of the existing corn laws became the grand point upon which the general election turned. The result was decisively favourable to the great party now in power, who, led by Sir Robert Peel, received, as the declared champions of the then corn law, the ardent support, not merely of the landed gentry, but of the farming tenantry almost to a man. Yet in spite of the apparent completeness of the victory gained by the protectionists, such was the impression made upon the public mind by a deplorable harvest—the fourth of decided deficiency in succession — and the unabated depression of commerce and manufactures, and so general had become the opinion that the actual system of restrictive law had failed, that the great pro-corn law leader, Sir Robert Peel, was himself compelled to propose an extensive change in the tariff, and to make some further relaxation in the corn laws. To enable him to prepare for these changes, which were obviously a surprise upon his own party, Parliament was adjourned from September, when it had met after the general election, to February, 1842, and the result was—as regards agriculture—the admission of foreign meat and cattle at moderate duties, and the modification of the sliding scale of duties on grain. In the mean time the autumn of 1841 had been as wet as the summer, so that an extraordinarily large proportion of the land upon heavy soils intended for wheat could not be sown, especially as the first months of 1842 continued equally wet. Yet from its previous high price the breadth of land meant for wheat was very large, and much of it was got in, though badly, in defiance of weather. The crops in the spring looked unpromising, and a fifth bad harvest being confidently predicted, speculation in foreign corn became rife, and the more so, as all the great speculators in that article during the previous four years had made large profits. "Extensive orders," I quote from the Mark Lane Express, of the 2nd of January, 1843, "were transmitted to all the continental "ports to purchase wheat at almost unlimited prices, "and quotations were speedily driven up in all parts "of Europe." The summer, however, proved remarkably fine, and something like a panic arose amongst the farmers, under apprehensions caused by Sir Robert Peel's measures, and the indications those measures afforded that the days of protection to agriculture were numbered.

"The finest weather possible," I quote from the same authority, "during the whole of the summer and "autumn, produced a wonderful improvement in the "growing wheat, and instead of a decidedly deficient "crop, which had been all along calculated on, a fair "acreable produce, of a quality perhaps never exceeded, "was secured. This, with Sir Robert Peel's new corn "law, occasioned so rapid a fall in prices, that it soon "became manifest the duty would not fall to the "minimum point; and, with a great depreciation in "the value of the article, importers had to pay an 8*s*. "duty. Then the panic [in the corn trade] begun, "failure succeeded failure, all confidence was de-"stroyed: speculators went first, then the factors who "had advanced heavily were involved, and such an "alarm was created, that corn paper*, however re-"spectable, was, for a period, almost unnegotiable in "the money market." Under such circumstances, a large quantity of foreign corn entered into the home market, competing unnaturally with British new wheat; prices rapidly fell at the end of December last to the average of 47*s*. 2*d*., a fall of 16*s*. 7*d*. on the quarter of wheat since the corresponding month of 1841. In other kinds of grain, the difference of prices was in about the same proportion.

---

*** A banking firm at Wakefield, the great Yorkshire corn market, has recently (February, 1843) issued a circular expressly to notify that they should decline to discount or place to the credit of customers any bill connected with operations in corn.**

The total quantity of foreign wheat imported in 1842, under the old law, was 1,326,173; and, according to Messrs. Sturge's circular, 3,039,521 * quarters had been entered for home consumption under the new law, which, with the fine quality of last year's crop, and the remarkably fine seed time just gone by, will, with an ordinary season, probably prevent any great rise of price during the current year. The number of acres sown with wheat this season is greater than for many years past, and hitherto the crops are everywhere looking well.

Having thus brought down the history of the corn trade to the present time, and before entering upon the consideration of the prospects of agriculture under the new laws which regulate the foreign trade in corn and meat, I will just glance at the effect and nature of our demand upon the corn exporting countries of Europe during the last five years. And the necessary information for that purpose is at hand; the government having, in November, 1841, dispatched Mr. Meek to the north of Europe for the purpose of obtaining information concerning the cost and supply of various agricultural produce in that part of the world. Mr. Meek's report coincides closely with those of Mr. Jacob, made upon the same districts in 1826 and 1828; for he states that, with the exception of Prussian Posen, there are no districts from which any great increase of corn is likely to be produced for exportation, except at rates which would "have a powerful tendency to equalise prices" here and on the Continent; and even that increase could

* So stated in the Mark Lane Express, but I suspect some mistake in the figures; the quantity was however very large, and the exact amount does not affect my argument.

only be expected under the influence of a steady demand, and that time and outlay would be necessary to bring it into operation. The districts in Prussian Posen, which Mr. Meek refers to as "unexhausted by tillage," are without good roads, the effect of which, in enhancing the cost of corn on the Continent, is so fully stated by Mr. Jacob*. I have mentioned the large importation into this country, which occurred on the 10th of September, 1841, and, as an illustration of the effect of our occasioual demand, Mr. Meek, speaking of Bremen, says, "In September last, at the time the "low duty was expected to take place, in the anxiety "of the corn merchants to export all that was possible, "*wheat was bought from the bakers, in as small* "*quantities as eight and ten quarters from each person;* "and an easterly wind enabled the vessels by which it "was shipped to arrive in time." In most of the corn countries, the English demand of the last few years had raised the value and price of land, and the prices of provisions, nearly fifty per cent.; and the result of Mr. Meek's inquiries is, that in ordinary seasons, about the same quantity of grain as has been obtained during the last four years, might be procured from the north of Europe at about 45*s*. a quarter. This presupposes foreign corn to be constantly admissible in England, and the season on the Continent to be an average one.

---

* Ante, p. 81.

## SECTION IV.

THE CORN LAW AND TARIFF OF 1842. PRESENT CONDITION AND FUTURE PROSPECTS OF BRITISH AGRICULTURE.

THE corn law of 1842 (5 & 6 Vict. c. 14), retains the principle of shifting duties, which was contained in that of 1828; the details merely being so altered, that the enormous nominal and practically inoperative duties of the former law are got rid of, and when prices range from 64*s.* to 69*s.* a quarter, the duties on wheat are 6*s.*, 7*s.*, and 8*s.* a quarter respectively. An alteration in the manner of taking the average prices has been made of the same kind, and with the same effect, as that introduced in the law of 1828, by adding a considerable number of small market towns to those from whence returns of sales are to be sent. The most moderate calculations estimate, that by this change the averages are lowered 2*s.* a quarter on wheat, while others rate the reduction of the average from this cause at 5*s.* a quarter. Probably the former is nearer the truth; for though the prices in the obscure markets, now included in the returns, will be a good deal lower than those of the larger markets, the quantities sold will be small in the same proportion: but importation by this operation is covertly retarded till prices rise full 2*s.* a quarter beyond the old averages*. This is the new scale; the highest duty on wheat is 20*s.* a quarter, which is to be levied whenever the average price is under 51*s.* the quarter; at 52*s.*, the duty is 19*s.*; at 53*s.* and 54*s.*, 18*s.*; from thence diminishing one shilling of duty with every shilling of advance in the average price, until such price reaches 66*s.* a quarter, when the duty, then reduced to 6*s.* a quarter, remains stationary until the average price rises to 69*s.* The same diminution of one shilling of duty for every increase of a shilling in the average price then recommences, and goes on until at 73*s.* the duty is 1*s.* a quarter, which ceases altogether on the average price attaining 74*s.*

About the usual proportions between wheat, barley, oats, and other grain are observed; the highest duty on barley, rye, beans, and peas being 11*s.*, when the average price is 26*s.*; and on oats, the highest duty is 8*s.*, levied when the average price is 18*s.*. Similar rests in the scale are established in respect of the duties on other grain as on wheat. Colonial wheat is admitted at 5*s.* duty, when the price shall be less than 55*s.* a quarter, decreasing at the rate of 1*s.* with every rise of a shilling in the average price.

On looking at the weekly average of prices, whenever grain has an upward tendency, it is impossible

---

* I see that Lord Radnor, with a view of showing what has been the effect of the new mode of taking the averages, has moved in the House of Lords for returns—first, of the averages by which duties are regulated under the new act; secondly, the weekly averages on which the duties would have been calculated under the law of 1828; and, thirdly, the weekly averages from the additional towns only, which under the act of 1842 were directed to make returns. When these returns have been received, the extent to which the late act has lowered the averages will be apparent.

not to be struck with the long periods during which the averages range between 64*s*. and 69*s*.; and the rests in the new scale bespeak an opinion in its framer's mind that a duty of from 6*s*. to 8*s*. can be levied upon the greatest portion of foreign wheat imported; and, notwithstanding the transactions of the last year seem to countenance such an opinion, there is no difficulty in showing its fallacy. The experience of the last thirty years has shown, that in this country the average price of wheat can never reach 64*s*., except from an anticipated or actual failure of the wheat crop; and so certainly has the price, after attaining 64*s*., risen to 70*s*. and upwards, that the speculators in foreign wheat may in general safely hold on until the lower duties of 3*s*., 2*s*., and 1*s*. only are chargeable. The fact that a large quantity of foreign wheat paid the 8*s*. duty last year in no way contradicts this conclusion, for the great entries then made were on account of the creditors of broken speculators and failing factors, the result of a complete break-down in the foreign corn trade from speculations undertaken upon erroneous premises, and when there was nobody to hold over the purchased corn. Now, the failure of this speculation was entirely caused by the harvest turning out so much more productive, both as to quantity and quality, than had been expected. The deficiency in the great wheat growing districts of the eastern counties has been satisfactorily proved; but sufficient allowance was not made for the vast growth of wheat in other districts, where the wet autumn of the previous year had been less injurious. This is distinctly pointed out as the origin of the numerous failures in Messrs. Sturge's circular, to which I have before referred, where they say, "The early and favourable

" harvest brought the new grain to market sooner than " was calculated upon, and the operation of the new law " resulted in 8*s*. as the lowest point at which the duty " became payable ; this added seriously to the previous " cost and charges, besides which it absorbed so much " capital, that it lessened the power of importers to " hold, and, in consequence, a much greater quantity " was pressed on the market than either consumers or " speculators were disposed to purchase. Under these " circumstances, *extensive forced sales were made in* " *some of the leading markets, at prices which incurred* " *a loss of from* 20*s*. *to* 30*s*. *a quarter*."

To assume, therefore, that importations under the new law will take place, except at the very lowest rates of duty, from the exceptional and accidental fact of the 8*s*. duty having been paid last year, would lead us into important error; and taking what appeared by the evidence of surveyors, in 1836, to be their calculated price of wheat in the indifferent seasons which preceded 1832, *viz*. 56*s*. a quarter as the average price, the duty of 16*s*. a quarter, then payable, would be as strictly prohibitory as the 24*s*. 8*d*. of the old scale. The modification of the corn law, then, is apparent, not real, whether the interest of the consumer who wants low, or of the farmer who requires steady prices, is considered. Indeed, it is agreed on all hands, that this law cannot be deemed permanent, and there are indications that before the landed interest will be induced to abandon their protective system, a fixed duty of 5*s*. or 6*s*. a quarter will be attempted, for the 8*s*. duty proposed by the late government is confessedly too high ever again to be seriously discussed. As regards the consumers, a fixed duty of 5*s*. on foreign wheat would in its operation be a tax of that amount upon every quarter of wheat sold in this country, whether of foreign or domestic produce; for no foreign wheat would be imported until the price in this country had risen at least 5*s*. a quarter beyond the average of continental prices, and the expenses of transport from the foreign port, with the ordinary merchant's profit. Now every account of the foreign corn markets tends to show that the sudden demands for wheat, which, under the sliding scale, this country makes upon those markets, offer far greater temptations to the foreign merchant than would exist under any system which did not occasionally permit import at nominal duties after a period of virtual prohibition; yet with that stimulus, and the accumulated surplus of the previous abundant years, the average yearly importations since 1838 have been little more than two millions of quarters; and large as such a quantity seems, and restricted as our consumption has been, from the universal depression of trade during all that time, the yearly average prices of the four years have ranged between 64*s*. and 70*s*. 8*d*. Will the country bear a tax of 5*s*. a quarter on its wheat—on every quarter consumed—with the average price ranging above 64*s*.? No one, looking at the temper of the times, the declared opinions of the most influential members of the government, and of the leaders of the Whig party, let alone the growing influence of the Anti-Corn Law League, can soberly believe that such an imposition will be submitted to for the now naked purpose of keeping up rents. It matters not that rents may not in the long run be kept up by a corn law, but so long as consumers on the one hand, and landowners on the other, believe that rents can be sustained by protective duties, and while an exorbitant rise in price is occasionally caused by those duties, a struggle injurious to both parties will be going on.

That consumers, and more especially our great manufacturing population, are in various ways seriously affected by any corn law, is a position nobody at this time attempts to controvert; the only question now is, how will the agricultural body themselves be affected by a free trade in corn? To a dispassionate examination of that question I would direct the attention of the reader. The new tariff has allowed the importation of live cattle, articles hitherto prohibited, at the following duties, *viz.* 20*s.* on each horse or ox; 15*s.* on each cow; 10*s.* on a calf; 3*s.* on a sheep; and 5*s.* on a hog. Fresh meat and salted beef are now admissible at a duty of 8*s.* per cwt., and bacon and hams at 14*s.* per cwt. These changes, when first announced, produced a complete panic amongst the owners of cattle, which the result has shown to be utterly groundless. Of salt beef and pork there will probably be a constant, and, perhaps, a considerable supply drawn from other countries; but that the British farmer should be alarmed by the most open competition with the cattle of any other country does appear to savour of the ridiculous. Hitherto the whole importation of cattle, up to the end of January, 1843, has amounted to only 4,867 head, of which 3,273 were oxen, 753 cows, 660 sheep, and 181 pigs; a result which proves that the terrors of those who feared, as well as the hopes of those who anticipated an abundance of cheap animal food, under the new tariff, were alike groundless. These imports are understood not to have proved profitable to the importers, and there is nothing in the character of the animals, or in the prices at which they can be sold, to tempt the grazier to prefer them to British cattle. That there were ample causes in operation to produce a great part of the fall in prices of cattle which has occurred is notorious, without attributing it to foreign competition; the most obvious of which was the inducement the high prices at which all kinds of animals had sold for several years offered to their production. This is the view taken of the subject by agricultural writers; for instance, the following passage in the Quarterly Journal of Agriculture of December, 1842, in reference to the fall of prices of live stock in Scotland says:—"That "causes exist sufficiently obvious to account for the "greater part, if not the whole, of the fall in the "price of stock, without calling in the aid of the "tariff, however *it* may *morally* have affected the "price, we firmly believe. It is well known that all "the cattle-markets have been *more abundantly supplied* with stock this than last year. This is a consequence naturally to be expected, from the high "prices of the few years back; but besides this, the "lambing seaso nwas so very fine this year that "scarcely a lamb was lost, while last year there were "thousands. This will, partly at least, account for the "recently glutted lamb-fairs of the south of Scotland. "It is well known to graziers that grass has not "fattened well this summer, and this might have been "expected as the effect of long drought upon a soured "state of soil; the condition of the stock has therefore "been low, the contrary of what was the case last "year." And very similar opinions have been expressed by most of the leading agriculturists at their various meetings. The cattle panic may, indeed, be said to have fairly passed away. An observation has, however, been made upon the policy which dictated the opening the British markets to foreign meat, whilst it was kept closed against foreign corn, in which I think there is considerable justice and force. It is said, that the tendency of the tariff and corn law, taken together, is to encourage the growth of corn in this country, and, so far as foreign competition goes, to discourage the raising and fattening of cattle, a system of husbandry the very reverse of that which science and recent experience have alike shown to be the most permanently successful; and I have heard no answer thereto from those who approve of the continuance of restriction against corn, and relax that against cattle, for it is a question only between such persons and the extreme protectionists. One of the advantages to the agriculturist of a trade in corn absolutely free, would be, that from time to time, quantities of inferior and low price grain might be imported and applied to cattle feeding to the great increase of the manure heap; now, under the plan actually adopted, this cheap corn must be consumed abroad, and the benefit of our market for the fatted carcase still offered to the foreign grazier.

When the inquiry of 1836 was instituted, at the instance of the landed interest, the agriculturists had been subject for four years to very reduced prices of corn, caused by four favourable seasons, of which 1834 was probably the most prolific of the present century; while, in the four or five years preceding, the crops had been below the average, and in one, at least, had been decidedly deficient. The cycle of about ten years, comprising about one-half of good and one-half of bad years, had very much a counterpart in the ten years which preceded it: the committee and witnesses of 1836 had the advantage, therefore, of looking back, not only to the great changes consequent on the transition of 1814, but over no less than four or five alternations from abundance to scarcity, and from scarcity to abundance again, in the crops of this country. The committee had passed in review before them three several periods, *viz.* from 1813 to 1816, from 1819 to 1823, and from 1831 to 1836, during each of which, prices of corn in this country were so low, solely from the abundance of the home growth, that the freest corn trade would have made little, if any, reduction in the price of grain; as well as the season of famine in 1816 and 1817, and the dearths and bad harvests of 1827, 1828, and 1829, when, whatever might have been the written letter of the law, no government would have desired or dared to have excluded foreign supplies; for we have seen, that in 1825, 1826, and 1827, when bad crops were feared, although the average had ranged considerably below the then import limit of 80*s.* a quarter for wheat, the ministers of that day felt it their duty practically to abrogate the corn law by permitting considerable importations of foreign corn. The field of inquiry of that committee had also been cleared of the more pressing evils suffered by the agriculturists from long continued mal-administration of the poor law, which had constituted a topic of so much complaint and embarrassment in 1821 and 1833. The currency question, too, had been practically set at rest, for though one or two members, and a few witnesses, gave vent to their figments upon that subject, all those advocates of an alteration of the standard, whose opinions were entitled to respect, had become satisfied, that whatever they would have done in 1819, no alteration could, in 1836, have been usefully attempted. Thus Lord Ashburton said, he did not then advise an adjustment of contracts, and that he "did not see any "interest any persons could have in the depreciation "of the standard, excepting that a debtor might be "said to have an interest in defrauding his creditor. "Nobody could honestly have any interest in the "depreciation of the standard." So Lord Radnor said, "I should see with apprehension any attempt to "alter the standard. I believe that all change of the "standard would be the source of very great calamity; "but if it be done at all, it should be done openly and "avowedly as a change of standard, and not covertly "and by the issue of paper." This, from their own witnesses, would give any reasoners but the currency doctors a *quietus*; and, practically, they are settled, for they can now obtain no audience for their theories.

There were, therefore, no extraneous topics of diversion under the shadow of which the advocates of protection could shelter or disguise their claim to a monopoly of the British corn market; the inquiry thus became a full and direct examination into the causes of the then low prices, and their effects upon the interest of agriculturists and the progress of husbandry.

The case of distress was opened by the Duke of Buckingham (then Marquis of Chandos), who called a number of farmers from the fertile vales of Buckinghamshire, and the rich wheat lands of Essex and Kent, who came prepared to prove that they could not then grow wheat with a profit; and many of them stated calculations of the cost of producing an acre of wheat, which, if sold at the prices of the day, would have entailed a loss upon the grower, and that in many cases without reckoning any payment for rent. To a landlord such statements would have been sufficiently startling, had not his every day's experience told him that these witnesses proved too much. The public, not acquainted with the precise condition of agriculture, set down the statements as nicely marshalled calculations made to serve a particular purpose, and ignorance or bad faith has not seldom been imputed to this class of witnesses. I do not think such imputations are merited. These estimates of loss, and the calls for "a remunerating price," came without exception from the occupiers of deep, strong, and, *in favourable seasons*, most fertile land — land so peculiarly adapted to the culture of wheat and beans, that it is usually designated "wheat and bean land," and has been generally applied, almost exclusively, to growing those kinds of grain. Such land suffers much from wet, whether during the season for owing or subsequently; but in dry years its culture is comparatively easy: then considerable crops may be grown with a small force of manure, and a large return is made for a moderate outlay. Less capital is thought necessary to cultivate land of this description than any other, and from the certainty with which a crop may be grown—subject to the influence of weather—its culture calls for a smaller exercise of skill and judgment on the part of the tenant in the cropping and management of his farm. Such lands have usually been, in the words of the committee of 1833, "old wheat land from time immemorial;" and this has been one cause of their present comparative inferiority, for during the high prices of the war the only art in farming them consisted in growing wheat as often as possible, a rotation commonly used being fallow, wheat, clover, wheat, beans, thus producing wheat twice in five years, a system which had been but slightly modified down to the investigation of 1836. Before the modern improvements in agriculture, meaning some fifty years ago, these heavy soils constituted practically *the* wheat lands of the country, and upon the suitableness of the season to their crops depended the degree of abundance or deficiency felt by the community; but when the growing population, aided by the obstructions of the war, caused the demand for wheat greatly to exceed the supply from the wheat lands, other soils, less fitted by nature for the growth of wheat, were by the application of capital and skill raised into competition with the strong soils in growing wheat. Up to 1814, all and more than all the wheat which could be grown upon land of any description being wanted, the wheat growers of the strong lands did not feel the competition which had been created at home, and their occupiers still continued to look to wheat, and wheat only, for remuneration. Rents, too, were relatively higher on the heavy soils, because from the simplicity in their system of tillage a larger share of the gross produce was, by the economical law which regulates rents, invariably paid to the landlord. Three rents were usually considered sufficient to remunerate the tenant on good wheat land, whilst four and five were the lowest gross return upon which the occupier of the lighter lands based his estimates. This arose from the larger capitals of necessity employed on the latter soils than on the former. In going through the evidence before the committees of 1821, 1833, and 1836, it is impossible not to be struck with the fact that, as a general rule, the loudest complaints and the largest demands for reductions in rents are made by the occupiers of land the most naturally fertile.

In the rich vales of Somerset, according to Mr. Hanning and others, 25 and 30 per cent. of abatement in rents was absolutely necessary to secure their payment, and even then in low years the farmer's capital was trenched upon; and in Buckinghamshire, Essex, and Kent, rents seem to have been altogether paid out of capital, or the tenants and estates have been ruined together; while on the chalk hills of Wiltshire and Hampshire, rents had not been reduced more than about 10 per cent., and cultivation was in a state of steady progression. In Scotland, more than in most parts of England, the farmers were adapting themselves and their modes of culture to the altered state of prices. The Scotch witnesses, one and all, spoke more hopefully of the prospects of the farmer than the English, and they all found their future expectations of profit upon keeping a large stock of cattle, which, not merely furnished a great supply of manure for the grain crops, but became themselves the source of a profit *which was a clear gain.* Indeed stock keeping has, of late, been so generally admitted to be the basis of good and profitable farming, that to cite the evidence to that effect, given before the committee of 1836, would be a work of supererogation. I shall therefore select my notices of that evidence from the parts which bear upon the assertions so confidently made by the protectionists, that a free trade in corn would throw large tracts of land out of cultivation, and annihilate much of the rental of Great Britain. I as confidently maintain nothing of the sort would occur. To the farmer it is a matter of indifference whether he pay a high or a low rent, provided it is calculated upon data which one year with another will give a correct average. To that end there must be steady prices; and it is mere trifling to take the prices of ten years, during which the quarter of wheat has been one year at 70*s*., another at 66*s*., and in others at 39*s*. and 46*s*. a quarter, and, striking an average of the whole, to say the average of the whole period is about 54*s*. as was lately done by the adherents of the corn law in the House of Commons. That the farmer may make real calculations, and not merely haphazard guesses as of late years have been necessary, the range of fluctuations in price must be limited to that caused by difference of seasons, and nothing will effect that end but to leave the farmers and dealers in corn to the unfettered exercise of their own intelligence, sharpened as it is sure to be by self-interest. Fluctuations in the price of corn raised upon a limited area, as within a single country, necessarily occur from the various character of different seasons, and every restriction, which has the effect of lessening the area from which supplies can be drawn, tends to aggravate such fluctuations. That the corn laws have done so in two ways is admitted; *viz.*, by unnaturally increasing or diminishing the growth of grain in dear or cheap seasons, and by promoted exaggerated speculations upon unfavourable appearances in the growing crops, which sometimes result in large supplies when not actually required, and always cause a great mass of corn to be thrown at once upon the market to the injury of the home grower. With a perfectly free trade, small timely supplies, coming in from week to week in the ordinary course of commerce, would prevent any great speculation on the growing crops, and would be sure to be closely proportioned to the probable wants of the community. This alone can give such a degree of steadiness to prices as will enable the farmer to make fair calculations for a lease of fourteen or twenty-one years. All the surveyors admitted the great difficulty they had in fixing rents for a long term in advance; and the very general abandonment of leases since 1814, which has taken place in England, more than any thing else proves the hazards which the corn laws have introduced into contracts between landlord and tenant. Tenants have been naturally afraid to bind themselves to money rents calculated at prices which so often eluded their grasp, and landlords have found in nine cases out of ten, that if the rent was too high the lease was binding only on the landlord, often compelling him to stand by whilst an insolvent tenant was scourging his farm by over-cropping, to the permanent deterioration of the land.

It was principally between 1821 and 1833, that the greatest abatements of rent were made, and that tenants had suffered the largest losses of capital; for, by the latter period rents had been in a great measure adjusted, or the weaker tenants had failed; and, in nearly every instance spoken to in 1836, the losses of capital and failure of tenants had occurred on the strong heavy soils, whilst there also had been the chief abatements of rent. Here, too, the fluctuations in price and the fall from war prices had been most severely felt; and much loss was at one time sustained from landlords not meeting the times by reducing the rent *soon enough*. As a sample of the evidence on this head, I take the testimony of Mr. C. C. Parker, a large farmer in Essex, and extensively employed as a land-agent. He is asked, "what is the condition of the "farmers in that part of the county of Essex with "which you are well acquainted?" and replied, "the condition of the farmers in part of my neigh-"bourhood has been very bad;" and, on further examination, said, that "since rents had been lowered, "not only the new but the old tenants, *having capital*, "had decidedly improved the condition of their farms; "that the reduction of rents commenced about 1823, "beginning with 10 and 15 per cent., and many 20 "and 30 per cent., and some 50 per cent., and even "more than that within the (then) last three or four "years: that he attributed the distressed state of those "farmers very materially to the landlords not prudently "lowering their rents *earlier than they had done;* and "that the total reduction of rent would have been less, "if the rents had been lowered sooner." Mr. Parker also observed, that "he knew farms that men of capital "were occupying, that were 25*s*. and 30*s*. an acre, and "they offered a pound; and those farms have been "since let for 12*s*. to 14*s*., and 15*s*. an acre; and he "believed, that had they been reduced to 1*l*. at that "time, those tenants would then have been in pos-"session of them, and *the farms would never have* "*been impoverished in their cultivation.* It has been "by persisting in the high rents, that the farms have "been worked out of condition, and then no person "would take them except at a very low rent." And he expressly stated, "*that he had never seen more im-*"*provement in draining, liming, and chalking than within* "*the last three years.*" This is very instructive: the last three years referred to by Mr. Parker were those of the very lowest prices, and the farmers *having capital* were directing their attention to precisely those improvements which would permanently ameliorate the texture of their heavy soils, and prepare it for a great increase of stock. Such facts, as those detailed by Mr. Parker, amply confirm all *à priori* reasonings against high prices.

Mr. Parker also said, that there had been a great change of tenantry in Essex, but that the tenants who had left had been either imprudent men, or persons induced by the "very high prices of corn to take farms "without any thing like sufficient capital for the management of them, hoping that if they could survive "one or two harvests the produce of their farms would "give them capital. Many persons were upon their "farms then, whose landlords had met the times by "reduction of rent, whose forefathers had occupied the "same farm from generation to generation, and that "most of them were prudent men and doing well." He also bore testimony to the improtance of keeping stock, and said, that the only "relief to the farmer" would be "rent being in proportion to the value of "produce."

Such is a fair specimen of the evidence of 1836, for nearly every witness confirmed these views upon some point or other. It should be mentioned, that Mr. Parker was an admirer of the corn laws, though, with his clear appreciation of the necessities of the times; it is difficult to understand upon what grounds.

Abundant testimony was also borne to the importance of draining the heavy lands; and the amount of expenditure in draining and liming solely by the tenant, which it was proved had taken place in Scotland, is quite surprising to English farmers. Farmers here and there in England also had drained their land, and they all spoke to its beneficial effects. Thus, Mr. Ellis, who holds a large farm near Leicester, when asked, "if he "had laid out much money upon that farm in draining;" replied, "I have drained nearly every furrow of it that "wanted draining, and I should say it all wanted drain-"ing except about forty acres." And to the further question, whether that draining paid him a fair interest for his money, he answered, "The best interest that I ever "got for any money in my life expended in farming." Now the great obstacle to the practice of draining in England is the enormous expense, amounting according to the Scotch witnesses to 10*l.* and 12*l.* an acre, which will never be incurred by tenants holding only from year to year. Indeed, tile draining partakes so much of a permanent addition to the value of the property, that I think landlords, under any circumstances, should bear a portion of the cost. But though the expense of tile draining may be greater than most tenants in England are prepared to encounter, it does not follow that they must allow their land to remain undrained. Mr. Ellis stated, that he had drained his farm with straw in the way he had seen practised in the county of Essex, and added, "I have a piece of land that has been drained "in that manner, which has been in tillage ever since: "I grew it with turnips, and I grew it with potatoes; "of course there was a good deal of cartage over it, "but it was as dry almost as any land you will see "during the late wet weather:" and drains so made will last twenty years. Mr. Ellis, also speaking of the superior condition of the farmer on light lands compared with the heavy land tenant, said, "The system of grow-

"ing wheat has altogether changed; I remember "twenty-five years ago a notion prevailed that light "land would not grow wheat; now, I believe, it is "found by experience that moderate light land, barley "and turnip land, *will grow upon an average of years* "*more wheat than what used to be called the old wheat* "*and bean lands.*" Yet Mr. Ellis grows on his strong land thirty-six and thirty-eight bushels of wheat per acre, and other grain and potatoes in equally large proportions. The neighbourhood of Leicester gave this gentleman some advantage, as he kept a dairy for supplying the town with milk; but he grazed largely also, and by growing potatoes and mangold-wurzel, heavily manured, in the place of a naked fallow, he had a full supply of food for his cattle in winter, and a great quantity of manure.

The history of the rise of rent on Mr. Ellis's farm shows how the growth of a manufacturing population increases the value of the neighbouring land. The farm, consisting of 374 acres, was taken in 1806 at a rent of 370*l.*; in 1810, it was raised to 444*l.*; in 1826, it was again raised to 700*l.* a year, and had been afterwards reduced to 650*l.* Within the period here spoken of the population of Leicester had increased from 22,000 to at least 45,000.

Again, Mr. George Robertson, a Scotch farmer and land surveyor, said, "The Scotch farmer had always "been looking about. When he saw that wheat did "not pay, he immediately altered his system; when "he found that he had not a remunerating price for "wheat *when the preparation was fallow, he took to* "*potatoes as a preparation for wheat, and he found that* "*profitable both for rearing and feeding cattle for* "*market.*" And this is just what the English occupiers of heavy land must do. A neighbour of mine in Hertfordshire, a shrewd and successful farmer, observed to me the other day on the subject of naked fallow, that "if the land won't pay to grow a green crop, it will "pay less to lie still;" and, accordingly, he has no summer fallows, and keeps an amount of stock quite unusual in that district.

It was a favourite inquiry with the ultra-protectionists on the committee of 1836 to ask the witnesses what was a remunerating price for wheat, and not a few of them were betrayed into naming 60*s*. or 65*s*. a quarter, or some other unattainable price, and which the rest of their evidence went to show to be quite unnecessary to profitable farming. Of course the farmer, like every other producer, is glad to get the highest possible price for his commodity, and he can hardly be blamed for entertaining a predilection for a law which promises him high prices, until he has found out that such promises are not performed.

When Mr. Robertson was questioned as to the remunerating price of wheat, he said, "It depends so much "upon the rotation adopted, because every crop must "be considered as remunerating in its relation to other "crops in the rotation; if one crop does not pay in "itself, yet perhaps it enables another crop, or the "whole crops in the rotation, to pay better, or the "whole course of crops to remunerate." And the same witness, when asked whether he thought that the farming in England was as perfect as it might be, replied; "I do not think so. There is one thing that "strikes me very strongly as to the management in "England, and that is, that generally in large farms

" there is a certain portion of grass land devoted ex-
" clusively to grazing sheep, the other part of the farm
" is under a rotation for cropping far too severe. The
" rotation is frequently a six-shift course, *and very few*
" *cattle are kept.* It occurs to me, that the rotation
" should embrace also a grass course, which would
" enable the farmer to rear cattle, to feed them, to con-
" sume his straw, and by having a greater portion of
" land under turnips and potatoes, to increase the
" quantity of dung and improve the quality of it, by
" which means the land would be kept in better order.
" I cannot see, by the system generally followed by the
" English farmer, *how he can get dung for manuring*
" *his fallow breaks.*" And he subsequently said, " I
" think the potato husbandry might be introduced on
" the cold wet clays of England, after draining, with
" advantage; they may fatten a great deal with pota-
" toes." And further; " I think even upon the cold
" clays grass might be introduced; we grow the finest
" turnips upon clay land, and the objection to poach-
" ing the land is done away with by storing them be-
" fore the frost sets in. The turnips carried home are
" given to the cattle tied up for fattening, and also to
" those in the straw-yards. *Any system of manage-*
" *ment upon clay land, without a sufficient quantity of*
" *stock, must lead to the ruin of the farmer.*" And yet
this is the sort of land which is commonly thought to
be unsuited to stock-farming. The witness also no-
ticed, that the rot in sheep, so much complained of
by the English farmers, would be got clear of by pas-
turing the flock on convertible breaks; and that pastures
long grazed by sheep alone get foul, and are improved
by being pastured with cattle. And a volume might
be filled with passages to the like effect. Now all

this applies to the deep heavy lands and wet cold clays, which are the only descriptions of land where competition with foreign corn is affected to be much apprehended. The truth is, that such a competition would enforce upon the tenants of those soils that system of husbandry, which would at all times be most permanently advantageous to them: if for every thirty acres of wheat they now sow, they were to substitute twenty acres of wheat and ten of mangold-wurzel, potatoes, or grass, for feeding cattle, they would obtain a far greater proportionate profit on their wheat land, with the profit of feeding or rearing cattle besides.

As a practical illustration of the benefits derived from sowing a more moderate breadth of wheat than is usual in England, I may mention the practice of a most successful farmer, who observed to me the other day, that he considered the mere amount of rent as a matter of comparatively little importance, for that the farmer's profits must depend upon his method of cultivation; and he referred to his own system as an example. His farm consists of a stiff and naturally retentive clay soil, which, to use his own expression, "is unkindly but not ungrateful." The course commonly adopted in the neighbourhood is fallow (generally a naked one), wheat, clover, wheat, beans; a rotation, which, notwithstanding the application of a good deal of London manure, is far too scourging, and, accordingly, from twenty-five to twenty-eight bushels an acre is esteemed a fair crop. My friend's system is altogether different. His land has been well drained, and he never uses a naked fallow; his preparation for wheat is two years of fallow or green crops, in succession, as, for instance, winter tares after clover, and rape, &c.

to be fed off after turnips, then wheat, followed by oats, with which the clover is sown. One half of the tares and turnips are fed off by sheep fattening on corn and oil cake, the other half being taken away for stall feeding cattle, and for working horses; many Welsh cattle are also fed yearly. By this system, the produce of wheat is most extraordinary. Once during the last fifteen years, the wheat crop averaged fifty-one bushels per acre; another year fifty bushels; and it has always been considerably over forty bushels to the acre. In one year the wheat crop (wheat and straw) produced in money 25*l.* per acre, and that in a year of not very high prices. Well might this gentleman say "that twenty acres of *good wheat* would pay the rent "of three hundred acres of land." And the same farm also furnishes a proof that such high produce can only be kept up by a steady perseverance in high farming, for the gentleman I have mentioned, being about to quit, has, during the last three years, taken peas and beans instead of pursuing his former plan of a second green or fallow crop, and he says the produce of wheat has already sensibly diminished, and that another round of crops on the same system would, as he believes, bring down his wheat crop to thirty bushels an acre. His neighbours have frequently wondered that he had the patience to wait so long for wheat; but the result has fully proved the advantages of such patient abstinence. It is clearly better to have one acre of wheat of fifty bushels, than two of twenty-five, or even thirty bushels each, for half the seed and other expenses of preparation are saved in the former case, while the second acre of land remains available for some other crop.

Few persons are aware of even the money value of the manure that is made during a winter from a few cattle tied up or in yards. I may mention, as an instance on a small scale, that I last year had three milch cows tied up and kept on hay, grains, and roots, two heifers in the straw-yard getting little besides straw, three weaning calves, two breeding sows, and an old jobbing cart-horse, more frequently running in the paddock than either in the yard or the stable; and besides this, one horse was kept in the stable for private use. Being about to remove at Michaelmas we had no use for the manure, and it was from time to time sold, as it accumulated in inconvenient quantities. Now, the manure made by these few animals sold for within a few shillings of *fifty pounds*. All this was made in the yard without poaching the land, or in any way interfering with the routine of tillage. When stock-keeping shall be more generally introduced upon heavy land, there will be a tendency in the rents of such lands again to rise more nearly upon a par with those of lighter lands, from the permanent improvement the former description of soils will derive from a more generous system than heretofore in use.

The condition of the light land farmer, as disclosed before the committee of 1836, even under the low prices of 1834 and 1835, was hopeful and improving. Thus, Lord Radnor, who resides much in the light land district about Salisbury in Wiltshire, said, he "did not think "the agricultural interest otherwise than in a flourishing condition, except where long leases were running, fixed at high rents, which occasioned distress; "but, generally speaking, he did not believe agriculture "to be distressed." Again, his Lordship, in answer to a question whether "the return to cash payments "had prejudiced the cause of agriculture generally," replied, "Not at all: my belief is, that the science of "agriculture has never ceased to go on progressively "flourishing ever since I can remember, and it is pro-"gressing now as much as ever. I rather think that "there has been a great start within this year or two "particularly; there has been greater activity in drain-"ing, which is one great symptom of improvement in "agriculture." His Lordship further said, "the agricul-"tural labourer was then better off than at any time in his "Lordship's lifetime." He also said, that his own rents had been adjusted, and were then principally corn rents, a system which some of the Scotch witnesses described as having been the salvation of the Scotch tenantry. Corn rents were extensively adopted in Scotland in 1822 and 1823, and they have certainly assisted the farmers of that part of the kingdom, more than any thing besides, to pass through the fluctuations of the subsequent years uninjured, though as I shall presently show, that corn is often, as regards the landlord, an unfair measure of the value of a farm. With reference to light land he said, "a great deal of land was brought into "cultivation on the high downs of Wiltshire on account "of the high prices, which are now in cultivation, *and* "*are increasing in cultivation every day*; and that is "very much owing to the improvement of agriculture." And both Lord Radnor and Lord Ashburton—both large owners of light land—expressed opinions that legislative enactment could not help the landed interest; the latter saying emphatically, "I really do not "know any thing you can do for the agriculturists, but

" to tell them honestly that no parliamentary relief is " possible."

This committee could not agree upon any report, but the chairman, Mr. Shaw Lefevre (the present Speaker of the House of Commons), proposed a report holding out those hopeful views and sound conclusions which the evidence so fully justified. He afterwards published the substance of his intended report in the form of a letter to his constituents. That letter has been widely circulated; but I must quote a few brief passages from it to show what conclusions were necessarily drawn from the evidence, for though a majority dissented from their chairman's report, they tacitly admitted its accuracy by abstaining from making any substituted report.

Mr. Lefevre said, the distress was " in a great mea-" sure confined to the occupiers of cold tenacious soils, " and to those farmers who rely upon their wheat crop " as their main source of profit." And he particularly referred to the modern improvement of light lands, which had rendered them fit " to produce wheat at a " less cost to the cultivator than the more tenacious " soils;" to the abundant crops of 1833, 1834, and 1835, as almost entirely the cause of the depression of prices; and to the fact that the corn laws had prevented the adjustment of rent sufficiently early. He further observed, that the yearly tenant was quite as dependent upon his landlord, upon a fall in prices, as the holder of a lease, " because he (the yearly tenant) can-" not realise the same amount for his stock as when " he entered upon his farm; and he will rather sub-" mit to the payment of too high a rent, in the hope "of a recurrence of high prices, than hazard the loss "of a considerable portion of his capital by a sale." The advantages both in Scotland and England, which had been proved to have resulted from stock farming, and the permanent improvements effected by draining, subsoil ploughing, with the consequent extension of turnip husbandry to clay soils, are severally noticed as leading to the conclusions at which he had arrived; *viz.* that with energy, skill, and capital, farmers had little to fear from low prices; and that the best thing the legislature could do for the agriculturists was to free their trade from shackles imposed by impolitic laws, and to avoid delusion and disappointment by any attempts to keep up artificially the prices of agricultural produce. These are the conclusions of a gentleman, who is not only a cautious and enlightened politician, but one of the most skilful practical farmers of the day.

Such having been the really hopeful state of agriculture in 1836, after four years of unusually low prices, we have since had the experience afforded by a cycle of four indifferent seasons with the accustomed concomitant, high prices of grain, which have led to the legislative changes stated at the commencement of this section. One moderately fruitful season and large importations have again brought low prices, and judging from former experience we must soon expect to hear reiterated complaints of agricultural distress. A material change has, however, occurred amongst the agriculturists themselves, since the publication of the evidence of 1836, for though no report was made, that evidence was felt to have been decisive against any claim to parliamentary interference; and up to the session of 1842, the efforts of the agriculturists were confined to the defence of the then existing corn law. From circumstances before alluded to, those efforts completely failed, and I have reason to think there is a growing wish, amongst the occupiers at all events, that the question should be set at rest by an entire removal of all restrictions on the importation of foreign corn. Such opinions have been expressed to me in the most unqualified manner by several farmers, who took the very active parts at the last general election in support of adherents of Sir Robert Peel, *upon the single ground of his assumed intention to maintain the corn law intact.*

Having thus shown, that legislative restriction has neither enabled the landed interest to retain the monopoly of the British corn market, nor to protect the British corn grower from prices falling at times to a level with, or even below, those of the Continent; and that such restriction has been coincident with the most violent fluctuations in price, and the severest pressure upon the consumer, it remains only briefly to trace what, in 1836, appeared to the witnesses, practically versed in the corn trade, to be the working of the corn law. And, finally, I propose to offer some suggestions, applicable to both landlord and tenants, on the probable operation of free trade in corn upon British agriculture.

Mr. James Fison, a corn and wool merchant in Norfolk, and whose business led him to be well acquainted with the condition of farmers in Norfolk, Suffolk, and parts of Essex and Cambridgeshire, stated, that the then low price of wheat had been caused by the abundant supply from the crops of 1833, 1834, and 1835, and he was inclined to estimate those three crops as equal to *four* average years. There was a great return per acre by reason of the fine season, a great increase in the number of acres sown, and the grain was of a superior quality, producing more flour than in average years. Here we have the simple effect of three successive good years producing, by mere home competition, such low prices of grain, that a large body of the agriculturists thought some additional interference in their favour on the part of the legislature was indispensable. But it very soon became obvious, that previous interference and the then existing corn laws had mainly contributed to occasion that distress of which the farmers complained. A premium on wheat growing had been promised by law in securing to the British grower a monopoly of the best market in the world; and when the stimulus thereby created co-operated with three fine seasons, the competition of British wheat growers alone was amply sufficient to reduce prices to the lowest point. Independently of corn laws, a succession of warm and dry seasons—which are always the favourable years for wheat in this country—have a tendency to promote the sowing of a large breadth of wheat, from the circumstance of the farmer being enabled in such years to prepare his ground for the seed with considerable advantage; and when those seasons follow a high range of prices, an undue proportional growth of wheat is inevitable. Against this cause of low prices, the extremest advocate of restriction scarcely ventures to suggest a parliamentary protection; yet the history of the corn trade has shown, that the probable occurrence of cycles of abundant years, of far longer duration than that of 1833, 1835, is never to be overlooked as an element in estimating the future prices of grain. Improvements in agriculture are year by year increasing the productive powers of good seasons, and probably counteracting, to a certain extent, the effects of unfavourable ones; but in cold wet years, such as constantly recur—most frequently several in succession—nothing can prevent an exorbitant rise of price in this densely peopled kingdom, but the knowledge that a foreign supply can be instantly and certainly obtained. Now the corn laws interpose such obstacles to the supply of corn in years when our own harvests are defective, and postpone *all* external supply until prices indicate so great a degree of scarcity, or alarm of scarcity, that, independently of the suffering and loss high prices of food always occasion, all the ordinary operations of commerce are deranged. This is generally admitted, and has been so often clearly proved, that it is unnecessary to do more than advert to it.

But though the corn law restrictions, by giving to the agriculturists in ordinary seasons a complete monopoly of the home market, are the immediate cause of those occasionally high prices which form the basis upon which land surveyors, and farmers themselves, calculate their rents and other fixed money outgoings, they are utterly inoperative in abundant seasons. Mr. Fison, whose means of observation had been so extensive, after stating his opinion, that the corn laws operated very unfavourably to the occupiers of the soil, thus described their effect:—"They give a " complete monopoly of the market, promising, as it " were, in consequence of that monopoly, high prices, " which promise they cannot realise, that is very " evident. Then they operate again to his disad- " vantage, because there is always some latent hope,

" that though prices are low now, they will advance " under the restrictive system; and thus it is, that if " the farmer goes to his landlord when he has " lost money in one year, and relates the case, the " landlord, perhaps, deducts 10 or 15 per cent., but " the landlord entertains a similar hope which the " farmer does, that the corn laws will help him at some " future time, though they do not at present, and, " therefore, he will not make a permanent reduction " in the rent; and if the next year happens to be a " pretty good one, the tenant goes again, hoping for a " similar reduction: the landlord turns round and " says, No, you are now making better prices, and I " shall not allow you this reduction of rent." And the same witness, when asked whether the farmers could grow wheat in competition with the growers of corn on the Continent, replied, "Yes; with the increased " intelligence that is going abroad, they would be " ultimately able to do that, because I do not contem- " plate that our prices are to go down to the prices of " the Continent, but that the prices of the Continent " will more nearly approximate to our prices;" and he added, in illustration, " there are two articles of agri- " cultural produce which are not protected by high " import duties; those two articles are rape-seed and " wool, and both are selling at fair prices." The examination then went on —

" Do you think it would be possible, with wheat at " 40*s*. a quarter, for the farmers to grow wheat to any " extent? Yes, I do."

" What reason have you for supposing the farmer, " supposing his rent to be fixed at a proper level, " could cultivate wheat at 40*s*. a quarter? *Rent I*

" *consider only the residue.* It is necessary to determine what is the proper level before that question can be answered*. I know farmers, young, enterprising, skilful men, who say they can grow wheat at 40*s*. a quarter, and who are doing very well now, having sold a part of their crop at 40*s*. a quarter; *but those are young men of skill* and intelligence; and the fact is, they make their rent, or nearly so, by stock. *The great error of the old race of farmers is, that they go, as it is called, to the barn-door for every thing.* Now I had an illustration of that the other day: there is a person I know very well, a shopkeeper, a man of property; there was a farmer near him, who held a farm of two hundred acres of land, an industrious plodding man, but he could not get a living, and he was literally obliged to give it up from his losses. This person who lived near, a man of business, said he should like to try it, and they told him 'Well, if you give the same price that he did, which was 1*l*. an acre, you shall have it, and we shall be very glad if you will.' He took it upon a lease of 1*l*. an acre, but employing double or treble the capital which the other tenant employed, he has made it answer his purpose exceedingly well; in proof of which, the agent of the estate said that he was *very sorry he had given this person a lease of it at* 20*s*., *for the farm was now so improved, that he could make* 30*s*. *an acre of it*"—an observation, by the bye, which said but little for the intelligence of the agent, *as with-*

---

* See p. 148, as to the comparative unimportance of rent to a good farmer.

*out the lease* the improvement would never have taken place. And Mr. Fison again said, "I have known "repeated instances of old tenants that have left their "farms because they could not live upon them; farm-"ing, comparatively, without stock, and employing "very little capital. Young men have come and "taken those farms, and have done exceedingly well "upon them by employing a great deal more capital, "and conducting their affairs in a more intelligent and "skilful manner." With reference to rape-seed, Mr. Fison thought the demand for it in this country was as certain as the demand for corn, and that the price was then full as high as the average price when there was a protecting duty of 40*s*. a quarter. This witness also said landlords had not looked sufficiently to persons of capital; they have thought more of the present advantage of a high rent than of the ultimate result to themselves in having persons of capital upon their estates; and he again and again reiterated what every other witness confirmed, that the chief distress existed amongst the occupiers of heavy soils. So Mr. Ellis, to whose evidence I have before referred, thought the corn law "gave the farmers an expectation that some-"thing is to come to their relief that can never arrive; "and on that account it holds up the value of land "fictitiously."

Such then were the views, with regard to the corn law, which had begun to be entertained by the more intelligent farmers and corn dealers in the great corn growing districts. I must now shortly advert to the evidence of two other witnesses engaged in the corn trade.

Mr. Rogers Ruding, principally engaged as a corn

factor in the import trade, said, "The (then) corn law "tended entirely to prevent our having a supply from "abroad, *except in cases of actual scarcity;* that it "was far from keeping a steady price, because at the "time of importation we necessarily have high prices; "and, immediately after the importation has taken "place, it alarms the agriculturists, who generally "send a large portion of the corn to market and occa-"sion a reaction. We have then low prices, and in "the event of good harvests very low prices indeed." And the whole scope of his evidence went to show, that by lowering the importation limit the great fluctuations we have hitherto experienced would be prevented: for instance, he is asked, "What would be the "effect of lowering the import price in bad harvests? "In bad harvests it would secure a regular supply of "foreign corn with less fluctuation of price to the "public.

"But with no proportionate increase of the price "of British corn? I do not consider that it would "prevent a proportionate rise in British corn. If "you have a bad harvest in this country *the foreign "supply, which would be trifling, would only prevent "enormously high prices.* The great alteration from "high to low prices has been chiefly from a succession "of abundant crops after importation, and sometimes "from erroneous ideas of the excess of produce, not from "excessive importations." And afterwards, in reply to a question as to the effect of importations after a bad harvest "checking," what the examiner designated, "the "fair price that the English farmer ought to have, from "having less corn than he had before?" replied, that "of "course any foreign importation would check the price

" of the English farmer, and therefore would not be be-
" neficial to him; but with a crop of three quarters in-
" stead of four, *let the importation be the largest ever*
" *known, the farmer would be certain of high prices as a*
" *remuneration for his short crop.*" Mr. Ruding also stated, that 10*s*. a quarter was the proper sum to be estimated as the expense of bringing wheat from the Baltic, except where the importer could sell it at once from the ship without the cost of landing and warehousing, that corn is occasionally subject to much damage in its passage, and that the rate of insurance varies according to the season from 6*d*. to 2*s*. a quarter.

Mr. Hayes, who had long been extensively engaged in trade as a miller, in reference to the foreign corn trade, said, " Foreign wheat, of the average quality of
" British red wheat, might have been bought in Dantzic
" (during the cheap years preceding 1836) at 23*s*. a
" quarter, *in the absence of all demand; but if you had*
" *wanted to have bought* 10,000 *quarters you would have*
" *raised the price immediately.*" And the same witness being asked what he would conceive to be a prohibitory fixed duty, answered, " *It depends upon the nature of*
" *the crop you have in this country.*" In many other respects he confirmed the testimony of other witnesses, and he fully agreed that the protection afforded to the farmer by the corn law was fallacious.

If then, as appears by the concurrent testimony of the great majority of witnesses examined before the committee of 1836, the principal effect of the then corn law was to postpone foreign importations in seasons of scarcity until prices became exorbitant, generally followed by a speedy reaction depressing the price, especially when coincident with a good harvest, below what would have been the natural rate with an unrestricted trade; if rents were fixed upon erroneous data; and if capital was misdirected in attempts to grow wheat on land not adapted for it, or to grow it too often on the soils, once called *par excellence* "wheat lands;" and if the consequence was to induce the occupiers of heavy soils — for it applies almost exclusively to them — to calculate upon returns which they never realise, and their landlords to demand rents the tenants could not permanently pay, whilst the power of the community to consume agricultural produce of all kinds is confessedly diminished by the corn laws, it would seem that in trusting to restrictive enactments and monopoly, rather than to the intelligent enterprise of British capitalists, the landed interests grasp at a shadow, and in so doing risk no small portion of the substance of their wealth.

There is nothing more instructive than the fact, that the tenants of light lands had nowhere—in north, south, east, and west alike—suffered from low prices in any thing like the same degree as the occupiers of the heavy soils, nor had the rents of land of the former kind fallen from their high range of 1812 in any proportion to those of the latter sort. It was to protect the heavy lands that the corn laws had been enacted; the lighter lands had a physical limit to their capacity for wheat growing, imposed by the absolute impossibility of producing it without long and careful preparation, to which ample capitals with numerous flocks or herds were indispensable.

In the result the light land farmer grew nearly as much wheat per acre—perhaps more, taking the average of seasons—as the heavy land cultivator; and though the wheat of the former was undoubtedly an important part of his produce, it formed *only* a part of his routine, and was kept in due subordination to a general system. On the other hand, the heavy land farmer staked his all upon his wheat crop; and his power, either to meet his rent or his other fixed money engagements, depended altogether upon the price that grain might realise: necessity dictated in the one case what prudence would have counselled in the other, had not the natural law of supply and demand been interfered with by restrictive regulations.

I think Colonel Thompson somewhere speaks of an observation made to him on a coach by a Lincolnshire farmer, "that all the rich farmers were found upon "poor land;" and as a general rule that is very nearly the truth, for no man thinks of undertaking the cultivation of a tract of light land without a full supply of capital, whereas the apparent facility of production upon heavier and richer soils tempts men not only to engage in farming them with too little capital, but to offer as rent too large a proportion of the anticipated produce. I am convinced that at this moment the estimation in which the heavy lands of secondary qualities are held is too low; first, because their occupiers have been unduly stimulated to look exclusively to wheat for profit; next, because they are generally occupied by a poor and unenterprising class of tenants; and thirdly, because the great competition which exists for farms has led the occupiers to make engagements for money rents, calculated upon expectations of the produce of abundant years and the prices of deficient seasons. These two conditions never happen together, and one way or the other the clay land tenant always suffers. Let the season be wet, and the crops on the heavy lands will ever be the most defective, and, though the price may be high, the low land farmer has either comparatively little wheat to sell, or its quality is so inferior that it fetches nothing: again, if there be a succession of dry years, when the deep lands are the most productive, the price falls so low that *all* the produce would barely realise the money rent, which has been calculated on a far higher range of prices. Now most of these miscalculations are directly attributable to the corn laws, and the way in which they have created a progressively increasing deterioration of such soils is described by Mr. Fison, who said the stiff land farms had been overcropped in consequence of the rents being kept up too high, and that the occupiers "*had paid their landlords what they ought to have paid* "*their labourers: if they had paid it to their labourers* "*they would have had value for the money*, whereas "they paid it to the landlord, and of course they had "nothing back, *and they have so much less to lay out* "*upon their farms*." The inevitable consequence of the state of things here described must be the ruin of the tenants, when the land would be thrown upon the landlords' hands worked out and impoverished.

I have said there is an apparent facility of cultivating clay land with small means, which increases the number of competitors for farms of that kind, and ultimately degrades the system of cultivation adopted upon them. This has been clearly and graphically brought out in a note by that intelligent agriculturist, Mr. H. Handley, appended to a review of the "Progress of Agricultural "Knowledge during the last four years," in the last part of the Journal of the Royal Agricultural Society of England, wherein he says,

"A main reason why clay farms have to a considerable extent fallen into 'inferior hands,' is the circumstance that they are the only farms which, from the moderate outlay required to enter, come within the reach of a certain class. If, for instance, a farming servant or cottager, either by marriage, bequest, or a long course of industry, shall have become possessed of a few hundred pounds, and desire to be himself an occupier, he is debarred from entering upon a grazing, a mixed, or convertible farm, by the capital necessary to purchase stock or artificial manures; but for a small clay-farm a team of horses and a few implements are alone necessary. He ploughs, sows, and reaps, and converts his straw into what he calls manure by the mouths and feet of a few starved calves or yearlings mainly aided by the winter rains, and then carts it on his land little better than rotted straw. No wonder the condition of small clay-farms should be low. Yet however disagreeable the enumerated drawbacks to a clay-farm, and I admit they are many, *there is none more grateful for capital expended*, either in draining or manure. Once drained, the art of clay-farming consists in the art of ploughing and the art of making manure. If, on the one hand, the clays could advantageously share their superfluous moisture to the thirsty, gravelly, or sandy soils, on the other hand they do not burn, like these, under a summer sun, and at all events retain, until required by the crop, whatever manure is put into them."

The reader, who has perused the foregoing pages, will be aware how much this seeming facility of production, this, so to speak, natural tendency to an undue growth of wheat on clay farms has been aggravated by the corn law.

That the corn laws do not benefit the *occupiers* of land was expressly stated by most of the witnesses, and was tacitly admitted by the rest of those who gave evidence in 1836; and it is, therefore, perfectly obvious, that in the long run they cannot benefit the landlord. True it is, that where land has been let to a responsible tenant, though at a rent which the course of events has shown to be too high, the full amount may be exacted to the end of the lease; and, in such cases, landlords may be satisfied to receive the stipulated payments, and trust to some turn of fortune in their favour at its expiration. Yet, even in such cases, the land will assuredly be overcropped and deteriorated, though the tenant may avoid legal breaches of the covenants of his lease. In other cases, if periods of low prices become frequent, as they probably will in spite of any corn law, tenants of inferior skill and small capital will sink under the pressure, unless it shall become plain both to landlords and tenants, that a new system and additional exertions are required. This, however, will not happen so long as either party retains a delusive reliance upon a law nominally protecting.

I firmly believe, that if the trade in corn was to be thrown open to-morrow, that there would be no real necessity for any important reduction of rents, except upon heavy wheat land; and there, it would only be required in order to allow the tenant time to adapt himself to a state of low prices likely to be permanent and steady, rather than from any difficulty in cultivating such lands, under a proper system, at the present rents, let the price of corn be ever so low. I would not advise the owners of such lands to consent to any lasting or serious abatements of rent under a temporary alarm; they had better allow a yearly sum to be laid out in draining or other permanent improvements of a similar kind; and in all future changes of tenants they must select the men of enterprise and capital to occupy their land, even at a few shillings per acre less rent than might be obtained from a less responsible and intelligent tenant. Experience, however, has shown, that the most skilful tenants and farmers who have the largest capital, are generally able and willing to give the highest rents. And it is reasonable that they should do so; for though the proportion of the gross produce raised upon any farm, which the man of capital will pay as rent, is less than the proportion paid by the inferior kind of tenant, yet the actual value of the landlord's share — the rent — will be higher, from the circumstance that the able capitalist will raise, perhaps, double the gross produce grown by the poor tenant. There are many estates on which the proprietor is unwilling to displace a tenant, though he is known to be cultivating his land in an indifferent manner; and I am satisfied, that to such feelings a considerable amount of rent is often sacrificed, though the oscillations of prices under the corn laws have hitherto prevented a clear perception of the fact, that, as a general rule, such sacrifices seldom avail much to the tenant's benefit. Free trade would dissipate all delusions of this kind. Landowners would understand that poor and slovenly farmers could no more compete with those of skill, capital, and activity, than a careless, bungling, or needy tradesman can rival one of contrary character. If, as a matter of feeling or pride, landlords allow their estates to be occupied by bad farmers, because they have been tenants a long time, the loss will be apparent, and capable of distinct appreciation.

Notwithstanding the pertinacity with which the landed interest have clung to the corn laws, there are symptoms abroad which show, that landlords are beginning to understand that rents have not in reality been kept up by such legislative protection. Thus, the Duke of Richmond, whose threat to unmake the present administration if the corn law were touched is well remembered, said to his Scotch tenants the other day, "That if any of his tenants shall next year find "himself placed in a disadvantageous position "from these changes [the corn law and tariff of 1842], "*I feel myself bound, as a man of honour, to accept his* "*resignation*; for I am not the man to let my lands, in "1840, under an old state of things, and hold the "tenant to his engagement for nineteen years under a "new state of things." All this seems very fair and reasonable, and was of course received at the rent feast with vociferous applause. But what has the Duke of Richmond, what have the great majority of landlords been doing since 1815 but letting their lands under one state of things, and holding, with more or less tenacity, their tenants "to their engagements, "under a new state of things?" How was it that land-surveyors, from 1815 to 1828, let their employers' lands under the idea that wheat, as guaranteed by act of Parliament, was to sell for 80*s*. a quarter, while, "in the real state of things," the tenants often netted little more than half that price? Such has not been the accidental or occasional state of things, but a constant, abiding system of alternation, which periodically subjected the tenant to the performance of engagements, when his produce sold low, which had been contracted under the expectation that it would sell high. No doubt landlords in particular localities have made large abatements of rent, but seldom in time for the tenants' safety and their own interest; and many of them, when the promises of their corn law have proved as faithless as lovers' vows, like the Duke of Richmond, have felt themselves bound, as men of honour, to accept the resignation of tenants. And what an alternative does this present to the tenant? He must sell off in a period of the lowest prices, to go into business again when perchance the corn law swing is at its highest. I have myself often heard a landlord meet the tenant's plain demonstration by figures, that the rent calculated on high prices ought not to be paid in full when prices had fallen, by the bluff retort, "I am willing to take your "farm off your hands." And landed proprietors well know that so great is the competition for farms, that, except under peculiar circumstances, such as the cases of very poor tenants on wet clay lands, they may safely offer such an alternative in cheap years to a farmer of capital. This certainly proves the landlord's belief, that his farm is not overlet, notwithstanding a reduction of prices, and it is with that view I have quoted the Duke of Richmond's speech; but is it any equivalent to the tenant for the failure of that basis upon which all his estimates have been made? Land-agents and farmers are alike able, by the aid of local information, to calculate very nicely what the yearly produce of a farm in its actual state is likely to be, whilst the tendency of valuers is to overlook accidental losses and deficiencies, which, in practice, are sure to occur, for the number of candidates for a farm is so great, that such minor errors in the calculation are sure to be overlooked by the farmer; and the landlord naturally regards with favour those *employées* who succeed in obtaining the highest rents.

The great competition for farms, which existed in the period of the very low prices preceding 1836, is mentioned by a great many witnesses. Thus Mr. Ellis, in reply to the question, "Supposing there were any "farms out of occupation at this moment, do you "think there would be many applicants for them?" said, "Yes, I think there is as great demand for "land now as there almost ever was; but very little "land has changed hands for the last two years."

Mr. Fison also assigned as one cause of the then depressed state of farmers on stiff lands, "the very great "competition that there was for farms," and added, "that is an acknowledged cause: when I have been "conversing with farmers, for instance, at the market "table at Bury St. Edmund's, a persons its there who "is a land valuer; he was telling me a short time "since, that they had a greater number of applications "for farms than they had had for many years before: "he said he had sixteen then on his list very pressing "applications; and he added, 'What appears very "curious to me is, that the majority of them are-applications from persons that have small farms of "100 or 200 acres begging me to get them larger "ones.'"

It will be obvious that such a degree of competition, as is here indicated, will compel farmers to offer the highest rents—in other words, the largest share of the gross produce—which they can possibly afford, after deducting the expense of cultivation with the lowest rate of profit; and, therefore, if it were possible by means of the corn laws or otherwise (which I have shown it is not) to secure permanently high prices for grain, the farmer would obtain no benefit, the pressure of competition compelling him to offer, as rent to the landlord, the uttermost farthing of the *residuum* which would remain after the deduction of expenses and the lowest profit. It is useless to adduce either arguments or authorities to prove that the general rate of profit in this country has long been exceedingly low; or that, from manifest causes, the ordinary rate of profit upon capital employed in agriculture is lower than that of capital engaged in any other business. The farmer, in making his calculations for taking land, must reckon upon offering as rent a very large proportion of its anticipated produce, and can only look for more than the lowest returns for his own capital and industry by increasing the gross produce of his land.

The only element in the calculation of a money rent then remaining is the price of produce, which, if it depended solely upon the variations in seasons, might be calculated to within a reasonable degree of certainty. But when prices are sometimes reduced to the lowest point through the great competition amongst the home growers, unnaturally stimulated by the corn laws—at others, by a sudden influx of foreign grain, the accumulated surplus of years—and are occasionally forced up to a range almost indicating famine — no calculations of price, which have the least pretension to accuracy, can be made. Surveyors, examined in 1821, 1833, and 1836, invariably stated the difficulty they found in fixing the prices of grain, for the actual prices have never squared with those promised by any of the successive corn laws. The tenant, however, may be certain, that in this state of doubt and difficulty the inclination of the balance, under pressure of competition amongst farmers, will be in favour of the proprietor. The tenant will never have the benefit of the doubt. Landlords, land-agents, and farmers, then, have been alike deceived and betrayed by corn laws; and the mischief of all reliance upon protecting duties is, that the protected interests, instead of putting their own shoulders to the wheel, always entertain lingering hopes that some act of Parliament remedy may relieve them from the consequences of their miscalculations.

The Scotch witnesses, who were examined in 1836, regarded the conversion of money rents into corn rents as one very important ingredient in their success; and certainly, under the operation of the corn laws, they were quite justified in saying that the change had been the salvation of the tenantry. But a rent measured by the price of corn is by no means, at all times and under all circumstances, fair towards the landlord. Upon stock farms, as several witnesses pointed out, the price of corn is no just measure of the amount of rent; and in proportion as land has approached the character of stock farms has been the success of the tenant and the maintenance of rents. I have reason to believe, that tenants are very generally becoming anxious to have their rents converted into corn rents; and, if the corn laws are to be maintained, such a conversion can alone save them from severe loss and distress in times of low prices: but are the landlords prepared for that result from their cherished protective duties? To show the landlords the hazard they run when they really embark with their tenants and unite in staking their incomes year by year upon the corn law prices, and which under a corn rent they must do, I will refer to Mr. Robert Hope's evidence, who said, that his rent, a corn rent fluctuating with the price of corn—was in the year 1835 within 10*l.* of the money rent paid by his father in 1793 for the same farm! Nobody pretends to say that such a reduction was necessary, even with the low prices of 1835, for improvements in land and in the art of husbandry have greatly increased the productive powers of all land since 1793.

Another witness, Mr. Brodie, showed, that on a farm, which he had taken in 1822 at the yearly rent of 1,500*l.*, his payments in the aggregate to 1835 would have amounted to 21,000*l.*, but from which he had been allowed abatements, commencing in 1827, amounting in the whole to 1,575*l.*, making his actual payments for rent 19,425*l.*; if it had been taken at the equivalent corn rent he had offered, he would have paid an aggregate of 16,125*l.* only, the actual receipts in fourteen years forming *a difference in favour of the landlord* of 3,300*l.* beyond what he would have received under a corn rent. The table, produced by Mr. Brodie to show the difference between his money rent and a corn rent, proves, that the price of corn has not come up to the estimates made by farmers themselves. Mr. Brodie said he took the average crops of wheat of 1818 and 1819, and estimating *the price at* 70*s.* 3*d.* a quarter, brought the rent to the sum agreed on, 1,500*l.* Now the rent he would have paid under a corn rent, that is, *if the expectations on which he founded his offer had made the actual basis of his contract,* would in no one year from 1822 to 1835, both inclusive, have amounted to 1,500*l.* The highest year was 1828 (a very bad season), when the grain was of most inferior quality, the corn rent would have been 1,497*l.* 16*s.* 8*d.*; only two other years reach 1,300*l.* and a fraction; three more are between 1,200*l.* and 1,300*l.*; three others between 1,100*l.* and 1,200*l.*; and three others are below 900*l.* And to this conclusion it must come, if the landed interest require their tenants' fortunes to be staked upon the fluctuating price of wheat under a law restrictive of importation.

Persons, who have not had a practical acquaintance with the management of landed property, have little idea of the immense difference there may be in the value of a farm in the hands of a good or a bad tenant, or of the extent to which a skilful farmer improves a property whilst seeking only his own individual profit. As an example, not many days ago I found that a farmer of my acquaintance, a man of skill and considerable opulence, was looking out for a fresh farm, and on inquiring the reason he quitted his present occupation, which is in high condition, I learned that a lease of fourteen years was just expiring, and that the landlord wanted 40*s*. an acre for the same farm which had before been let at 10*s*. an acre, whilst the tenant was not willing to give more than about 25*s*. the acre. Another person had, however, been found to take it at 30*s*., just three times the rent at which it had been let fourteen years ago. True, the farm was then much out of condition; part of it is rather cold clay land, and the previous occupier had "ploughed, sowed, and reaped," till he scarcely got seed for seed; and the now going off tenant had made large and spirited outlays upon the farm, which he does not deny to have been amply returned to him during the currency of the lease. Probably there are few parishes in England in which, to some extent, the same sort of thing is not of occasional occurrence. One farmer shall make a good living at a high rent on a farm, which another could not have occupied with a profit had he lived rent free. But when these things are fully understood, which they are now beginning to be, the landed interest can never expect the country to submit to be taxed, to the extent of some 10*s*. a quarter on its consumption of grain in all years of scarcity, to countervail the inertness or ignorance of the proprietors of heavy land, and their tenants.

That the landed interest, and the agriculturists at

large have been bestirring themselves ever since the low prices of 1834 and 1835, and especially since the investigation of 1836, must be plain to the most careless observer of passing events, and the progress which has been made in the diffusion of agricultural knowledge, during the last five years, is remarkable. In 1838, the English Agricultural Society (since dubbed Royal) was founded under the auspices of Lord Spencer and other great landholders, who had been distinguished for their devotion to practical agriculture; and which, taking for its motto "Practice with science," has been eminently successful in forming a medium for the communication of the best existing practices in husbandry. The society now numbers upwards of 5,000 members, into whose hands the journal published half yearly goes as of right, and which is besides sold to the public in the ordinary way. As the Highland Society of Scotland, at the beginning of the present century, was at once the evidence of improving husbandry, and the cause of its rapid diffusion in that country, so the formation of the English Society marks an epoch in the progress of agriculture in South Britain; and by its annual meetings and its journal will do much to place a knowledge of some of the best processes of agriculture within the reach of all English farmers. I refer, however, to this society chiefly for the purpose of showing, that the evidence given in 1836 has not been altogether lost upon British agriculturists. They are evidently setting their houses in order for a free trade in corn; a measure, which after the tariff and corn law of 1842, can only be delayed a comparatively short time. Nor has British agriculture aught to fear from foreign competition, which will merely have the effect of compelling the general adoption of the best practices of the best cultivated districts; with such local or temporary variations, as the situation or season may suggest to farmers sharpened by self-interest and a wholesome knowledge, that upon themselves only, and not upon protecting duties, they must rely for profit.

The farmers may be assured that those who advise such self-reliance are their true friends; and the landed interest, generally, will soon discover, that the counsellors who teach them to rest upon protecting laws for prosperity are both unwise and unsafe advisers. There is no man of common observation, whatever his wishes or opinions upon the subject may be, who can hope to retain that modified—apparently modified, but practically stringent—monopoly given by Sir Robert Peel's late corn law, through another series of failing harvests. Yet so long as any corn law lasts, there will be none of that permanent adjustment of rents and other money payments, which is absolutely necessary to the progressive improvement of agriculture, and to its profitable pursuit; while the attention of all parties interested in land will be directed too exclusively to wheat growing, and the injurious incitement to plant wheat, in land not sufficiently prepared for that crop now offered by prices occasionally high, will continue. When gambling speculations upon mere price shall no longer form one of the elements in letting and hiring farms, and successful farming shall be universally understood to consist in such a system and such rotations as will return the largest produce for a given outlay,—when farmers, sufficiently calculating for the difference of seasons, shall be willing to embark in large expenditures with a view to distant returns,—when that steadiness and wholesome feeling, which induce tenants to desire and landlords to grant leases, shall return, then, and not till then, can the landed proprietor be assured, that the value of his property will advance in a ratio proportioned to national prosperity.

That agriculture can be permanently prosperous whilst the national resources are declining, forms an anomaly too preposterous to be worth discussing; and the landed interest would soon find, if our trading and manufacturing industry should decay, how little corn laws and restrictive legislation have promoted that wealth for which the British landholder is so remarkable. And the fact, that the nation was able to make great advances in wealth during the war and to pay a tax of enormous amount to the landholders besides,—a tax which was over and above their full share of the general prosperity,—is no argument for the maintenance of the exaction under a new state of circumstances. The manufactures of Great Britain were then first occupying new ground,—on the fresh vegetable soil of the world so to speak,—and the rate of profit, which the competition of accumulated capitals within *a limited and decreasing* field has now so much reduced, then enabled the trade of the nation to bear the burthen of the war, and *of the high price of food as well;* but that is hopeless now. Rivals meet our manufacturers in every foreign market, and tariffs and prohibitions (reflected images of our own corn laws) year by year exclude us from markets of great demand, and the commercial interests of the nation daily find that nothing but the indefatigable exertion of intelligence, caution, and active enterprise can enable them to maintain their footing. Is it likely, then, supposing the corn monopoly of the British landlords to have been as real and beneficial, as it has been shown to be illusory and detrimental, to the agricultural interest, that the labour and commercial industry of the kingdom will consent to be taxed and restricted for the single purpose of exempting the occupiers of land from the necessity of exerting an intelligent activity other classes have found so indispensable to themselves? And this is not a question which will bear to be bandied about and made the subject of party warfare: it can never be permitted that party politicians shall fight over the comparatively insignificant point of whether there shall be an 8*s*. fixed duty, or a scale of duties, sliding from 20*s*. downwards, and that, in the meantime, the substantial evil *a protecting duty* shall be retained.

Both are equally mischievous; or if by ingenious hypothetical reasoning it can be shown that a trifling amount of evil less occurs under the one than in the other, the practical difference is so slight as not to be worth notice; for both extend the range of fluctuation, both effectually prohibit importation until the danger of a deficiency in this country became imminent; both would keep up that inducement to the misdirection of agricultural capital and industry, which has been so fully shown to be one of the great evils of the corn law; and neither could prevent, as the conjoint effect of that misdirection and of good seasons, such occasional gluts of wheat as at times to depress the British markets unnaturally. And there must be an *immediate* as well as a total repeal of all corn duties, if British agriculture is to be prosperous; for so long as the notion of protection lingers in the minds of farmers and landlords, that steady Anglo-Saxon determination, which has enabled Englishmen, in all other occupations, to accomplish so much, will never be directed towards those improvements in husbandry, which are now so indispensable to agricultural success. I believe, from my own observation, no less than the evidence of 1836, that the agriculturists were then ripe for a free trade in corn, and that had the corn laws been repealed at that time, the condition of farmers at this moment would have been far better than it now is. That opportunity, however, was lost, and the agriculturists will probably undergo a fresh series of fluctuations before they get upon the safe ground of freedom. We must fully calculate that a period of agricultural distress is at hand; I know that farmers are looking to abatements of rent at the coming half year's audits; and should the summer season prove as fine and genial as the seed time and winter have been seasonable, prices will unquestionably be very low, and there will be much distress amongst that class of farmers, who have not ceased to found their hopes of profit on scarcity and high prices.

Now, then, is the time to repeal the corn law. Home competition has reduced the price of grain to a moderate rate, and if we are blessed with a good harvest, wheat may, and probably will, fall lower than it was in 1835. The most sensitive agricultural alarmist will, therefore, be unable to conjure up any phantom of greater abundance than that produced by the home growth. The repeal of the corn law would now create no panic, and free trade, by a gentle and gradual pressure, would direct the exertions of farmers towards that intelligent system of husbandry wherein their permanent prosperity is alone to be found. All the beneficial effects, which free trade in corn is fitted to produce on commerce and manufactures, would at once begin to operate, and a clearer prospect of national prosperity, a prospect more free from adventitious circumstances whether of good or evil, will be opened, than has ever been hitherto attained. On the other hand, if, either through public indifference, or from the half measures of party politicians, the corn laws be allowed to linger on the statute book—practically inoperative, as we have seen, to prevent agricultural distress in abundant years—until the cycle of the seasons shall bring round two or three deficient crops, it is certain, that a total and instant repeal will be quickly forced upon the government of that day. But this will not be effected until all the evils of scarcity have again been endured by the community, new engagements at high rents entered into by farmers, wheat culture again unduly extended, monetary derangements and ruinous corn speculations once more rife, and, finally, an agricultural panic which the experience of several years may be required to allay. It is plain there never was a time, especially as regards the interests of the agriculturists, more favourable for the decisive step than the present. What do we fear? Is it cheap corn? If so, we have it notwithstanding the corn laws. But the mischief is, that though for this year we may have abundance, a bad harvest must half starve us before we can get relief.

That the British agriculturist is by no means so ill prepared to adopt the only stable means of success, as some of his self-styled friends would have believed, a brief survey of the present state of English husbandry will make manifest. Perhaps, there is no source from which I could take a statement of the actual condition of English agriculturists (for in Scotland farmers have become pretty well alive to the exigences of the times) so little open to suspicion or cavil, as the article by Mr. Philip Pusey, M.P., one of the members for the agricultural county of Berks, " On the Progress of " Agricultural Knowledge during the last four years," which appears in the last number of the English Agricultural Society's Journal, published in January of the present year. The purpose of the article is to inquire what has been the progress of agriculture since the establishment of the Society; and, incidentally, how far the working of the Society has assisted in promoting agricultural knowledge; and it completely confirms the views I have taken of the comparatively backward condition of the heavy soils, and the steady progress of agriculture in general. Mr. Pusey justly remarks, that the foundation of all improvement upon wet lands is drainage; and in the foregoing pages I have shown that the owners and occupiers of wet and heavy soils are those who are most frequent and loud in their demands for protection. " It is only seven years since," proceeds the article, " we heard in England, chiefly " through the present Speaker of the House of Com-" mons, that a manufacturer in Scotland, now well " known as Mr. Smith, of Deanston, had found the " means of making all land, however wet and poor it " might be, warm sound, and fertile; and that this " change was brought about by two processes, tho-" rough draining and subsoil ploughing. His rule of " draining was this, that we are not merely to endea-" vour to find out hidden springs, and to cut them " through by a single drain, which in some of our " books appeared to be regarded as all that was neces-" sary; but that, as the whole surface of retentive soils " is rendered wet, not by accidental springs, but by the " rain, the whole surface of the field must be made

" thoroughly dry by under drains running throughout " at equal distances; any field, however wet, might be " so dried, provided these under drains were cut suffi- " ciently dry."

The soil having been thus rendered dry, the subsoil is stirred by a plough, which is simply the frame of a plough without the mouldboard, following in the furrow made by the ordinary method of ploughing; the effect of which is to admit the air, light, and water to the previously impervious subsoil, and so to change and ameliorate its character, that portions of it may be afterwards fully brought to the surface by deep ploughings, while the roots of plants can run into it and the water penetrate through it to the drains.

Probably there are few persons who have not, within the last few years, read more or less of this grand agricultural discovery, for such in truth it is, but only those who have had some experience of the difficulty with which clay-land is worked will entirely apprehend its value. Such land, when thus ameliorated, can be ploughed with fewer horses; in many districts the team may be reduced from *four* (I saw *five* in one plough-team the other day in Buckinghamshire) to *two*: it can be worked in weather which was before quite impracticable; and the crops are not only positively more abundant, but are far less dependent upon seasons, while they invariably ripen earlier, always a point of importance on deep land. The general adoption of this plan upon strong lands which are fitted for it—for it appears to have done harm on some land of a peculiar kind—will probably have as great an effect in increasing the productiveness of the clay lands of the country, as the turnip husbandry on the light soils had on land of that kind in the beginning of the present century. But there is a circumstance which would seem to render its general adoption impossible, notwithstanding the exhortations of landholders and the ablest disquisitions upon the subject, which is the expense. On the soils which most require draining the cost of that process alone, if done with tiles, is from 10*l.* to 12*l.* and 15*l.* the acre; an outlay which it is merely fanciful to suppose will be incurred by the tenant while the fluctuations of price caused by the corn laws continue to render the farming heavy land a hazardous speculation, and the yearly value of such land scarcely a subject for calculation: and it may be safely predicted that the universal adoption of this great agricultural improvement will only be coincident with free trade in corn.

It is notorious that the manuring of land alone will not increase its productiveness beyond a certain point, and that being reached, additional manure does harm, but when strong deep land has been drained and subsoiled, so that any extra quantity of the under soil, which may be required, can be safely brought to the surface, the extent to which manures may be applied, may, for practical purposes, be deemed boundless. Neither is manure upon wet land of much use. For instance, on my own farm, the previous holder of which, though an indifferent farmer in other respects, always applied a great deal of stable manure from London, but was especially negligent in draining and carrying off the surface water, I found on ploughing up a rather wet piece of land, that the straw of the dung put in two years ago remained not at all decomposed, but turned up like a thin coating of old thatch: and this is more or less the case in all wet strong land.

Valuable as Mr. Smith's system promises to be, it forms a curious illustration of the observation made in the Journal article, that "if the best practice of each "different district could become general in the country, "a very great improvement in farming would be at "once effected;" for it is now ascertained, that this very system of frequent draining was practised in Suffolk forty years ago, and has long been, and is now common in Essex, where its value is well understood. The Essex draining, however, being done with straw and bushes only, is not so permanent as that with tiles proposed by Mr. Smith, requiring to be renewed in about fourteen or sixteen years; neither are the drains made so deep, nor filled up in such a manner as to admit of subsoil ploughing, which is at least as important to increased fertility as draining itself. Though, at present, the chief expectation of benefits to be derived from draining rests upon the inducements it holds out to enterprising tenants, there are sufficient examples of the great advantages landlords may derive from outlays in draining and irrigation, on a scale much more extensive than can ever be undertaken by a tenant under any farming lease. Thus the accounts given in the English Agricultural Society's Journal of Sir James Graham's draining operations at Netherby, Cumberland, and Lord Hatherton's at Teddesley, in Staffordshire, where, in the latter instance, at an expense of about 1500*l*., a tract of land was raised from the yearly value of 10*s*. to 30*s*. an acre, while the water from the under-ground drains, being thrown over a water-wheel, turned a threshing-machine and did other work in the barn*. The particulars of the great additional value caused by an

---

* Second volume of the Journal of the Agricultural Society of England, 277.

extensive and scientific plan of irrigation to the Duke of Portland's meadows, at Clipstone Park, Notts, are also detailed in the same work *. Yet there are various indications abroad, that, when once the attention of the landed proprietors shall have been turned to the subject, and when extensive and combined plans for carrying off the redundant moisture of the heavy soils, and for applying the accumulated waters to various uses, shall have developed the enormous latent value of their possessions, rapid and hitherto unimagined improvements will be made throughout the low land districts of England. The act of Parliament enabling owners of entailed estates to charge them with money borrowed for the purpose of draining, the numerous scientific publications on land-draining which have been published within the last few years, the notice Mr. Smith's (of Deanston) practice has attracted, and some proposals which have been put forth for a land-drainage company, all show that the landed interests only require to be relieved from their fallacious reliance on the corn laws, and all those illusory expectations of gain from protecting duties, in order to seek, by means of the healthy development of their own resources, that steady prosperity they have failed to secure by anti-commercial restrictions †.

* First volume, ibid, art. 39.

† Another purpose to which landowners may profitably apply wet clay land of an inferior kind, now generally of little value, is planting. Such lands are often peculiarly adapted for the growth of certain kinds of valuable timber, as oak, and, I believe, larch thrives well upon them. Some of the most unmanageable tracts of land in the country are those which are called wealds—Saxonice woods—and forests, and it is more than probable that there is no way in which the worst portions of such districts could be rendered so valuable, both to their owners and the public, as by planting them.

Before quitting this subject, I must quote an observation of Mr. Pusey's, which also supports the views I have disclosed in these pages. After enumerating many of the disadvantages of wet clay land, he says, "If I were a working-farmer, nothing would induce "me to enter on a cold, wet farm, unless there were a "fair prospect of its being drained, either with *my own* "*money under a long lease*, or with the aid of the land-"lord." But what farmer, who intends to remain solvent and independent five years hence, would now

---

There is in North Wilts an extensive district of cold, wet, and most unproductive clay land, called Braydon Forest, which formerly belonged to the crown, but is now the property of Mr. Joseph Neeld, M.P. This land was broken during the war, and proving most unprofitable in tillage, was chiefly laid down again somewhere about 1821. Up to the year 1826, when the late Earl of Clarendon, who held the property under a crown lease, disposed of it to Mr. Neeld, I was well acquainted with this tract; and, believing that it might furnish an illustration of the pernicious effect of that indiscriminate conversion of all kinds of soils into tillage, which occurred about 1811 and 1812, I applied to Mr. Joseph Neeld, M.P., the proprietor's brother, for information as to the present state of the property. That gentleman was then absent from England, and it was not until after these sheets had passed through the press that I received from him a letter, in which he obligingly referred me to the local manager for the full information I had sought. It was too late to obtain that information for the purposes of this tract; but I must transcribe Mr. Neeld's account of the successful planting of a small part of the property: he says, "The property of my brother, at Braydon, remains much in the "same state of cultivation as in Lord Clarendon's time, that is to "say, where no plantations have been made. My brother has con-"verted 400 acres into plantations, which have thriven wonderfully, "and are much admired. The soil is a wet clay, and it is surprising "how the plantations have succeeded." There is no doubt that the value of plantations has been too much overlooked by English landed proprietors, and I think this, like other omissions and misdirections of rural industry, may be distinctly traced to the inordinate desire to grow wheat which is promoted by the corn laws.

venture to take a long lease of "a cold wet farm," knowing, as he does, that he would be obliged to engage to pay a rent calculated on prices he may not obtain five years out of twenty? And while such lands can be let without draining, the landlords—the majority of whom cannot afford the outlay—will never, to any great extent, furnish the means. Here and there individual landholders may promote such improvements at their own expense; but, looking at land in the aggregate, its permanent improvement will only take place in the hands of occupiers. To enable the occupiers of the clay lands of England to become improvers, the first requisite plainly is steadiness of price, which can only result from a free trade in corn.

The breaking up *weak* pasture land is mentioned as an improvement which might be extended throughout England with advantage to owners and occupiers, and in that observation I quite concur; but that indiscriminate conversion of our better pasture lands to arable tillage, which it is now rather the fashion to recommend, must be resorted to with much caution; and the landlord should be very certain as to the means and the skill of his tenant before he permits such a conversion. There are many farmers of the present day, who will pay a fair rent and make a living upon pasture land, but who have neither skill nor capital to manage the very same farm under a convertible system. The superior quality too of both butter and cheese, which is made from old pasture land, is notorious. Besides, the system of cropping upon all land of such quality as is permanent pasture of much value, is in England far too scourging, and it would be well to eradicate from the minds of the majority of farmers, that anxiety for growing grain which so often defeats its own object: this will never be effected so long as any corn laws, which offer a premium upon corn culture, shall be in existence.

Passing, then, from the heavy soils, the article enumerates improvements made in various districts on those of an opposite kind, light land and lands too loose. Thus marle, chalk, and clay have been extensively applied to sandy soils in Bedfordshire, Norfolk, Suffolk, Hampshire, and, above all, in the fen districts of Lincolnshire, where the application of marle, or clay, has enabled good wheat to be grown, where formerly nothing but light oats could be raised. Chalk is also largely applied to clay land, and with excellent results. The means of fertilizing soils by amalgamation have long been practised in certain districts, whilst in others, equally well situated for such improvements, they seem to be entirely unknown.

To the Society belongs the merit of having shown, by actual experiment, that the wheel-plough*, though of much greater weight than the swing-plough, is considerably lighter in draught to the cattle, and does much better work, though the contrary had been for many years the received opinion. It was also proved that, great as the Scotch are in husbandry, their ploughs were the *most* severe implements to the cattle. The difference in favour of wheel-ploughs was found to be

* I had always taken it for granted that the swing-plough was the most approved implement, and used it exclusively, until I read an account of the experiments of the Society. My ploughman, a Suffolk man, always accustomed to a swing-plough, was induced, not without considerable difficulty, to use a wheel-plough; but having once used it, he finds it so much easier for his horses, and, in other respects, such a decided improvement, that he has become a complete convert to wheel-ploughs.

as one horse in three. Lord Spencer is said to have made the observations which led to the experiments upon this subject.

Here we have a fact established, which is of great importance to husbandry, as saving horse labour, generally a source of unnecessary expenditure on English farms. The same experiments have also established another position of some value, namely, that where horses plough at the pace of $2\frac{1}{2}$ miles an hour, the draught is no greater than when going at the pace of $1\frac{1}{2}$ miles in an hour, though, in the former case, nearly twice the quantity of earth was moved, and almost double the work done.

Again, an Oxfordshire agriculturist, Mr. Hannam, is recorded to have reduced the number of horses on a farm of three hundred and seventy acres from *sixteen* to *eight*, simply by the use of two-horse ploughs and single-horse carts. Independently of the annual saving in horse-keep, the economy of capital effected by these means is very considerable. Thus, on such a farm as Mr. Hannam's, besides the first cost of eight horses, which cannot be reckoned less than 20*l.* each, or 160*l.*, the ordinary description of carts and waggons used in the neighbourhood would cost 295*l.*, while the prime cost of the carts would be 128*l.* only, making a total saving upon entering a moderate-sized farm, on these two items of investment alone, of no less than 327*l.* All this shows what may be done in reducing farming outlay without lessening production, when the necessity for observation and intelligent calculation in agricultural matters shall have become obvious to the mass of farmers.

But, perhaps, it is in the raising green and root crops that English farmers have most to learn from the diffused knowledge of the best practices of the most improved districts. In the north, a crop of roots is raised on ridges by the application of artificial manures, at an expense of from 12*l.* to 15*l.* an acre, whilst, in the south, a crop of swedes will be raised at a less charge than 2*l.* per acre for manure. By the former system, 25 and 30 tons of swedes, and upwards, are grown to the acre, while, by the latter, 15 tons is considered a large produce. Not only are the after-taken corn crops of the rotation greatly benefited by the heavy dressings given in the north to the root crops, but the increased quantity of cattle provender thereby raised, goes to the production of a force of manure double that obtained in the south from the same quantity of land.

There is no expenditure which the ordinary classes of English farmers seem to grudge more than that applied in raising roots, especially upon land where grain crops can be frequently grown, such as strong clays, yet there is none that would ultimately repay them better. The too frequent recurrence of turnips, in the four-course system of the lighter soils, has also caused that crop to be a very uncertain one; and, in the article I have noticed, a more extended use of mangold-wurzel and the cultivation of the white or Belgian carrot are recommended to vary the monotony of that rotation.

As good farming is now generally admitted to depend upon the quantity of stock which can be kept all the year round, it may be well to show, by the evidence of Mr. Pusey, the progress which has been made in providing for them through the winter.

"Such is the information received on those roots by which our stock are sustained in winter; and I cannot but look back to the former history of farming on this point. The castles of the old barons were victualled at Michaelmas with salt beeves and sheep, because there was little hay for their winter keep. Afterwards more hay was made, and fresh meat was obtained throughout the year. When our population exceeded the extent of our meadows, the common turnip was introduced, but as this does not well resist the frost, it would last only till February. Then came the swede, which carries on till the end of March. Another class of summer food, clover, had been also introduced, but would not be ready so soon; vetches, therefore, were sown in autumn, to be fed off in spring. But there is still an interval to be filled, for vetches do not come in as soon as swedes are ended. Mangold-wurzel, indeed, will carry us through this space of time; but it appears also, that while winter feed may be prolonged, spring feed may be hastened by growing an early variety of vetches; and Mr. Williams, a farmer of Ilsley, informs us, that last year he had vetches three feet high, in the beginning of May, on a backward soil in a high situation."

The circle of artificial food is thus completed throughout the year.

In the department of live stock the improvement which has taken place within the last few years is surprising. Cattle and sheep have been so well bred, and kept so well from the hour of their birth, that a steer or a sheep is now often brought to market, well fatted, at two years old, whereas formerly four, five, and six years old beef and mutton were alone eaten. This material and beneficial change has been effected by the use of oil-cake, corn, and roots in feeding, and care and judgment in breeding all descriptions of stock. The value of well-bred stock, which is far beyond what the mere difference in weight would indicate, arises chiefly from this quality of early maturity. The gradual introduction of the improved breed of short-horn cows into all the best dairy districts of England is going on, and the benefits derived therefrom are forcing even the most bigoted farmers to adopt the better breeds*.

The interest excited amongst the higher classes of agriculturists by the scientific investigations of Liebig and others, into the nature and chemical operation of manures and the analysis of soils, if of less immediate and practical utility, bespeaks a higher standard of mental cultivation amongst agriculturists than existed at any previous time, and will eventually lead, to those close examinations of the various processes and accurate records of facts in husbandry, which are requisite to give it the character of a science.

Now, though individual cultivators had been, for some time, in the practice of enlightened systems of husbandry, and were thereby enabled to bear up against the ruinous fluctuations caused by the corn laws; yet it was not until that complete disclosure of the real origin of agricultural distress, and of the hollowness of all expectations of profit founded on protective laws, which were made in 1836, that any general movement was communicated to agriculture. Then a desire for improvement, to counteract the effects of low prices, arose amongst the landed gentry; one of the consequences of which was the formation

* Meeting, the other day, a friend much employed in the west of England as a land-agent, and talking with him on the progress of agriculture in his district, he gave me many illustrations of the activity with which farmers there were improving their systems; amongst the rest, he said, "You know J. W. (a dairy farmer notorious for his adherence to "ancient ways"), well, he has become alive to the necessity of improved stock, and has lately given 85*l.* for four short-horn cows." To those who know the class of farmers here alluded to, this fact speaks volumes.

of the English Society, whose proceedings have both given an impulse to improvement, and diffused the knowledge of useful practices already in operation. "I am certain," says Mr. Pusey, "that four years "ago no one knew how much good farming there was "in the country;" and he adds, "now that these "things are come to light, we may hope that they will "not only be spoken of, but be practised more gene- "rally; that draining tiles will be greatly cheapened, "more drains be cut, more chalk be laid on the downs, "the wolds, and the clays; marle on the sand, clay on "the fens and heaths, lime on the moors, many of which "should be broken up; that old ploughs will be cast "away, the number of horses reduced, good breeds of "cattle extended, stock fattened where it has hitherto "been starved; root crops drilled and better dunged, "new kinds of those crops cultivated, and artificial "manures of ascertained usefulness purchased."

In all this, every one must cordially agree, as well as in the following sentiments—"It is the knowledge of "these weapons, *which we have actually in our hands*, "that may make us look back with satisfaction to the "efforts we have already made, and *forward with* "*cheerful confidence to the improvement of husbandry*, "*through the collective experience of our farmers.*" But there is one obstacle to the healthy self-reliance from which alone these improvements can spring. On this self-reliance only can agricultural prosperity be based, and though such reliance, and improved husbandry its consequence, may extend amongst the more educated of the agriculturists, the general adoption of the means of success pointed at in the above quotations, will never take place amongst the more numerous and less intelligent body of English farmers, until all those fallacious hopes and erroneous calculations, the offspring of the corn laws, shall have ceased to misdirect their attention.

One word upon leases: — In the article above quoted, Mr. Pusey has more than once alluded to the necessity of leases of considerable duration wherever large outlays by tenants are anticipated, and this very obvious preliminary to all permanent improvement upon a large scale, has been much dwelt on by all who have lately written or spoken upon husbandry. But for the last twenty years tenants have been, at least, as unwilling to take, as landlords to grant leases; the one class fearing to pledge themselves to high rents on the faith of protection prices, the other hoping, by means of their corn law, to avoid any permanent reduction of rents. Political considerations also have been said, and I believe truly, to have had much to do with the landowners' indisposition to grant leases; but the maintenance of the corn law has been the grand object for which the landowners have desired to exercise political influence over the tenantry: and notwithstanding the advocates of protection have, of late, been fond of putting forward the farmers' interest as a plea for the corn laws, they have most of them entertained a shrewd suspicion, that the farmers, sooner or later, would arrive at the conclusion, that all the losses of fluctuating prices and artificially high rents may be traced to the corn laws. Hence, the check political has been so constantly held over the farmers. My own opinion, however, is, that this motive for refusing leases has been over-estimated. But, whatever may be the cause or combination of causes, the disuse of leases is notorious, and forms a serious drawback to agricultural improvement; yet to expect that they will again become general, whilst a corn law and its consequences, fluctuating prices exist, is to suppose that cultivators have learned nothing from the trials and hazards of the last twenty-five years. And, perhaps, until the period of transition has passed away, this is not to be regretted. The leases most usual were barbarous and cumbrous instruments, utterly unsuited to the present state of agricultural knowledge. Though often impeding and obstructing improvements by the tenant, I have never known them sufficient to protect the land against over-cropping, and consequent deterioration, in the hands of an indifferent or over-rented tenant. Then, the terms common in England, of seven, ten, twelve, or fourteen years, are too short to give that permanent interest to the tenant which is the corner-stone of all improvements in husbandry. So clearly is this now understood, that we may be sure, whenever the agricultural interest shall be freed from the incubus of a "protecting" duty on foreign grain, leases will again be resorted to with equal readiness by both farmer and landlord. Then it will be advisable, as indeed it is now whenever a lease is made, to consider with how little of restriction and positive stipulation as to the mode of culture, the landlord may protect his land against unfair treatment. With the exception of a few simple, general provisions, adapted to the locality and nature of the farm, I believe all that will be necessary is, for the tenant to be interdicted from growing in the last three years of the term more than the proper proportions of exhausting crops, and from misapplying his manure. Except at the end of the term, no tenant can injure his farm without damaging himself; and, if ordinary care is exercised in first letting the farm, a landowner may safely trust to his tenant's self-interest to keep the land in good condition, provided he be not stimulated to any particular mode of mismanagement by legislative enactment. It is also worthy of consideration, whether it might not materially promote the interest of both parties to adopt leases of very considerable duration, as thirty, forty, or even fifty years, with certain periodical, say decenial, advances of rent; which would, not only, give the landowner his fair share of the increase in the productive power of their common property, but would act as an incentive to the tenant to prepare himself to meet the definite and pre-arranged advances of rent by increased production. I have no doubt, that in this way a very great additional value may be given to land in every part of the kingdom, for a leaseholder at rack-rent for a very long term, has, for most of the purposes of practical enjoyment, all the fixity of possession of a freeholder; and, it is certain, land is never so productively employed as when the occupier has a full, but fair, yearly rent to pay.

# CONCLUSION.

From the foregoing examination, founded almost exclusively upon facts and data furnished by persons practically versed, and directly interested in agriculture and the corn trade, the following conclusions seem to be irresistible:

That the chief part of that permanent improvement in agriculture and of that rise of rents, which has occurred in modern times, commenced with, and has been consequent upon, the growth of commercial and manufacturing industry in this country, and that such benefits to the landowner are solely based upon the national prosperity thereby occasioned; while the exorbitant prices to which grain attained during the war were completely fortuitous, and were mainly caused by deficient seasons, concurring with extraordinary obstructions to foreign supplies, which arose out of the particular events of the contest.

That the most complete monopoly of the home market will not secure permanently high prices to the British agriculturist; but, on the contrary, that the occasionally high range of prices, which, under such a monopoly, a deficient season produces, has a tendency to force an undue and unnatural extension of wheat tillage, and thereby to depress the price of bread-corn, in years of abundance, to an extent that would never occur under a free trade in corn.

That the monopoly prices promised by the corn laws, both of 1815 and 1828, were never practically enjoyed, for any considerable period, by the occupiers of land in Great Britain, whilst all their fixed money engagements have been calculated with reference to the promised, not to the real prices of grain; and besides, that the community will not bear, in times of scarcity, an effective maintenance of the corn monopoly, for a period sufficiently long to compensate the farmer for the unnatural depression prices undergo in years of abundance. This was clearly shown in the admission of foreign grain, by the Government, in 1825, 1826, and 1827; in the remodelling of the corn law in 1828; and in the recent change in the corn law in 1842, all of which, though insufficient to meet the necessities of the respective occasions, were evidences, that no stringent corn law will be submitted to by the nation when under the pressure of even a partial deficiency.

That though the full extent of monopoly prices successively promised by law, would not be endured by the public for any considerable time, yet the restrictive operation of the corn laws has been stringent enough to cause great advances and violent fluctuations of price, which have proved most injurious to the consumer, and destructive of all rational calculation in the business of the farmer.

That though the farmer, who by accident had taken his farm during a low range of prices, if his rent had been fixed with reference to the then existing prices, might be apparently benefited by even a short period of high prices; yet that, in fact, he is no gainer, for the competition of farmers for farms enables landlords and land-agents, in practice, to disregard the very low priced years, and to calculate money-rents with reference to the prices of seasons of comparative scarcity, and to the act of Parliament price of corn.

That the variation in the productiveness of the crops of this country, in different seasons, is so great, that, while in deficient, and perhaps in average years, a certain amount of foreign supply is required to prevent the evils of dearth, the home crops, in abundant seasons, have been so productive as to reduce the prices of grain in this country, to, at least, the level of the European market.

That the shifting duties of the existing system of corn laws have caused large accumulations of foreign grain,—often beyond the effective demand of consumers,—to be suddenly thrown upon the British market, at periods most detrimental to the British grower, and which, under an open trade, would have come in gradually, and would have been absorbed in consumption, with the effect of keeping prices steady and equable.

That the corn laws have prevented timely adjustments of rent, and have thereby permanently injured the landlord and tenant, more particularly on those soils which were formerly almost exclusively regarded as "wheat-lands;" that they have induced farmers to rely for profit upon a great breadth of wheat, to the neglect of stock-farming and improved systems of husbandry; and that they have created a habit, in the minds of those connected with land, of looking to the legislature for some undefined or unattainable remedy for occasional distress, rather than to their own energy and enterprise.

That the uncontrolled power, which the landed interests have had to legislate for the protection of agriculture, has not abled them to prevent the periodical recurrence of real and severe distress amongst the tenantry; but that, on the contrary, protection has either caused or aggravated agricultural distress, by interfering with the manner in which capital and industry would otherwise have been applied to land.

That it is not for the interest of the farmer that prices of corn should be high, for whether they are high or low, the existing competition for farms would prevent him from realising more than the ordinary rate of profit, after payment of rent and other outgoings, calculated according to the actually existing prices; but it is most important to him that prices should be steady, without fluctuation beyond what must follow from variations in the seasons; and that such steady prices would be best secured by a constant and regular importation of grain.

That all recent improvements in agriculture have taken place in spite of the corn laws, and by pursuing plans directly the reverse of those which the corn laws have tended to encourage; that the agriculturalists, who have had least reliance upon the corn laws, have been the most successful, and that the farmers, who have been most remarkable for their adherence to old systems of husbandry, or for want of capital or skill, have been the most apprehensive of free trade in corn.

That though the corn laws were avowedly passed to keep up rents, there are good reasons for believing that, if they had never existed, rents in Great Britain would have been as high, if not higher, than at present.

That a fixed duty on corn would, to a considerable extent, have the same effect in producing fluctuations of price, by misdirecting the application of agricultural industry and capital, as well as by aggravating the incidence of scarcity and increasing the depression of prices in years of abundance, as the sliding scale of duties; and would, when any foreign supply may be required, operate as a direct tax upon the whole of the corn consumed in this country, equivalent to the duty levied upon the portion imported.

That, under the most completely free trade in corn, the largest quantity of foreign grain that could be profitably imported would be so small, when compared with the total consumption of this country, that the utmost effect it could produce on the British market would be to prevent sudden variations in the price of corn, and exorbitantly high prices in deficient years; but that, in productive seasons, it is doubtful whether the inferior agriculture of the Continent could compete at all with that of Great Britain.

That by looking solely to a large acreable return for a given outlay, which is the direction in which science is leading agriculture, the British farmer would place his business upon a stable foundation, and be enabled to set all competition at defiance.

That the immediate repeal of the corn law is not only desirable, as the means of placing agriculture upon a sure foundation, by at once enforcing those improved systems of husbandry, and adjustments of engagements, which alone can make agriculture permanently prosperous; but that the present time, from the comparatively low prices and the healthy appearance of the growing crops, is peculiarly favourable for the adoption of free trade in corn*.

And, finally, that the high value of land in this country has always been coincident with, and is directly attributable to, the great wealth created by our commercial and manufacturing industry, and the comparatively wide diffusion of that wealth amongst the mass of the community; but not to any artificial restrictions, which have been shackles and obstructions on, not aids to, our productive power.

---

* A very intelligent farmer, who has also been, for many years, largely engaged in the corn trade, in Essex and Hertfordshire, tells me, that there is now full *one-fifth* more land sown with wheat, than in any one year within his recollection. This is universally the case, and, with a moderately good harvest, will assuredly produce very low prices for some time to come.

LONDON:
E. WOOD, PRINTER, POPPIN'S COURT, FLEET STREET.

# AN ATTEMPT

TO ESTIMATE THE

# EFFECTS OF PROTECTING DUTIES

ON THE

# PROFITS OF AGRICULTURE.

BY

JOHN MORTON, F.G.S.

AUTHOR OF THE NATURE AND PROPERTY OF SOILS,

AND

JOSHUA TRIMMER, F.G.S.

AUTHOR OF PRACTICAL GEOLOGY AND MINERALOGY, AND PRACTICAL CHEMISTRY FOR FARMERS AND LANDOWNERS.

---

Diique Deæque omnes, studium quibus arva tueri,
* * * *
Et vos, agrestum presentia numina, Fauni,
* * * *
Munera vestra cano.

Aid us, Protectionists and Farmers' friends,
We shew the good to which Protection tends.

*FIFTH EDITION.*

LONDON:

JAMES RIDGWAY, PICCADILLY.

1846.

*John Morton (1781–1864)*[1] *and Joshua Trimmer (1795–1857)*[2]

John Morton was born in Ceres, Fifeshire, the second son of Robert Morton and Kath Pitcairn. He was educated in the local parish school until the family moved to Flisk. Morton first farmed in Kilmany, Fifeshire, and in 1810 moved to Dulverton, Somerset where he farmed until 1818. In 1818 he became agent to Lord Ducie's Gloucestershire estates, a position he held until his retirement in 1852. Morton planned and managed the Whitfield example farm and established the Uley agricultural machine factory where he developed the Uley cultivator and other farming appliances. In 1812 he married Jean, sister of Dr Thomas Chalmers who in 1843 led the disruption of the Church of Scotland.

Morton is said to have walked over most of the English counties noting their geology. In 1838 he published *On the nature and property of Soils: their connexion with the geological formation on which they rest; the best means of permanently increasing their productiveness, and on the rent and profits of agriculture*, London: Ridgway, 1838, and in 1839 he was elected Fellow of the Geological Society. To the 3rd edition of 1843 he added *an account of the proceedings at Whitfield Example Farm; the system of agriculture recommended on the estates of the Earl of Ducie: a letter to Mr. Pusey's tenants; and the mode of cultivation adopted on Stinchcombe farm.*

Joshua Trimmer was born in North Cray, Kent, the eldest son of Joshua Kirkby Trimmer. In 1814 he managed a copper mine in North Wales, then a farm in Middlesex, and from 1825 until about 1840 he was an overseer of slate quarries near Bangor and Carnarvon. Like Morton he combined an interest in agriculture with the study of geology, and is said to have made important advances in the classification of superficial deposits of the earth's crust. Trimmer was made Fellow of the Geological Society in 1832. His first published work was *Practical Geology and Mineralogy; with instruction for the qualitative analysis of Minerals* (1841), followed by *Practical Chemistry for Farmers and Landowners* (1842), *Proposals for a Geological Survey, specially directed to agricultural objects* (1850), *The Keythorpe System of Land Drainage, its principles, efficiency, economy and opponents* (1857), and various articles on geology and agriculture.

According to Somerville,

[Cobden] communicated new views to me which had neither seen before, nor comprehended clearly even when he introduced them. But he always introduced new views as questions for my consideration, not as positive certitudes. Of this kind was the question of how far the farmers taxed each other for each other's supposed protection? How far the wheat-growing farmer taxed the cheese-making farmer and the sheep farmer? the oats and the barley growers, the wheat growers? and so on. When this subject was first opened to me, I doubted whether the free traders had a case in it. Mr. Cobden was sure they had. He suggested this subject to Mr. Morton of Whitfield Example Farm, Gloucestershire, who confessed this view of the question to be new to him; but at the same time he said he thought there was truth and force in it. He undertook the task of examining it closely, and, in doing so, made a series of calculations, which were published, and did more, I believe, than any single publication whatever, to convince thinking minds, not before convinced, of the fallacies of protection.

Alexander Somerville, *The Whistler at the Plough* (1852), London: The Merlin Press, Fairfield, N.J., U.S.A.: Augustus Kelley, 1989, p. 6.

[1] Entry by Bernard Barsham Woodward in *D.N.B.* vol. 13, pp. 1051–2, and Frederic Boase, *Modern English Biography*, vol. 2 (1901), London: Frank Cass, 1965.
[2] Boase, vol. 3.

# PREFACE.

The writers of the following pages happened to be in communication soon after Mr. Cobden's announcement of the new view which he had taken of the system of agricultural protection, namely, that it is a system of mutual plunder, under which the growers of the different descriptions of agricultural produce rob one another; and it was agreed to test a proposition so novel and plausible, by working out the question in detail, each for that kind of farming with which he was most familiar.

The unexpected results obtained, encouraged them to extend the inquiry to the other systems of husbandry prevalent in the best farmed districts of Britain; and to lay the results of their joint labours, in their joint names, before the public, in the hope that they might have the effect of diminishing that alarm with which so many of their agricultural friends contemplate the prospect of those changes which are inevitable, and of inspiring the landed, as well as the monied interests, with confidence in the application of capital to the improvement of the productive powers of the soil.

This want of confidence, and the persuasion that the prosperity of agriculture depends upon artificial prices, are the chief causes which drive the surplus capital of this country into any channel of speculation, however uncertain and hazardous, in preference to the safe and profitable investment which the improvement of our own soil affords.

# EFFECT OF PROTECTING DUTIES

ON THE

# PROFITS OF AGRICULTURE.

1. On a question which has been so repeatedly discussed as that of the Corn-laws we have long ceased to expect anything new. The monotony of the Agricultural Debates of the past session, has however been agreeably relieved by several striking novelties. Among these may be enumerated the indications given by Sir Robert Peel and Sir James Graham of the tendency of their future policy to the gradual abolition of the protective system; the declaration of Lord John Russell that protection is the bane of agriculture; the argument of Mr. Cobden that the effect of protecting duties is merely to defend the cultivators of one British county against those of another; and lastly the notice given by Mr. Escott that he shall move early in the next session of Parliament for the free admission of maize or Indian corn. To these significant hints that the days of the Corn-laws are drawing rapidly to a close, we may add the suggestion thrown out by Mr. Sotheron, at an agricultural meeting, that the system of agricultural protection, may possibly not last more than two years.

2. If such be the prospects of the farmers, it behoves them to consider well the value of the protective system; in order that if they cannot carry on their business without that of which there appears every prospect of their being speedily deprived, they may rally all their forces, and make a desperate effort to maintain it; and that on the other hand, if it be of

no value, or if it be, as some contend, a serious loss to them, they, the tenant farmers of England, may throw their weight into the scale, to accelerate that change which seems inevitable, and, by so doing, relieve themselves, at once, of a burthen which oppresses them.

3. Mr. Cobden has declared the system of protecting duties to be a system of mutual plunder, between the growers of the different descriptions of agricultural produce.

4. If his views of the protective system be correct, it will go far towards establishing the truth of Lord John Russell's assertion, that protection is the bane of agriculture.

5. We propose, therefore, in the ensuing pages, in order to test the validity of Mr. Cobden's assertion, to consider in detail, the effects of protecting duties, on the interests of some of our chief agricultural districts; and to inquire whether there are any which gain by those duties, at the expense of others. We shall endeavour also, to estimate the amount of loss to those districts which lose by protection, if such there be.

6. The first point to be ascertained is the amount of the protecting duties on the different descriptions of agricultural produce.

7. This will be easy enough with respect to every kind of produce except corn. Over corn, however, the sliding scale has thrown such a cloud of mystification, that it is impossible to bring any two persons to agree as to the amount of protection afforded under the late or present Corn-law.

8. Fortunately, however, it is not essential to the value of our reasoning, that we should arrive at an exact conclusion upon this point. It will be sufficient if we agree upon a given amount of protection; *and apply it equally to both sides of our argument.*

9. By a Parliamentary return of the foreign wheat and other grain entered for home consumption between 1828 and 1841, the duration of the late Corn-law, we are fur-

nished with the average rates of duty actually paid upon each description of grain imported.

10. The following is the aggregate of the importations from 1828 to 1841, with the average amount of duty paid:—

| | Qrs. | Amount of Duty Received | Average rates of duty per qr. |
|---|---|---|---|
| Wheat . . | 13,555,471 . . . . | £3,779,417 . . | 5*s.* 7*d.* |
| Barley . . | 2,826,397 . . . . . | 659,559 . . | 4 8 |
| Oats . . . | 3,534,627 . . . . . | 1,137,940 . . | 6 5 |
| Peas . . . | 919,227 . . . . . | 266,374 . . | 5 10 |
| Beans . . . | 1,071,369 . . . . . | 371,698 . . | 6 11 |

11. The rates of duty which we shall use in the following calculations will be for wheat 5*s.* 6*d.*, oats 6*s.* 6*d.*, barley 4*s.* 8*d.*, peas 5*s.* 10*d.*, beans 6*s.* 11*d.*, being a close approximation to the protection indicated by the preceding returns.

12. Our estimate of the duty on wheat may perhaps be objected to as too low, by those who remember that the late sliding scale afforded an apparent protection for several years in succession of from 20*s.* to 40*s.* a quarter.

13. The real test, however, of the extent to which the sliding scale has succeeded in its avowed object of keeping up artificial prices, is a comparison of the prices of wheat in this country and abroad during a period of several years.

14. There is probably no better test of what the price of wheat would have been in this country, in the absence of all restrictions on importation, than is afforded by the Channel Islands, where the trade is perfectly free; those islands sending the corn of their own growth free to this country, whenever the importation is profitable, and receiving foreign corn duty free for their own consumption.

15. By a Parliamentary return, it appears that the price of wheat in Jersey, during the ten years from 1832 to 1841, averaged 48*s.* 4*d.* the quarter. The average price

in England, for the same ten years was 56*s.* 8*d.* being a difference of 8*s.* 4*d.* the quarter. But it will at once be conceded, by all who are acquainted with the subject, that a constant demand from England, under a free trade, would have raised the level of foreign grain, at the very least, 2*s.* to 3*s.* the quarter, and this brings the price up to within 5*s.* or 6*s*, of our own average; which corroborates our estimate of the protection at 5*s.* 6*d.* the quarter.

16. Having thus sufficiently determined the amount of protection enjoyed under the last Corn-law, and assuming that it has not been increased by the present sliding scale, we proceed to estimate the value of protection to our different agricultural districts.

17. The first case which we shall investigate will be that of 400 acres of light land in Norfolk, in the eastern district of that county, where the cultivation is not in general so high as in West Norfolk.

18. In commencing this inquiry we must remember that the farmer cannot possibly derive any benefit from the fictitious value given by protecting duties to any part of his produce, except the surplus which he has for sale, after providing for the maintenance of the men and animals employed in cultivation. It matters not to him, provided the quality be the same, whether the hay consumed by his horses be worth £3. or £6. the ton; whether the oats with which he feeds them would sell for 20*s.* or 40*s.*; or whether his seed wheat be valued at 40*s.* or 80*s.* the quarter. The prices of these portions of the produce, are only of consequence, as indicating the price of that portion of the same kinds of produce which he sells.

19. As little does it matter what may be the price of the wheat and bacon with which he feeds the ploughmen whom he boards in the house. Neither, if, after the custom of Northumberland, and some other northern counties, he

employs hired householders, resident upon the farm, and paid their wages in kind, will he gain anything by the enhanced price of that portion of the produce consumed by them.

20. The only advantage which the farmer can derive from the artificial enhancement of the price of the food of agricultural labourers, is when competition for employment enables him to pay them money wages, insufficient to purchase their fair share of the produce.

21. Either the farmer repays his servants, in the form of increased wages, the amount of protecting duty paid by them on the agricultural produce which they consume, or the system robs them to that amount.

22. This robbery, moreover, is not committed for the farmer's benefit, but for that of his landlord; because since rent consists of the surplus produce, after deducting the cost of cultivation, and a fair remuneration to the tenant for his time, skill, and capital, whatever depresses the value of wages relatively to the price of agricultural produce, operates to increase rents.

23. Such advanced rents, however, are not all clear gain to the landlord, they are subject to many serious deductions in the form of increased poors' rates, increased county-rates, for gaols and criminal prosecutions, the cost of maintaining a rural police, and losses by incendiary fires. They are subject, also, to many enormous deductions in the form of electioneering expenses, for the maintenance of the protective system, and to deductions for the protecting duties on every description of agricultural produce consumed in their families, and in the famlies of all the tradesmen with whom they deal, which of course are added to their bills.

24. In the calculations which follow we shall assume, that whatever the agricultural labourer pays, in the shape of protecting duty, on the bread which he consumes, and on his cheese—when he is fortunate enough to be a con-

sumer of cheese—he receives back again, in the shape of higher wages than he would be paid were the price of his food not artificially raised.

25. We have made this assumption the basis of our calculations, respecting the effects of the protective system on labour, because it is the most favourable view which can be taken of that system; but we believe the fact to be quite the reverse. If the protectionists demur to this assumption, they place themselves on the opposite horn of the dilemma, that THE EFFECT OF AGRICULTURAL PROTECTION IS TO ROB THE AGRICULTURAL LABOURER.

26. Hitherto we have supposed a case in which the farmer raises the whole of the protected agricultural produce which he employs in cultivation, as seed, or food for his servants and cattle; but if, from the nature of his soil and climate, he is obliged to purchase from other districts, a greater amount of protected articles than he sells, it is clear that he must be a loser by the difference.

27. Now this is precisely the case with the farmers of the light lands of Norfolk; they sell no protected articles, produced by themselves, except wheat and barley.

28. They buy from the pasture districts most of the bullocks which they fatten, and it is only some parts of the county which breed their own sheep.

29. They purchase the oats consumed by their horses; and they purchase large quantities of artificial manures and of food for purchased cattle, in order to increase the quantity and quality of the manure.

30. If therefore, the returns of the farmer be increased, by the protective system, his expenses are likewise increased, by the amount to which those duties enhance the price of his seed-corn.*

31. His expenses are increased, for the benefit of the oat growers of the Lincolnshire Fens, and of Scotland and

* See par. 63.

Ireland, by the amount of the protecting duty on every bushel of oats which his horses eat.

32. He pays tribute to Cheshire, Derbyshire, Gloucestershire, Wilts, and Somerset, to the amount of ten shillings the hundred weight, upon all the cheese consumed by himself and his labourers.

33. For the benefit, or supposed benefit of Kent, Essex, and a few other southern counties, the price of all the clover-seed he sows is enhanced, by a protecting duty of ten shillings the cwt.

34. For the benefit of a few thousand acres in Kent, and in less than six other counties, he pays a protecting duty on the hops consumed by himself and his labourers. The protecting duty on hops is the difference between the import duty of £4. 10*s.* on foreign hops, and the excise duty of 18*s.* 8*d.* on hops of English growth; that is £3. 11*s.* 4*d.* the cwt.

35. As the arable farmer of East Norfolk is a buyer of lean cattle and sheep, as well as a seller of fat beef and mutton, the most favourable view which can be taken of the protecting duties on foreign cattle and meat, is either that they have no effect at all, upon the market, from the inability of foreign countries to supply us, or that the duties on fat and lean stock neutralize one another.

36. The least favourable view is, that while a fat and a lean ox are admitted at the same duty, and corn is excluded, the system operates as an inducement to the foreign breeders to send their cattle over fat instead of lean, thus depriving the British Farmer of the benefit of the manure produced while they are fattening.

37. The cultivator of 400 acres of light land in Norfolk purchases annually, at least 40 tons of oil cake, with which to feed his bullocks and sheep, for the sake of improving their manure. The bullocks are chiefly Highland and Galloway, Scots and Short-horns bred in the North; the

remainder are Devons and Irish, together with some Homebreds from the pasture districts of Norfolk.

38. The complaint of the arable farmers of Norfolk is, that they are obliged to pay so high a price for their lean stock that they rarely make any profit by fattening them; and that they are to them mere manufacturers of manure.

39. A great benefit, would therefore be conferred on the arable farmers of Norfolk, by such an influx of cattle from Belgium, Holland, Germany, and Spain, as would, keep down the price of lean stock to such a point as would in conjunction with cheap cattle food, leave them a profit on fattening their manufacturers of manure; provided those cattle were equal in quality to the Scots and Short-horns they now receive from the North.

40. The prospect of this, however, is, we fear, but distant: there are two impediments to it; the augmented demand of a rapidly increasing population, which enhances the price of meat, and by consequence, of lean stock, and the tardiness with which the diffusion of improved breeds of sheep and cattle spread among the bulk of the farmers of any country. We may take the case of cattle imported from Ireland, as an example of the manner in which the demands of our increasing numbers keep a-head of the supply. Twenty years ago the total importation of live cattle from that country amounted to 17,000 head. We can remember when the low prices of 1822 and 1823 were attributed by butchers, graziers, and statesmen, to the seventeen thousand horned invaders of that period. In the reign of Charles the Second, when the importation was much smaller, the English Parliament voted them a nuisance; in 1841 the numbers annually imported into Liverpool alone had increased to 100,000 head; and yet, with our increased population—when the manufacturers are in full employment and at good wages,—notwithstanding a diminished Government demand for the army and navy,

notwithstanding the prohibition removed against importation of live cattle and fresh meat from the Continent, and with duty reduced on American provisions—measures which excited such a panic among the agricultural interest—this increased importation from Ireland has been insufficient to keep down the price of meat—witness the present state of Smithfield market—to such a point as the interests of the consumer require, or to keep down the price of lean stock to such a point as would enable the tenants of those light lands which cannot be cultivated advantageously without the manure of a large quantity of live stock, to purchase that stock at such a price as would give them a profit on feeding it.*

* The following calculations, extracted from two articles in the North British Review for May and August, 1845, on the improvement of land, as an employment for capital, are well worthy the consideration of those who still feel alarm at the effects of the importation of foreign food on the interests of British agriculture, and have not considered the power of increasing population fully employed at good wages, to cause a continually augmenting demand with which the supply will with difficulty keep pace: "Two pounds of meat," says the writer, "consumed weekly by each of the two hundred thousand mouths, added annually to our population, would occasion an augmented demand increasing annually at the rate of 34,000 oxen of six hundred weight each, whilst increased wages affording to five millions of our underfed existing population the means of purchasing only one pound of meat, each weekly, would cause a further annual demand of 386,000 oxen of the same weight, or an equivalent quantity of mutton and pork. Again, as to the surplus produce of Ireland, it would soon be reduced to a negative quantity, if the cultivators of her soil were consumers of bread and meat; five ounces only of beef consumed weekly by each of the eight millions of her people, would cut off her export of live cattle, supposing it to be double that which now

41. The Irish cattle afford an example of the tardiness with which improved breeds are diffused. Though considerably improved, during the last twenty years, they are still so far inferior to our best breeds, as to cause the farmers of Norfolk to buy them, not from choice but from necessity, in consequence of the higher relative price of Devons, Scots, and Short-horns. It is therefore obviously their interest, that our Continental neighbours should improve their breeds of sheep and cattle, in order to render them suitable to our markets; and that they should resort with them in a lean state, like the drovers of Scotland and Ireland, to the weekly market on the Castle Hill, at Norwich, or the annual fair at St. Faiths.

42. The improvement of the Continental breeds and the rearing of cattle for the English market will, however, be a slow process; and most of the present generation will be laid in their graves, before the imported foreign cattle will, either in numbers or quality, equal the importation from Ireland. In the mean time the rapid increase of population will occasion a demand for meat which will far exceed the supply, and which will be of no benefit to the arable farmer of Norfolk, because the price of the lean stock which he is obliged to buy will advances at an equal rate.

43. It would be more in accordance with the present state of continental agriculture to send us lean cattle and corn, than to employ the corn in fattening them, and to send them over fat. While, therefore, the entire removal of restrictions on the importation of corn and cattle, would

---

enters England by way of Liverpool, and supposing that instead of being lean kine, they were fat oxen of six cwt. each; again the 318,700 quarters of wheat, and wheat flour, and the 2,327,782 quarters of oats imported from Ireland in 1841 would give scarcely 1½ pecks of wheat and little more than 2½ bushels of oats for the annual consumption of each of her "potatoe-and-point-fed population.""

benefit the cultivators of our light soils; the partial relaxation of the protective system, which admits the foreign fat ox, but refuses to receive the corn with which the lean beast might be fattened, gives a bonus to the foreign breeder to fatten his ox before he sends him over. We thus inflict a triple injury on the cultivator of the light arable lands of England, by preventing him from purchasing his raw material—the lean beast and his food—in the cheapest market, and bringing in the manufactured article—fat meat—to compete with that which he has produced under disadvantages occasioned by those very Corn-laws, the maintenance of which he has been taught to believe is necessary to save him from ruin.

44. We may form some estimate of the benefit which our Norfolk farmer would derive from the free importation of oats, beans, and maize, none of which he grows, from the results which have attended the use of peas and linseed made into a compound, on the plan of Mr. Warnes of Trimingham, as a substitute for linseed cake, in the feeding of sheep and cattle.

45. A large tenant farmer near Norwich informed us, that in 1843, the produce of twenty acres of peas, with the linseed from eight acres of flax, fattened as much stock as he could have kept with purchased oil-cake to the value of £300, and he also informed us, that during the winter of that year, the use of this kind of food reduced the price of cake by £2. the ton. Other parties have assured us that this was a low estimate of the reduction of price thus occasioned. The general failure of the hay and turnip crops, in 1844, caused oil-cake to advance again in price, notwithstanding the extended use of the compound of Mr. Warnes. We are, therefore, forming a very low estimate of the effect of an unrestricted importation of beans, maize, and oats, in reducing the price of oil-cake, by fixing the reduction at £2. the ton.

46. There is another road to the same conclusion: seven quarters of oats weigh a ton, the protective duty on which, at 6s. 6d. the quarter, amounts to £2. 5s. 6d.; we may, therefore, safely calculate the effects of a free importation of this and other grain, capable of being used as substitutes for oil-cake, as equal to the reduction of the price of that article by £2 the ton.

47. At this rate, the benefit which the cultivator of an arable farm of 400 acres of light land, in Norfolk, would derive from the free importation of cattle-food would amount to £80, supposing him to consume only 40 tons of oil-cake. The pecuniary benefit which the occupier of this farm would derive from the expenditure, in cheap cattle-food, of the sum now applied to the purchase of artificial manures, we shall place hereafter in several points of view.

48. We proceed now to consider the extent to which protecting duties on oats enhance the cost of keeping farm horses. A light land farmer in Norfolk cultivates 400 acres with twelve horses, and he does not feed them so highly as in most other counties, giving them *only one bushel of oats each weekly*. The consumption of his farm horses will, therefore, be 78 quarters, to which must be added two bushels a week for his riding horse, making a total of 91 quarters, which will be raised in price by protecting duties 6s 6d. the quarter, £29. 11s. 6d.

49. We shall now proceed from the consideration of the effects of protecting duties on the food consumed by the Norfolk farmers' cattle, to their effects on the food consumed by the agricultural labourer of Norfolk. In calculating the extent to which these enhance the cost of production to the farmer, on the assumption that the protecting duty paid by the labourer on the agricultural produce consumed by him, is repaid by him in his wages, we have first to ascertain whether the Norfolk labourer lives chiefly on bread, or whether he is a regular or constant consumer of meat, butter, bacon, and cheese.

50. To answer the latter question with strict truth, it must, we fear, be answered in the negative. Wages, in Norfolk, are, 9*s*. a week for labourers, and 10*s*. for ploughmen, who work longer hours. Labourers having families of from four to six children, have stated to us, in reply to inquiries as to the manner in which this sum was expended, that their weekly consumption of flour varied between 3 and 3½ stones.

51. If we take the Norfolk labourer's weekly consumption of flour at three stones, and if we suppose him to consume, during the year, 1 cwt. of cheese and an equal quantity of bacon—though how it is to be paid for out of 9*s*. a week we know not—we shall find, estimating 3½ cwt. of flour as equal to one quarter of wheat, which pays a protecting duty of 5*s*. 6*d*., that this labourer will be taxed to the protective system as follows:—

| | | | |
|---|---|---|---|
| Flour, 156 stones, paying 5*s*. 6*d*. for 28 stones, or 3½ cwt. . . | 1 | 10 | 7 |
| Cheese, 1 cwt., duty 10*s*. per cwt. . | 0 | 10 | 0 |
| Bacon, 1 cwt., duty 14*s*. per cwt. . | 0 | 14 | 0 |
| | £2 | 14 | 7 |

52. If, however, the labourer consumes 3½ stones of flour weekly, no bacon, and only ½ cwt. of cheese during the year, the account will stand thus—

| | | | |
|---|---|---|---|
| Flour 182 stones, duty 5*s*. 6*d*. for 28 stones | 1 | 15 | 9 |
| Cheese ½ cwt. . . . . . | 0 | 5 | 0 |
| | £2 | 0 | 9 |

53. The mean of these two diet tables, neither of them so good as that of the convict,* will be £2. 7*s*. 8*d*., which,

* The convicts in the dock-yards receive weekly:—Biscuit, 28 ounces—Oatmeal, 49 ounces—Beef, 56 ounces—Cheese, 12 ounces—Beer, 3 pints.

multiplied by twenty, for 400 acres, allowing five labourers to the hundred acres, will give £47. 13*s*. 4*d*.

This is the amount of protecting duties paid on the food consumed by the labourers employed upon this farm.

54. To this we must add the protecting duty on the malt and hops consumed by them, unless they are to drink water. If we allow the twenty men employed upon 400 acres, seventeen hogsheads of beer, as the annual consumption of themselves and their families, which will be "the slightest taste in life" over one pint a day, among all the members of each family, the malt required for this quantity, at one quarter to two hogsheads, will be 8½ quarters, which being the produce of an equal quantity of barley, will have paid a protecting duty of 4*s*. 8*d*. the quarter.

55. The hops necessary for this quantity of beer may be called ¾ cwt., which will have paid a protecting duty (see par. 34.) of £3. 11*s*. 4*d*. the cwt., in favour of the hop growers of Kent, Sussex, Surrey, Hampshire, Worcestershire, and Herefordshire.

56. The following will, then, be the amount of protecting duty on the beer of twenty agricultural labourers:—

| | | | |
|---|---|---|---|
| Protecting duty on 8½ quarters of barley (grown in Norfolk) at 4*s*. 8*d*. per quarter . . | 1 | 19 | 8 |
| On ¾ cwt. of hops not grown in Norfolk . . | 2 | 13 | 6 |
| | £4 | 13 | 2 |

57. If, therefore, the labourer be repaid the amount of protecting duties, charged upon what he eats and drinks, to enable the landed interest to enhance the price of food to the non-agricultural classes, the cultivator of 400 acres of light land in Norfolk, will be obliged to repay his labourers, for protecting duties, the following sums—

| | |
|---|---|
| Protecting duties on the food of twenty* men and their families . . . . | 47 13 4 |
| Protecting duties on their beer . . . | 4 13 2 |
| | £52 6 6 |

58. We will now collect together the several items which the cultivator of 400 acres of light land in East Norfolk pays in the shape of protecting duties on articles of agricultural produce consumed upon the farm, as well as the amount of protecting duties which he receives in the increased price of those articles which he sells.—These are only wheat and barley.

59. We charge nothing to the account of protection on sheep and cattle, because in the particular case under consideration, as well as in East Norfolk in general, they are not bred upon the farm, and therefore, the protecting duty if charged at all, should be charged on both sides of the account, that which is received with the one hand for the fat animal, being paid with the other to the breeder.

* "Twenty men and their families." It is not to be understood that the *whole of the families are employed on the farm*, but the labour of the men who are employed must support their families. It may, perhaps, be objected that the Norfolk farmers do not employ so many as five men to the hundred acres. It must be remarked, however, that we have charged nothing for protection on the food of women and boys employed, or of extra labourers in harvest, hay-time, and turnip-hoeing. The wages of twenty men, at 10*s*. a week, would amount to £520., or twenty pounds more than 25*s*. an acre. We have seen resolutions of certain Farmers' Clubs, in that or the adjoining county, which declared, that "if they had remunerating prices they could employ labour profitably to the amount of £2. or £2. 10*s*. per acre." We allow them remunerating prices—that is to say, as remunerative as the Corn-law of 1828 could give.

In other cases which will come under consideration, we shall charge the protecting duty of 3*s*. a head on sheep and 20*s* on cattle, among the items received by the farmer from the protective system on animals bred upon the farm, but not upon those purchased.

60. Under the head of tradesmen's bills, farmers, who keep accounts, class their payments to the blacksmith, wheelwright, and harness-maker. These, in Norfolk and Suffolk, are usually considered to amount to about one hundred pounds on a farm of 400 acres. The charge is high, but as it appears the general calculation, we shall adopt it.

61. It will be a low estimate of the effect of protecting duties on this item, if we call it ten per cent, or ten pounds. It must be remembered, that this includes, not only the protecting duties on the food consumed by the blacksmith, wheelwright and harness-maker, and their workmen, but also the protecting duties upon the food of all the labourers who have worked in preparing the raw material, from the raising of the coal and iron, the felling of the timber, and the tanning of the hide. It includes, also, the enhanced price of all wood-work, arising from the timber duties, which are kept up partly to encourage the growth of trees in hedgerows, to the farmer's cost.

62. The sum of two pounds, which we have charged for the farmer's expenses in maintaining the protective system, such as subscribing to Central and Branch Agricultural Protection Societies, attending Demonstration Dinners, and signing petitions, must, we are sure, be deemed very moderate, by all who have had any experience of such matters. "We poor farmers," said a Lincolnshire friend of ours, as we paid our dinner bill of a guinea a head, upon the occasion of some great agricultural gathering, "we poor farmers have just eaten up a sack of oats apiece and 28 lbs. of mutton."

### Recapitulation.—Norfolk.

63. The following will be the amount paid by the cultivator of 400 acres of light land in East Norfolk, in the shape of protecting duties on agricultural produce consumed by himself, his labourers, and cattle: and first with respect to seed, as we have allowed the protective duties on the gross produce of the farm, without deducting the seed, we must here charge the same duties on the corn sown.

| Seed-corn. | Bushels. | | Acres. | | | £. | s. | d. |
|---|---|---|---|---|---|---|---|---|
| Wheat | 2½ | × | 100 | = | 31¼ quarters at 5*s* 6*d* | 8 | 11 | 10 |
| Barley | 3½ | × | 100 | = | 43¾ ditto at 4*s* 8*d* | 10 | 4 | 2 |
| Clover red | 12 lbs. | × | 100 | = | 1200 lbs. | | | |
| White | 8 | × | 100 | = | 800 | | | |
| | | | | | lbs. 2000 say 17¾ cwt. at 10*s* | 8 | 17 | 6 |
| Trefoil | 8 lbs. | × | 100 | | 800 say 7⅛ cwt. at 5*s* | 1 | 15 | 9 |
| Rye-grass, | ½ bushl. | × | 100 | = | 50 bushls. 12½ cwt. at 10*s* | 6 | 5 | 0 |
| | | | | | | £35 | 14 | 3 |

| | £. | s. | d. |
|---|---|---|---|
| Horse keep, (par. 48) | 29 | 11 | 6 |
| Oil-cake for sheep and cattle, (par. 45 to 47) | 80 | 0 | 0 |
| Tradesmen's Bills, 10 per cent on £100. (par. 60) | 10 | 0 | 0 |
| Sundries, (par. 62) | 2 | 0 | 0 |
| Labourers' food (par. 50, 51, 52) | 47 | 13 | 4 |
| Labourers' beer, (par. 54, 55, 56) | 4 | 13 | 2 |
| | £209 | 12 | 3 |

64. Amount received from protecting duties on the produce which this farmer sells.

| | £. | s. | d. |
|---|---|---|---|
| Wheat 4 qrs. × 100 acres = 400 quarters at 5*s* 6*d* | 110 | 0 | 0 |
| Barley 5 qrs. × 100 acres = 500 ditto at 4*s* 8*d* | 116 | 13 | 4 |
| | £226 | 13 | 4 |

65. Deducting the amount paid for protection from the amount received by it on the produce sold, we find that the occupier of this farm gains £17. 1*s*. 1*d*. by the protective system.

66 This, however, is taking a very imperfect view of the effects of the system. It merely includes the burthen of protection on the cost of cultivation. There remain to be considered the effects of the system on the rent, and on the expenditure of the tenant's profits—or the housekeeping expenses of his family.

67. His rent may be called £500 per annum. It is fixed at that amount on the assumption that by means of protective duties, an average price of 56*s.* can be secured for wheat, instead of which the average does not range above 50*s.* The rent therefore is too high by £54.*

68. In our estimate of the effect of protecting duties, in enhancing the amount of the payments to tradesmen whose assistance is necessary in the work of cultivation, we have stated reasons why ten per cent is a very moderate allowance for the increased charge occasioned by protecting duties on the food, not only of the blacksmith, wheelwright, and collar maker, but of all the workmen, employed in producing the raw material, the iron, wood, and leather, which they bring to the complete state of manufacture.

69. For the same reasons, estimating the expenditure of the family of the tenant occupying a farm of this size at £400 a year, we consider that we are well within bounds, in charging £40 of this to the account of agricultural protection —protecting duties on the bread, butter, cheese, bacon, malt and hops consumed by the tenant, his wife, children, house-

* In the event of the abolition of the present delusive system of fixing rents by reference to an ideal act-of-Parliament standard of prices, which on the average of years is never realized, and the abolition of the protective laws which gave birth to the system, the farmer would either get a reduction of rent, or an equivalent for it in better terms, such as improved tenure, diminution of game, removal of useless fences, trees, &c. and power to convert poor pasture land to arable.

hold servants, and guests, protecting duties on the food of his grocer, tailor, shoemaker, and other tradesmen,—protecting duties on the food of all those employed in the manufacture, from its raw to its finished state, of every article of wood, iron, wool, flax, cotton, &c., upon every article in fact of dress or furniture which he uses. Those advocates for protecting duties on agricultural produce, who deny that they are thus repaid to the tradesmen with whom the farmer deals, place themselves in the same dilemma, as that which has been stated in the case of the agricultural labourer, par. 25, namely that the tradesmen are robbed to the amount of those duties.

70. The farmer will pay then for protection in the form of

| | | | |
|---|---|---|---|
| increased rent . . . . . . . . . . . | £54 | 0 | 0 |
| Increased housekeeping and expenses . . | 40 | 0 | 0 |
| | £94 | 0 | 0 |

and this sum added to £209. 12*s.* 3*d.* the increased cost of cultivation arising from protecting duties, will amount to £303. 12*s.* 3*d.*, from which deducting £226. 13*s.* 4*d.* received from protecting duties on the produce sold, we have £76. 18*s.* 11*d.*, as the loss of the tenant by the protective system.

71. This, however, is not his whole loss. Besides the forty tons of oil cake purchased to improve the manure of his cattle, the tenant of this farm expends at least £200 in the purchase of artificial manures, such as rape cake, bones, and guano. If, by the removal of restrictions on the importation of corn, he were enabled to purchase oats weighing forty pounds the bushel for 15*s.* the quarter, the £200 now expended on artificial manures, would buy 266 quarters of oats, which would enable the green crops to fatten 170 sheep, and 17 beasts more than the farm carries at present. The manure produced by them would be more

beneficial than the bones, rape cake, or guano which could be bought for £200.

72. If we estimate therefore the loss which the tenant of such a farm sustains by being precluded by the protective system from the purchase of low priced corn merely at the amount of duty on these 266 quarters of oats it will be £86. 9*s*., which added to the £76. 18*s*. 11*d*., of par. 70, will give £163. 7*s*. 11*d*., as the sum he would gain by a free importation of corn. This however is too low an estimate.

73. If we suppose the sheep and beasts to be purchased in such terms that they merely return their prime cost, and the cost of the corn consumed by them, the £200 now expended on artificial manures will be saved and the account will stand thus :—

| | | | |
|---|---|---|---|
| There would be gained by the removal of restrictions on impo.tations, as in par. 70 . . | £76 | 18 | 11 |
| There would be saved by purchasing corn instead of artificial manures . | 200 | 0 | 0 |
| | £276 | 18 | 11 |
| 74. The purchase of the additional live stock would require an additional capital of £400, deduct therefore ten per cent on this for interest and casualties . . | 40 | 0 | 0 |
| There remains . . . . . . | £236 | 18 | 11 |

This is equal to a profit of 11*s*. 10*d*. per acre to be gained by the repeal of protecting duties.

75. If we suppose only the moderate profit of 3*s*. each on the 170 sheep, and 30*s*. each on the 17 beasts to be made above their prime cost and the cost of their corn, it would amount to £51, which added to the £236. 18*s*. 11*d*. of the last paragraph, will give £287. 18*s*. 11*d*. or 14*s*. 4*d*. the acre.

76. Such would be the gain, which the cultivator of 400

acres of light land in East Norfolk would derive from the repeal of protecting duties on agricultural produce; and such would be the gain under similar circumstances upon a farm, of the same size, upon similar soils in Sussex, Surrey, Berks, Wilts, Hants, Dorset, and every county in the country, where the turnips are consumed upon the ground, if the better system were adopted of drawing a portion of them to be consumed by beasts in the yard, fed largely with oil-cake or corn. The cultivators of the turnip soils of those countries only suffer less from the protective system, because they employ less labour, and purchase neither corn, nor oil-cake for feeding cattle. It is to the cultivation of these light lands, carried on in this manner, that Mr. Pusey alludes in the following passage (Journal Royal Agricultural Society, Vol. I. p. 3.) "There is many a light land farm in the south of England of 500 acres on which 100 acres have not produced turnips worth more than £200 or £300, while the more spirited cultivation actually practised in Yorkshire, might have yielded 20 tons of swedes or 30 tons of turnips per acre."

77. The farmers of the Southern counties who adhere to such a system, will perhaps object to our statement of 40 tons of oil cake for the consumption of a farm of 400 acres as too high; we can assure them, however, that it errs on the side of under, rather than over, statement, and that the most spirited cultivators of the light lands of Norfolk and the adjoining counties consume cake in much larger proportions; take for instance the case of Mr. Hudson of Castle Acre, in Norfolk, (Journ. R. Ag. Soc. vol. v. p. 307) who consumes annually on 1500 acres, two hundred tons of linseed cake for his beasts and sheep, besides 100 tons of rape cake and bones. When he first entered upon the farm in 1822 he kept only 30 head of cattle, and about 800 sheep; he now fattens annually about 200 beasts and 2500 to 3,000 sheep; Mr. Jonas, likewise, of Ickleton in Cam-

bridgeshire (Farmer's Magazine, vol. 10, p. 30.) talks of keeping "constantly" on a farm of 1700 acres, on which 400 acres of turnips are grown, 200 beasts, to be fed with one fourth of the turnips drawn, and with oil cake and corn, the beasts to weigh not less than from 70 to 80 stones. Now, as it is well known, that a beast of that size consumes from 12 to 20 lbs. of cake daily, say 14 lbs. on an average, it would require 450 tons of cake to keep them "constantly," if constantly means through the whole year, or 225 tons if it means half a year; these proportions would give 112½ or 56¼ tons respectively on a farm of 400 acres, whereas our statement goes only to 40 tons.

LINCOLNSHIRE.

78. We will now consider the case of a Lincolnshire farm of 1100 acres. Our calculations will be based upon data derived from the very highest authority; namely, two statements published, first in the Mark Lane Express, and subsequently in the Farmer's Magazine for April 1842, (vol. 5, p. 372.) The first of these statements is entitled "A CALCULATION, shewing the profit on a Lincolnshire heath farm of 1100 acres of land, according to the present system of cultivation, the produce being sold for *remunerating prices*, the CAPITAL necessary for working the same to the greatest advantage being £7,700 or £700 per hundred acres."

79. The remunerating prices here spoken of are 60*s*. the quarter for wheat, 35*s*. for barley, 6*d*. the lb. for mutton, 1*s*. the lb. for wool, and 7*s*. the stone for fat hogs; with these prices, and rent 20*s*. the acre, labour 12*s*. a week, 18*s*. in harvest, bone dust 2*s*. 9*d*. the bushel, rape cake £7.10*s*. the ton, oil cake £11. 10*s*., beasts bought for straw yard £13. and lambs for turnips 26*s*. a profit is shewn of £863. 18*s*. 4*d*., besides 5 per cent. interest on the capital.

80. The other statement is called "A CALCULATION, showing the loss on a Lincolnshire heath farm of 1100 acres of land, according to the present mode of management, the

produce being sold at the reduced prices owing to the passsing of the NEW CORN BILL. The CAPITAL necessary for working the same to the greatest advantage £6,600 or £600 per 100 acres."

81. The prices charged in this statement are, wheat 44*s.* 6*d.* and barley 25*s.* the quarter, mutton 4½*d.*, wool 10*d.* the lb.; with these prices, rent remaining 20*s.* the acre, and labour reduced to 10*s.* a week, (15*s.* in harvest) bone dust 2*s.* 6*d.* the bushel, rape cake £7., linseed cake £10. 10*s.*, beasts bought for the straw yard £11., and lambs for the turnips 23*s.*; a loss is shewn of £519. 5*s.* 11*d.* making a difference of £1383. 4*s.* 2*d.* arising from the loss of agricultural protection, by the tariff and the Corn law of 1841 and 1842.

82. To each of these statements the following certificate is appended: "We the undersigned occupiers of land in this neighbourhood have carefully examined this document and do not hesitate to say we believe it to be strictly correct.

Lincoln, March 18th, 1842. (Signed)

| | Acres. | | Acres. |
|---|---|---|---|
| Thos. Greetham occupier of | 800 | David Blackbourn . . | 1150 |
| William Longstaff . . | 1100 | T. W. Wiles . . . . | 1460 |
| Paul Francis Pell . . | 1100 | Edwd. Clarke . . . | 370 |
| Jno. Brown & Saml. Slater | 2100 | Edward Gibbeson . . | 400 |
| Charles Clark Pears . | 900 | Leonard Harland . . | 300 |
| William Brown . . . | 800 | William Wilson . . . | 400 |
| George Waddington . | 500 | Thomas Clarke . . . | 1000 |
| Edward Stafford Boothby | 350 | William Seagrave . . | 500 |
| William Lamb Aubourne | 500 | John Greenham . | 700 |
| Do. do. . . . | 250 | Francis Marshall . . | 430 |
| Edward Clarke . . . | 800 | Saul Turvey . . . . | 308 |
| William Lacy . . . | 850 | Messrs. Marfleet . . | 1130 |
| Charles Clark . . . | 800 | Frederick Shaw . . | 350 |
| Charles Tonge . . . | 1200 | John Eland . . . | 480 |
| William Foster . . . | 1200 | J. G. Stevenson . . . | 720" |

83. "N.B. Market day—Wheat at a nominal price, best malting barley 25*s.* the quarter, and best seed oats 9*d.* per stone, in anticipation of the proposed Corn bill; the duty on malt is *now* about 90 per cent."

84. The produce stated in each case is wheat 3¼ qrs. the acre, barley 4¾; the quantity of bones 4400 bushels, of rape cake 69 tons, of linseed cake 23 tons, exclusive of that consumed by 700 lambs, which from the data given, we estimate at 12 tons, making 35 in all. Now we happen to know farms of inferior soil in Lincolnshire, but more highly cultivated, on which the average produce of wheat and barley is much higher; the quantity of artificial manures purchased much less, or none at all; the quantity of oil cake much greater; and the capital per acre, employed in cultivation nearly double that stated in these two documents. As we cannot suppose that thirty British Farmers holding so respectable a position in society would affix their names to a deliberate misstatement of facts, even for the purpose of upholding the cause of Agricultural Protection, we can only conclude that their management involves some peculiarities of expenditure and returns, which distinguish it from that of the best farmers in Lincolnshire, who employ at least one-third more capital than these farmers of Lincoln Heath.

85. This being premised we proceed to estimate the effects of protecting duties in enhancing the farmer's expenditure, under the following heads, as stated in this document:—seed corn; food purchased for horses, sheep, and cattle; food of labourers boarded in the house; food of labourers not boarded; food of smith, wheelwright, and collar-maker; rent, and the expenditure of the farmer's profits.

86. Having ascertained these, we shall then, as in the case of Norfolk, determine the amount of protecting duties received by the tenant of a Lincoln Heath farm of 1100

acres on the produce sold by him. The one sum deducted from the other will show the profit or loss derived from the protective system, according to the mode of cultivation indicated in the above statements.

87. Lastly, we shall endeavour to estimate the effects of protection under a system of management more in accordance with the best cultivation of Lincolnshire; spending less on bones and rape cake, and more on food for additional live stock.

88. *Seed Corn*, &c.

| | | | | | |
|---|---|---|---|---|---|
| Wheat | 103⅓ qrs. at 5*s*. 6*d*. . | | 28 | 8 | 4 |
| Barley | 137⅓ qrs. at 4*s*. 8*d*. . | | 32 | 1 | 8 |
| Red Clover | 60 stones | | | | |
| White | 215 stones | | | | |
| | —— 275=cwt. 34⅜ at 10*s*. | | 17 | 3 | 9 |
| Trefoil | 61⅓ | cwt. 7⅝ at 5*s*. | 1 | 18 | 1 |
| Rye Grass | 6½ qrs. | . . | 6 | 10 | 0 |
| Tares | 7½ qrs. | . . | 3 | 15 | 0 |
| | | | £89 | 16 | 10 |

89. *Labour*—

Eighteen Men boarded in the house, their board charged at £15: Wheat, 44*s*. 6*d*. We therefore allow them to consume:—

| | | | |
|---|---|---|---|
| Wheat, 6 bushels × 18 men=108=13½ qrs. at 5*s*. 6*d*. | 3 | 14 | 3 |
| Bacon, 3½ cwt. × 18 do. = 63 cwt. at 14*s*. . | 44 | 2 | 0 |
| Cheese, 1⅝ cwt. × 18 do. = 29¼ cwt. at 10*s*. . | 14 | 12 | 6 |
| | £62 | 8 | 9 |

90. *Five Women Servants* charged the same board as the men, consume therefore the same provisions:—

| | | | |
|---|---|---|---|
| Wheat, 6 bushels × 5 women=30=3¾ qrs. at 5*s*. 6*d*. | 1 | 0 | 7 |
| Bacon, 3½ cwt. × 5 do. =17½cwt. at 14*s*. . | 12 | 5 | 0 |
| Cheese. 1⅝ cwt. × 5 do. = 8⅛ cwt. at 10*s*. . | 4 | 1 | 3 |
| | £17 | 6 | 10 |

91. *Malt*—

| | | | |
|---|---|---|---|
| 35 quarters at 4*s*. 8*d*. . . . | 8 | 3 | 4 |
| Hops charged £14., price at the time £4. 10*s*. per cwt., quantity therefore, say, 3 cwt. at £3. 11*s*. 4*d*. per cwt. (par. 63) | 10 | 14 | 0 |
| | £18 | 17 | 4 |

92. *Labourers not boarded.*

Fifteen regular labourers, 40 weeks at 12*s*., twelve weeks at 18*s*.; whose families, of 5 each, will consume—

| | | | |
|---|---|---|---|
| Wheat, 6 bush. × 5 × 15=450=56¼ qrs. at 5*s*. 6*d*. | 15 | 9 | 4 |
| Butter, ¾ cwt. × 15=11¼ cwt. at 20*s*. . | 11 | 5 | 0 |
| Bacon, 4½ cwt. × 15=67½ cwt. at 14*s*. . | 47 | 5 | 0 |
| Cheese, 3¾ cwt. × 15=56¼ cwt. at 10*s*. . | 28 | 2 | 6 |
| | £102 | 1 | 10 |

93. *Fifteen Boys,* consuming—

| | | | |
|---|---|---|---|
| Wheat, 6 bush. × 15 = 90 = 11¼ qrs. at 5*s*. 6*d*. | 3 | 1 | 10 |
| Bacon, 3 cwt. × 15 = 45 cwt. at 14*s*. . . | 31 | 10 | 0 |
| | £34 | 11 | 10 |

94. *Extra labour in harvest* and turnip hoeing, charged £130, equal to the labour of, say four men, all the year, at 13*s*. Food consumed by their four families of five each—

| | | | |
|---|---|---|---|
| Wheat, 6 × 5 × 4 = 120 bush. = 15 qrs. at 5*s*. 6*d*. | 4 | 2 | 6 |
| Bacon, 4½ cwt. × 4 = 18 cwt. at 14*s*. . . | 12 | 12 | 0 |
| Cheese, 3¾ cwt. × 4 = 15 cwt. at 10*s*. . . | 7 | 10 | 0 |
| Butter, ¾ cwt. × 4 = 3 cwt. at 20*s*. . . . | 3 | 0 | 0 |
| | £27 | 4 | 6 |

95. *Beer* consumed by the men not boarded, the same quantity as by those in the house. The protecting duty on the malt and hops, £18. 17*s*. 4*d*.

96. *Horse, sheep, and cattle food,* purchased—

Farm horses 34
Riding horses 3
—

| | | | |
|---|---|---|---|
| 37 × 2 bush. × 52 weeks, 481 qrs. at 6*s.* 6*d.* | 156 | 6 | 6 |
| Oil-cake for beasts, 23 tons (par. 46) at £2. . . | 46 | 0 | 0 |
| Ditto for lambs, charged by the head, amounting to 140, price of cake £11. 10*s.* per ton, quantity therefore 12 tons at £2. . . . . . . . | 24 | 0 | 0 |
| | £226 | 6 | 6 |

97. *Tradesmen's bills*, ten per cent. (par. 60, 61) on £170. . . . . . £17 0 0

98. *Sundries*, attending Demonstration Dinners, and subscribing to Agricultural Protection Societies (par. 62) . . £2 0 0

99. *Rent.* The rent is stated at £1100, the remunerating price of wheat is 60*s.*; unless, therefore, this rent be too low for that price, the reduction of the price to 50*s.* should produce a reduction of rent to the amount of . £183 0 0

100. *Expenditure of profits.* The expenditure of the tenant's profits we estimate at £500. a year. At least ten per cent. of this must be charged (par. 69) to the account of protecting duties on the food consumed by all the tradesmen with whom he deals, recharged to him £50 0 0

RECAPITULATION.

101 *Protecting duties paid by the cultivator* of 1100 acres of light land in Lincolnshire—

Seed (par. 88) . . . . . . 89 16 10

Food of labourers, boarded—

| | | | | | | |
|---|---|---|---|---|---|---|
| Brought forward | | | | 89 | 16 | 10 |
| 18 men (par. 89) | 62 | 8 | 9 | | | |
| 5 women (par. 90) | 17 | 6 | 10 | | | |
| Malt and hops (par. 91) | 18 | 17 | 4 | | | |
| | | | | 98 | 12 | 11 |
| Labourers, not boarded— | | | | | | |
| 15 regular men (par. 92) | 102 | 1 | 10 | | | |
| 15 boys (par 93) | 34 | 11 | 10 | | | |
| Extra labour, harvest and turnip-hoeing (par. 94) | 27 | 4 | 6 | | | |
| Beer of men not boarded (par. 95) | 18 | 14 | 4 | | | |
| | | | | 182 | 11 | 8 |
| Cattle food (par. 96) | | | | 226 | 0 | 0 |
| Tradesmen's bills (par. 97) | | | | 17 | 0 | 0 |
| Sundries—Demonstration Dinners, &c. (par. 98) | | | | 2 | 0 | 0 |
| Rent increased by protecting duties (par. 99) | | | | 183 | 0 | 0 |
| Tenant's expenditure of profits increased by protecting duties (par. 100) | | | | 50 | 0 | 0 |
| | | | | £849 | 1 | 5 |

102. *The Lincolnshire farmer receives from protecting duties on his sales—*

| | | | |
|---|---|---|---|
| Wheat, 893¾ qrs. at 5*s.* 6*d.* | 245 | 15 | 7 |
| Barley, 1306¼ qrs. at 4*s.* 8*d.* | 304 | 15 | 10 |
| Sheep bred on the farm (par. 59) 500, at 3*s.* | 75 | 0 | 0 |
| Beasts bred on the farm (par. 59) 8, at 20*s.* | 8 | 0 | 0 |
| Hogs, 25 × 25 stone = 78⅛ cwt. at 14*s.* | 54 | 13 | 9 |
| | £688 | 5 | 2 |

| | | | |
|---|---|---|---|
| 103. *The tenant pays for protecting duties* (par. 101) | 849 | 1 | 5 |
| *He receives from protecting duties as above* | 688 | 5 | 2 |
| | £160 | 16 | 3 |

He therefore loses, by being protected, £160. 16*s*. 3*d*., or 2*s*. 11*d*. the acre.

104. Such is the loss to the tenant of 1100 acres of light land in Lincolnshire, under the system of cultivation indicated in a document drawn up to prove the necessity of protecting duties to the welfare of the farmer.

105. The system of cultivation, however, is different, as we have said, from that pursued by some of the best Lincolnshire farmers; the capital employed much smaller, and the average produce lower; we will, therefore, proceed to calculate what would be gained upon a farm of this size by the repeal of all protecting duties on agricultural produce, in conjunction with a system of cultivation, under which more money would be expended on cattle-food and less on artificial manures.

| | | | |
|---|---|---|---|
| 106. If we estimate this gain only at the amount of the protecting duty on the 1496 quarters of oats, at 15*s*., which the sum of £1122. now paid for bones and rape-cake would purchase, at 15*s*. the quarter, this at 6*s*. 6*d*. the quarter, would amount to . . . . . | 486 | 4 | 0 |
| 107. But to this must be added the loss under the present system of cultivation, from protecting duties, which would be saved by a repeal of them (par. 103) . . . | 160 | 16 | 3 |
| Also, the saving of the £1122. expended in bones and rape-cake, the manure of the sheep and beasts fed with the oats, being far more efficacious than artificial manures . . . | 1122 | 0 | 0 |
| | £1769 | 0 | 3 |

| | | | |
|---|---|---|---|
| Brought forward . . . . | £1769 | 0 | 3 |
| 108. The quantity of oats given above would with the present green crops, fatten 1000 sheep and 100 beasts, which would cost, at the prices of the Lincolnshire Heath farmers' statements (namely 23*s.* for lambs, and £11. for beasts) £2250. Deduct, therefore, 10 per cent. on this additional capital for interest and casualties . . | 225 | 0 | 0 |
| | £1544 | 0 | 3 |

109. This gives more than 28*s.* the acre, as the gain to the tenant by repeal of the protecting duties, in conjunction with an improved method of cultivation; on the assumption that the additional sheep and beasts *merely return their prime cost, and the cost of the oats, without any profit.*

110. It may, however, be safely concluded that, in addition to this, the farmer will reap that moderate profit to which we before alluded (par. 75) of 3*s.* a-head upon the sheep, and 30*s.* a-head upon the beasts.

111. To this let any one add the increase which would take place in the acreable yield of wheat and barley immediately upon the adoption of this, which we are sure is an improvement on the present system and management.

112. We leave him to contemplate the enormous extent, to which he will thus have demonstrated that the occupier of 1100 acres on Lincoln Heath would benefit, by a removal of the present system of agricultural protection.

113. The total gain from all these sources would exceed two pounds per acre.

114. Those who may be disposed to dispute the possibility of improved cultivation, cannot escape the conclusions drawn from the statistics of this farm, furnished by thirty Lincolnshire farmers themselves, if it be admitted that the protecting duties on the food of the labourers not boarded in the house, are repaid in their wages, and if it be admitted that the extensive substitution of corn for oil-cake as cattle-food, would reduce the price of cake £2. per ton.

## Dairy Farming.

115. We have traced the effects of the protective system upon the light soils under the most improved cultivation. This superior cultivation, though confined to a few districts, was proved, before the Agricultural Distress Committee of 1836, to have been one of the causes of the low prices, which it was feared would drive the clays, long considered the proper wheat soils, out of arable culture, and cause them to be converted to pasture.

116. Let us therefore try the results of agricultural protection upon land of this description, which has been under grass time out of mind. We shall take a Gloucestershire Dairy Farm of one hundred acres, as representing this kind of farming.

117. A farm of this description and size keeps thirty cows; the produce sold is cheese, whey-butter, bacon, and fat cows. The servants employed are boarded in the house.

The protecting duties on the gross produce of the farm will amount to the following sum—

| | | | | |
|---|---|---|---|---|
| 30 cows, producing 3 cwt. of cheese | 90 cwt. at 10*s* | 45 | 0 | 0 |
| Whey Butter | 9 cwt. at 20*s* | 9 | 0 | 0 |
| Bacon 8¾ score per cow, say | 47 cwt. at 14*s* | 32 | 18 | 0 |
| One-fifth of the cows fattened annually, 6 Cows × 7 cwt. | 42 cwt. at 8*s* | 16 | 16 | 0 |
| | | £103 | 14 | 0 |

118. The agricultural produce consumed upon the farm consists of the food of two men, three women, and one boy, consuming as follows—

| | | | | |
|---|---|---|---|---|
| Wheat, 6 bushels × 6 = 4½ qrs. at 5*s* 6*d* | | 1 | 4 | 9 |
| Bacon, 3½ lbs. each per week, say 10 cwt. at 14*s* | | 7 | 0 | 0 |
| Cheese, 3½ lbs. ditto 10 cwt. at 10*s* | | 5 | 0 | 0 |
| Malt, 3 quarters at 4*s*. 8*d*. | £0 14 0 | | | |
| Hops, ¼ cwt. at £3. 11*s* 4*d* | 0 17 10 . . . | 1 | 1 | 10 |
| | | 14 | 16 | 7 |
| Beans for fattening Hogs, 1½ bushel for each cow say . . 6 quarters at 6*s*. 11*d*. | | 2 | 1 | 6 |
| Tenant's own expenditure increased 10 per cent by protection (par. 100) . | | 10 | 0 | 0 |
| | | £26 | 18 | 1 |

119. The Gloucestershire dairy farmer of one hundred acres, therefore—

| | | | |
|---|---|---|---|
| Receives from the protective system . | 103 | 14 | 0 |
| He pays for protection . | 26 | 18 | 1 |
| He therefore gains by protection | £76 | 15 | 11 |

120. This is equal to a clear protection in favour of Dairy-farming of 15*s*. 4*d*. per acre; the present rent of the land being about 20*s*.

121. Had this been a breeding farm, the items would have been somewhat different, but the results would have been nearly the same. There would, for instance, be in

some cases only half the quantity of cheese, butter, and bacon produced, but besides the annual sale of cast old cows, there would be a three-year old beast sold for every cow kept, the protecting duty on which would be £1 × 30 = £30.

### Whitfield Farm, Gloucestershire.

122. We will now endeavour to ascertain how the protective system would affect this Gloucestershire dairy-farm, if broken up and converted into an arable farm, on which corn is grown alternately with roots and clover. Such is Whitfield, of which the following are the statistics taken from the accounts for the past year.

123. It employs regularly 12 men, 7 women, and 3 boys, and its extra hands in harvest, may be considered equal to the constant work of 3 men, 3 women, and 1 boy. The wages of men are from 12*s* to 14*s* per week.

124. The crop of wheat consisted of 575 quarters grown upon 120 acres, no other grain being produced upon the farm. The consumption of purchased food has been oil-cake 20 tons, oats 201 quarters, pease 5 quarters, maize and barley 15 quarters.

125. The total quantity of land to which these details apply is 240 acres, there having been, till this year, 20 acres of the farm still under permanent pasture.

126. Whitfield Farm pays protecting duties on articles of agricultural produce consumed by its labourers, cattle, and tenant's family as follows :—

127. *Seed.*

| | | | |
|---|---|---|---|
| Wheat 120 Acres × 1½ Bushels = 180 bshls. = 22½ qrs. at 5*s*. 6*d*. | 6 | 3 | 9 |
| Clover Red 12 lbs. ×40 acres = 480 lbs. | | | |
| White 8 ×40 acres = 320 | | | |
| 800 say 7 cwt. at 10*s*. | 3 | 10 | 0 |
| Trefoil 4 lbs. × 40 acres = 160 say 1½ cwt. at 5*s*. | 0 | 7 | 6 |
| | £10 | 1 | 3 |

128. *Labourers.*

12 regular men
3*
—
Total 15, representing fifteen families of five individuals each, whose consumption is—

| | | | |
|---|---|---|---|
| Wheat 6 bshls. × 5 × 15 = 450 = 56¼ qrs. at 5*s.* 6*d.* | 15 | 9 | 4 |
| Meat ¾ cwt. × 15 = 11¼ cwt. at 8*s.* . | 4 | 10 | 0 |
| Butter ¾ cwt. × 15 = 11¼ cwt. at 20*s.* . | 11 | 5 | 0 |
| Bacon 3¾ cwt. × 15 = 56¼ cwt. at 14*s.* . | 39 | 7 | 6 |
| Cheese 3¾ cwt. × 15 = 56¼ cwt.† at 10*s.* . | 28 | 2 | 6 |
| | £98 | 14 | 4 |

129. *Women and boys.* 10 women, 4 boys.

| | | | |
|---|---|---|---|
| Wheat 6 bshls. × 14 = 84 × 10½ qrs. at 5*s.* 6*d.* | 2 | 17 | 9 |
| Bacon ½lb. × 365 days = say 1¾ cwt. × 14 = 24½ cwt. at 14*s.* . . . . | 17 | 3 | 0 |
| Cheese . . 1 × 14 = 14 at 10*s.* | 7 | 0 | 0 |
| Butter . . ¼ × 15 = 3½ × 20*s.* | 3 | 10 | 0 |
| | £30 | 10 | 9 |

130. *Labourers' beer.*

| | | | |
|---|---|---|---|
| Fifteen families consuming each one quart daily amongst all its members; fourteen women and boys consuming 3 quarts daily amongst them, total 18 quarts × 365 days = 1642 gals. say 30 hogsheads, at two hogsheads to the quarter, requiring 15 quarters of malt—protecting duty 4*s.* 8*d.* the quarter . | 3 | 10 | 0 |
| Hops, say 1¾ cwt. protecting duty £3. 11*s.* 4*d.* the cwt. . . . . . | 6 | 4 | 10 |
| | £9 | 14 | 10 |

* The harvest labour is equal to that of three men for 52 weeks.

† The consumption of these articles here given, is the average of the statements of the men employed on the farm respecting the food consumed by their families.

131. *Food for cattle and sheep.*

| | | | | | | |
|---|---|---|---|---|---|---|
| Oil cake | 20 tons | at £2 = (par. 46) | . | 40 | 0 | 0 |
| Peas | 5 quarters | at 5*s.* 10*d* | . | 1 | 9 | 2 |
| Maize & barley | 15 ,, | at 4*s.* 8*d.* . | . | 3 | 10 | 0 |
| Oats | 201 ,, | at 6*s.* 6*d.* . | . | 65 | 6 | 6 |
| | | | | £110 | 5 | 8 |

RECAPITULATION.

132. *Whitfield pays for Protection—*

| | | | | | | |
|---|---|---|---|---|---|---|
| Seed . . . . . . | | | | 10 | 1 | 3 |
| Food for Labourers | 98 | 14 | 4 | | | |
| Women & boys | 30 | 10 | 9 | | | |
| Their beer | 9 | 14 | 10 | | | |
| . . . | | | | 38 | 19 | 11 |
| Food for cattle . . . . . | | | | 110 | 5 | 8 |
| Tradesmen's bills . . . . . | | | | 2 | 10 | 0 |
| | | | | 261 | 16 | 10 |
| Consumption of the tenant's family 10 per cent. on £200 . . . | | | | 20 | 0 | 0 |
| | | | | £281 | 16 | 10 |

133. *It receives from Protection—*

| | | | |
|---|---|---|---|
| Wheat 575 qrs. at 5*s.* 6*d.* . . . . | 158 | 2 | 6 |
| *Loss by Protection* . . . | £123 | 14 | 4 |

134. Whitfield farm, therefore, which in its former state of a dairy farm, gained by the protective system at the rate of 15*s.* 4*d.* per acre, is taxed by that system at the rate of 10*s.* 3*d.* per acre now that it is converted into an arable farm, employing a larger proportion of labour, and paying its labourers sufficient wages to enable them to be consumers of bacon, cheese, and beer, besides bread.

EAST LOTHIAN.

135. Having thus ascertained that the working of the protective system is detrimental to the cultivators of South

Britain, both upon light arable soils, and npon strong soils converted from a state of pasture to tillage, let us next trace its effects upon the high cultivation of Scotland, taking for our example the district of East Lothian, the evidence of whose cultivators, before the Agricultural Distress Committee of 1836, formed such a striking and favourable contrast to that of their Southern brethren.

136. The secret of their strength lay in their corn-rents and their corn-labour. The money value of their rents and labour, like that of their seed corn, and cattle food, rose and fell with the price of corn; they were forced into no squabbles with their men about a reduction of wages; they were not compelled to stand at the audit with bated breath, waiting to know whether they were to receive, at the pleasure of the landlord or his agent, an eleemosynary return of ten, fifteen, or twenty per cent., or whether they were to pay out of diminished prices the full money rent to which they had put hand and seal. They measured out a certain quantity of corn to their labourers and to their landlord, as to their stable and their seedsman; its price was as much a matter of indifference to them as to their sower and their horses. Bound by no fixed money engagements, they were as indifferent about a depreciation of the currency as about an artificial enhancement of prices by protecting duties on imported agricultural produce.

137. The following calculation shows the amount to which the respective shares of produce allotted in East Lothian, to the land, the landlord, the labourer, and the tenant, are affected by an advance of price equal to the amount of protecting duties on the various kinds of produce, consumed in cultivation, paid as rent, or expended as profits.

138. We take the case of a farm of 420 acres, that being the quantity cultivated under the Lothian system, with six pairs of horses; the rotation of crops, produce, and seed are derived from returns to printed queries ad-

dressed by us some years ago to cultivators in various parts of Britain, when we were preparing a work not yet completed, as a contribution to the Statistics of Agriculture.

139. In assigning twelve men to the cultivation of these 420 acres we have deviated a little from the East Lothian return, which gave 2 men, — women — and boys, to the hundred acres, the greater part of the filling and spreading of dung, as well as the thrashing and turnip hoeing having been performed by the two latter. To simplify the calculation, we have omitted the women and boys, and substituted for them one man to the hundred acres, or nearly so.

140. The rent we have taken in wheat, oats, and barley, in the following proportions: wheat 105 quarters, oats 294 quarters, barley 210 quarters.

141. The wages of farm servants in East Lothian consist of a small money payment, the only portion affected by fluctuations in the supply of labour and demand for it; a house, for which is given the labour of the wife in harvest, the money-value of which may be about three pounds; the keep of a cow summer and winter, the free carriage of coals; one-sixteenth part of an acre, well dunged and planted with potatoes; and as much ground for flax as can be sown with a peck of seed.

142. The quantity of corn received by the hind, as these hired householders are called, in the north of England and in Scotland is—

| | | | | |
|---|---|---|---|---|
| Oats | 10 bolls* | equal to | 7½ | quarters |
| Barley | 3 | ,, | 2¼ | ,, |
| Peas | 2 | ,, | 1 | ,, |

143. The value, therefore, of the corn paid to the twelve men, will be enhanced by the protective system to the following amount—

* The boll of oats and barley = 6 bushels, of peas 4 bushels.

*Labourers' Food—*

| | | | | |
|---|---|---|---|---|
| Oats 7½ qrs. × 12 × 90 qrs. at 6*s* 6*d* | | 29 | 5 | 0 |
| Barley 2¼ „ × 12 = 27 . 4*s* 8*d* | | 6 | 6 | 0 |
| Peas 1 „ × 12 = 12 . 5*s* 10*d* | | 3 | 10 | 0 |
| | | £39 | 1 | 0 |

144. *Seed Corn—*

| | Acres. | Bushels. | | Quarters. | | | | |
|---|---|---|---|---|---|---|---|---|
| Wheat | 140 × | 2½ = | 350 = | 43¾ | at 5*s* 6*d* | 12 | 0 | 7 |
| Oats | 70 × | 5 = | 350 = | 43¾ | at 6*s* 6*d* | 14 | 4 | 4 |
| Beans | 70 × | 3 = | 210 = | 26¼ | at 6*s* 10*d* | 8 | 19 | 4 |
| Clover Red | 70 × | 12 = | 840 } | lbs. 1400 | cwt. 12½ at 10*s* | 6 | 5 | 0 |
| White | 70 × | 8 = | 560 } | | | | | |
| Trefoil | 70 × | 8 = | 560 | . | 5 at 5*s* | 1 | 5 | 0 |
| Rye grass, 35 bushels, say | | | | . | 9 at 10*s* | 4 | 10 | 0 |
| | | | | | | £47 | 4 | 3 |

145. *Cattle Food—*

| | | | |
|---|---|---|---|
| 12 Farm horses, 1 riding-horse = 13 × 2 bush. × 52 weeks = 1352 bush. = 169 quarters, at 6*s* 6*d* . . | 54 | 18 | 6 |
| Oil cake, 30 tons, at £2. (par 46) . | 60 | 0 | 0 |
| | £114 | 18 | 6 |

146. The gross produce of the farm will be raised in value by protecting duties to the following amount—

| | Acres. | Bushels. | | Quarters. | | | | |
|---|---|---|---|---|---|---|---|---|
| Turnips | 70 | | | | | | | |
| Wheat | 70 × | 30 = | 2100 = | 262½ | at 5*s* 6*d* | 72 | 3 | 9 |
| Seeds | 70 | | | | | | | |
| Oats | 70 × | 56 = | 3920 = | 490 | at 6*s* 6*d* | 159 | 5 | 0 |
| Beans | 70 × | 30 = | 2100 = | 262½ | at 6*s* 11*d* | 90 | 15 | 7 |
| Wheat | 70 × | 30 = | 2100 = | 262½ | at 5*s* 6*d* | 72 | 3 | 9 |
| | | | | | | £394 | 8 | 1 |

| | | | | | | |
|---|---|---|---|---|---|---|
| Brought forward | | | | £394 | 8 | 1 |
| 147. The produce consumed in cultivation is increased in value by protecting duties to the folllowing extent— | | | | | | |
| Labourers' food (par 143) | 39 | 1 | 0 | | | |
| Seed . . | 47 | 4 | 3 | | | |
| Cattle food . | 114 | 18 | 6 | | | |
| | | | | 201 | 3 | 9 |
| | | | | £193 | 4 | 4 |

148. Thus far, therefore, the East Lothian farmer appears to be a gainer by the protective system. There is, however, one item yet to be considered, which forms no part of the cost of production, but is, or ought to be, the portion of the produce which remains, after deducting the cost of cultivation, and the tenant's remuneration for his time, skill, and capital; it is often however a great embarrassment to the farmer when it is a money-payment, which does not vary with the price of produce, and must be provided for, owing to reduced prices, by the sale of a larger share of produce than was contemplated at the letting of the land—that item is RENT.

149. The rent of the East Lothian tenant would be raised by an advance of price, equal to the amount of the protective duties on the different kinds of grain in which it is reserved; this amount would be as follows—(par 140.)

| | | | | | | |
|---|---|---|---|---|---|---|
| Wheat 105 quarters, at | 5*s* 6*d* | . | 28 | 17 | 6 |
| Oats 294 ,, | 6*s* 6*d* | . | 95 | 11 | 0 |
| Barley 210 ,, | 4*s* 8*d* | . | 49 | 0 | 0 |
| | | | 173 | 8 | 6 |
| 150. Add to this the portion of the produce employed in cultivation raised in value by protecting duties (par 147) | | | 201 | 3 | 9 |

| | | | |
|---|---|---|---|
| Brought forward | £374 | 12 | 3 |
| Add also family expenses, estimated at £400. increased by protection 10 per cent. | 40 | 0 | 0 |
| | 414 | 12 | 3 |
| 151. Deduct the increased value of the gross amount of the produce of the farm arising from protecting duties | 394 | 8 | 1 |
| | £20 | 4 | 2 |

152. Well then may the East Lothian tenant be indifferent to "protection." Owing to his payments in kind, the respective shares apportioned to his landlord, his labourers and himself are divested of all money-value; he sees that the amount of produce retained by him is after all the main point; that so far as he is concerned, the advance of price would be merely nominal, and that his landlord would be the gainer by it. With the tenants of the South, however, the case is different. The mystery in which the subject is involved by their money-labour and their money-rents, and the payment of those rents to three different landlords, the landowner, the church, and the poor, throw sand in their eyes, and cause them to look upon their interests as identified with high prices, which, if they could be maintained by protecting duties, would be more detrimental to them than to the farmers of Scotland. Why they suffer more from the protective system than the farmers of the north, is a question to be discussed hereafter.

### THE GROWERS OF CLOVER SEED AND HOPS.

153. We have now traced the effects of the protective system on the profits of farming, in connexion with the chief products of arable and pasture land; we have ascertained that on arable land, whether light or strong, under

high culture, the protective system is pernicious, by increasing the cost of production, and by raising rents more than it raises the value of tenants' share of the produce; we have seen, moreover, that the only description of land which actually gains by the protecting duties, is pasture land, employing few labourers, and consuming little or no purchased cattle-food.

154. In the course of our inquiries we have noticed the protecting duties on clover seed and hops, as contributing to swell the cost of producing the staple commodities of the soil. We will now, therefore, endeavour to ascertain whether the growers of these two articles derive benefit from the duties on them, which are a burthen on the rest of the agricultural community—we are not now considering the effects of the hop duty on the non-agricultural classes. Clover seed and hops, however, must be regarded as the mint, anise, and cummin, of agriculture. They ought, rather, to be classed with such trifles as liquorice, chicory, and saffron, carraway, coriander, and canary seed; which are, properly speaking, mere garden produce, unworthy to be placed in opposition to the growth of corn, beef, and mutton, in which the welfare of agriculture, and the food of the whole population are at stake.

155. We might take our stand on this high ground, as assertors of the freedom of agriculture from the trammels of the protective system; we might call for the abolition of the duties on clover seed and hops, as injurious to the most numerous and important class of cultivators; but the calculations into which we have been led, have convinced us that even the growers of clover seed and hops derive no benefit from them. In this, as in every other department of agriculture, not only is the protective system a system of mutual plunder, a robbing of Peter to pay Paul, but it is a robbing of both Peter and Paul in order to make them pay themselves. Whether they grow only a few of the protected

articles and purchase the others necessary to the due cultivation of the soil, or whether they raise the whole of them on their own farms, the case is much the same; cash is taken out of Button Park on the right, to transfer it into Button Park* on the left. They, good easy men, expect to grow rich by the process; but, during the transfer, a large portion of their money is abstracted by a party whom we will call Mr. Nobody, for nobody really benefits by the ill-gotten gains, and nobody is a personage who has long been celebrated for mischief. They find their pockets growing sensibly lighter, and instead of perceiving the real cause of their losses, they set up a cry of agricultural distress, call loudly for more protection, which brings more friends about them, and a further abstraction of cash; and then they go to Parliament, on an errand nearly as hopeless as that of those not very wise gentlemen, who having lost their money and watches in the streets of London, they know not how, are very fond of running to the police office, "to ask the magistrate's advice," or to "give their case publicity through the medium of the press." The satisfaction received in each case is nearly the same. If the "worthy magistrate" happens to be in a good humour, he regrets their loss, assures them that it is not a case in which he can interfere; advising them for the future, to take more care of their pockets. If he happens to be in a bad humour, he tells them not to come "whining" there; he cannot have his court made an advertising office.

### Clover Seed.

156. The growth of clover is confined to the Southern Counties, and that would be strong presumptive evidence

* For the benefit of the uninitiated it may be necessary to explain, that Button Park is a farmer's phrase for the breeches pocket.

that it is not profitable, for these constitute the district from which the cry of agricultural distress is always the loudest. It is grown under a modification of the four course rotation; in which beans, peas, or vetches, occupy one half of the portion of the farm usually allotted to clover.

157. The benefits of growing clover seed, whatever they may be, consequently apply only to one-eighth of the farm. The average crop cannot be stated at more than 1½ cwt. per acre, the protecting duty on which is 10*s.* per cwt

158. The gross amount of the clover seed grower's protection, therefore, does not on the average exceed 15*s.* an acre on one-eighth of his holding, or £37. 10*s.* upon a farm of 400 acres, a small affair truly in the returns of a farm of that size.

159. But even this paltry sum of 15*s.* is subject to deductions comparatively considerable, arising out of the protective system. Against the protecting duty on the gross produce, must be set the protecting duty on the seed sown by the farmer himself, and the duties on the food of the labourers—we mean the extra labourers employed in harvesting and thrashing the crop. The former cannot be stated at less than 1*s.* 6*d.*; and if we call the latter 3*s.*, we shall be well within the mark; for clover seed, in our precarious climate, is a troublesome crop to harvest, and always expensive to thrash. There then goes 4*s.* 6*d.* out of the 15*s.*

160. But there are other serious drawbacks to the profits of growing even protected clover seed. Clover fed with sheep, or made into hay, is one of those crops, which, so far from exhausting the land, form a good preparation for a crop of wheat. Allow it to mature its seed, and it exerts an exhausting influence. So sensible are they of this in Essex, that many landlords prohibit the growth of a crop of wheat after clover seed, without the intervention of a fallow.

161. Let us, therefore, calculate the returns made for the rent, labour, and expenses of the two years:—

1st. By a crop of clover hay followed by wheat.

2nd. By a crop of clover seed followed by a fallow.

3rd. By a crop of clover seed followed by wheat.

We shall, in each case, give the grower of clover seed the benefit of such remunerating prices as the present protecting duties profess to secure; namely clover seed 84*s*. the cwt, and wheat 56*s*. the quarter; and we shall allow him a liberal value, namely half the price of clover hay, for the clover straw, stover, or whatever he calls it, from which the seed has been thrashed.

162. To his rival, on the contrary, we shall allow no higher price for his wheat, than 50*s*. the quarter; that is, the present remunerating price of the protectionists, less the protecting duty. The account will then stand thus—

163. Clover twice mown for hay followed by wheat.

| | | | |
|---|---|---|---|
| Hay two tons at £3. for consumption on the farm | 6 | 0 | 0 |
| Wheat 3½ quarters at 50*s* (unprotected) . | 8 | 15 | 0 |
| | £14 | 15 | 0 |

164. Clover mown once for hay, once for seed, and followed by a fallow.

| | | | |
|---|---|---|---|
| Hay 1 ton first mowing at £3. . . | 3 | 0 | 0 |
| Clover seed 1½ cwt. at 84*s*. . . | 6 | 6 | 0 |
| 1 ton of Clover straw . . | 1 | 10 | 0 |
| Fallow . . . | 0 | 0 | 0 |
| | 10 | 16 | 0 |
| Difference on two years in favour of the Hay Crop | 3 | 19 | 0 |
| | £14 | 15 | 0 |

165. In this case Peter clearly robs himself of £3. 19*s*. or £1. 19*s*. 6*d*. the acre, by growing clover seed.

166. If, however, we suppose him to live under a land-

lord who allows him to grow wheat after clover seed, without the intervention of a fallow, the case will be somewhat different. His wheat crop will be less, than had he fed his second crop of clover or made it into hay, but if we allow him to grow for a time as much wheat as after hay, the following will be his returns—

| | | | | |
|---|---|---|---|---|
| 167. | Clover seed crop as before . . | £10 | 16 | 0 |
| | 3½ quarters of wheat at 56*s.* (protected) | 9 | 16 | 0 |
| | | £20 | 12 | 0 |

168. In this case the value of the two crops is £5. 17*s.* more than when wheat followed clover made into hay. Peter therefore pockets £2. 18*s.* 6*d.** the acre by growing protected clover seed and protected wheat; and what is more his crops have all gone to market; none of them have been consumed in the yard; and that is one of the merits of the system in his eyes. He has got them all in hard cash. None of them are buried in the land, in the form of that invisible thing called condition.

169. So far all is well, and encouraged by his success he perseveres in the system, and after a few rotations finds the result of taking as much as possible out of the land, and putting nothing in, to be the reduction of the produce of the wheat crop to such an extent that *on his land*—it is always the land, not the farming that is in fault—it will no longer remunerate him to grow wheat at a price which remunerates others who follow a less scourging rotation. He therefore goes up to London to ask Parliament for a protecting duty on wheat, never to be less than 30*s.*† the quar-

* Over one-eighth part of the farm which produces clover.

† This amount of fixed duty was actually proposed by some of the witnesses before the Agricultural Distress Committee of 1836.

ter: and is sent back with the civil, but unsatisfactory answer before alluded to.

In the meantime, his declaration, before the Committee, that he is bordering upon insolvency brings upon him every creditor to whom he owes a shilling; and the end of the clover seed growing is that Peter is sold up; and his landlord finds the farm so run out that he cannot meet with a tenant who will take it, except at a reduction of rent to which he is not inclined to submit. He therefore takes it into his own hands, and thus a plausible foundation is laid for stories with which to work upon the feelings of future Agricultural Distress Committees, about millions of acres going out of cultivation. The landlord's endeavours to bring the farm into condition only make matters worse; and he is at last obliged, sorely against his will, to let it on a twenty-one years' lease, at a great reduction of rent, to a tenant of capital, who brings it into condition by following Peter's rotation, with the trifling exception of the clover seed. Peter's gain, therefore, from this his favourite crop, ended in ruin to himself and a great loss to his landlord.

170 To keep up the system and to render us "independent of the foreigner" for clover seed, a tax is levied in the shape of protecting duties, not only on red clover, but upon white clover, trefoil, and rye-grass from every farmer in the United Kingdom, who sows artificial grasses, and does not save the seed of them. This tax our preceding calculations have shewn to be about 3*s.* an acre on the clover crop, or of 9*d.* the acre, over the whole farm under the four course rotation.

171. We must not suppose, however, that this protecting duty is the only inducement to grow clover seed. There are other temptations to the practice. It affords a more expeditious method of converting the clover crop into money, with a smaller capital than would be required for

its consumption with live stock; added to which, once in about a dozen years, a large crop and high prices coincide, which produce much greater returns than we have calculated on, crops below the average are forgotten, those above it remembered, and for the chance of a large but uncertain gain, a certain loss is incurred every year.

172. But we have already devoted too much space to clover seed and must proceed to hops.

### Hops.

173. Besides the large revenue levied upon hops, and the extensive speculations to which the fluctuations in the price of so precarious a crop give birth, there are many extraneous circumstances which cause an exaggerated importance to be attached to this branch of agricultural industry; but, on the other hand, the excise duty to which hops are subject, furnishes correct statistical information respecting them, which is a great desideratum in the other departments of agriculture, and which enables us to reduce these exaggerated pretensions to their true value, and to demonstrate the disadvantage of protecting duties, and high artificial prices to the growers of even the most highly protected article to be found in the agricultural tariff.

174. Not to weary the reader with the details of investigations, which have cost us much labour, we shall content ourselves with a general statement of the results.

175. The average annual value of the hop crop does not exceed one part in one hundred and forty of the average annual value of the total agricultural produce of the United Kingdom.

176. The average number of acres under hop culture, during the last thirty years, has not exceeded 47,870, on which the average annual produce has been 6 cwt. 1 qr. 3 lbs., and the average price £6. 19*s*. per cwt.

177. The extremes of produce during the period have

been 11 cwt. 5½lbs. and 1 cwt. 8¾lbs., and it is a curious fact that they occurred in consecutive years. The extremes of price have been £27. the cwt. and £4. 4*s*.

178. The labour of the hop culture, exclusive of the picking, cannot be estimated as affording constant employment to more than fifteen men to the hundred acres; whereas the same land, under arable culture, would or might, employ one third of that number.

179. The conversion of one hundred thousand acres of land from pasture to arable, would employ the surplus hands dismissed from the hop culture, if the discontinuance of protecting duties should cause its total abandonment; and that quantity of pasture we must break up *annually*, if we would feed our increasing population with home-grown food.

180. The hop culture, highly as it is protected, has been denounced as unprofitable, upon the whole, by every agricultural writer who has treated of the subject, in every county in which they are grown; and experienced hop growers have concurred in these opinions, if indeed they did not originate them, declaring that a large portion of the hop-grounds are planted upon soils on which they never can pay, because uncongenial to them, that hop-growing is the gambling of farming, and that the chief inducement to engage in it is the chance of the prizes of the hop-lottery, in the pursuit of which, the certainty of blanks is overlooked.

181. The pecuniary evils described as attendant on the hop-culture, are the drain of manure and of capital which it occasions from the rest of the farm; and the neglect which the other operations of husbandry suffer when they come in collision with the hop-ground to which every thing else is considered subordinate.

182. The moral evils which the same authorities point out as attendant on the hop-culture, are the gambling

habits which it introduces among the farmers, and the demoralization of the peasantry, occasioned by the swarms of itinerant pickers with which they are brought in contact, in those districts where the cultivation is carried to such an extent that the resident population is not sufficient to harvest the crop.

183. This excessive concentration of the hop-culture in particular districts, by which the peasantry of those districts are demoralized, and the hop-culture as a whole rendered unprofitable, by its extension to soils on which the produce is uncertain, the quality inferior, and on which the plants will not yield more than ten or twelve good crops, while on the proper hop-soils the duration of the plantation may be deemed perpetual, is to be traced to the encouragement held out to the growth of hops on those inferior hop-soils, by protecting duties.

184. These soils, even without an excise duty would not be cultivated as hop-grounds, with an average price of hops equal to the difference between the protecting duty and the present price.

185. The expenses of hop-cultivation are increased, like the expenses of cultivating every other crop, by the amount of protecting duties on the labourers' food; they are increased by the protecting duties in favour of the owners of coppice—a very profitable application of poor soils—on imported spars or poles capable of being used as hop-poles, equal to fifty per cent. on the present value of home-grown 14-feet poles, and from twenty to thirty per cent. on 16-feet poles; they are increased by whatever enhances the value of oil-cake; for the hop-growers of Kent have long used cake for the purpose of raising manure, not to be applied to the growth of turnips and the reproduction of manure, but to be employed in the hop-grounds.

186. In 1797, when Marshall wrote his "Agriculture of the Southern Counties," the price of agricultural produce

was nearly the same as in 1844, and English oil-cake, now worth on an average £10. the ton, was then considered extravagantly high at £5. and £6.

187. This advance in the price of oil-cake, in the face of increased and increasing importations of foreign cake, is attributable to the increased demand arising from the extended but, at the same time, only partial use of cake, and is a proof of the benefit which the hop-growers would derive, in common with the light land arable farmers, from an extensive importation of cheap cattle-food as a substitute for oil-cake.

188. The expenses of hop-growing are partly fluctuating and dependent on the amount of crop, such as excise duty, picking, drying, and marketing; partly constant, such as the labour of cultivation, manure, and the renewal of poles; these, together with rent, tithe and local taxes, must be borne by the tenant, even though the crop should not be worth the gathering.

189. The fluctuating expenses may be stated thus—

| | | | | |
|---|---|---|---|---|
| Duty | 0 | 18 | 8* | |
| Picking, drying, and marketing | 0 | 12 | 0 | |
| | £1 | 10 | 8 | per cwt. |

190. The constant expenses are as follow:—

| | | | | |
|---|---|---|---|---|
| Labour | 4 | 0 | 0 | |
| Manure | 4 | 0 | 0 | |
| Renewal of poles | 6 | 0 | 0 | |
| | £14 | 0 | 0 | per acre. |

* To this five per cent. was added by Vic. 3, ch. 27.

191. The amount of protecting duties on the food of the labourer may be estimated, at the medium of the highest and lowest diet tables of our preceding calculations, as amounting to 14*s.* 6*d.* the acre; and with the abolition of these duties, and of those duties which now enhance the cost of hop-poles, with the removal of the restrictions on the importation of cattle-food, which would diminish the demand for oil-cake, and with the aid of the energies now applied to the manufacture and importation of artificial manures, of which commerce and science are daily increasing the number and diminishing the cost, it is not too much to expect that the constant expenses of a hop-ground might be reduced to the following extent:—

| | | | | |
|---|---|---|---|---|
| Labour . . . . . | 0 | 14 | 6 | |
| Renewal of poles 33 per cent. . | 2 | 0 | 0 | |
| Manure . . . . . | 1 | 10 | 0 | |
| | £4 | 4 | 6 | per acre. |

Thus making the constant expenses of cultivating an acre of hops £9. 15*s.* 6*d.* instead of £14.

192. The average produce of hop-ground, for the last thirty years has been, as we have before stated, 6 cwt. 1 qr. 3 lbs.; but as some grounds have greatly exceeded that average, the yield of others must have been as much below it. If we call the produce of the best grounds 8 cwt., and that of the inferior 4 cwt., we shall have the following as the returns and expenses of an acre of inferior hop-ground, at the present, and at the reduced prices, and with and without the excise and protecting duties.

193. With the excise and protecting duties, present prices, and present expenses, the following will be the account.

| | | Returns. |
|---|---|---|
| 4 cwt., at £6. 19*s*. . . . . . . | | £27 16 0 |
| | Expenses. | |
| Constant expenses . . | 14 0 0 | |
| Fluctuating expenses | | |
| Duty 4 cwt. at £0 18*s* 8*d* with 5 per cent. additional by Vic. 3. chap. 27 . | 3 18 8 | |
| Picking, &c. 4 cwt. at 12*s*. | 2 8 0 | |
| . . . | | 20 6 8 |
| Excess over expenses of cultivation to pay rent, tithe, rates, and tenant's profit. . . . . . . . | | £7 9 4 |

194. With the excise and protecting duty abolished, the constant expenses reduced to £9. 15*s*. 6*d*., as in par. 191, and the price reduced to £3. 7*s*. 8*d*. the cwt., being the difference between the present price, and the amount of protecting duty, we should have,

| | | Returns. |
|---|---|---|
| 4 cwt. at £3. 7*s* 8*d* . . | | 13 10 8 |
| Constant expenses . | 9 15 6 | |
| Picking, drying, and marketing 4 cwt. at 12*s*. . . | 2 8 0 | |
| | | 12 3 6 |
| Excess for rent, tithes, rates, and profits . | | £1 7 2 |

195. From this it is evident, that with excise and protecting duty abolished, and expenses reduced according to the scale calculated as in par. 191: these inferior hop-soils would cease to be hop-grounds and revert to arable culture. In other words the protecting duty keeps them under the hop-culture.

196. On the other hand, we find Mr. Pooke, an extensive hop-grower of long experience, declaring to Arthur

Young that with a price of £4. the cwt., hop ground averaging 8 cwt. to the acre, yielded no profit. The following was his estimate.

| | | | | | | |
|---|---|---|---|---|---|---|
| | | | | Returns. | | |
| 8 cwt. at £4. . . . . | | | | 32 | 0 | 0 |
| | Expenses. | | | | | |
| Constant expenses, labour, poles, and manure . | 18 | 2 | 6 | | | |
| Picking, drying, duty, and sending to London our market, £1. 10*s*. per cwt. . . | 12 | 0 | 0 | | | |
| . | | | | 30 | 2 | 6 |
| Excess of returns above expenses to pay rent, tithe, and tenant's profit . . . | | | | £1 | 17 | 6 |

197. With the excise and protecting duties abolished, the expenses of cultivation reduced to £9. 15*s*. 6*d*. the case of hop-ground of this quality would stand thus.

| | £. | *s*. | *d*. | Returns. | | |
|---|---|---|---|---|---|---|
| 8 cwt. at . | 3 | 7 | 8 | 27 | 1 | 4 |
| | Expenses. | | | | | |
| Constant expenses | 9 | 15 | 6 | | | |
| Picking and marketing 8 cwt. at 12*s*. . | 4 | 16 | 0 | | | |
| . | | | | 14 | 11 | 6 |
| | | | | 12 | 9 | 10 |

198. So that the better description of hop-ground, which when burthened with the excise and protecting duty, only yielded an excess of return over the cost of cultivation, amounting, for an expenditure of £32. to £1. 17*s*. 6*d*. for rent, tithe, rates, and profit, will, with the same weight of produce, a lower price, expenses reduced, and the excise and protecting duty abolished, yield for an expenditure of

£14. 11*s*. 6*d*. an excess of returns over the cost of cultivation equal to £12. 9*s*. 10*d*.

199. The effect of the removal of the protecting and excise duties on hops would probably be to cause land averaging 8 cwt. to the acre to be the lowest description of soil that would be applied to the hop-culture.

200. The abandonment of the inferior hop-soils, sounds, no doubt, very dreadful; but it must be remembered, that it means no more than the discontinuance of planting hops on soils of that description. Those at present in cultivation, would die a natural death at the end of ten or twelve years from the date of plantation. But, like Parliaments, they are seldom suffered to live out their full term. Their history is commonly this. A succession of deficient crops produces high prices, and a farmer is tempted to make a plantation on such soils. By the time the plantation reaches maturity, the tide has turned, we have had a succession of good crops, and low prices, and in a pet, he grubs the whole plantation, and determines, for the future, to confine himself to the growth of corn, beef, and mutton.

201. For this his land is still worth the rent it was worth before, nay more, for like the land of Æsop's dying farmer, who told his sons that somewhere on his farm, he would not say where, he had buried a treasure, for which he advised them to dig; the extra cultivation and manuring which it received for the hops—the treasure which was not found—bring to light a real treasure in the abundant crops of corn which it now produces.

202. The oil-cake and extraneous manures formerly bestowed upon the hops are now applied to the growth of turnips, and reproduction of manure, whereby the produce of the remainder of the farm is increased. The whole farm, also, participates in the benefit derived from the removal of protecting duties on the labourers' food, which enhance the cost of cultivation, if repaid in wages; and

since the competition for land will always prevent tenants from making more than a certain amount of profit on their capital, whatever diminishes the cost of production, or increases produce, or effects both together, causes an advance of rent. To the tenant, therefore, during his occupancy, and to the landlord at the termination of it, these inferior hop soils will be more profitable under an efficient system of culture than when partly devoted to the growth of hops forced, by the aid of the protective system.

203. There is, however, another view to be taken of this forced cultivation of hops, for which the owner of every acre in England not devoted to hops is taxed, in common with all the consumers of beer; and that is the dimiuished consumption of malt and hops caused by the high prices which the protecting duties on those articles combine with the excise duties to produce.

204. Barley is taxed for the benefit—or supposed benefit—of the owners and occupiers of the light soils, 4*s.* 8*d.* the quarter. And malt is taxed for the benefit of the revenue, 2*s.* 7*d.* the bushel, in all 25*s.* 4*d.* the quarter.

205. The excise and protecting duties on hops amount together to £4. 10*s.* the cwt.

206. The effects are felt in the diminished consumption of malt and hops. The increased consumption of these since 1811, is not in proportion to the increase of population.

207. The population of England and Wales was, in round* numbers, in 1811, 10,100,000, in 1841, 15,900,000.

208. The consumption of malt, in England and Wales,

* The true numbers are, population 1811—10,150,615; 1841, 15,911,725; consumption of malt 1811 25,979,328 bushels; 1840, 34,086,053 bushels.

was in 1811, 25,900,000 bushels, in 1840,* 34,000,000 bushels.

209. To be in proportion to the population it ought to have been 40,700,000 bushels.

210. The average annual growth of hops, for the five years ending 1811, was 267,021 cwt. the produce of 38,333 acres.

211. The average growth of hops for the five years ending 1844 was only 257,768 cwts., the produce of 44,243 acres; but during the five preceding years, there had been a greater breadth of hop-ground planted, and higher yields than during any other similar period of the thirty years. We may therefore suppose there was a stock in hand, carried over from them, and we will take the average of the last ten years as the present consumption. This is 334,083 cwts.

212. To be in proportion to the increased population of England and Wales since 1811, it ought to be 420,359 cwts.; but this does not shew the whole of the diminished consumption; as we have not taken into the account the increase of the hop consuming population in Scotland and Ireland; both of which, however limited in their consumption of hops, compared with England and Wales, are supplied from England; and it includes the hops used in the beer brewed, in increased and increasing quantities, for Australia and the East Indies.

213. If we divide 420,359 cwts. by 6½ cwts., the average produce per acre of our present hop-grounds, it will give 67,257 acres as the quantity of hop-ground, of that description, which we might have under cultivation, instead

* We have not returns of the consumption of malt in England and Wales for later periods, nor accounts of the population of Scotland and Ireland before 1821.

of our present average number of 44,243, or the greatest number we ever had in cultivation, which was 57,323, in 1837.

214. If, however, we divide the 420,359 cwts. by 8 cwts. supposing the effect of the removal of the protection to be the abandonment of the inferior hop-grounds, and the derival of our supply from soils of superior quality, our population might still be consumers of the produce of 52,544 acres of such superior hop-soils, which exceeds our present extent of hop-ground, good and bad, by 8,000 acres. There is ample room, therefore, under a free trade, not only for an importation of foreign hops, but for an extended growth of British hops, and we have abundance of soil well suited to the culture near sources of extraneous manure, and in the midst of a redundant agricultural population, to whom, if thus dispersed, it would afford employment, and supersede the nuisance of the itinerant pickers.

215. But we have not yet done with the effects of high excise and protecting duties on the consumption of hops. Not only has the consumption of malt and hops not increased in proportion to the increase of population, during the last thirty years, which will be described in history as the period of agricultural protection and agricultural distress, but the consumption of hops appears not to have kept pace with the consumption of malt.

216. The 25,900,000 bushels of malt, and 267,021 cwts. of hops of 1811, give $96\frac{9}{10}$ bushels of malt to 1 cwt. of hops.

The 34,000,000 bushels of malt of 1840 and the 334,083 cwts. of hops, taking the consumption on the average growth of the last ten years, give $101\frac{7}{10}$ bushels to a cwt. of hops. If, however, we take the consumption from the growth of the last five years, it gives $131\frac{9}{10}$ bushels to a cwt.

217. Without attaching too much importance to these proportions, there is certainly something here to excite suspicion, that our attempts to render ourselves independent of the foreigner for hops, have ended in rendering us dependent upon him for drugs. Quassia, cocculus Indicus, and grains of Paradise may be very good things, but for ourselves we prefer hops in our beer, though some of them should be grown in Flanders.

218. The quantity of malt which our population are debarred from consuming, by this double taxation for revenue and agricultural protection, is equal to the annual crop of 167,500 acres of barley producing five quarters to the acre. Its production would require the cultivation of 670,000 acres of additional land, or an additional produce of half a quarter an acre on 1,675,000 acres of barley.

219. Consider this, owners and occupiers of light lands, and calculate whether you would gain most by a continuance of protecting duties on the food of your labourers, the food of your cattle, and your own food, or by a repeal of all protecting duties, in conjunction with a repeal of the excise on malt and hops.

220. You may learn of Mr. Mechi in more ways than one. He has taught the farmers of Essex how to make Tiptree-Heath produce crops equal to those of the best land in the county. When a nobleman, lately conversing with him on agricultural matters, said, " Mechi, you should open a shop at the west end, we would patronize you." " I am much obliged to you, my Lord," was the reply, " but all the beards of the aristocracy are of no value to me; it is the *millions* I want to shave."

221. When will farmers learn to look to the millions, when will they learn that increased consumption is of more value in maintaining prices, than an artificial diminution of supply; when will landlords learn that increased produce, raised at comparatively smaller cost, is more effi-

cacious *in advancing rents than protecting duties,* which increase the cost of production as fast as they increase the price of produce.

222. Some of our agricultural friends are strongly impressed with the belief, that great injustice is inflicted on the agricultural interest by fiscal restrictions on the growth of hops, tobacco, and beet-root sugar.

The diminished consumption of malt and hops—diminished in comparisonwith the increased population,—which we have shewn to arise from the excise and protecting duties on those articles, renders unnecessary any declaration that in their opinions with respect to hops we fully concur.

223. A total remission of all duties on malt and hops, is desirable for all classes, and would be cheaply purchased by an additional income tax to the amount of the revenue derived from them; or a continuance of the present income tax when its time shall have expired.

224. With tobacco and sugar, however the case is widely different.

225. If all the tobacco imported, were raised in England, its cultivation would not employ more than 23,000 acres. The average produce is little more than 1,000 lbs. an acre; it requires for its production land of the very best quality, and the expenses of cultivation are great; and, though tobacco growing would without doubt be very profitable if the Government would allow it to be grown duty free, while the foreign article, worth, exclusive of duty, no more than 7½*d.* the pound, continues to pay a duty of 3*s.* the pound, yet the evidence given before a Committee of the House of Commons, by the advocates for the culture of tobacco in Ireland, proved most satisfactorily, that British grown tobacco could not compete with the foreign, paying an excise duty of 1*s.* the pound against the 3*s.* charged on the latter; and, that the competition would be equally hopeless were British and Foreign tobacco alike exempted from duty.

226. It is much the same with the beet-root sugar. The returns collected by M. Dumas for the Government of France, where peculiar circumstances forced the culture, and where the climate is more productive of sugar in beet-root than with us, have been reduced by Professor Kane, in his "Industrial Resources of Ireland," to British weights, values, and measures.

227. From these it appears, that to a manufacturer of beet root sugar, who paid 16*s.* 8*d.* the ton for beet root, and 12*s.* the ton for coals, and who sold the refuse pulp (one-fortieth part of the beet root) to the farmer for cattle food, at 6*s.* 3*d.* the cwt.; the skimmings of the boiler for manure, at 6*s.* the cwt.; and the treacle at 1*s.* 8*d.* the cwt.; the prime cost of the sugar would be 26*s.* 6*d.* the cwt., or 2¾*d.* the lb.; and as the average price of Colonial sugar, exclusive of the duty, does not exceed 31*s.* 1*d.* the cwt., there would be very little inducement to undertake the manufacture of beet-root sugar, on payment of the duty levied upon imported sugar, namely 27*s.* the cwt., or with Colonial and home grown sugar, both duty free.

228. As regards the grower of beet-root for sugar making, it is to be observed that the crop most productive of sugar does not exceed 12 tons the acre. "Thirty or forty tons may be forced by high culture, but in such cases there is little or no sugar; it has been used in forming the woody matter of the roots; and hence the light crop described above is finally the most productive."

229. Whether a crop of beet-root of twelve tons, at 16*s.* 8*d.* the ton; the whole to be carried off the land, and making no return of manure, would hold out much temptation to the growth of it, is a question which need scarcely be asked of any farmer who knows in what his true interest consists.

230. The revenue derived from the present duties on tobacco and sugar, amounts to more than nine millions sterling. If they were reduced one-half, the revenue derived from them would certainly equal, probably exceed its pre-

sent amount. It is too much to expect that the Government should abandon them without an equivalent, merely to enable our farmers to convince themselves, by experiment, of the utter hopelessness of attempting to compete with the growers of these articles under their proper climates. Let the agriculturists, rather, agitate for a total repeal of all duties on malt and hops, whether for revenue or protection; and the reduction of the duties, on tobacco and sugar to one half of their present amount; and there can be little doubt that with the aid of the great mass of consumers, of all classes, they will succeed.

### General Conclusions.

231. We will now return to the staple products of agriculture, in order to review the results exhibited by our calculations of the effect of protecting duties in their production, under the different systems of management practised upon the the light arable soils of Norfolk and Lincolnshire, the stronger soils of East Lothian, a Gloucestershire dairy-farm, and the same land broken up and converted into an arable farm, observing the various degrees in which protecting duties increase the returns, and the cost of cultivation, labour, and rent.

232.

| | Acres. | Total increase on cost of cultivation. | | | | Per acre. | | | Total increase on returns. | | | | Per acre. | | | Rent increased per acre. | |
|---|---|---|---|---|---|---|---|---|---|---|---|---|---|---|---|---|---|
| | | £. | s. | d. | | £. | s. | d. | £. | s. | d. | | £. | s. | d. | s. | d. |
| Norfolk . | 400 | 209 | 12 | 3 | or | 0 | 10 | 5 | 226 | 13 | 4 | or | 0 | 11 | 4 | 2 | 8 |
| Lincolnshire | 1100 | 616 | 1 | 3 | .. | 0 | 11 | 2 | 688 | 5 | 2 | .. | 0 | 12 | 6 | 3 | 4 |
| Dairy . . | 100 | 16 | 18 | 1 | .. | 0 | 3 | 4 | 103 | 14 | 0 | .. | 1 | 0 | 8 | | |
| Whitfield . | 240 | 261 | 16 | 10 | .. | 1 | 1 | 9 | 158 | 2 | 6 | .. | 0 | 13 | 2 | | |
| East Lothian, | 420 | 201 | 3 | 9 | .. | 0 | 9 | 6 | 394 | 8 | 1 | .. | 0 | 18 | 9 | 8 | 3 |

233. In our former statements of the amount of loss per acre which the tenant sustains from the protective system, we included the increase of his housekeeping expenses, or expenditure of profits. This is excluded from the statement given above, from which is also excluded the

loss which the tenant incurs by having his money-rent based upon an average price for wheat, higher by several shillings the quarter than that which he receives.

234. With respect to Lincolnshire we have confined ourselves to the statements of the thirty Lincoln Heath farmers, omitting in their case, as in that of Norfolk, the amount which they are precluded from gaining by keeping, according to a practice which is at present the exception but might become the rule, a larger quantity of live stock fed with cheap corn purchased with the money now expended on artificial manures.

235. On this, as in every thing connected with agriculture, there will be differences of opinion. The points at issue are, whether corn can be substituted for oil-cake in fattening sheep and cattle; whether the manure thus produced would be equal in its effects to bones and rape-cake; and whether upon the soil of Lincoln Heath, an increased produce of 8 bushels of wheat and of 4 bushels of barley, per acre, could thus be obtained above that given in the statement of those thirty farmers.

236. If these points be conceded, and the practice of some of our best farmers leaves no doubt on our minds respecting them, the total loss to the tenant from the protective system, including that which he incurs from having his rent founded upon average prices, which upon an average of years he never receives, together with that occasioned on the expenditure of his profits, will amount to the sums per acre which we have stated elsewhere (par. 73), namely, on the Norfolk farm 11*s.* 10*d.* per acre, and on the Lincolnshire farm (par. 109) to 28*s.* per acre, supposing the additional live stock to pay nothing for feeding beyond their prime cost and that of the purchased corn.

236½. Those who dissent from these views must admit, that by the statement of the Lincoln Heath farmers themselves, the sole advantage derived by them from the protective system, which they declared to be the only thing that could save them from ruin is this, that it increases their returns by 1*s*. 4*d*. an acre more than it increases the cost of cultivation, and that in consideration of this 1*s*. 4*d*. levied from the non-agricultural consumers, they pay a rent too high by more than 3*s*. 3*d*. the acre. From this conclusion there is no escape, with the data furnished by them, of the produce and cost of cultivation, if it be true that the amount of protecting duty paid by the labourer on his food is repaid in his wages, and if it be true that a large importation of grain suitable for cattle food would reduce the price of oil-cake £2. per ton.

237. We are often told that the object of the protective system is not to keep up rents, but to benefit the agricultural labourers, by preventing millions of acres of arable land being thrown out of cultivation, which means being converted to pasture. The result of our calculations shows the effect of the protective system to be the very reverse of this, namely, to discourage the conversion of pasture into arable land. They show that the system of farming, of which the Gloucestershire dairy-farm is the representative—a system under which the tenant merely collects the natural produce of the soil with the employment of as little capital and as little labour as possible,—is that in which the greatest excess of returns over expenditure arises from the protective system, the value of the returns being increased £1. 0*s*. 8*d*. the acre, while the expenses are only increased 5*s*. 4*d*.

238. This kind of farming, therefore, enjoys a clear protection of 15*s*. 4*d*. the acre; and as the rent of such land does not exceed 20*s*. or 25*s*., three-fourths or three-fifths of it may be said to be made up of protecting duties.

239. On the other hand, when the same land is broken up, yielding grain and forage crops alternately, employing more capital and more labourers, at wages which enable them to live as well as the few who, under the former state of husbandry, were boarded in the farm-house,

the cost of production becomes raised by protecting duties more than the value of the returns by 8*s.* 7*d.* the acre.

240. It is evident, therefore, that even supposing the protecting duties on food to be repaid in wages, THEY INJURE THE AGRICULTURAL LABOURERS BY DIMINISHING THE DEMAND FOR THEIR LABOUR, AND CONSEQUENTLY DEPRESSING THE VALUE OF IT.

241. Let us examine in detail the comparative extent to which the cost of labour, estimated by the head and by the acre, is increased by protecting duties, under the different systems of cultivation under consideration, and we shall see that the greater the amount of labour bestowed upon the land, and the better the labourers' fare, the higher the protective tax becomes. And yet we are told protecting duties are for the benefit of the agricultural labourer.

| 242. | Protecting duties on their food. | | | Per man. | | | Per acre. | |
|---|---|---|---|---|---|---|---|---|
| Norfolk, 400 acres— | £. | *s.* | *d.* | £. | *s.* | *d.* | *s.* | *d.* |
| 20 men not boarded . . | 52 | 6 | 6 | 2 | 12 | 3* | 2 | 7 |
| Lincolnshire, 1100 acres— | | | | | | | | |
| 23 men and women boarded | 98 | 12 | 11 | 4 | 5 | 9 | 1 | 9 |
| 19 men not boarded† . | 148 | 0 | 8 | 7 | 15 | 9* | 2 | 8 |
| 15 boys not boarded . . | 34 | 11 | 10 | 2 | 6 | 1 | 0 | 7 |
| | | | | | | | 5 | 0 |
| Dairy-farm, 100 acres . | 14 | 16 | 0 | 2 | 9 | 4 | 2 | 4 |
| Whitfield arable, 240 acres— | | | | | | | | |
| 15 men not boarded, £98 14 0; Their proportion of beer . . . 7 6 | 106 | 0 | 0 | 7 | 1 | 4* | 8 | 10 |
| 14 women & boys, £30 10 9; Their proportion of beer . . 2 8 10 | 32 | 19 | 7 | 2 | 7 | 1 | 2 | 8 |
| | | | | | | | 11 | 6 |

* These sums represent the amount of protecting duties on the food not of an individual but a family of five.

† Pars. 92, 94, 95.

| | Protecting duties on their food. | | | Per man. | | | Per acre. | |
|---|---|---|---|---|---|---|---|---|
| East Lothian, 420 acres— | £. | s. | d. | £. | s. | d. | s. | d. |
| 12 hired householders . | 39 | 1 | 0 | 3 | 5 | 1 | 1 | 6 |

243. From the above and the preceding table, it appears that the arable farm on which we find the protective system increasing returns the most, and the cost of cultivation the least, is that of East Lothian;* there also the protective tax on the labourer's food is lower per man than on any other arable farm, except that of Norfolk, and lower per acre than on any of them. This arises from two causes: first from the inferior kinds of grain constituting the accustomed food of the peasantry, and secondly, from those economical arrangements which enable a large produce to be raised with the employment of a small amount of manual labour.

244. The last has the most influence, since the cost to the Northern farmer of a labourer eating to his fill of oatmeal porridge and milk, is greater than the cost to the Norfolk farmer of a half starved labourer fed with wheaten bread.

245. This will appear from the following estimat of the money value at present prices of the wages of a hind in East Lothian and Northumberland, where the wages are paid alike in kind, and amount to nearly the same sum, though the descriptions of grain which they receive are somewhat different.

| East Lothian | | | | | | Northumberland. | | | | | |
|---|---|---|---|---|---|---|---|---|---|---|---|
| Oats $7\frac{1}{2}$ qrs. | at 20s. | 7 | 10 | 0 | | Oats $4\frac{1}{2}$ qrs. | at 20s. | 4 | 10 | 0 |
| Barley $2\frac{1}{4}$ | ,, 25s. | 2 | 16 | 3 | | Barley 3 | ,, 25s. | 3 | 5 | 0 |
| Peas 2 | ,, 3s. | 3 | 12 | 0 | | Peas $1\frac{1}{2}$ | ,, 36s. | 2 | 14 | 0 |
| | | £13 | 18 | 3 | | Wheat 3 bshls. | | 0 | 18 | 9 |
| | | | | | | Rye 3 | ,, | 0 | 12 | 0 |
| | | | | | | | | £11 | 19 | 9 |

* The hinds of East Lothian and Northumberland are consumers of bacon, the produce of hogs fed with a portion of the corn and potatoes which they receive as wages, on this we have not charged protecting duty.

| | | | | | | | |
|---|---|---|---|---|---|---|---|
| Brought forward | 13 | 18 | 3 | Brought foward | 11 | 19 | 9 |
| Potato & flax ground | 2 | 0 | 0 | Potatoes 36 bshls. | 1 | 16 | 0 |
| Carriage of coals | 0 | 16 | 0 | Carriage of coals | 0 | 16 | 0 |
| Cottage and garden | 3 | 0 | 0 | Cottage & garden* | 3 | 0 | 0 |
| Keep of Cow . | 8 | 0 | 0 | Keep of Cow | 8 | 0 | 0 |
| Cash . . | 4 | 0 | 0 | Cash | 4 | 0 | 0 |
| | £31 | 14 | 3 | | £29 | 11 | 9 |
| Deduct cottage, as the wife's labour in harvest is given for it | 3 | 0 | 0 | | | | |
| | £28 | 14 | 3 | | | | |

246. These wages cost the farmer a trifle over 11*s.* and 11*s.* 4*d.* a week, but they give the labourer a much greater command over the necessaries of life than he would derive from wages to the same amount, paid in money, to be expended at the village shop; they possess, moreover, this advantage over the higher money wages of Lincolnshire, that they suffer no interruption from sickness and bad weather.

247. This, at first sight, may seem a loss to the farmer: if a loss to anybody it is to the landlord, since a high scale of wages causes a diminution of rent, unless an increased produce be raised to compensate for it. But against this loss, from sufficient wages thus paid, there is the set off of lower poor rates. Mr. Grey, of Dilston, in his paper on the agriculture of Northumberland (Journ. R. Ag. Soc. vol. II. pt. 2) has insisted strongly, not only on the pecuniary advantage of this mode of payment to both master and servant, but on the moral advantages which result from it, in conjunction with the possession of a cow, from the

* The Northumbrian hind is bound to have a woman always at hand, to work on the farm when required, who receives 1*s.* a day in harvest and 10*d.* at other times.

habits of economy and prudence which it engenders, and the removal of temptation to dissipate earnings at the ale house; he insists also, and he speaks from experience, on the good feeling which it engenders between master and servant, and its effects in superseding the necessity for parochial relief; declaring that he never knew an instance of a regularly hired hind applying to the parish, however numerous his family, unless disabled by permanent ill health or accident, and that the expenses of the purely agricultural poor in the districts where this practice prevails, do not amount to sixpence in the pound.

248. It is only in the North, where wages are thus paid in kind, that the labourer can ever derive benefit from an advance in the price of food; because being entitled to as much grain, besides the keep of a cow, and other advantages, as is more than sufficient for the consumption of a family, unless it exceed the average number, he has often a surplus due to him at the end of the year, for which he is paid by his master the average price; and, however high the price of the provisions, he is secure of an ample supply of them.

249. The Scottish and Northumbrian peasant consume, it is true, but little wheaten bread, but they have what Cobbet, in his popular phrase, called the bellyful—of wholesome food, porridge, eaten hot under their own roof, with the milk of their own cow, varied with oaten cakes, or bread made of a mixture of pea and barley meal, relished with home made cheese, and butter, and bacon of their own feeding. *They* are not obliged when they have fattened the hog to sell him; and, without going the full length of the writer in a recent article in Blackwood's Magazine, who considers wheat the inferior grain, and wheat eaters an inferior race, we very much question whether the hind of Northumberland and East Lothian would be disposed to change his fare, for the dry bread diet, and

it is little better, of Norfolk, or the cold potatoes of Sussex eaten under a hedge.

250. We are not, however, recommending an oaten diet to the labourers of the South, nor even a return to the rye bread which constituted the food of a large portion of the peasantry of Norfolk before the commencement of Lord Leicester's improvements. The landowner and the farmer, have raised their style of living, our horses, sheep, and cattle are better lodged and fed than they were a century ago, and why should not the agricultural labourer participate in the benefits derived from improvements in agriculture? Whatever the grain which is established as his customary food, of that he ought to have a sufficiency for the support of a family under all fluctuations of price; and nothing secures that so effectually as wages paid in kind.

251. The following would be a scale of wages in kind, adapted to the habits of the South, in which wheat would be substituted for the oats which constitute the principal diet of Scotland, and enter largely into the consumption of the labouring classes in most of the English counties north of Trent.

| | | | |
|---|---|---|---|
| Wheat, 5 qrs. 50*s.** . | 12 | 10 | 0 |
| Barley, 3 " 25*s.* . | 3 | 15 | 0 |
| Potatoes, 40 bushels . . | 2 | 0 | 0 |
| Keep of Cow . . | 8 | 0 | 0 |
| Cottage and garden . . | 3 | 0 | 0 |
| Coals, 2 tons, or an equivalent quantity of wood . . . | 2 | 10 | 0 |
| Cash . . . | 4 | 0 | 0 |
| | £35 | 15 | 0 |

252. These items, at present prices, would cost the

* By the custom of Northumberland the hind is entitled to the best corn grown upon the farm, after that used for seed.

farmer about 13*s*. 8*d*. a week, that is, they would be equal to the present money wages of Lincolnshire and Whitfield; two shillings a week more than the oaten diet of the North, and one-half higher than the 9*s*. a week, the present wages of Norfolk. But they would be of more value to the labourer than their cost to the farmer; the wheat would be sufficient for the consumption of an ordinary family, the cow would supply them with cheese or butter, beside their consumption of milk; and the potatoes, with the refuse of the garden and the barley, would furnish them with bacon.

253. Whenever this mode of payment shall be established in the South, the labourer may be interested in an increase in the price of corn, as he will, under ordinary circumstances, have an excess to dispose of; then we may hope to see him independent of the parish, and laying by something for a wet day. Till then it is cruel mockery to talk to him about making provision for sickness and old age out of 9*s*. a week.

254. Had such a scale of wages, and such a mode of payment been established in Norfolk, at the close of the last century, securing to the labourer a sufficiency of food during the period of agricultural prosperity, and obviating the necessity of altercations about a reduction in the money value of wages, when the revulsion came, the agricultural population of Norfolk would not have been in the state described in the following extract from Mr. Bacon's work on the agriculture of that county.*

255. " Unhappily, while other classes were gradually progressing, the moral and physical condition of the labourer was as gradually retrograding, until at one period

---

* The Report on the Agriculture of Norfolk, to which the prize was awarded by the Royal Agricultural Society of England.

a complete disorganization of the rural districts of Norfolk was threatened. In order to trace this retrogression, its effect upon agriculture, and its action upon a naturally honest and industrious class, we must go back forty or fifty years, when occupations were not so extensive, when the demand for labour was above the supply, and production more adequate to consumption. At that period, most of the farm servants were lodged in the houses, the occupations were comparatively small, the master and servant often worked together, and hence arose mutual respect and attachment, which mutual dependence and mutual aid almost invariably create. The system of weekly wages was the first blow towards weakening the ties which had hitherto bound the farm servant, under all circumstances, to his employer. Expelled from the long cherished "home of the estate," and thus cut off both from those social communications which ensure confidence, and that supervision which imposes a wholesome restraint, the labourer sought a new dwelling, too often an improvident marriage, and his interest centered in his own hearth. As a natural consequence, population increased, not at first perhaps in proportion to the demand for labour, augmented by enclosures, but certainly beyond the rate of wages, which underwent no addition corresponding to the rise of price in the necessaries of life. It ought, however, in justice, to be stated, that in almost all the inquiries which have been made upon this point, we have invariably found the rate of wages higher in proportion, when the price of corn was low, than when high prices have been obtained. The following table of wages paid on a farm for the last forty years, may be received as representing the customary rate of weekly payment during that period."

256. The Average price of Wheat per quarter received, and Labourer's weekly Wages paid from 1804 to 1844, on a light land Farm.

| Date. | Average price of Wheat, per quarter. | Labourer's Wages, per week. | Dat | Average price of Wheat, per quarter. | Labourer's Wages, per week. | Date. | Average price of Wheat, per quarter. | Labourer's Wages, per week. |
|---|---|---|---|---|---|---|---|---|
| 1804 | 44 10 | 8 0 | 1818 | 82 11 | 10 6 | 1831 | 66 0 | 10 6 |
| 5 | 92 8 | 10 0 | 19 | 71 8 | 10 6 | 32 | 60 0 | 10 6 |
| 6 | 60 10 | 9 0 | 20 | 65 6 | 10 0 | 33 | 57 0 | 10 0 |
| 8 | 71 0 | 9 0 | 21 | 56 3 | 9 0 | 34 | 46 8 | 9 0 |
| 7 | 65 0 | 9 0 | 22 | 39 10 | 8 0 | 35 | 40 0 | 9 0 |
| 9 | 87 0 | 10 6 | 23 | 49 0 | 9 0 | 36 | 52 0 | 9 0 |
| 10 | 100 0 | 12 0 | 24 | 58 8 | 9 0 | 37 | 52 0 | 10 0 |
| 11 | 83 1 | 10 0 | 25 | 64 8 | 9 0 | 38 | 69 0 | 11 0 |
| 12 | 120 1 | 15 0 | 26 | 58 0 | 10 0 | 39 | 64 8 | 10 6 |
| 13 | 110 8 | 13 6 | 27 | 56 0 | 10 0 | 40 | 63 0 | 10 6 |
| 14 | 64 1 | 10 0 | 28 | 60 0 | 10 0 | 41 | 60 0 | 10 6 |
| 15 | 63 0 | 10 0 | 29 | 65 0 | 10 0 | 42 | 52 0 | 10 0 |
| 16 | 66 2 | 10 0 | 30 | 62 0 | 10 0 | 43 | 48 0 | 9 0 |
| 17 | 106 5 | 12 6 | | | | | | |

257. "The labourer then gradually compelled to confine his exertions to the bare support of existence, grew careless of higher considerations; first in the respect of his superiors, who had, in his way of thinking, thrown him off, and then of his own. Thus were the first stones loosened in the "agricultural homestead" of England, which has since been so fatally shaken from base to roof. Labour competition was still further increased by the discharge of soldiers and seamen, after the peace, as well as by that of artizans whose employment had been created and continued by the manufacturing impulse and monopoly enjoyed during the war; and the consequence was that wages were reduced to the lowest possible rate. In addition to the surplus labour, came low prices, with a period of agricultural ruin, and, in the struggle, the labourer, under the law of settlement bound to one spot, was reduced to the minimum of subsistence. What followed? Broken in spirit, sunk to the depth of degradation and distress, he was compelled

to have recourse to parish allowance, granted with a sparing hand, both on account of the number of applicants and the distressed state of the tenantry themselves. Then came the further infliction of working on the roads, or in the gravel-pit, the almost only passport to a scanty allowance. These causes fully account for that moral and physical depravation, and that exasperation which has since inflicted such evils on the proprietor and the tenant, and such misery upon the labourer. A fourth party, the overseer, placed as he was between the rate-payer and the pauper, had a hard duty to perform, and was too frequently the unwilling medium of inflicting injustice as well as suffering; for it was out of these circumstances that wages came to be eked out by the substitution of payment from the poor rates.

258. "Perpetual disputes between the tenantry and the labourers, and parishes, ended in an appeal to magisterial power, and litigation only added to the pressure under which the county laboured; while the vice and the crime engendered by these many causes, and fostered by recklessness, was fast hastening the population to that disorganised state, which, in 1830, exhibited itself in the destruction of machinery, and similar acts of violence. The strong arm of the law was, of necessity, called in, and the insurrection was ostensibly controlled; but, almost nightly fires, throughout the county, shewed the spirit to which it had given birth, and succeeded in the object at which it aimed—to excite the fears of the wealthy.

"Such is the brief history of the labourer in husbandry, during the interval since 1805.

259. "While the wealth of the landlord, and the profits of the tenant had been rapidly augmented by the influence of increased practical knowledge and skill in culture; and, while general education had elevated the intellectual position, and refined the habits of the higher and middle classes,

the labourer had been subject to a neglect which had as rapidly sunk him in the scale of society--a neglect which recoiled on his superiors with double force at a later period, when it was beyond the power of the occupier to remedy the evils engendered by depression; he, himself, being involved in almost irretrievable ruin.

260. "No more powerful instance can be given of the state of the agricultural poor, than that in 1831, in 473 parishes, 2714 men, exclusive of women and children, were out of employment; that is to say, about one-eighth of the whole population of those parishes.

"From the following table of commitments to the several county prisons, from 1800 to 1843, an estimate may be formed of the state of crime; due allowance being made for the increase of population."

261. The results of these tables may be thus briefly enumerated:—

| | | | | |
|---|---|---|---|---|
| 1800 | to | 1808, | 2336 | committals. |
| 1809 | to | 1817, | 3323 | ditto. |
| 1818 | to | 1826, | 8535 | ditto. |
| 1827 | to | 1835, | 12654 | ditto. |
| 1836 | to | 1843, | 11038 | ditto. |

262. That this increase of crime entailed a great burthen to the owners and occupiers of land, is evident from the Criminal and Civil Departments of the County expenditure. These have risen from £6,496. in 1800, to £19,378 in 1842, and had reached in 1841 to the sum of £27,110.

26. After stating that the alteration in the Poor Law, caused a just and important change in the position of the farmer and the labourer, that both have discovered their errors, and have become aware of their mutual dependence; that the condition of the labourer has become improved; and being now convinced that he will receive the full benefit of his industry, he has grown more steady, diligent, and obliging; and that in all the returns received from farmers

in different parts of the county, a unanimous opinion is expressed that a great and beneficial change has been produced in the morals, habits, and feelings of the labourers; the author thus describes the system at present pursued in regard to boarding(?) and lodging farm servants.

264. "A cottage, not very far from the farm, is occupied by the foreman or bailiff, who receives the farm servants, is responsible for their conduct, and takes care that they are in the house at proper hours. His wife cooks for all, takes care of the beds, washes sheets and towels, all of which are provided by the master. For this the foreman and his wife live rent free, receive a shilling a head from each lodger, which is considered part of his wages. The team men and lads are thus paid—the men receive from six to seven shillings a week for board wages, and yearly wages varying from £6. to £7. The lads five shillings a week for board, and yearly wages from 20*s*. to 50*s*."

265. This is something like the "boothie" system of those parts of Scotland, where the hind system does not prevail. It may be more economical for the farmer, but it wants all the moral advantages of the system of employing hired householders resident upon the farm, a description of servants which, from the testimony of all who have had any experience of them, are far superior in steadiness and industry to these young men.

266. The Norfolk plan is inferior, however, to the boothie system in this, that while under that, the young men are entitled to an allowance of meal, which is more than they consume, receiving the balance in money, at the average price of the year, under the improved Norfolk system, they are paid money wages with which to board themselves.

267. Where the hind system prevails, a sufficiency of food for the support of a family becomes the standard of wages, and is paid to all, whether married or single. In

those cases where a "double hind" is engaged, that is the services of a father and a grown up son residing with him —a species of hiring considered equally advantageous to both master and man,—the young man receives the same allowance of grain as the father, and six pounds a-year in lieu of the keep of a second cow.

268. Where money wages prevail, as in Norfolk, a sufficiency of food for a single man becomes the standard, and the labourer with a family lives on those wages how he can. The wages of the team men in the above case amount to from 8*s*. to 9*s*. 8*d*. a week, exclusive, we believe, of lodging, while the married labourer only receives 9*s*., to provide food, clothes, and lodging for the whole family.—Prior to 1835 he received from the parish an allowance proportioned to the number of his children. That allowance is now cut off, but he has not yet received an equivalent for it in wages, although, in glancing over the preceding table of wages and prices, it is evident that the former are now somewhat higher in proportion to the latter, than during the period of agricultural prosperity.

269. Rents may advance from improvements in agriculture, and an increase of prices may increase profits to tenant holding on lease at low money rents, as they were increased between 1805 and 1815: but agriculture will never be in a healthy state, till the agricultural labourer be secured a sufficiency of food for the support of a family under all fluctuations of prices; and till that sufficiency become the standard of wages for all, whether married or single. Without this sufficiency neither cattle-shows nor cottage allotments, nor Cottagers' Horticultural Societies, nor Associations for the Reward of Industry, nor Benefit Clubs, nor Savings Banks, nor even Schools for the education of children, will avail any thing. To THE LABOURER MUST BE RESTORED THAT SHARE OF THE PRODUCE OF WHICH THE PERIOD OF HIGH PRICES DEPRIVED HIM.

270. To enable the labourer to command sufficient wages, it is necessary that the numbers seeking employment should be diminished, or, which is the same thing, the demand for their labour increased. The concession to the tenant of security of tenure, and the confidence which natural prices will inspire, will, by extending agricultural improvement, open a new field for agricultural labour; but if space permitted, it would be easy to show that the utmost extension of the demand for such labour, which can be looked for from improved cultivation, will employ but a limited portion of our annual increase of numbers, and that from the extension of manufactures, or from emigration, the crowded state of the labour market can alone obtain material relief.

271. Nevertheless, the mode in which wages are paid, exercises an important influence on the moral and physical condition of the agricultural labourer.

272. While in one highly cultivated district, Norfolk, rents have advanced at the expense of the agricultural labourer, there is another highly cultivated district, where they have advanced at an equal rate, without injury to the labourer; because his share of the produce was secured to him by the custom of paying wages in kind—that is Northumberland.

273. The following table from the paper of Mr. Grey of Dilston, in the Journal of the Royal Agricultural Society, shows the rental of a portion of the Greenwich Hospital Estatos in that county, exclusive of the mines and fishings, at intervals of twenty years, from 1772 to 1841. To this we have added the average price of wheat at those periods, from which it appears, that irrespectively of price, there has been a considerable advance arising from improved cultivation and not obtained, for reasons which we have already stated, at the expense of the agricultural labourer. There has been there no muzzling of the ox that treadeth out the corn.

| | 1772-3. | 1793-4. | 1805. | 1814-5. | 1835-6. | 1840-1. |
|---|---|---|---|---|---|---|
| | £. | £. | £. | £. | £. | £. |
| Newton . . . | 450 | 750 | .. | 1400 | 1150 | 1200 |
| Turviclaws . . | 340 | 550 | .. | 900 | 830 | 900 |
| Chillingham Barns, part of it clay . | 400 | 550 | .. | 900 | 800 | |
| East Lilburn, turnip loam . . . | 300 | 800 | 1600 | 1200 | 1050 | |
| Wooperton, turnip loam . . . | 240 | 400 | 1200 | 800 | 800 | |
| Fenton Demesne, part wet and strong . | 350 | 500 | .. | 600 | 600 | |
| Fenton Townland . | 450 | 800 | .. | 1600 | 1050 | 1050 |
| Doddington, South . | .. | 750 | .. | 1500 | 1200 | |
| Doddington, North . | .. | 1200 | .. | 2000 | 1500 | |
| Horton, turnip loam . | .. | 650 | 2000 | 1800 | 1715 | |
| Average Price of | *s.* *d.* | *s.* *d.* | *s.* *d.* | *s.* *d.* | *s.* *d*. | *s.* *d.* |
| Wheat . . . | 52 5 | 49 11 | 87 7 | 69 2 | 43 10 | 66 4 |

274. The following statements, from Mr. Bacon's work, show that in Norfolk rents are as high now as during the period of agricultural prosperity. He has given the number of assessable acres in the county, the estimated rental and rateable value, returned by the parishes, and acted upon under the old assessment up to 1842; the new assessment decided on by the magistrate in 1843; and finally, the assessment under the old property tax of 1815, and the new property tax of 1842. They are as follow—

| | | |
|---|---|---|
| Assessable Acres . | 1,688,807 | £. |
| Gross estimated rental . . . | | 1,787,822 |
| Rateable value . . . . | | 1,548,693 |
| Assessment in 1843 . . . . | | 1,778,422 |
| Assessment under the old Property Tax . . | | 1,439,977 |
| Assessment under the Income Tax of 1842 . | | 1,945,558 |

275. In speaking of East Lothian, we remarked that the bold and erect front shewn by the farmers of that district, during the low prices of 1836, when all around them were bent to the dust, was due to their corn-labour and corn-rents. Corn-labour is beneficial both to farmer and labourer.

Under a system of money-rents and money-wages, the farmer finding himself uneasy during a period of depressed prices, naturally endeavours to diminish his expenses, and in so doing falls first upon the labourer, as most within his power, either reducing the pay, or diminishing the number of his workmen. Under a system of corn-wages the labourer still enjoys his share of the produce, and its money value is silently and insensibly adjusted to the altered value of the farmer's returns. On the other hand, during a rise of prices, it prevents the increase of rents and profits at the labourer's expense.

276. In the same manner, rents dependent on the price of corn, cause the burthen of depressed prices to fall, where it ought to fall, on the landlord instead of upon the tenant and labourer; and they enable landlords to grant that security of tenure which is essential to good cultivation, without running the risk of giving the tenant inordinate profits, and thereby injuring themselves, as many landlords were injured during the war, by the increase in their rentals not keeping pace with the increased expense of living.

277. The advantages of rents regulated by the price of corn, are not now urged, by either of the writers of these pages, for the first time; they were advocated by one of them in a work on Soils, published in 1838, and by the other in a letter published in 1823 in the *Morning Chronicle*, under the signature of a "Tenant at Rack-rent."

278. At that period he, or rather his father, held, for a term of twenty-one years, a leasehold farm of 300 acres, the rent of which was fixed, in 1816, from the average of the preceding twenty years, with the supposed guarantee by Parliament of 80*s*. as the future average price of wheat. In 1823 the futility of this guarantee was but too apparent; and farmers were looking around, in all directions, for relief from the pressure of agricultural distress. The system of

eleemosynary returns at rent-day was commencing; but was confined to the wealthier or more liberal landlords.

279. In the letter above mentioned, the writer denied that the distress arose from the defective corn laws, or could be removed by any alteration of them; he attributed it to the change in the currency, and contended that high prices were no longer to be expected, and were not essential to the tenant's prosperity, which was rather to be sought in a reduction of expenses to the scale of the reduced prices. He argued that some of these, such as seed and horse-keep, contained within themselves the principle of self-adjustment; that others, such as labour and poors' rates, were more or less dependent on the price of produce; and that the only outgoing which the farmer had it not in his power to reduce was rent.

280. He therefore demanded, since Parliament had led the tenantry to expect the price of 80*s*. for wheat; since the House of Commons had moreover denied the depreciation of the currency, which was then admitted, though differences of opinion still existed as to its amount, that an act should be passed enabling leasehold tenants to tender their landlords the value, as declared in the London *Gazette*, of two bushels of wheat, for every pound sterling of rent reserved, in all leases of lands signed before 1820.

281. Among the writer's friends the project was derided as visionary; and it met with little more favour from the farmers, among whom it was advocated by him at market meetings, where agricultural distress and its remedies formed the constant theme of discussion. With them, the favourite remedy was, "Keep out the foreigner," and they were well disposed to regard the Scotch and Irish as foreigners; for they complained bitterly of the admission of the corn and cattle of those countries, which paid no poors' rates, to compete with theirs which bore "all the burthen of the church and the poor." They did not like corn-rents;

they were too much like tithe; and some of the knowing ones, who were looked up to as oracles, cited cases within their knowledge, of tenants who had been ruined by corn-rents, in years of deficient crops, which raised their rents when they had little produce to sell. The rents to which they appeared to give the preference were low money-rents, secured by lease, which enabled them to take their chance of an advantage over the landlord under an advance of prices.

282. Very shortly after the publication of that letter—not it is believed in consequence of it—the late Lord Fitzwilliam converted his money-rents into corn-rents; but the system made little progress in England, and was not much heard of till after the examination of the Scottish witnesses before the Distress Committee of 1836. Since then the subject has attracted considerable attention, and the advantages and disadvantages of corn-rents have been much discussed.

283. The advantages consist in securing to both *tenant and landlord*, during fluctuations of price arising from political causes, that share of the produce which each covenanted for; the disadvantages attending rents dependent on the price of corn, are that they aggravate, either to the tenant or landlord, the fluctuations of price arising from fluctuations of seasons, frequently raising the tenant's rent, in the case of a deficient crop, when he has little produce with which to pay it, and in years of low prices, arising from abundant harvests, unnecessarily diminishing the landlord's income.

284. To remedy these inconveniences various plans have been proposed; such as reserving the rent in several kinds of grain; making it dependent on the average of three or four years besides the past year; reserving half the rent in corn and half in money; making the rent of one half year dependent upon the averages of several preceding

years, and the rent of the second half year, dependent upon the average of the current year;—and lastly, by fixing a maximum and minimum price between which the variations of rent should be limited, which is the plan now generally adopted in Scotland.

285. There can be no good farming without a lease; and in the present uncertain state of agriculture, dependent as some believe for its very existence on the fiat of a minister, no prudent man will sign a lease of a farm at a rent which he considers will require a higher average price of wheat for its payment than 50*s.* the quarter.

286. So attractive, under these circumstances have the once despised corn-rents become, that they have tempted several Farmers' Clubs to break their tether, for the purpose of grazing in the prohibited field of questions affecting the relations between landlord and tenant. In every club where corn-rents have been discussed, a verdict has been given in their favour, with some one or other of the above modifications; and now that corn-rents are beginning to acquire popularity among the farmers of the South, we trust they will bestow a little attention on the question of corn-labour, and only take land on such terms as will enable the principle of LIVE AND LET LIVE to be carried into effect between master and servant, as well as between landlord and tenant.

287. On the other hand, when landlords are asked for abatements of rent, they will do well, if the claim be a just one, to give them, speedily and liberally; so as to enable the labourer to enjoy sufficient wages, and it is their interest, as well as their duty, to see that he has it. They will do well also to give their abatements of rent in such a form as will secure an increase in the value of their property, by draining, marling, liming, &c. according to circumstances; and insisting on the abandonment of useless expenses in cultivation,

which have nothing to plead in their defence but ancient custom.

288. In conclusion, we would exhort those in whom the approaching destruction of the protective system excites such terrors, to calculate for themselves, the extent to which protecting duties increase the cost of cultivation and the value of returns under that system of farming with which they are best acquainted. We have supplied some data; the rest they possess themselves. They cannot enter fairly on the calculation without being convinced that to the tenant, the system is on the whole, more injurious than beneficial; that to the labourer it is decidedly detrimental; that no one can gain by it but the landlord; that he cannot be permanently benefited by that which injures the tenant and the labourer; that he often loses on one description of land what he gains on another; that his utmost gains are not to be compared with those which he would derive from the security conferred on agricultural pursuits by natural prices; the increased confidence and energy that would attend them; the increased capital that would flow into them; and the increased produce, raised at diminished cost, which these would call forth.

289. To fortify their minds against the fears which now assail them, we would bid them look back at some of those hobgoblins which once terrified them so much; but with which they have now become as familiar, as the birds who build their nests on the scare-crows set up to frighten them.

290. There is wool. Is its price, we would ask, better or worse now, when, after a long struggle, the trade in it is perfectly free, than when it was protected with a duty of sixpence the pound? Where is the glut of Canadian wheat with which we were threatened; or the American flour which was to be smuggled across the frontier? Were not the Canadian shippers watching our markets, till the late

rise, with no little anxiety, for a decision of the question whether their shipments would be free from loss? There is flax too—poor flax—unprotected either in the seed, or fibre; are not protectionist landlords, whose leases have long prohibited its culture, now adding another chapter to the anomalies of agriculture, by advising their tenants to sow it, in order to remunerate them against the loss attending the growth of protected wheat?

291. When, we would ask again, did beef and mutton bear a better price, than since live cattle and fresh meat, long prohibited, have been admitted at a moderate duty, and the duty on salted beef and pork has been reduced one-half? Is it not notorious that nothing short of a price of 7*d.* the pound could draw three thousand head of cattle from the whole continent of Europe, and that even that drain, trifling as it is, has raised the price there?

292. But, the present high prices, we shall be told, are a re-action arising out of the panic, which caused farmers and graziers to reduce their stock, by hurrying sheep and cattle to market, lest Sir Robert Peel should render them unsaleable; or, lest, like wheat at Lincoln market, on the memorable 18th of March, recorded by thirty farmers of Lincoln Heath, they should be reduced to a nominal price.

293. And who, we would ask, caused the panic, and who were the farmer's best friends? Those who told them to be steady for they had nothing to fear; or those who alarmed them with tales of Spanish oxen; and pledged their reputation as practical men, in opposition to free-trade theorists, for the mountains of pork, which, when they lived in the back-woods of Canada, they would gladly have sold at two cents the pound? Why does not some of it come? Can it be kept back by the same cause, the cost of transport, which induced the same practical authority to burn as much bird's-eye maple in clearing his land, as would in London have made him one of the richest commoners in England?

294. The din that was raised at the alteration of the tariff, and the panic which it caused, to their no small loss, among the landlords and farmers, can be compared to nothing but that described by Cowper in the "Needless Alarm"—The passage is rather long, but it is so appropriate that it appears to have been written for the occasion, and therefore we shall conclude by quoting it.

The sheep recumbent and the sheep that grazed,
All huddled into phalanx stood amazed,
Admiring terrified the novel strain,
Then coursed the field around, and coursed it round again.

* * * *

But recollecting, by a sudden thought,
That flight in circles urged advanced them nought,
They gathered close around the old pit's brink,
And thought again, but knew not what to think.
Awhile they mused—surveying every face,
Thou had'st supposed them of superior race,
Their periwigs of wool and fear combined
Stamped on each countenance such marks of mind.

* * * *

At length a mutton statelier than the rest,
A ram, the ewes and wethers sad addressed:
Friends, we have lived too long, I never heard
Strains such as these, so worthy to be feared.

* * * *

Or heard we that tremendous bray alone,
I could expound the melancholy tone,
Should deem it by our old companion made,
The ass, for he we know has lately strayed,
And being lost perhaps and wandering wide
Might be supposed to clamour for a guide;
But oh those dreadful yells what soul can hear,
That owns a carcase and not quake for fear,
Demons produce them doubtless; brazen-clawed,
And fanged with brass, the demons are abroad.
I hold it, therefore, wisest and most fit,
That life to save, we rush into the pit.

# POSTSCRIPT.

1. In the foregoing pages we have treated exclusively of protection to agriculture. It must not, however, be forgotten, that the protective system, embraces all articles of colonial produce; for which the agricultural population, in common with the rest of the community, pay an enhanced price; for the benefit, or supposed benefit of the inhabitants of the Colonies.

2. The protecting duty on sugar is 10*s.* a cwt., which with its effects in impeding trade may be considered equal to a tax of 1½*d.* the pound upon all the sugar consumed in this country, over and above the revenue paid to the Exchequer. This is not only a serious addition to the farmer's housekeeping expenses, and a cruel privation of what ought to be a daily ingredient at the peasant's board, but it operates very injuriously to the market-gardeners and the fruit-growers of Kent, Hertfordshire, &c. by limiting the consumption of pies, puddings, and preserves, and thereby lessening the demand for their produce.

3. There is a heavy protecting duty on timber for the benefit of Canada; on coffee, for the benefit of Jamaica and Ceylon; on currants, for the benefit of the Ionian Islands: in short, every production imported from our Colonies is protected to the extent of from 50 to 100 per cent. as compared with the duty upon foreign produce.

4. These protecting duties are paid by the agriculturists as well as by other classes, and they materially add to the expense of carrying on their business and enhance the cost of their living.

5. If we have succeeded in proving that "protection" to agriculture is a burthen upon the shoulders of the agriculturists, we need not go into an argument to shew that the same system has failed to secure prosperity to the colonists. The continued cry of distress from the West India Islands places this question out of the pale of controversy.

6. There are also protecting duties on silks and other manufactures.

7. It cannot be for a moment doubted that the removal of all protecting duties, whether colonial or manufacturing, will accompany the discontinuance of protection to agriculture.

8. This the agriculturists have a right to expect. They cannot expect, however, that colonial and manufacturing protection should be abolished, and that protecting duties on agricultural produce should be maintained; but hitherto our movements, in the direction of free trade, have consisted chiefly in admitting foreigners to compete with certain articles of home manufacture in which manual labour forms a large portion of the cost of production; while protection is still maintained on the food of the manufacturing artizan, the protecting duties on corn, butter and cheese, being left untouched, and those on meat and bacon, being only partially reduced.

THE END.

NORMAN AND SKEEN, PRINTERS, MAIDEN LANE, COVENT GARDEN.

# CONSOLIDATED INDEX

## VOLUMES I–VI

**The bold figures indicate the volume; the page numbers refer to the folios at the foot of the page.**